In the Beginning...

David Heidenstam was born in Grimsby and grew up in Norfolk, England. Trained as a political scientist, he has worked as a labourer, security guard, park-keeper, editor, house renovator, village postman, sailboat-delivery cook/crewman, EFL teacher, and warden of backpackers' hostels in Ireland.

IN THE BEGINNING...

A stage play

David Heidenstam

Grey Dolphin Press

Cover design: Emir Orucevic (Pulp Studio)

Set in Gentium Book Basic by Grey Dolphin Press
Main cover typeface: Gilligans Island Regular

Grey Dolphin Press logo typeface:
Champagne and Limousines © Lauren Thompson
www.nymphont.com

ISBN: 978-0-9955934-2-8 (pbk.)
A CIP catalogue record for this book is available from
the British Library.

First edition
2023 2022 2021 2020 2019   1 2 3 4 5 6 7 8 9 10

Printed in Poland by booksfactory.co.uk

Published by Grey Dolphin Press, 2019.
www.greydolphinpress.com   admin@greydolphinpress.com
Amherst, Harnham Lane, Withington, Gloucestershire, GL54 4DD,
U.K.

God and Satan have been alone – and one person –
the universe just the play of their united mind.

Now God has decided to separate 'good' from 'evil'

And the battle requires a battlefield...

My thanks to booksfactory.co.uk, for their expertise. To Emir Orucevic, for once again creating a striking cover to a very specific brief. And two very belated thanks. To S, whose care, years ago, gave me the time to search for a home in the English countryside, where the writing of this play was to begin. And to M, who never complained at my returns to the family home between the stages of my life. And who, reading the first mss. of this play, sent back from backpacking for safe-keeping in episodes in airmail letters, thought that it was, at last, "the real thing".

Contents

*A part of the Garden of Eden, over 24 hours
on the 5th and 6th days of Creation...*

*

To the reader...

Like any play, this was written to be performed. Read on the page, some passages – such as the farce of the naming scene – demand a leap of imagination, of visualisation. This text tries to help, by including many more stage directions than usual.

Among these are many 'pause' directions. They mostly just mean an actor would take a 'beat', as it would be termed: a moment's hesitation before speaking. On the page, they may seem intrusive. But the brief moments spent reading them give equivalent hesitations where they are needed – helping to slow the reading to the right pace.

The directions also try to highlight any differences, between the apparent content of a line and how it might be said. But more generally: this script contains some deliberately but dangerously 'poetic' lines. These may well need to be undercut by TV-style naturalism (especially in a small-scale production) or the effect is more likely to be bathos.

*

Act One

ACT ONE, SCENE ONE: Evening.

ENTER GOD AND SATAN

GOD and SATAN walk on slowly, stopping to look around, as if enjoying a stroll in an unfamiliar place.

GOD (*after a time*). I think I'll like to walk here in the evenings.

SATAN says nothing.

Don't you?

SATAN. ..Yes; I think you will.

GOD glances at him. After a moment he arrives under the apple tree. He looks up, admiring the fruit; reaches up to handle one; and finally picks it. He looks at it, then turns to Satan.

GOD. Have an apple.

SATAN (*after hesitating*). Thank you.

SATAN takes the apple. GOD picks another from the tree, sits on a rock, and prepares to eat. SATAN stands staring at the apple in his hand.

GOD. We can make each day a little cooler; till we have the temperature right.

3

SATAN *sits, and produces a pocket knife, to peel and pare his apple.*

SATAN (*abstracted*). What is the 'day', again?

GOD (*his mouth full*). The.. bit with light in.

SATAN (*realising he hasn't been concentrating*). Ah, yes.

GOD. You approve?

SATAN. Your creativity outstrips the dictionary.

SATAN *peels his apple.*

As to the climate.. – I'll leave that judgement to you.

GOD. Yes; it'll be hard to make everything comfortable.

GOD *sighs happily.*

You know, I think this is the best hour of all. Life sits down and rests its legs. The cosmic dance gets a little less energetic!

SATAN *says nothing.*

You disapprove?

SATAN. ..No. Only – you will always like and dislike now.

GOD. So will you.

SATAN (*looking up and straight at him*). But perhaps not the same things.

After a moment SATAN *looks down again. He has finished peeling his apple. With a single stroke of the knife, he splits it open, then stops.*

GOD (*as he finishes his apple*). Ah – it's not..?

SATAN sits looking at the exposed core. Then he gently reaches down and places the apple on the ground.

Never mind. Here (*getting up*) – try another.

SATAN. No. It doesn't matter. Thank you.

A pause, then GOD *realises he is still holding the core of his apple. He looks at it, then gently lobs it into the foliage.*

Decay begins.

GOD. New life.

SATAN. You've made sure the two are wonderfully confused.

A pause. GOD *looks around.*

GOD (*vaguely*). A garden is a lovesome thing, God wot.

SATAN (*after a moment*). I notice you're not saying what you've been up to since tea.

GOD *looks at him.*

You've been 'creating' again. I can tell. You've got that look in your eye.

GOD (*smiling*). You make it all sound rather disreputable.

SATAN (*continuing rather than replying*). I wasn't born yesterday.

GOD. Well – you'll see in a while.

SATAN. Anyway, your garden's doing well.

GOD. Yes, I do like a garden. Did I show you these?

They are roses.

SATAN. Ah, yes.

GOD. Smell them. Go on.

SATAN. Very nice.

GOD. They're almost perfect.

SATAN. You've certainly got green fingers.

GOD. I don't know though! Look at those.

SATAN. Well, they've only had a couple of days.

GOD. Still – they've been a bit of a disappointment. Perhaps they need more of a mulch.

SATAN. What's this called?

GOD. I thought – 'tobacco'.

SATAN. Good for anything?

GOD. Oh no, no, I don't think so; it's just itself. I should have done some tidying really, but you know how things have been.

SATAN. A good chemical would keep things back. For a time, anyway.

GOD. Well, yes. But I really want to get a compost heap going. Put the goodness back in. I suppose it should get hot enough, inside, to kill the seeds?

SATAN. Hard to say. You're the scientist.

GOD. We really need a gardener. Someone who knows.

A pause. GOD *reaches and picks another apple.*

You won't try another apple?

SATAN. No. Thanks.

GOD. If you're sure.

SATAN. Actually I'm a bit tired of apples.

GOD. Yes, of course..

There's satsumas.

SATAN. No. Really.

GOD. Well...; ah, I know.

SATAN. It's all right, I..

GOD. No, you must try this. Here, hold this a moment.

SATAN *takes the apple.*

Now.. – where did I..? Ah! Yes. Here we are.

GOD *moves some foliage aside and peers at the ground.*

Somewhere here.

SATAN. I hadn't really noticed these before.

GOD. No, they're modest things. Don't put on a big show. But quite appealing in their way. Let's see; I gave them all names. This is.. Yes, this is 'old man's beard'.

SATAN. Which?

GOD. That's this one. Careful.

SATAN. Sorry.

GOD. Don't want to go breaking anything.. Yes. And this one – that's 'jack in the pulpit'. And this is 'monkshood'.

SATAN. What's this one?

GOD. 'Love lies bleeding'.

SATAN. I don't know how you do it..

GOD. Oh, it's just..

SATAN. Just the names would beat me.

GOD. It's just a knack, I suppose.. Now, let me see.

SATAN. What were those things you were turning out this morning?

GOD *is probing into the soil.*

GOD. The whales?

SATAN. No, *after* breakfast.

GOD. Oh – molluscs.

SATAN. That's it. Oy-ster. Oct-o-pus.

GOD. Here we are.

SATAN. And those.. – 'Insects'. Locust. Death-watch beetle. Coffin fly.

GOD *gets up.*

GOD. There we are.

SATAN. What is it?

GOD *brushes dirt from something, and holds it out for Satan to take.*

GOD. Try it.

SATAN *takes it and looks at it dubiously.*

Go on, just peel off the..

GOD *helpfully holds out a hand, to relieve Satan of the apple. SATAN gives it to him, then peels the skin from what God has handed him. He nibbles a corner tentatively, pauses reflectively, then smiles.*

SATAN. What's it called?

GOD. Umm.. – garlic.

SATAN. It's really quite.. – sophisticated.

SATAN *nibbles some more, and his smile broadens. He offers some to God.*

Would you..?

GOD (*showing the apple in his hand*). No, thanks. It's rather a personal taste.

GOD *starts eating the apple, while* SATAN *eats the garlic.*

We should have names, too.

A moment's pause, while SATAN *swallows.*

SATAN. We should?

GOD. Yes. Why not? I can be called..

GOD chews some apple reflectively.

..'God'. And.. you can be called.. the.. 'Devil'.

SATAN. What do we need names for? We – know each other already!

GOD only smiles.

'God'.. – and..?

GOD. The 'Devil'.

SATAN. One syllable for you; two for me.. Two, I suppose, for duplicity.

An awkward pause.

Well.. – the 'Devil'.

SATAN holds out his hand and smiles.

The Devil.

GOD. God.

   GOD *and* SATAN *shake hands, laughing.*

Good, good.

SATAN. Pleased to meet you.

   They laugh again.

Quite like old times.

GOD. An auspicious occasion.

SATAN (*reflectively*). The Devil..

   SATAN *looks thoughtful – then suddenly sneezes.*

GOD. Bless you!

   SATAN *sneezes twice more, as he gropes in a pocket and produces a handkerchief.*

Are you all right?

SATAN. Yes. Yes. Sorry. I..

   SATAN *almost sneezes again, but manages to contain it.*

GOD. I knew I should have made it that bit less humid. If you've caught a cold, I'll never forgive myself.

SATAN. No, no, I'm all right, really. Just a sneeze.

SATAN *is still wiping his nose, recovering.*

GOD (*still concerned*). Well..

SATAN. Probably the garlic!

GOD. Sit down for a moment, anyway. Here.. Watch out for the nettles!

SATAN *sits on a rock by the pool, finishes recovering, and puts his handkerchief away. A pause. He seems to notice something on the pool's surface, and chases it good-humouredly with a fingertip.* GOD *watches:*

(*smiling*) The waterboatmen.

SATAN. You're getting to be quite a craftsman.

GOD. Oh.. It's rather pleasant, actually. Having a skill. Doing something with your hands.

SATAN *suddenly looks rather depressed.* GOD *notices, but pretends not to; he tactfully turns aside, and peers into the pool.*

That's funny, actually.

GOD *peers closer.*

(*vaguely*) Well, there's the pike, at least..

GOD *turns back to Satan.*

Are you all right? Perhaps..

SATAN. Yes; yes. No, I was just...

GOD. How about a game of something?.. Poker?.. Backgammon?..

SATAN. No; ..thanks.. No: perhaps I'll turn in soon.

GOD. What time is it?

SATAN *looks at his watch.*

SATAN. Twenty-thirty.

GOD. Ah; now – wait just a minute.

SATAN (*wryly*). Another miracle?

GOD. No, no, it's just..

GOD *pauses, and looks into the middle distance expectantly. Nothing happens.*

Perhaps..

SOUND: *suddenly there is the call of a cuckoo.*

GOD *smiles.*

After a moment the cuckoo sounds again.

SATAN. What on earth is it?

GOD. The first cuckoo.

SATAN. Is that some sort of event?

GOD *holds up his hand – wait. A pause.*

Then SOUND: *from a different direction, a brief trill from another species of bird. Then another, from another direction. Then a third. They build up – workmanlike trills of evening birdsong. Then this is gradually replaced by the sound of wings, as tens, then hundreds, then thousands of birds flock in the evening air.*

SATAN *has stood. He is staring up, breathtaken.*

What is it?

GOD. Birds... The birds.

SATAN (*eventually*). Another new word.

A pause.

(*to himself*) The opulence of creation.

SATAN *continues staring;* GOD *also watches. Gradually the sounds die. At last they seem to have faded completely. A silent moment; then, alone and pure but indistinct, the song of a single bird. It finishes. A silence.*

GOD. They've settled down.

SATAN (*quietly, after a time, still breathtaken*). Is there a.. word for the sounds, too?

GOD *looks at him, then smiles.*

GOD. Why don't you make one?

SATAN *looks at him. A pause.*

SATAN. What about..... – music?

GOD. All right. Music.

SATAN *suddenly smiles broadly, very pleased. After a moment:*

SATAN. You don't mind?

GOD. No, no.

SATAN. Music.

GOD. All in a day's work!

A pause. LIGHTS: *begin to dim.*

SATAN. The sun's going.

GOD. Yes.

A pause.

Almost Saturday.

SATAN (*after a moment, quietly, still abstracted*). Why do you start your days with... – the end of the day?

GOD. Because there we're using the Jewish calendar.

SATAN. It's a little confusing.

GOD. Yes, I suppose so. It's just one of those.. – traditional things.

    A pause.

There she goes.

    LIGHTS: *dimmed, reddish; dim white spot around God.*

Is she on time?

    SATAN *nods, without looking at his watch.*

SATAN (*after a pause*). Spot on.

GOD (*pleased*). You could set your watch by her.. I wonder what the weather will do tomorrow. The sky seems redder than ever. Perhaps that means something.

..Well – I think I'll be getting to bed. Things are going to be pretty busy in the morning.

SATAN. What will you do?

GOD. Oh.. I don't know yet. But it'll be.. – something good.

Sleep well.

SATAN *nods.* GOD *starts to move off:*

Don't stay up too long, with this damp getting up.

GOD *turns and looks at Satan for a moment, then turns and exits.*

EXIT GOD

SATAN *does not move.*

SOUND: *suddenly there is the hooting of an owl.*

SATAN *turns his head stiffly, to stare in that direction; otherwise, he is unmoving.*

LIGHTS: *fade.*

(End of Act One, Scene One.)

*

ACT ONE, SCENE TWO: Morning.

The stage is completely dark.

SOUND: *a cock crows three times, then silence.*

LIGHTS: *fade up to bright morning light.*

GOD is sitting on a rock. By his feet are a knapsack, a vacuum flask, a clean cup and saucer, and an apple core. He has several sheets of paper in his hand, and looks alternately between these and the auditorium, running a finger down the top sheet as if checking an inventory.

SOUND: *fade up background – morning chorus of birds.*

ENTER SATAN

SATAN enters quietly, unseen by God. He pauses and watches for a moment, then approaches.

SATAN. You're up bright and early.

GOD smiles in greeting.

GOD. Yes, I thought I'd be up and doing. It's the sort of day that makes you glad to be alive.

SATAN registers the sound of the birds – which at this moment is rather loud and discordant.

SATAN. Will it be like this every morning?

GOD (*joking*). You don't feel a profound oneness with life?

SATAN. No, well, I'm not as good in the mornings as you are.

   SATAN *glances out towards the auditorium for the first time – then stares.*

My God..

You *have* been busy.. I hope you know what you're up to.

GOD. Oh, they'll sort themselves out.

   GOD *rises, stretching.*

The more the merrier. I like things round me. How about some coffee?

   SATAN *is still staring out towards the auditorium.*

SATAN. What?

GOD. Coffee.

SATAN. No, no, I won't take yours.

GOD. I made plenty. Look, I brought a second cup.

SATAN. Well..

   GOD *unscrews the plastic mug of the vacuum flask, and then the stopper. He starts pouring coffee into the cup and then into the plastic mug.*

GOD. How's the cold?

SATAN. Oh, it was nothing. I see the goldfish are back.

GOD. Yes, I.. reorganised things a bit.. No sugar?

SATAN. No. Just as it comes. Thank you.

GOD offers the cup and saucer, and SATAN takes them. GOD produces a bag of sugar from knapsack or large pocket. He retrieves a teaspoon from inside, and spoons several heaped spoonfuls into his mug. Then he puts spoon and sugar away again, and produces a glass bottle of milk with screw top.

SATAN notices.

What's that?

GOD. Mm.. – something I came up with this morning. I think it may go quite well with coffee.

GOD pours a touch of milk into his mug, then tries it.

Ah.

SATAN. Good?

GOD. Try some.

SATAN. Well..

GOD *offers his own mug.*

GOD. Here. Try a sip of this. See if you like it. Don't mind the sugar!

SATAN *tries God's coffee; he pulls a face.*

SATAN. I'll never know how you like things so sweet.

SATAN *hands the mug back to* GOD.

Interesting.. But –

GOD. You'll stick to black.

SATAN. I think so. Thanks.

GOD *and* SATAN *stand sipping their coffees. After a moment,* GOD *looks out at the auditorium again, as if his thoughts have returned to work in hand.*

SATAN *notices.*

Monarch of all you survey!

GOD. It's all go!

SATAN. They're nice.

GOD. Horses.

SATAN. And those.

GOD. Horses of a different colour.

SATAN. Don't overdo it.

GOD (*vaguely*). I don't know much about art, but I know what I like.. (*answering him*) – Oh, I'll take a rest in a day or so. You get teething problems, you know.

SATAN (*smiling*). Like the pike.

GOD. Well, yes. And – things you're not sure about.

SATAN. Those?

GOD (*nodding*). Cloven hooves.. Not chewing the cud..

SATAN. What's the trouble?

GOD. Oh, nothing really. I'm just not sure if I've made them unclean enough.

SATAN. That's the trouble with work. Before you know where you are, you can't call your soul your own.

GOD. All the same – this won't do.

  GOD *drains his mug.*

SATAN. I'd have said it would!

GOD. There's still most of the names to do. Might as well make a start.

Would you like to help? Give me a hand?

SATAN. Me? I wouldn't know a..

   SATAN *gestures vaguely, unable to think how to finish.*

GOD. No, I mean..

SATAN. Like yesterday?

GOD. If you don't mind.

SATAN. No, no. Just say the word. I quite like paperwork.

   He is quite eager.

GOD. Well, then. This is the first batch. You take this, and..

   GOD *hands* SATAN *a sheaf of papers, then starts searching his pockets.*

SATAN. It's all right. I've got a ballpoint.

GOD. I always seem to be losing mine.

SATAN. Where do we start?

   GOD *looks at the papers that Satan is holding, and points to a place.*

GOD. Umm.. Here.

SATAN. What about the.. – birds?

GOD. Oh, I did them first thing.

SATAN *flips back through the sheets.* GOD *points.*

SATAN (*reading*). 'Bird of paradise'.. 'albatross'.. 'vulture'... – 'Dodo'?? – Not up to your usual standard! Which was that?

GOD (*embarrassed*). Oh, he.. Wasn't in the flypast.

SATAN (*not noticing, turning the sheets*). All right, so it's.. Marsupials. Which are they?

GOD *points to the auditorium.*

GOD. Over there. They tend to hop.

SATAN. So I see.

GOD. They were only an experiment, really. For filling up a minor continent.

I've done those ones, though..

GOD *turns back to the papers Satan is holding.*

If we start – here.

SATAN. All right, then. So it's..

SATAN *flips back through the previous sheets, to find the*

headings. He pronounces them with some confidence, as if by now accustomed to scientific Latin. Still, he is clearly encountering these particular words for the first time, and so takes them carefully – the longer ones a syllable at a time.

Class, Mammalia.. Subclass.. – Metatheria.. Order, Marsupialia.. Suborder.. Suborder, Polyprotodontia.. Family.. Peramelidae.

GOD. Ah.. – the.. bandicoots.

SATAN. Bandicoots?

GOD. Yes.

SATAN makes a mark on the top sheet.

SATAN. You ought to tick them off, when you've done them, you know. Keep things in apple-pie order.. Genus.. Perameles.

GOD is standing to one side of the stage. He peers at the front rows of the audience.

GOD. The.. long-nosed bandicoots.

SATAN. Long-nosed.

SATAN looks higher up the sheet.

No subfamily or tribe then?

GOD. Ah, no; not this time.

SATAN. Bit inconsistent.

GOD. You have to go as the spirit moves you.

SATAN. Well then.. – Perameles.. Perameles nasuta.

SATAN joins GOD. They stare at any convenient member of the audience, in the front rows.

GOD. The.. common long-nosed bandicoot.

SATAN. Perameles fasciata.

As before, using another occupant of the front rows, working towards the centre. GOD considers carefully:

GOD. The.. Eastern.. barred.. long-nosed.. bandicoot.

Perhaps GOD or SATAN or both descend into the auditorium. In any event, they continue to work along the front rows, SATAN pointing, GOD peering.

SATAN. And Perameles gunni.

GOD. The.. Tasmanian barred long-nosed bandicoot.

They move sideways again. SATAN turns back towards those they have already passed.

SATAN. Move along, please, once you've got your names.

O.k. Peroryctes next.

GOD. The.. New Guinea bandicoots.

SATAN. And we've got –

   SATAN *indicates a member of the audience.*

– Peroryctes longicauda.

GOD (*coughs*). The.. er.. long-tailed New Guinea bandicoot.

SATAN. And Peroryctes raffray-anus.

   Slight expression of distaste from SATAN, *tactful concealment of distaste by* GOD.

GOD. The..

   GOD *and* SATAN *look at each other.*

GOD.   )
) ..*common* New Guinea bandicoot.
SATAN.)

SATAN. Then Microperoryctes. Just one of those. Microperoryctes murina.

GOD. Oh, yes: the New Guinea mouse bandicoot.

SATAN (*throwaway*). I do hope New Guinea doesn't mind specialising in bandicoots.

(*consulting his papers*) The.. Echimypera.

SATAN *glances back towards those they have already passed.*

Please move along.

GOD (*apologetically but not uncertainly*). The New Guinea spiny bandicoots.

SATAN. Are you sure you're in the right mood for this?

SATAN *looks back again.*

Come on. Move along. And keep off the grass.

His "Come on" is clearly not directional, for he also gestures slightly to wave them on their way.

GOD. They're all nocturnal really, of course. Not used to being out during the day.

SATAN. Yes, well, it was a lot simpler with the fish.

All right then; we've got.. – Echimypera clara.

GOD *looks at the next member of the audience, and smiles in recognition.*

GOD. Ah, yes; Clara's spiny bandicoot.

SATAN *looks at God, and holds for silence.*

SATAN (*into the silence*). Clara?.. What's 'Clara'?

GOD looks embarrassed, but says nothing. SATAN seems suspicious, but goes back to his list.

And.. – Echimypera kalibu.

GOD. Um.. Echi..

SATAN. Echimypera kalibu.

A pause while GOD stares at the next member of the audience, then looks at the ground. The pause lengthens.

GOD (*eventually*). I don't think I can think of a name for that one.

Another pause.

Sorry.

SATAN. No name?

GOD. Well..

SATAN. It can't be that..

GOD and SATAN apparently peer at the member of the audience. A pause, then they look at each other. A pause.

GOD. Why don't you?..
(*together*)
SATAN. You're the creative one!

Another awkward pause.

SATAN. All right: I'll just put an asterisk by it.

SATAN marks with his pen. GOD and SATAN start to turn to the next person, but then SATAN turns back.

(*to the member of the audience*) No, no – you'd better go now.

(*gradually transferring his gaze to an apparently departing animal*) Yes, go on. No, I'm sorry, I can't do anything now. That's right, don't hold everyone up. That's it.

We'll call you.

(*shouting after*) We'll let you know.

GOD. Do you think it was a bit upset?

SATAN pointedly ignores this, shaking his papers into order.

SATAN. Macrotis.

GOD. Sorry?

SATAN. Mac-ro-tis.

SATAN points to the next section of the front rows.

GOD. Oh. Um.. Yes: the.. rabbit bandicoots.

SATAN. Macrotis leucura.

SATAN indicates a suitable member of the audience.

GOD. The.. *small* rabbit bandicoot.

SATAN. And macrotis lagotis.

Rhymes that. Bit unfortunate in a scientific work.
Macrotis lagotis.

GOD. The..

GOD.   )
) ...common rabbit bandicoot.
SATAN.)

SATAN. Now. Just two more genera.

SATAN *indicates the next section of the front rows:*

Thylacis first.

*Then he turns away again, this time to beckon to those they
haven't reached yet.*

Come on. Look alive.

Meanwhile GOD *looks at those Satan has just pointed to.*

GOD. Ah yes, the..... – *short*-nosed bandicoots.

SATAN *turns back and looks at him.*

SATAN. 'Short-nosed'.

I hope this is just a rough first draft.

Suddenly SATAN, stony-faced, points to three members of the audience in rapid succession.

Obesolus!

GOD (*nervously*). The.. Southern.. short-nosed bandicoot.

SATAN (*almost threateningly*). Macrourus!

GOD (*with a touch of desperation*). The... brindled bandicoot.

SATAN. Chaeropus ecaudatus!

GOD. The.. the.. the.. pig-footed bandicoot!

GOD pants, out of breath. SATAN smiles.

SATAN. Better?

GOD nods.

'Pig-footed'!

Nothing like a bit of pressure.

GOD. Thanks.

SATAN. So – that's the bandicoots.

SATAN consults his papers.

The next family's the.. – Caenolestidae.

SATAN *gestures to another section of seats.*

GOD. Oh, they're the rat opossums.

(*still recovering*) Actually, we needn't really bother with them. There's only a few. I think they can just be named after wherever they're found.

What comes next?

SATAN *turns a page.*

SATAN. The.. Vombatidae.

GOD (*wearily*). Ah, yes, the wombats.

SATAN *is standing on tiptoe, beckoning further back, as if they are not ready in line.*

SATAN (*long-sufferingly*). Come on. Look sharp there.

GOD. I didn't think they were Polyprotodontia.

SATAN. Well, that's what.. Oh.. No. Sorry. I turned over two pages.

GOD. Ah.

SATAN. After the rat opossums, we're onto the Diprotodontia.

GOD. Good job we spotted that. It could've played hell with the ecology.

SATAN. So we need the.. Phalangers first.. No. Go back.

SATAN *gestures desperately.*

SOUND: *melee of animals moving – but the sounds of bodies only, no cries except perhaps a few small grunts or squeals of discomfort.*

EFFECTS: *dust begins to rise.*

GOD. Look, it doesn't matter. We can take the wombats first.

SATAN (*not disagreeing*). If they get out of line, we won't know where we are.

If GOD and SATAN have previously descended into the auditorium, they should by now have mounted back onto the stage.

GOD. What's the first wombat?

SATAN. Vombatus ursinus.

SOUNDS: *get louder. The voices of GOD and SATAN rise to compete. GOD speeds things up.*

GOD. That can be the common wombat. What's next?

SATAN *is at the far end of the stage, pointing down.*

SATAN. Vombatus ursinus platyrrhinus. He's up here. They don't move very fast.

EFFECTS: *dust gets thicker.*

GOD. O.k.: the.. Australian common wombat.

SATAN (*pointing further off*). And tasmaniensis.

GOD (*shouting*). The Tasmanian common wombat!

SATAN (*ditto*). And one other genus, Lasiorhinus.

SATAN *peers into the distance.*

EFFECTS: *Satan is almost hidden in a cloud of dust.*

SATAN *points triumphantly, coughing on dust:*

Lasiorhinus latifrons!

GOD. The.. the.. hairy-nosed wombat!

GOD *starts coughing too.*

Look, why don't we take five?

EFFECTS: *dust gradually subsides.* SOUNDS: *die away.*
Voices become quieter.
SATAN *gestures doubtfully.*

SATAN. We've hardly scratched the surface.

GOD. Well, the rest can be left till later, it won't matter too much.

Besides – it's getting much too warm for this sort of thing.

SATAN. Well..

GOD (*to auditorium*). It's all right. You can go now.

SATAN *gesticulates, still harassed.*

SATAN (*shouting*). We'll be in touch. We'll let you know.

GOD (*shouting after*). Have a nice day!

GOD *and* SATAN *apparently watch the confusion depart.*

SATAN. I don't mind the paperwork.

GOD. It's just too warm for that sort of thing.

GOD *sits down on a rock.*

Come on; sit down. Mind the ants.

After all, it is the weekend.

SATAN *sits.* GOD *relaxes:*

Phew.

My feet were killing me.

A pause. SATAN *brushes dust from his clothes.*

You could have a dip in the pool.

SATAN (*agreeing*). It's a temptation.

  But he does not move. After a moment:

GOD. An apple?

SATAN. No thanks.

GOD. Some garlic?

SATAN. I can see I'm going to have a savoury reputation.
Too early in the day. No – thanks – I'm quite content.

  GOD *lies back and stares up at the sky.*

GOD. This is the life.

SATAN. You've had a busy week.

  Dialogue building up as patter.

GOD. It's been a bit of a rush job.

SATAN. You took a lot on.

GOD. It was just a one-off.

SATAN. Work hard, play hard.

GOD. I quite like working to a deadline.

SATAN. Well – no rest for the wicked.

A pause.

GOD. How about some chess?

SATAN. Oh, I...

GOD *sits up.*

GOD. Unless you'd prefer Scrabble?

SATAN. No, no. Chess's traditional.

GOD. Come on then.

SATAN. You've got your travelling set?

GOD. Never without it.

GOD *produces a travel chess set from pocket or knapsack, and starts to open it up.*

Come on. We can have a little on it, if you like. Say.. – 50p? Just for spice.

SATAN *acquiesces. They set up the pieces.*

These portable sets are a real godsend.

GOD *offers Satan his fists, for the selection of colours.*

Your choice.

SATAN. You know what's going to happen!

SATAN chooses. GOD opens his fist.

You see?!

GOD. Have white for a change.

SATAN. No, no.

SATAN turns the board around.

Actually, I think I really prefer black. I like it when you get the first move.

GOD hesitates for only a second before moving.

Old faithful.

GOD. Tried and true!

The game continues during the conversation. A pause, while SATAN and GOD each make a quick move. Then GOD again:

How's the music coming on?

SATAN looks taken aback.

I thought I heard a little something, last night.

SATAN. For a moment I thought you'd been dabbling in the occult. I didn't disturb you?

GOD. No, no. I just happened to be doing some thinking.

SATAN. I'm sorry. I always seem to come awake around midnight.

GOD. No, you know me: I was never exactly a light sleeper.

SATAN. Well..

GOD (*encouragingly*). It sounded..

SATAN. There's a way to go.

GOD. Still..

SATAN. It's just a matter of harmonics, really.

GOD. Is that another new word?!

SATAN. Sorry! How things – vibrate. You've.. created some interesting possibilities.

A pause. The rapid opening moves of the game are now over. A pattern forms in which one player is concentrating on the board while the other relaxes.

Getting your queen out early..

So. What will you do now?

GOD. Oh – I don't know. Devote myself to good deeds!

SATAN. You could write a book about it.

GOD. That's a thought!.. Under some pseudonym.. Ah, but I'm no writer.

SATAN (*joking*). You could always collaborate. Hire a ghost.

Or paint. You know – watercolours. They're quite respectable.

GOD. No, no, you're the artistic one. No, I'll find some hobby. A pet, perhaps.

I thought I might breed pigeons.

  GOD *is bent over the board.*

SATAN. Watch out for my knight.

GOD. It's your rook that worries me.

SATAN. You're getting a bit bald, you know.

GOD. Really?

SATAN. Just a touch on top.

GOD. The worry, probably!

SATAN. The heat, more likely!

GOD moves a piece, and rises. He strolls at random for a moment, pauses, looks at a banana, and finally picks it. He considers it expressionlessly, then peels it, and sits at the board again.

After a moment, SATAN moves a piece, and rises in turn.

All yours.

SATAN strolls, stretching his legs; then sits away from the board, relaxing.

(*eventually*) You know, there's something quite odd about sitting here, watching you eat a banana.

GOD (*swallowing*). They're quite nutritious.

Full of potassium.

The SOUND *of a hen clucking, just off stage. It begins slowly, with quiet metronomic clucks, builds, then stops.*

SATAN. And what – on earth! – was that?!

GOD can apparently see the hen.

GOD. Well, I *think* it's a Rhode Island Red.

GOD tries to tempt it over, rubbing thumb against fingertips as for a dog or cat.

But I could be wrong.. Come on. Here girl. Come to uncle.

SATAN has got up as if to investigate. GOD turns back to the board:

Well, if the mountain won't come to Mohammed, it will just have to stay where it bloody is.

SATAN shakes his head in mock bewilderment. He strolls, pauses by a grape vine, looks at the grapes without interest. Then crouches, his attention caught by something on the ground beneath.

SATAN. What's happened to these?

GOD (*glancing over*). Oh, they've been lying around. Take some fresh from the vine.

But SATAN picks one of the grapes from the ground. He sniffs it, looks at it, sniffs again – then nibbles a bit very tentatively.

SATAN. No. They're.. – good.

SATAN eats the rest of the grape.

Yes. Try one.

SATAN picks a bunch from the ground, crosses, and hands one to God. GOD looks at it.

Watch out for the pip.

GOD tries it tentatively.

Well?

GOD. They are rather good, aren't they?

GOD eats the rest of the grape.

Ha. Some fungus I suppose. Well – the age of miracles isn't past.

GOD reaches forward, and moves a piece decisively.

SATAN digests the move.

SATAN (*after a moment*). Oh. A sly move.

Still concentrating on the board, SATAN passes GOD a handful of grapes, then sits down with the remainder.

A sly move.

But..

SATAN moves a piece equally decisively.

GOD. Oh.

SATAN. Ah.

GOD. Ahha.

SATAN rises, flipping a grape into his mouth.

SATAN. Follow that.

SATAN *ambles off, humming, and finds himself by the roses.*
He admires them for a while.

During the rest of the game, both SATAN *and* GOD *continue*
to eat the occasional grape, even replenishing their supply
from beneath the vine.

SATAN *eventually, admiring a rose:*

What's this again?

GOD (*glancing over, preoccupied*). A.. nose.

SATAN. That's right.. Go, lovely nose.

SATAN *looks vaguely doubtful.*

It doesn't sound quite right.

GOD *smiles and shrugs, preoccupied - but obviously thinks*
he is right.
SATAN *again:*

Well - a nose by any other name would smell as sweet.

SATAN *bends closer to the flower.*

I like your insects.

GOD. I thought you felt we were getting a bit crowded!

SATAN. Perhaps. But they hardly contribute. In fact..

SATAN *crouches to the ground, looking around.*

..it's the miniaturisation that appeals, really.

Meanwhile GOD *makes his move, and rises.*

I'll never know how you fitted everything in.

GOD *joins him, and crouches, as* SATAN *rises to return to the board.*

GOD. Have a look at this.

GOD *apparently picks an insect from the ground, and rises.*

Careful; there's a sting in the tail.

SATAN. There usually is!

GOD. You like it?

SATAN. Very clever.

GOD. You see how the..

SATAN. Ah, yes, yes.

GOD. And look here. The reproductive organs on this one are rather..

SATAN. Oh, neat! Very neat!

They laugh.

He'll have fun with that.

> GOD *crouches and gently replaces the insect.* SATAN *starts to cross towards the board:*

A little bundle of appetites!

> SATAN *reaches the board, and sits.*

There's madness in your method – I'll give you that.

> SATAN *studies the board. Meanwhile* GOD *is picking more grapes from the ground, and considering them with interest.*

That's a point, though.

> *A pause.*

GOD. What?

> *But* SATAN's *attention has returned to the board. He hums unthinkingly:*
> *'Plaisir*
> *d'aaa*
> *-mour..'*
> *A pause.* SATAN *still studies the board.*

SATAN. Why appetites?

> SATAN *turns towards God.*

Why reproduction?

I mean – you can always make more.

GOD. Ah.

SATAN. Any time that you want.

GOD. Well.. – I suppose it keeps them busy! A sense of purpose. You know. But in any case –

GOD *pauses.* SATAN *moves a piece, then turns his full attention to God.*

I don't want to be always 'interfering'. Butting in.

A pause.

SATAN (*eventually, hesitantly, but with force*). But if you – stopped – 'interfering' – even for a moment – it would all – vanish.. – like a dream.

GOD. Ah.

SATAN *rises to his feet.*

SATAN. Like the dream it is.

A pause. Then GOD *begins to move slowly towards the board.*

GOD. Yes.. But that isn't what I meant, you know. Just that I want it all to be.. consistent.. Bound by its own laws..

So there's always a.. pattern they act.. in. And on.

The shoe shouldn't fit the shoemaker, you see.

> GOD *sits.*

SATAN. I see. The god's in the machinery. No deus ex machina.

> GOD *is studying the game.* SATAN *plucks a leaf rather forcefully from the tobacco plant.*

Your trouble is you're getting religious.

> GOD *looks up and smiles.*

GOD. Takes all sorts!

> SATAN *is absentmindedly chewing the tobacco leaf. After a moment he realises what he is doing. He takes the leaf from his mouth, looks at it curiously, and throws it aside.*

> *Meanwhile* GOD *turns back to the game.*

Why do you always get my bishops?

> SATAN *ignores this. A thoughtful pause.*

SATAN. ..So you make them into.. bundles of appetite. To run on rails of chemistry.. And when they breed..

GOD. It'll be just as if they did it. All by their little selves.

SATAN. The fire forgets the spark. It's too busy burning by its own laws.

GOD *moves on the board.*

GOD. That's freedom.

SATAN. Of a kind.

A pause. GOD *is still studying the move he's made.* SATAN *again:*

(*to himself, quietly*) The rotting generations.

GOD rises. SATAN *is standing looking at the sky.*

What's that?

GOD (*looking*). A cloud.

SATAN (*after a time*). Quite impressive.

GOD. I think it's got something to do with the hydrogen cycle.

SATAN (*impatiently, slowly crossing to the board*). Yes, yes, yes. No doubt. Webs of necessity.

SATAN sits and studies the board.

(*for himself*) "Oh what a tangled web we weave.."

LIGHTS: *dim for a moment.* SATAN *glances up again.*

Seems to be not unconnected with the thermometer either.. No; I don't understand. Not why. What does he know of patterns? Consistency?.. Or care?

GOD. But.. intellectually?..

SATAN. Oh yes.

GOD. It's more...

SATAN. Satisfying. Like a ..good chess game.

SATAN *studies the board and frowns. A pause.*

Yes.

A pause. SATAN *looks up.*

Is that what you're doing? Playing games?

SATAN *looks back down, and moves a piece.*

GOD (*laughing*). Ah – we'll see, we'll see.

GOD *and* SATAN *look at each other.* SATAN *looks back down at the board.* GOD *crosses towards it.*

SATAN. Oh.

GOD *reaches the board.* SATAN *shrugs hopelessly.*

GOD. Oh, take it back. Go on. Have another.

SATAN *is shaking his head.*

Go on. Anyone can make a mistake.

SATAN. No, no.

A moment's pause. Then SATAN lies his king on its side.

Resigns..

There's no game unless you play it.

GOD. Well..

SATAN sits back, puts a hand to his head, then rises and crosses to near the roses. There is a hint of drunkenness in his movements. He stares at the roses.

SATAN (*at random*). My love is like a red, red nose..

SOUND: *a bird's cry from overhead.*

SATAN looks at his clothes.

Ah.

SATAN peers up at the sky, then back at his clothes.

A dissenting opinion.

GOD (*laughing*). I think you just discovered gravity.

GOD crosses to Satan and, laughing, scoops water from the pool to wash the stain from Satan's clothes. SATAN just stands, rocking slightly.

SATAN. As a law it's excellent, no doubt. But as the basis of a waste disposal system, don't you think it leaves something to be desired? Perhaps I do think we're getting crowded.

GOD (*still chuckling*). All part of life's rich pattern, my friend. The weft and the .. woof. There we are. Good as new. The more the merrier, I always say.

SATAN *stands staring strangely into God's face. A pause.*

SATAN. Brother...

SATAN *puts one hand on God's arm.*

I owe you 50p.

A pause. Then SATAN *pats his pockets with his free hand, vaguely searching.*

..Do you take credit cards?

SATAN *sits down abruptly on a rock by the vine. After a moment he reaches forward, picks up some more grapes from the ground, and looks at them quizzically. He looks at God, and then holds out the grapes to him. They look at each other, laughing.* GOD *takes the grapes.*

Then SATAN *reaches down, takes more grapes, carefully selects one, and pops it into his mouth.*

GOD *smiles, studies his grapes, also selects one, tosses it into his mouth, and ambles away.*

SATAN *leans back and looks up.*

It's a busy world, between the skull and the sky.

SATAN *slides down the rock to the ground.*

(*for himself, but openly*) I understood the garden.

(*after a moment, seriously*) Look...

GOD. Look!.. There! A yellowhammer. Behind the.. Ah, pity. We must have frightened it.. You don't usually get them so far south.

A pause. SATAN *slowly and deliberately gets to his feet.*

SATAN (*quietly*). If you'd been alone, it would have come and sat on your shoulder, and sung its soul out in your ear. They would cover you like a coat, were I not here.

GOD (*after a moment, quietly*). Too many grapes, my friend.

A pause. Then SATAN *is clearly sober.*

SATAN. No. Your world rejects me. Wherever I go I am a stranger.

GOD *and* SATAN *look at each other.*

(*eventually*) You mean – I reject myself.

(*for himself*) So wherever I go, I must stay a stranger.

A pause.

You've set creation on a pretty dance.

GOD. Don't you see the beauty of it? Green and new.

SATAN. You know I can't. I'm not allowed to. No: I see the.. – egotism of matter. The squirming 'I' in the smallest squirming worm.

GOD (*diffidently*). The same spark.

SATAN. In wretched wrappings.

A pause.

GOD. Yes; I suppose we see things differently.

SATAN. Before, we saw everything whole.

Look. Tell me. Why are we playing this game? We only have to step back. Fit together.

..Can't we make peace?

GOD *still does not speak.*

(*with a touch of desperation*) All I want is a quiet life.

A pause.

GOD (*eventually*). We must be separate. Don't you see?

SATAN. Why should I..?!

It's all worked well enough; till now.

..Look. Divide – good.. from – (*he hesitates, and gestures to cover the missing word*) .. and this.. creation follows. All right; I know. The battle requires a battlefield. The first separation requires the rest. Life.. shatters into a million fragments. And none of them can ever get home again.

(*more fiercely*) You can't end the dance. Not without us *ending* it.

　GOD *still says nothing.*

Just let me understand, then. Because I have to watch you. Trotting to and fro. Smashing it all. Smashing our world; into a million splinters. We were one being. Our universe was.. – one mirror. You made us two; so you could smash it. Smaller and smaller and smaller. Why? My friend. Why, why, why, why, why?

GOD (*after a moment, simply*). To make a better mirror.

　A pause.

SATAN (*eventually*). I see. And how will you put it together again? Alone.

GOD. I can't. But I can write the instructions in its heart.

　A silence.

SATAN. You.. think.. You.. (hope..)

SATAN *understands.*

Ohh – vanity!! Vanity. All this – *this* – in the vain hope –

(*quietly*) that one day it will find its way back together again. And reflect only you.

GOD. No..

..It may be a false hope. But it is not a vain one.

A silence.

SATAN. I suppose you think you have no choice.

GOD. That's the one thing I always have. Whatever happens, I will always see choice. And you – I think – will always – choose! – to see necessity.

SATAN. Your choice!.. Your vanity!

(*simply*) Brother. Come back.

GOD. There was no freedom.

SATAN (*genuinely taken aback*). There was *only* freedom!

You think this..

SATAN *picks up a worm.*

has freedom? As free as a fish in a frying pan.

SATAN *drops the worm.*

The freedom of the gutter. Well: God save us from saints!
Once all being danced in us; and now you want to be a
good headmaster.

A pause.

GOD. How do you see egotism, without seeing freedom?

SATAN. Oh, I manage!.. Life – lives itself too much. You
can see its – wilfulness; everywhere.

GOD. You're a devil to argue with.

I see how weak the will is. And how poor.

A long pause.

SATAN (*eventually, wryly*). Any archbishop would be on
my side.

GOD. Archbishops will always be on your side.

SATAN *looks at him, then turns and heads towards the exit.
But he halts, and turns again.*

SATAN (*as if it is a criticism*). You've made a world to love
you.

GOD (*after a moment*). Can you make one, to love you?

GOD *and* SATAN *stare at each other. Then* SATAN *abruptly turns and exits.*

EXIT SATAN

   A long silence.

(*eventually*) It is not good for God to be alone.

   LIGHTS: *fade.*

(End of Act One, Scene Two.)

*

Act Two

ACT TWO, SCENE ONE: Afternoon.

SOUND: *As the interval nears its end, a single repeated drumbeat begins, transmitted through the theatre. It sounds about every three seconds – insistent, though not menacing.*

Then a few seconds' silence as the house lights go down.

Complete darkness. Then LIGHTS: *abrupt white light, so powerful – and so directed towards the auditorium – that it is impossible for the audience to see the stage.*

ADAM *is centre stage, hidden in the light. The voice of* GOD *is amplified, so that a quiet, almost conversational tone fills the whole theatre.*

GOD (*offstage*). You are Adam, and I have made you

I am your God

I made the world, and everything that is in it

I was before the world began, and will be when it has passed away

I made the worlds, and everything that is in them

I was before the worlds began, and will be when they have passed away

I am in all things that live, and in all things that have no life

I breathe in them, and without my breathing they could not be.

You are man, and I have made you

To have both hand and mind, alone of the creatures

To grasp the world, alone of the creatures

To till the world, alone of the creatures

To know the world, alone of the creatures

Alone of the creatures, to know you search for me.

Your mind will seek order, and see order in the world

And in the world is that order, without which you could not be

Your mind will seek beauty, and see beauty in the world

And in the world is that beauty, without which you could not be

Your mind will seek love, and see love in the world

And in the world is that love, without which you could not be.

SATAN (*off-stage*) – (*A terrible long descending cry.*)

ENTER GOD (UNSEEN)

GOD *enters while the lights still prevent the audience from seeing the stage.*

LIGHTS: *return to summer noonday.*

GOD *is discovered onstage with Adam.*

ENTER SATAN

SATAN *enters, running.*

SATAN (*in anguish*). What have you done?? What have you done??

GOD (*after a moment*). He will be like us.

SATAN (*in utter indignation*). *You know that he will not!!*

Whatever you do. He can't be. Ever.

GOD (*after a moment, smiling*). Pigs might fly.

A pause. Then GOD *turns to Adam.*

Adam – this is my – friend, the Devil. The Devil – Adam; Adam – the Devil.

SATAN (*eventually*). Your servant.

SATAN *and* ADAM *reach forward to shake hands. An awkward pause.*

GOD. Well.. – I was just going to show Adam what's good

to eat around here. Let's see: there's bananas.. And straw-
berries.. and oranges.. and dates.. and blackberries.. – the
bananas are ready when they're yellow like that, you see,
and the.. oranges when they're.. – that colour... and
passion fruit.. and pears; and some vegetables over here –
lettuces, and if you dig a bit you'll find carrots and.. and..
radishes.. and.. – Remind me to explain to you about
milk sometime. You're lucky, really; we've been a bit
starved for choice. But everything's coming into season
about now.. Now, do be careful, make sure you wash the
vegetables: don't want any upset stomachs. – The water's
quite safe around here, by the way. – And of course peel
any of the fruit if it's got a hard skin on it. And watch out
for the stones in the dates. Which reminds me, there's
plums and peaches around somewhere. And apricots. In
fact, you could look after things a bit if you like – keep
things tidy. A little light gardening, you know. Anyway,
look – have a look around; nose about a bit

A puzzled expression flickers for a moment over SATAN's
face.

– if you feel like it. It will help you find your legs – or help
your legs find you!

ADAM *moves off. A pause.* SATAN *takes out a black packet
of filter cigarettes, opens it, takes one out, and lights it.*

Meanwhile ADAM, *after glancing about for a moment, puts
his hands to his face, and checks the location of his eyes, nose,
and mouth.*

During what follows, ADAM *goes on investigating his body and his surroundings. First he looks into the pool, as the fish catch his attention. Then he realises he can see something of his reflection in the water, and bends to peer at his face for a moment. Then, rising, he looks at his hands, and compares the one with the other.*

Then he loses interest in his body, and goes back to looking about him. He investigates plants and rocks, looks at the trees and the sky, touches and smells, breathes deeply and stretches and scratches. He takes notice, takes pleasure, amuses himself.

SATAN (*quietly, having lit his cigarette*). So. You've added some human interest. I hope you're satisfied.

GOD (*after a moment*). I'm sure that can't be good for you.

SATAN. There's a worm in most pleasures.. It won't kill me, though.

What will you call him?

GOD (*surprised*). Adam.

SATAN. No. All of them.

Their eyes meet.

GOD. Men.

SATAN. Men?

GOD. Yes.

SATAN. Well, you could at least have made him a veget-
arian. You and your salads.

GOD. You're so sure I didn't?

SATAN. I see his needs. What they'd need to be. In a..
harder garden. It's only your needs I never see.

A pause. SATAN *looks at Adam.*

This week's deliberate mistake.

A pause.

Perhaps I am too serious.

A pause.

GOD (*quietly*). You know I can not make anything that is
not good.

SATAN. And you know that what you see as good, I see as
a mass of stinking lies.

A pause.

Yes, well...

A pause. LIGHTS: *dim for a moment.* SATAN *looks up at the
sky. Then he takes the cigarette from his mouth, looks at it,
throws it to the ground and treads it out.*

You're the boss.

.. Anyway – doesn't he get any/[any more] clothes?

GOD (*consciously lightening the mood*). Oh, of course, of course. It's only that there hasn't been time yet.

Sometimes life's too short for sewing.

SATAN (*wryly, perhaps a little bitterly*). You're turning goodness into a career.

GOD. Perhaps you can make one of criticism.

SATAN. Thank you, but the 'prospects' are rather poor.

A pause. ADAM is looking upwards, shielding his eyes, as at the sun, and with appreciation.

Still, perhaps you'll get some competition. I think we've just discovered Nature worship.

GOD. Well – he'll still need some comfort in the night!

SATAN. That, I imagined, was to be provided for!

GOD smiles.

So. No more chess games.

GOD (*his mind elsewhere*). Oh, I'm not so sure.. And – well: one more and we'll have enough for bridge!

SATAN. Ah: who gets to partner?

GOD *smiles but does not answer.*

GOD (*matter-of-factly*). As for the clothes – it's scarcely an urgency. Ours just go with the job, after all. And there's nothing in his heart he wants to hide from.

(*looking down at his own clothes*) In fact, I sometimes think..

SATAN. Not now we've got mosquitoes, thank you!

GOD. True enough.

SATAN. A covering's a convenience, in a cruel world.

An awkward moment. GOD *and* SATAN *eye each other speculatively. Then* ADAM *suddenly sneezes.* GOD *looks round, worried;* SATAN *gives a wry smile.* ADAM *sneezes again.*

GOD. Adam!

SATAN (*aside*). Nature knows its cues.

ADAM *sneezes a third time, as he approaches God.*

GOD. Adam – come here. Are you all right?

ADAM *smiles in good-natured helpfulness.*

SATAN. It's probably just an allergy. Hay-fever or something.

GOD *feels Adam's forehead.*

ADAM. How do the trees stand up?

GOD. Or the humidity. They go beneath the ground. Don't think you've got a temperature. Say 'ah'.

ADAM. Ahhh.

GOD *is peering down Adam's throat.*

SATAN. Some air conditioning wouldn't go amiss.

ADAM (*his head tilted back*). How high is the sky?

GOD *steps back uncertainly, as if not knowing what to do next.*

SATAN (*with heavy irony*). I'll make out a card for him, if you like. Patient number: one. Sex: male. Age...

GOD (*preoccupied*). Twenty-one.

SATAN. Address: Eden. G.P.: God. No congenital defects. No inherited disorders. No infections, so far, of smallpox, poliomyelitis, encephalitis, yellow fever, bubonic plague, syphilis, or athlete's foot. No history to date of metabolic, digestive, cardiovascular, respiratory, or mental disorder. Or gynaecological, come to that. No established pattern of alcohol or drug abuse. None of the ills to which flesh will be heir. Temperature, normal. Pulse, normal. Respiration, normal. Blood pressure, normal. Haemoglobin, normal. Urine, normal. No known allergies. No old injuries. No remarks.

GOD. Sorry.

SATAN. How do you feel?

ADAM (*not sure what he's experiencing*). I'm...

SATAN. Hungry.

ADAM. Yes.

> SATAN *steps across, picks a banana, peels back the skin, and passes it to Adam.* ADAM *sniffs it carefully, tries it tentatively, then proceeds to munch it with obvious enjoyment.*

SATAN (*pacifically*). Perhaps it is the pollen. (*sighing*) After all, it's that time of year.

> *A pause.*

(*suddenly forceful*) You can't start *caring*, you know. Just because he's the prototype. Not if you're going to go stuffing souls into meat.

ADAM (*looking at the banana skin*). The colour's have names.

GOD. Yes – well, the basic ones. 'Red', 'blue', 'green'. You know.

ADAM. Show me; please.

GOD. Oh. Well – yellow, you know. Red – well, they're red. The.. roses.

SATAN *finally realises the confusion of 'nose' and 'rose'.*
GOD, *of course, hasn't noticed.*

Green is the grass. And blue is what the sky is. Oh, and those little fellows (*pointing up*), they're white. There, that'll get you started.

ADAM. What colour is this?

GOD. Green.

ADAM. That was green.

GOD. They're both green. It's a fairly broad..

ADAM *reflects.*

ADAM. And this?

GOD. Green.

ADAM. And this?

GOD. Green. Mind the ants.

ADAM. And this.

GOD (*nodding*). Green.

ADAM. And this.

GOD. Well, no, that's a sort of khaki.

ADAM (*reflectively*). Green.

A pause, while ADAM *reflects. Then he points to some of his own body hair.*

And this grass?

GOD (*chuckling*). Brown/[black]/[blond].

ADAM moves slightly apart, looking at the colours around him.

GOD is smiling. SATAN produces some garlic from his pocket.

SATAN (*after a moment, peeling the garlic*). Does he realise, do you think?

GOD turns to look at him. Meanwhile ADAM stops to look at an apple.

That he's got built-in obsolescence.

GOD does not answer. SATAN begins to eat the garlic. After a moment, GOD turns to watch ADAM, who is just picking the apple.

..Well, I expect he knows what his body knows.

ADAM looks at the apple with interest – and then begins to throw it a little way into the air and catch it again.

GOD. Adam.

ADAM *turns, still holding the apple.*

I forgot. I must show you what you should not eat.

GOD *and* ADAM *move together.*

Now – one thing you might be tempted by, but I really
must warn you against it..

GOD *puts out his hand and takes the apple – but simply, it
becomes clear, to make sure Adam is concentrating.*

and that's the cucumber. It can give you a hell of a time.
Then, most other things that aren't good for you, you'll
be able to tell easily enough; the taste will be –
unappealing; or the smell. I mean, you're not going to go
eating aconites, for example – mind, it's a bit damp
underfoot; or arum lilies; or..

SATAN. Garlic.

GOD. Well, yes. No. You'll be able to catch those out
easily enough. But some things can be a bit deceptive.
The berries, for example. Now, most of them are fine; but
there's one or two you've got to watch for. This one here,
now, that's deadly nightshade.. – yes, that's right.. – and
if you ate it you'd probably find it quite tasty, but I'm
afraid it would... ummm. Well, that's its gift. Yes. And
then those little fellows are mushrooms (*picking one*) and
these are toadstools (*ditto*), and sometimes if you're not
careful they can really be quite tricky to tell.. apart.. Yes.
In fact, I think the best thing there – if you're going to
use them, in a salad or casserole or anything – is to try

them out on me or.. (*glances towards Satan*) on me first. If I don't come to any harm, at my age, I'm sure you won't! That's about it really. I expect it all sounds a bit complicated, just like that; but I know you'll get a.. feeling for it in no time. Well, now; perhaps *I'll* take a stroll – stretch my legs. But I won't be far – just give a shout if you need anything. I'm always happy to give advice, you know. You only have to ask.

GOD *holds out the apple to Adam.*

ADAM (*out of politeness*). Or Mr. Devil.

An awkward pause.

SATAN. No. It's God you must listen to.

A pause. GOD *withdraws his hand – still holding the apple.* SATAN *again:*

(*for himself*) Thou shalt have no other gods but me.

GOD *hears this. He and Satan are close enough to speak apart.*

GOD. I wish I'd said that.

SATAN. You will, Lord, you will.

GOD *and* SATAN *look at each other.*

GOD (*after a moment, to Adam, but still looking at Satan*). That reminds me. I'm afraid I've been neglecting my responsibilities. Adam – listen to me. You see that tree. Its fruit is called the apple. Adam, I am your God and I say this to you – you shall not eat the fruit of that tree.

ADAM *looks at the tree, and then at the apple in God's hand.*

ADAM (*eventually*). It will make me ill?

After a moment GOD *turns to Adam.*

GOD (*eventually*). No. Its fruit is good. It will only make you.. – see differently. But – I say that you should not.

ADAM *bows his head.*

SATAN (*to himself*). Well, that'll be a blow to market gardeners.

ADAM *turns and stares up at the tree. Again,* SATAN *and* GOD *can speak privately.*

And why can't he eat apples? May one ask?

A pause.

GOD (*eventually*). Because it'll be easier for him; if there's something he shouldn't do.

A pause. Meanwhile ADAM *turns aside and stares abstractedly into the pool.*

SATAN. I see... Well, well. I suppose one can say it's an original sin.

GOD (*after a moment, flatly*). I think that I should take a walk.

   GOD *starts to exit.*

(*to Adam*) You shouldn't stay in the sun too long, you know. Not on your first day.

   ADAM, *still staring into the pool, does not react.* GOD *exits.*

EXIT GOD

   A pause. Then ADAM *realises he is alone with Satan. He shows slight signs of unease.*

SATAN (*after a moment*). Are you afraid of me?

ADAM (*eventually*). Something makes me want to keep away from you.

SATAN. I expect it's the garlic!

   ADAM *does not smile.*

(*simply*) Then you must keep away from me..
What were you doing?

ADAM. ..I was watching the fishes.

SATAN. And?

ADAM. ..I was wondering what they know.

SATAN (*after a moment*). Yes, well – you'll have to ask them that. I'm a stranger here myself.

> ADAM *turns back to the pool. Crouching down, concentrating on the fish, he inadvertently touches the water. He draws back startled.*

ADAM. It's..

SATAN. Wet.

ADAM. Yes.

SATAN. That's its gift.

> *A pause.*

Do you find everything – beautiful?

ADAM. I don't think I know that word.

SATAN. No; I suppose you have no need for distinctions like that.

> SATAN *changes his tone.*

Well, perhaps you will. Nothing wrong with words. Always be grateful God's an Englishman. You might have been saddled with Sanskrit.

ADAM (*understanding nothing*). An...?

SATAN. Oh, yes – although of course he'll have a Jewish mother. Oh, don't think I'm prejudiced, though: some of my best friends will be English..

ADAM (*abruptly*). – Why did God make me?

SATAN. ..Ah, you'd better ask him that. He's a bit of a law unto himself. (*brightly*) Perhaps he needed a friend.

ADAM. Aren't you his friend?

SATAN. Me?... I suppose I'm the official Opposition.

(*simply*) You see, I don't think he's doing the right thing.

   A pause. ADAM *stares into the pool, thinking.*

ADAM. The colours in the water. The sun makes them.

   A pause.

What happened before I was made?

SATAN. God made other.. – creatures.

ADAM. And before that?

SATAN. He made the Garden.

ADAM. And before that?

SATAN. The day and the night.

A pause.

ADAM. And – before that?

SATAN. There was just..

SATAN shrugs.

ADAM. There was just the two of you.

SATAN. There was just the one of us. And we were one being, without action, without end; and all the universe was our mind's life.

A pause.

ADAM. It must be very different for you.

SATAN. It's very different for everyone.

A pause.

ENTER GOD

GOD enters, unseen – but does not seem to listen.

SATAN (*cont.*). Still – I'm sure we'll be friends.

ADAM. I don't think you are. But I'm sorry.. – if you're not happy.

SATAN (*after a moment*). I see I've got a lot to learn.

(*painfully*) Don't be too sorry.

SATAN realises God has entered. A silence. GOD says nothing.

(*eventually*) Where have you been?

GOD (*a very long way away*). Walking; among the universes.

GOD comes back to himself, and looks gently from one to the other; then is abruptly filled with power.

(*to Adam*) *Be still.*

ADAM falls into a trance.

LIGHTS: start to fade.

GOD turns to Satan.

Leave me; till the light returns.

SATAN looks at him, then turns away.

EXIT SATAN

LIGHTS: still gradually fading.

A pause. GOD visibly returns to his customary persona.

Now. It needs to be something fairly – redundant.

GOD takes hold of Adam's hand. Still in a trance, ADAM sinks to the ground – then, with GOD supporting him, lies out flat.

A toe, perhaps?.. A trivial muscle?.. The appendix?.. A tonsil?..

He seriously considers this.

Ah, no – this has the right mix of tissue, I think.

LIGHTS: *the darkness becomes complete.*

My son the surgeon.

ENTER EVE

LIGHTS: *return.*

EVE *is on stage, lying alongside Adam.*
After a moment, GOD *leans forward and breathes above her nostrils.*
He sits back. A pause.

ENTER SATAN

SATAN *appears at the side of the stage, apparently unnoticed.*

(GOD, *cont., half singing, quietly*) "If you were the only.."

(*humming*) ("*Girl in the world*
("*And I was..*")

EVE *begins to move.*

SATAN (*referring to Eve*). I suppose you think that's funny.

SATAN *moves forward.*

Oh dear, oh dear.

GOD (*after a moment, very lightly*). Pretty, surely?

SATAN. But hardly practical.. What's it to be called?

GOD. ..Woman?

SATAN. So this is the softback.

(*interested despite himself*) I like the finish.
Is it still waterproof?

GOD. Oh, yes. More so if anything. Hello, my dear.

SATAN (*still to God, trying out the word*). Woman?

SATAN *realises* EVE *is looking at him.*

(*bowing*) The lady of the house.

GOD. How are you feeling?

EVE, *getting up, does not reply.*

Adam: you can wake now.

ADAM *wakes. He does not see Eve.* SATAN *holds out a hand,
to help him up – they are so close it is automatic for him to do
so.*

ADAM. There was a light. I was with the fish. And the birds.

SATAN. In your head.

ADAM (*eventually, soberly, realising*). It was a different world.

SATAN. Well: your dreams are better than mine.

ADAM *turns, and sees Eve. A pause.*

GOD. You may speak.

They do not.

SATAN (*to himself*). And what else did you get for Christmas?

GOD. I'm sorry – I suppose I should make some introductions. Eve, this is Adam. I'm God. And this is the Devil. This is Eve, everyone.

SATAN. My pleasure.

GOD. Forgive our – informality. So much – company – is something new. Well – shall we all sit down?

ALL *sit, except for* SATAN, *who lights a cigarette.*

My feet are having a difficult day.

A pause. ADAM *is looking intently at Eve.* SATAN *is standing aside, facing the auditorium.*

SATAN (*glancing at Adam and Eve, then speaking wryly to the auditorium*). "Splendid weather, for the time of year."

GOD *begins to fetch out a bundle of sewing from his knapsack.* ADAM *gets up, picks a satsuma, and offers it to Eve.* EVE *takes the satsuma.*

EVE. Thank you.

SATAN (*as before*). "Do you come here often?"

EVE *smiles at Adam, but does not know what is expected of her.* ADAM *takes it back and begins to peel it enough to separate out a small segment.*

GOD. It's all right, my dear, he already washed his hands.

It's for eating, you know. But perhaps you're not so hungry.

ADAM *offers the segment to* EVE, *and she takes it. Then* ADAM *separates another piece, pops it into his mouth, and eats it in a straightforward way.*

EVE *hesitates, then, with some unconscious grace, leaning towards her hand, touches the segment to her lips. Then eats it tentatively, keeping her hand in front of her mouth. An action as much practical as decorous - since she might want to spit it out again.*

GOD *meanwhile is preoccupied with trying to thread a needle.*

SATAN (*for himself, turning away, and glancing around generally*). Yes, well; the miracle's in the detail perhaps.

GOD *is still taken up with preparations for sewing.*

GOD. Very good, satsumas. Full of vitamin C.

SATAN (*for himself*). Some people wouldn't know a miracle if it was shoved up their nose.

ADAM *offers Eve another segment.* EVE *smiles and shakes her head.*
ADAM *rises, to go to the pool. He discards the satsuma, then dabbles his hands to clean them.*

GOD. Anyway, Adam will tell you what's good to eat, around here. If that's all right, Adam, with you. Personally I'm going to put my feet up. I think it's time I took a break.

(*for himself*) It'll be Easter before we know where we are.

During the following, ADAM *returns to Eve.* EVE *rises to join him.* ADAM *begins to show Eve the pool and the various foods.*

SATAN (*smiling*). No more creating?

GOD (*ditto*). Only these.

GOD *holds up what he is working on: it is a large pair of baggy underpants.*
SATAN *smiles.*

SATAN. You'll want to keep in practice.

GOD. No, no. Enough's enough.... Do you think these will shrink?

SATAN. What are they?

GOD. Oh, cotton.

SATAN. In this climate.

GOD. Nothing synthetic, certainly.

SATAN (*going back to the question of shrinkage*). Yes, I shouldn't wonder.

GOD. Well; one can only hope so!

A pause. SATAN *takes the pack of cigarettes from his pocket, looks at it, but puts it away again. After a moment he sits.*

Getting cooler at last.

SATAN *nods vaguely. A pause.*

Still, I'm glad it turned out nice again.

A pause.

We can make sure it's a bit milder tomorrow.

    A pause.

SATAN (*dreamily*). "When that I was and a little tiny boy
"With hey, ho, the...."

    SATAN *pauses, uncertain how to finish the line.*

"A foolish thing was but a toy
"For the....

"sun it shineth every day..
    "It

"shineth every day."

    A pause.

I wish I didn't have to shave so often.

    A pause.

GOD. That was rather good.

SATAN (*embarrassed, realising he's spoken aloud*). Oh.
Well. Needs some working on yet.

GOD. You should write it down. Make a name for
yourself!

SATAN (*smiling*). No, no, I'm just a scribe.

A pause.

The happy couple.

GOD (*after a moment*). She's certainly the apple of his eye.

SATAN (*after a moment*). Two pegs to hang on... You couldn't make some more coffee, could you?

   GOD *reaches forward and touches the vacuum flask.*

Thanks.

   SATAN *opens the flask, and pours himself some coffee, obviously piping hot.*

GOD (*quietly*). Don't you see her beauty?

SATAN. I see how she must seem to him.

   SATAN *finishes using the flask.*

(*sitting back, a different reply*) Yes, of course. Your choice. Since you made us as men.

   GOD *looks at him, then rises.*

GOD. Adam. Eve. Coffee?

SATAN. Aren't they a bit young for stimulants?

GOD. Legally, they're adults.

GOD *is rinsing the mug of the vacuum flask in the pool, then filling it with coffee from the flask.*

SATAN. The law is a...

GOD. Bandicoot?

SATAN. Something like that.

GOD. There you are. You'll have to share a cup. Milk.. and – a touch of sugar, I think. Just yell out if you want it sweeter.

GOD *puts down the flask.* SATAN, *having watched for a moment, is taking out a black leather notebook.*

GOD *again, still to Adam and Eve:*

(*smiling, confidentially*) Don't worry if you don't like it!

GOD *picks an apple.*

You can try cocoa tomorrow.

SATAN *meanwhile is searching for a pen.*

GOD *returns, sits, takes a bite from the apple, then considers his sewing.*

SATAN *opens his notebook, holds his pen ready.* LIGHTS: *dim for a moment.* SATAN *looks up at the sky, apparently noting another cloud.* GOD *again:*

What's that?

SATAN. Oh, just a diary.

SATAN turns his head to look at Adam and Eve.

Ow!

SATAN has stung himself on a nettle.

Meanwhile ADAM and EVE, with their heads together over their cup of coffee, are standing looking at the apple tree. ADAM, prompted by God's eating, is obviously explaining to Eve that they must not eat apples.

Sometime during the following ADAM and EVE turn from this and, sitting, begin at EVE's instigation to groom each other like chimpanzees, searching and smoothing each other's hair, and gently cleaning each other's eyebrows.

SATAN sucks his hand.

(*throwaway*) Your nettles!

(*humorously*) My writing hand!

GOD, in the midst of his sewing, lifts one finger.

GOD (*not at all seriously*). Teach you to watch it.

SATAN (*clearly healed*). Thanks.

GOD. Mustn't stifle fresh talent.

SATAN *smiles, opens the notebook again, and begins to write.*

After a moment:-
SOUND: *a loud cackling from a hen, offstage – this time the hiccupping call of a hen that has just laid an egg. It builds into a squawking cacophony.*

GOD *and* SATAN *look up, but* ADAM *and* EVE *are too engrossed to pay any attention.*

GOD. Ah.

GOD *puts down his sewing, stands, and briefly exits, while* SATAN *watches.*

GOD *returns with a hen's egg in his hand.*

There you are. Not bad for her second day... Nice and fresh...

(*roguishly*) That'll put some..

He seems to censor what he was going to say.

.. – protein in his diet.

GOD *glances across at Adam and Eve, and notes their preoccupation.*

Well, later perhaps.

GOD *puts the egg somewhere safe and sits again.*

SATAN *looks back down at his open notebook – and smiles at the aptness of what he had just written:*

SATAN (*for himself*). "Male and female created he them."

SATAN *looks up from the notebook to find* GOD *looking at him, and realises he has spoken aloud.*

GOD (*after a moment, lightly*). Could I hear some more?

SATAN. Oh..

GOD. If it's not intruding.

SATAN. Oh, it's.. Well..

SATAN *hesitates.*

Well, I just started off like this.

SATAN *turns back the pages, then reads in a very flat, matter-of-fact way.*

Umm.. "In the beginning, God created the heaven and the earth. And the earth was without form, and void; and darkness was upon the face of the deep. And the Spirit of God moved upon the face of the waters."

SATAN *looks up at God.*

GOD (*nodding*). Yes. Yes... Bit abstract, isn't it?

SATAN (*disappointed*). Well – it's only a rough first draft.

It wasn't really the beginning, of course. But before that there weren't any beginnings... Or ends.

A pause.

GOD. Well – at least language is..

GOD pauses, then smiles as he stumbles on the conceit:

Fresh-laid for you.

SATAN. That won't prevent the children scrambling it!

EVE rises, from the grooming. As if stretching from sitting, she performs a slight quick dance step – then hides her face in her hair.

(*for himself, quietly*) "Clothed with the sun.."

GOD (*quietly*). That's nice.

SATAN. Oh – feel free.

SATAN jots it down at the back of the notebook.

Give us enough language and we'll all hang ourselves.

GOD and SATAN watch as ADAM and EVE begin to skylark in a mock fight. Then GOD turns back to his sewing: he holds up the finished garment.

GOD. That's it.

GOD *has other garments, presumably finished, in his lap.*

SATAN (*ironically*). The more the merrier.

GOD (*laughing*). No, no. Enough's enough.

EVE. Adám, Adám.

EVE *laughs, and splashes water on ADAM from the pool. She splashes again, and some of the water falls close to God and Satan. Seeing this, she hesitates; then, smiling, deliberately splashes a little water over them. GOD smiles benignly; SATAN chuckles. They sit wiping water from their faces.*

N.B. Throughout this, Eve must not seem in any way coy or flirtatious. She simply has, for the moment – having just been created! – the playful good humour of the young. It is, if anything, tomboyish. She will grow up quickly enough.

SATAN. You've got diamonds in your beard, old friend.

This line can stand even if God is played clean-shaven.

EVE *tries to look shyly penitent, but keeps breaking into grins.*

Then EVE *suddenly steps forward, takes GOD's hand, and makes him rise. Taking hold of GOD, she makes him start to dance with her. GOD is willing but rather clumsy. SATAN watches, laughing.*

Ha! Better than a play!

Then EVE *drags* GOD *back to Satan.*

She returns to ADAM, *and shows him how to hold her.* EVE *and* ADAM *begin to dance.* EVE *looks at God and Satan for them to do the same.*

GOD *and* SATAN *look at each other.* SATAN *curtsies:*

Enchanté.

GOD. Who's leading?

SATAN. You've just had the lesson.

GOD *offers* SATAN *his arm, and the two couples dance.*

The dancing gradually speeds to a whirl, then collapses in confusion.

All, except SATAN, *end up sitting on the ground. All are laughing, out of breath.* SATAN:

That broke the ice.

GOD. All good clean fun.

More laughter, which gradually dies.

SATAN (*very reflectively, to himself, sobering for a moment*). So do all our actions ape a vanished truth.

Then, as if making an effort, SATAN *smiles again – and*

suddenly produces a set of pan pipes. He blows a scale – up and then down.

GOD. Hey! You finished.

SATAN. A poor thing but mine own.

SATAN passes the pan pipes to GOD. GOD looks at them, blows a note, smiles, and hands them back. SATAN blows a quick trill, and pauses.

Then, as if making a decision, SATAN straightens, and begins playing a hornpipe or jig. The others beat time.

The music continues for a while, and towards the end SATAN breaks into a brief ironic caper, prancing satyr-like.

The music ends. SATAN sits abruptly, exhausted but smiling. The others all clap, laughing.

GOD. Bravo! Bravo!

SATAN (*breathless*). Give the Devil his due.

GOD reaches out and takes the pipes, and looks at them with interest.

All a matter of harmonics.

GOD. Isn't science wonderful!

GOD claps Satan on the shoulder, passes back the pipes.

Well – the life and soul of the party.

SATAN (*diffidently*). No neighbours to mind, if we raise the roof a bit.

   SATAN *is still getting his breath back, but plays one more flourish on the pipes.*

   After a moment, EVE *sings the flourish, with ornamentation.*

   Everyone looks astonished – including Eve.

SATAN (*after a moment*). A little less coloratura?

   EVE *sings again – not reacting to Satan's comment, just experimenting.*

GOD. Well, well, well.

SATAN. A bit of work on the breathing.

GOD. I knew there was some talent somewhere in the family.

SATAN. She could get anywhere, with a voice like that.

   EVE *sings another couple of notes. But she breaks off, staring out towards the auditorium.*
   She looks to one side, and as if into the distance – not at where the audience is sitting.

GOD. What is it?

ALL *turn their attention in the direction of Eve's gaze. Those sitting rise to their feet.*

Oh: the animals. Coming to drink.

ADAM *and* EVE *move a little towards the edge of the stage.*

Now we're past the worst of the heat.

A pause.

EVE (*quietly, after a time*). So many. So many.

A pause.

ADAM. You made them.

GOD. Yes.. This morning... Seems like a lifetime ago. The heat's made them thirsty.

EVE (*as if deciding something*). Yes. They are good.

A pause.

ADAM. It would be good to go down. Talk to them.

GOD (*after a moment*). Go down. But they cannot speak. They have no words. They are creatures, like the birds and the fish.

SATAN (*quietly*). The birds have.. – voices.

GOD. That is their gift.

A pause.

ADAM. You could give them voices.

EVE. Ours are too little; in all of this.

A pause. GOD *looks at Adam and Eve.*

GOD (*reflectively, nodding with approval*). Thou art a stiff-necked people.

Adam – make me a staff.

ADAM *breaks a suitable length of wood from the garden – for example, a length of stout cane from a clump of bamboo.*

SATAN (*for himself*). A surfeit of power, for a peaceful life.

SATAN *smiles.*

Ah well; it will – disarm the ladies.

ADAM *gives* GOD *the staff.* GOD *looks at Adam and Eve.*

GOD (*after a moment*). According to their natures, then.

GOD *turns to the auditorium, and advances to the front of the stage.*

A moment's pause.

Then GOD *begins to strike the staff against the stage in a slow, steady, forceful rhythm. Each impact is very loud –*

exaggerated, if necessary, by amplification.

SOUND: *From the first stroke, the calls of animals begin, amplified to fill the entire house. Each stroke of the staff adds, as convenient, one, or two, or three more calls. All are of flightless land animals – mammals, reptiles, insects – and every kind of call is there: an elephant's trumpet, a lion's roar, the lowing of a cow, a donkey's bray, the chirrup of a grasshopper – and, at the end, the hiss of a snake. The naturally loud sounds may seem to come from a distance, but the softer ones – and especially the hissing of the snake – should seem to be very close. The sounds build up – the earlier continuing under the later – into a final cacophony of noise.*

SATAN (*perhaps during the braying of the ass*). The rest is – bedlam!

SOUND: *The calls reach their climax, and gradually die away.*

SATAN *has now become motionless with introspection.*

Silence.

(*to himself, sombrely*) A full heart can make wrong seem right.

A pause. ADAM *and* EVE *have been standing together, behind* GOD. *Soon after the sounds begin, they reach out to hold hands. Now they turn to each other to kiss.*

SATAN *turns towards God, and so sees their kiss.* GOD *is still looking out towards the auditorium, unaware.* SATAN *again:*

(*sadly, with full conscious irony*) The time of noses.

A pause. Then SATAN coughs quietly, to attract God's attention.

Ahem.

GOD looks at Satan.

(*quietly*) A young man's fancy.

GOD turns and sees. A pause. The kissing is very gentle.

(*wryly*) They find love in lips.

GOD (*after a moment*). Why not? They are not animals. And, like animals, they are out of time.

But the kissing becomes more resolute. GOD and SATAN turn away.

It's all right. I married them when they weren't looking.

SATAN (*lightly*). So much for freedom, after all. Ah, well – you're making the rules.

The kissing pauses. ADAM, with an air of scientific curiosity, experimentally touches one of Eve's breasts.

(*clearing throat*) However... – I think...

GOD. If you prefer.

GOD *and* SATAN *begin to move across the stage.*

ADAM *and* EVE *begin to move towards one of the exits.*

They'll discover the body's possibilities. Being also animals. It doesn't need thought for that.

SATAN. Back to necessity again.

GOD. That's why it's not important.

GOD *pauses, and looks at Satan.*

They're nothing if not innocent.

SATAN (*after a moment*). Come on. Four's a crowd.

GOD. All right; I'm coming. But – after all, my friend, after all..

GOD *places a hand on Satan's shoulder.*

Hymens are like rules.

GOD.   )
) Made to be broken.
SATAN.)

SATAN. Do you suppose that's politically correct?

GOD (*smiling and shaking his head*). Always the scrupulous letter. Never, never the spirit!

GOD *and* SATAN *reach the far side of the stage.* ADAM *and* EVE *exit on the opposite side.*

EXIT ADAM *AND* EVE

A pause. Then the rhythm suddenly changes.

GOD (*cont., prosaically*). Will you give her the apple?

SATAN *stares.*

SATAN. My God!! Don't you have any heart?

GOD. Yes. But you will have to choose.

You know you can.. tempt her more easily. Since she is the more innocent.

SATAN (*after a moment, nodding*). Yes. She's never been alone.

(*fiercely*) You *know* what will happen. If I do.

GOD. No. I don't. That's one thing I never know.

SATAN (*agreeing*). No. I understand life. Better than you do. That's why it will always hate me; however hard I try.

(*dispassionately, as if making a point of logic*) Let me be loved. You are loved. Let me be loved.

GOD (*quietly*). How can you be loved if you cannot see love?

SATAN. You think that sin is a vocation?!.. Don't I know it's there? Even in lips! Oh, I know it's a nonsense, a fantasy, a useful delusion of the ego. But I can still feel it; here; in the garden. It blows in my face as I walk.

A pause.

Indeed – you make virtues of necessities.

A long pause. LIGHTS: *dim again for a moment.*

Another cloud!!

GOD. There shouldn't be too many of them. Well – not anywhere important.

SATAN. Why not? He'll turn any necessity into a philosophy.

GOD smiles.

You'll see. "Lonely as a cloud.." "Every cloud has a.. (*shrugs*) pigskin lining." You'll see; you'll see. Philosophies are a lot simpler than love.

GOD. Not simpler.

SATAN looks at God.

SATAN. Man cannot live by butter alone.

You sit in your web, and only see the dewdrops. You leave me to see the silk snares everywhere.

GOD *turns away.*

GOD (*after a moment, to himself*).
It is not love that does not give
And, giving, finds itself again...

GOD *turns back.*

Where would you look for love?

SATAN. To her. And him. Since my brother can not.

GOD (*after a moment, gently*). Then you must love them.

SATAN (*quietly, knowing he condemns himself*). And how can I love fools?

A *silence.*

Well, well, well, well, well.

A *pause.*

GOD (*quietly*). Will you.. tempt them.. with the apple?

SATAN (*with dignity*). If I don't.. they'll still be filled with love; and despise me with it.

GOD. And if you do, and they.. fall?

SATAN (*simply*). They'll see a little as I do; and hate me as their love dies.

GOD. I see.

SATAN. Heads you win; tails I lose.

GOD. If that's how you see it.

SATAN. It's true, God help me!

GOD. You lie in truth like a pig in dung.

SATAN. All I have is my honesty!

GOD. All you have is your fear!

A long silence.

SATAN (*wryly*). You're a devil to argue with..

A pause.

Even to be *understood* a little.

GOD. Ah..

  SATAN *approaches God.*

SATAN (*quietly*). Brother. In the name of all that's sacred.
Come back to me. Don't leave me with this.... – cross.

  GOD *draws back decisively.*

GOD. Get thee from me, Satan.

GOD *turns and exits.*

EXIT GOD

SATAN *stands motionless. A pause.*

ENTER EVE

EVE *enters unseen behind* SATAN. *She approaches him from behind, and puts her hands over his eyes.*

EVE. Guess who?

SATAN (*dryly*). I can't imagine.

EVE *removes her hands.* SATAN *turns.* EVE *smiles.*

Well, well; it's a small world. Hello.

EVE. Hello.

A pause.

SATAN. Where's Adam?

EVE. Sleeping.

SATAN. Ah.

Will you walk with me?

EVE. Yes. All right.

They take a pace or two.

SATAN (*joking*). Alone at last.

A pause. SATAN is now beneath the apple tree.

Actually, I'd hoped for a chat with you.

SATAN reaches up to pick an apple.

A word in your ear.

SATAN gestures – not *implying the apple.*

Some fruit? A banana?

EVE. No. Thank you.

SATAN. I find it hard to talk to Adam.

He smiles.

Perhaps I'm more of a ladies' man!

SATAN looks at the apple.

Still, your man sees straight.

SATAN sits, and places the apple on the rock beside him.

EVE (*not naively*). How else would he see?

SATAN looks at her. A pause. EVE sits.

SATAN (*brightly*). I can't offer you a cigarette. Or they'd say I was really leading you astray.

EVE (*after a moment*). Why?

SATAN. What? Smoking? In public? With nothing on? My dear – what would the neighbours say?

I'd never hear the end of it.

EVE (*after a moment*). You mean – God told *you* not to smoke.

SATAN *looks at her for a moment as if he doesn't understand.*

SATAN (*eventually, amused*). Oh, he wouldn't do a thing like that! No, he just thinks it can't be healthy.. Not as healthy as.. – apples. Knowing my luck, he's probably right.

EVE (*after a moment*). He's not God for you, then.

SATAN (*quietly, after a moment*). Let's say it doesn't usually come to that.

Anyway – it's probably an overrated pleasure!

(*for himself*) Pleasures mostly are.

(*brightly*) Well; quite a day for you. Born and married.

EVE *is amused.*

(*puzzled*) Did you understand that?

EVE. No. But you were – being yourself.

SATAN (*after a moment*). I see. Well, don't laugh too soon; you might be needing someone to babysit.

Then he runs on for his own amusement, with EVE *clearly understanding nothing.*

Still, I did think he could have made more of the wedding. Though I suppose, in a way, you were in white..

EVE (*abruptly, cutting in*). – What do they taste like?

SATAN (*shaken*). What?!...

EVE. Cigarettes.

SATAN. Oh. (*shrugs*) I don't know. I expect you'll try one sometime.

A pause, in which it seems from EVE's *gaze that she is about to ask what apples are like.*

(*pretending not to notice*) Things aren't like other things.

She does not ask. The moment passes.

Try a grape. Some of these.

He means those on the ground.

EVE. Would God approve?!

SATAN. Probably not!

EVE *makes a mock bow.*

EVE. You're very kind!

SATAN. You mean, I'm too polite!

You could have some garlic. But then it might be Adam, who wouldn't approve.

Though why anyone should approve or disapprove, Eve, I don't quite know. If I understand it right, most things are good for something, in God's world!

EVE. And...

A long pause – but as if Eve is playing with Satan, not hesitating.

apples?

SATAN. Oh, they're probably.. – good for the teeth, or something equally farcical. A great believer in goodness, our friend God. Personally I prefer coffee.

EVE. And smoking.

SATAN. True enough!

A pause.

EVE (*gently, looking at the ground*). You've got a friend.

SATAN (*jumping up, though not afraid*). I hate it, when they coil at my heels like that.

   A silence. After a moment, SATAN *moves away. He looks about sombrely. A pause.*

He keeps things from you, you know. (*shrugs*) He keeps things from himself.

   A pause.

EVE. Like – eating meat?

   SATAN *looks startled.*

They're only games he plays. On the surface of things. It doesn't change what's underneath.

SATAN. Surfaces kill. And the apple, then; isn't that a game?

EVE. Perhaps. But..

SATAN (*wry, nodding*). There's no game unless you play it.

   SATAN *stands abstracted.*

EVE. Why do you wear a second skin?

SATAN (*not thinking*). Because it's tougher than what's underneath.

A pause.

(*to himself*) Oh well – all's fair in religion, I suppose.

A pause. SATAN, *still abstracted, rubs his hand over his chin.*

Perhaps I'll grow a beard.

His abstraction going:

Would it suit me, do you think?

EVE. A little one, with a point?

SATAN. No! Something – bushy and.. – extrovert!

EVE (*amused*). I can't imagine!

What will you do?

SATAN (*surprised*). Me? Oh.. – I'll be uncle.

EVE (*gently, smiling*). I don't think you mean so much, of what you say!

SATAN. Sez who? Sez you. – Don't smile: I haven't got my sunglasses on.

(*genuinely*) I'm sorry: it is your honeymoon.

(*brightly*) A little precipitous, perhaps. But – I suppose one can say you were made for each other..

EVE (*cutting in*). – Why mustn't we eat apples?

SATAN *shudders.*

SATAN (*angrily*). I don't know. Perhaps they're fattening, after all. He doesn't always fill me in, you know.

SATAN *plucks a flower rather forcefully. A pause.*

(*quietly*) No. I think it's just – another game. Something you shouldn't do. For the sake of it.

(*looking directly at Eve*) You're very..

SATAN *turns away, and clearly changes what he was going to say.*

Very pretty, you know. I hope Adam – appreciates you properly.

EVE (*after a moment*). What's the matter?

SATAN. What?

EVE. Why are you still pretending things?

A pause.

SATAN. I'm sorry.

SATAN *begins to pluck petals from the flower.*

Sometimes God and I don't see eye to eye.

EVE. Why?

SATAN. Because we... – see things differently!

He's like Adam. He thinks I've got halitosis of the soul.

EVE (*after a moment*). And what do you think of him?

SATAN *looks surprised. A pause. He realises what he is doing to the flower.*

SATAN (*wryly*). She loves me!.. She loves me not!

Oh, he's a bit of a nutter. But his heart's in the right place.

(*eventually*) What do you think of him?

EVE. I think he's a good man.

A pause.

SATAN (*eventually*). And...?

EVE. I think you smile when you're unhappy.

SATAN (*after a moment, half smiling*). And what do you know of unhappiness?

EVE. Only what your body tells me.

SATAN. So we've all got a lot to learn.

A pause.

EVE. You mean, we'll be unhappy.

SATAN. I expect I'm wrong.

EVE. You see; you do pretend.

We could eat an apple, couldn't we. That's what you've wanted to say... And would we 'see things differently'?

SATAN. You'd see you didn't have to do everything he said!

(*quieter*) Indeed you would. You'd see the things I see.

   A pause.

EVE (*gently but decisively*). I think we'll stay with what we see; if all we see is true.

   A long pause.

(*suddenly*) Dance with me.

SATAN. What? Well. Ha. I suppose. I hope Adam isn't going to mind.

   EVE *shows Satan the hold.*

EVE. Like this. That's right.

SATAN (*embarrassed*). Nothing like leather... Who's leading? Don't want to start off on the wrong foot.

They begin.

I'm sorry, I ought to be undressed for the occasion... Sorry... My mistake.. I think I need some lessons.

EVE. Try without me.. That's it.. You have to put your heart into it.

SATAN. I don't think I'm much good at dancing!

SATAN stops breathless.

No. Sorry. It's not for me... Well, at least my head's still going round... You'll teach us all to spin.

SATAN recovers, smiling and mopping his face; then touches his heart thoughtfully.

EVE. All right?

SATAN (*gesturing that it's nothing*). A little heartburn.

EVE (*smiling*). Too much apple.

SATAN. I suppose you've got to laugh, really.

After a moment, the rose bush catches SATAN's attention. Suddenly he starts to laugh.

EVE. What's funny?

SATAN. I'm sorry. I can't explain.

SATAN's *laughter subsides gradually. Then his expression becomes reflective.*

EVE. What is it?

A pause.

SATAN. For a moment...

SATAN bows his head, thinking – but after a moment his attention seems caught by something on the ground. He crouches down, and seems to clear the earth around it, grasp, and tug.

The object appears from behind foliage or rock or other convenient piece of scenery. It is a large bone.

(*quietly*) The prototypes. He must have buried them.

SATAN studies the bone.

Tyrannosaurus rex.

A pause.

(*for himself*) I always feel I'm trespassing.

SATAN returns the bone to the ground.

(*for himself, quietly*) Dust to dust.

SATAN looks up and sees EVE watching.

Only models, little one.

A pause. They look at each other.
SATAN abandons this gentleness.

(*quietly*) You'll need me, you know. You will do.. Life
doesn't need me. Life needs nothing; except itself. But
you, you'll need me. You and Adam. You'll have to see
things as I do.

A pause. Then EVE turns away.

EVE (*after a moment, quietly*). I can't think, when your
tongue darts like that.

Why did he make us? Adam and me.

SATAN (*flatly*). I wish I knew.

(*quietly*) You've come into a merry inheritance.

A pause. EVE, abstracted, bends to smell a rose. She has her
hand near her face – to hold the rose, or hold back her hair
perhaps. As she straightens, her attention is caught for a
moment by the skin of her wrist – she smells it reflectively. A
flicker of reminiscence crosses her face.

EVE. Skins have perfumes.

SATAN (*briskly*). So does sweat. There'll be more sweat
than sweetness, in the world.

A pause.

(*quietly*) All this. You'd think it was a paradise.

EVE. And – isn't it?

SATAN (*shrugging*). If it's got fools in it.. Worlds aren't for paradises. Mix mind and matter, and you get some pretty misery.

(*more forcibly*) You won't always have his breasts to hang from, you know.

(*quietly, turning away*) I do care, you see.

EVE. About principles? yes.

A pause.

SATAN. Well – we can only care about what we care about.

A pause. EVE *glances at the sky.*

EVE (*matter-of-factly*). Is the sun falling?

SATAN (*flatly*). It'll be back tomorrow.

A pause.

EVE. You know – I think you're the sentimental one.

SATAN (*after a moment*). Oh, don't mind me – I'm just an old goat.

SATAN *suddenly snatches at the air with one hand – as if to catch a fly. He opens his hand, but apparently has not caught anything. He smiles.*

(*joking, throwaway*) It's a job. Beats being alone.

EVE. If you don't like to be alone with yourself.

SATAN *turns fiercely on Eve.*

SATAN. And Adam? He doesn't tell you the colour of your eyes, I suppose!

(*gently*) Well.. You'll never have a mirror.

SATAN *turns away.*

(*quietly and slowly*) I do know, you see. That I must be wrong. That all of – this – must be right; and beautiful; and good. Even though I may never see that. Even though its foundations stink.

Even if it hates me; and always must. Like a healthy mind hates mortality.

EVE (*after a moment, gently*). I think your heart never fills you.

SATAN. Her master's voice.

A pause. Then SATAN *gives up. He turns to leave.*

EVE. You could forgive him.

SATAN (*flatly*). You need somewhere left to stand, for that.

Abruptly, just tidying up, SATAN picks up the apple that he left lying on the rock, looks at it blankly, and heads towards the exit.

EVE. And if we eat that apple?

SATAN stops as if shot, but does not turn.

SATAN (*eventually*). You'll see as I do. How his games hurt.

EVE. And?

SATAN (*after a moment*). He'll cancel it all. He'll have to. He'll take us back.

We'll all be one being again.

A long pause. Then EVE begins to approach SATAN from behind.

EVE. You think it will ..help you, then?

SATAN begins to tremble. EVE comes up very close behind him.

If we do?

OFF: *a faint calling sound from ADAM, off-stage.*

EVE *pays no attention. Standing close behind Satan, she*

reaches and takes the apple from his hand, as it hangs by his side.

EVE *slowly looks at the apple, then back at Satan.*

I'll take it to Adam. We can eat it together.

OFF: *another call from* ADAM, *closer.*

Go now. It will be as I say.

A moment's pause. Then SATAN *exits in a rush, his face hidden.*

EXIT SATAN

A pause.

OFF: *another call from* ADAM, *closer.* EVE *does not move.*

A pause.

ENTER ADAM

ADAM *enters.* EVE *turns:*

Hello.

EVE *and* ADAM *speak very gently, smiling.*

ADAM. I was calling you.

EVE. You didn't say my name.

ADAM. Woman – who else would I be calling to?

A pause.

(*flatly*) I dreamt you were with me.

EVE. I was with you.

ADAM (*nodding*). But we have different worlds, in our sleep.

They look at each other. After a moment, ADAM sees the apple in Eve's hand. He looks back at her, startled.

EVE (*quietly*). We can eat it together.

A pause.

He thinks.. – it will help him – if we do.

ADAM takes the apple.

ADAM (*after a moment*). If God wants us to.

After a moment, ADAM takes a bite.

EVE (*after a moment, quietly*). No. The other one.

ADAM stops, with the piece of apple still unchewed in his mouth.

EVE reaches out, takes the apple from Adam, and takes a bite.

For a moment EVE pauses in the same way, the piece of apple in her mouth.

Then she reaches out and takes Adam's hand, looking into his face.

Her eyes fixed on his, EVE clearly and decisively begins to chew.

ADAM *takes courage, and does the same.*

They stand hand in hand, looking into each other's eyes.

EFFECTS: *a wind begins to blow.*

LIGHTS: *become colder.*

EFFECTS: *leaves blow across the stage.*

LIGHTS: *fade.*

(End of Act Two, Scene One.)

*

ACT TWO, SCENE TWO: Evening.

During the necessary scene changes, there is first MUSIC, then:-

SOUND: *the sound of birds, flocking and calling in the evening air – as in the opening scene, but in the background, as if subdued by distance. This lasts until the stage is ready for the scene to begin.*

Silence again.

LIGHTS: *approaching sunset.*

ADAM *AND* EVE *ARE ON STAGE*

Evening, towards sunset. Most of the trees have lost their leaves. The flowers and much of the grass have died. Dead leaves and a few rotting apples litter the muddy ground.

ADAM *and* EVE *are wearing animal skins. They have a small pile of 'belongings' on the ground – objects concealed in wrappings of leaves and placed in bags and pouches, also of skin.*

As the scene begins, ADAM *and* EVE *are squatting on the ground,* ADAM *with his back to the auditorium.*

After a moment, EVE *rises, and goes to the pool. Mechanically, she washes her face; then stops, pauses a moment expressionlessly, as if assessing what her body is telling her, rises and exits.*

EXIT EVE

After a moment, ADAM rises, and turns. His face is painted with lines and whorls of white or earth colours. The effect is ugly, but perhaps also pathetic. In any case, not so fierce or inhuman as to make it ludicrous when he speaks.

He stand purposelessly for a moment. Then his attention is attracted back to the ground. He crouches, picks up a stone, and apparently begins to scratch random patterns with it in the dirt, then roughly scratch them out again.

Frustrated, he strikes at the ground with the stone. Then he is about to discard it, in boredom, when he stops suddenly and looks at it. He makes the striking action once more, very gently; then looks at the stone again. Then he puts it carefully into his belt.

ENTER EVE

EVE returns, shuffling, and crouches again. ADAM and EVE look at each other, then away. A pause.

ADAM (*eventually*). Time we were going.

EVE does not move. ADAM gets up, and begins to load his back with bundles.

SOUND: *the cry of a wild animal in the distance – more lonely than bloodthirsty.*

ADAM pauses, looking up, then goes back to his task.

EVE *gets up, and loads herself down with the remaining bundles.*

ADAM *is waiting for her.*

EVE. Come on then.

ADAM *and* EVE *move off. Then, as they are about to exit, EVE stops. She turns.*

LIGHTS: *abruptly full on.*

(*at the top of her voice, blood-curdling, simultaneous with the lights*) GOD!!!

A pause. Then EVE *seems to be looking at someone just off-stage, at the far exit.*

(*quietly*) You forked us with matter. You must bear the consequences.

LIGHTS: *fade back to a little darker than before.*

EVE *turns. She and* ADAM *leave.*

EXIT ADAM *AND* EVE

ENTER GOD *AND* SATAN

GOD *enters slowly, from the exit to which Eve spoke. He is followed after a moment by* SATAN.

They are dressed in garments like monks' habits. The colours are nondescript, God's pale, Satan's dark. Their faces are half hidden by the hoods. Each carries a burning torch, which sends a flickering light across the stage.

EFFECTS: a wind begins to flap their garments against their ankles.

A silence. Then together, almost ritually, GOD and SATAN lower their hoods.

During what follows, GOD may free himself of his torch – perhaps placing it in the 'branches' of a tree at the side of the stage. SATAN, as he intends to leave at any moment, should keep hold of his torch throughout.

SATAN (*eventually, watching in the direction taken by Adam and Eve*). Fresh fields and pastures new.

A pause.

GOD. You won't stay?

SATAN. No. In a while I have to follow them.

GOD. And I have to wait for them here... Well, you'll have a long journey.

SATAN. And you'll have a long wait.

A pause.

GOD. We'll meet again.

SATAN. To compare notes. Chat about old times. No. Thank you.

GOD. What will you do?

SATAN. I can always sell something door-to-door!...

I've got a home, now. In their heart.

No doubt I'll warm to my work.

   SATAN *turns back towards the exit that Adam and Eve have taken. A pause.*

A bad time for travelling.

GOD. There'll be a moon. They wanted to get away.

   A pause.

SATAN (*suddenly, simply*). Have more compassion on them.

GOD (*after a time*). No. That's their job. Not ours.

SATAN (*after a time, very simply*). It's all gone wrong.

   A pause.

GOD (*gently*). No. I think it's.. gone as well as could be expected.

   SATAN *turns on him.*

SATAN. *WHAT – TRICK – NOW ??!!*

GOD (*after a time*). There are no tricks.

But they made a choice. Perhaps it was the right one.

A long pause.

SATAN (*slowly*). The apple...

SATAN *breaks off.* GOD *waits, but sees that he is not going to continue.*

GOD (*eventually*). Yes. That single deference..

SATAN (*interrupting eagerly*). Would've –

SATAN *breaks off.*

(*reluctantly*) ..saved them.

GOD (*quietly*). From ever being free.

A pause.

SATAN (*eventually*). How to have your cake and eat it!

A pause.

I see. Don't you want them – ..religious?

GOD (*after a time, gently*). I think what I mean by religion, and what you mean, are two different things.

SATAN. Don't you want man *dependent* on you?

GOD. He is dependent on me.. But he'll never know how much, unless he's free to find out.

SATAN. Free to fear you. Free to take his pleasures sadly. Free to fill his life with futile taboos.

GOD. Yes. A pity. Punishment is one of his ideas; not one of mine.

SATAN. They'll hate your freedom. They'll have no use for it.

GOD. Perhaps. But if we judge that for them – they won't be man.

A pause. Then SATAN *strides quickly towards the exit, to follow Adam and Eve. But, right at the exit, he stops abruptly, and half turns back.*

SATAN. Then...

A pause, while he thinks through to his conclusion.

(*triumphant, completing his turn*) I did nothing wrong!!

GOD. Oh yes. Yes. Your reasons were wrong.

The road to hell is paved with bad intentions.

(*almost throwaway*) You thought you didn't love them. And gave up.

SATAN *begins to shake.*

(GOD *still, almost for himself*) If you hadn't given them the apple – I think they'd have taken it for themselves.

GOD *turns away from Satan.*

But..

(*for himself*) Nothing's lost. Nothing's ever meaningless. Mind's.. – previous to matter. The honest mind is what matters. The dishonest one mars the universe.

SATAN *hasn't been listening.*

SATAN. You... think...

GOD *turns back to him.*

GOD (*after a moment, gently*). It sounded like it. But – I suppose you thought it would have felt good. And got love back.

A long silence, while SATAN *gets control of himself.*

(*not so gently*) You wanted to have love; not to live it.

SATAN (*quickly, struggling for sarcasm*). And what might *that* mean?

GOD *shrugs.*

GOD. Being naked in front of things.

SATAN (*in throwaway, suddenly shaking again, and so painfully and even weirdly that there is nothing at all funny in it*). Great for mosquitoes.

A pause. Then SATAN *turns on God.*

(*suddenly, fiercely, back in his own mind*) And what love was there in *my* birth?... It's hard not to have illusions, about what you've never known!

GOD. And if you'd had your 'love' – how long, before you'd have wanted to be loved alone?!

A very long pause.

SATAN (*quietly*). You know your.. – world – ..will never grow back together again. Become a mirror.

GOD. It is free to..

SATAN. Forget freedom!! See what we *know*. Choose that! For a moment.

GOD (*eventually*). No. You are in it; you are right. Love binds it, but cannot bond it.

SATAN begins to cry, and desperately tries to hide it.

SATAN. Win some, lose some.

A pause.

For ever, then.

GOD *does not reply. A pause.* GOD *and* SATAN *look towards the last of the sunset.*

LIGHTS: *the light is fading fast.*

GOD. It's been a long day.

SATAN (*eventually*). Yes. Yes.

GOD (*glancing at the sky*). What will it do tomorrow?

SATAN (*eventually*). Much the same, I suppose.

A pause.

GOD. Well. Time for bed.

SATAN (*referring to God*). Another day, another dollar.

GOD. Yes. Don't.. – work too late.

SATAN. No... Starting to rain... What day is it now?

GOD. Oh – Sunday.

My day of rest.

LIGHTS: *fade.*

(END)

AFTERWORD

Writing of this play began in Lydbrook, England, in the late 1970s, continued in Egypt in the winter of 1981-82, and was completed in April '82 on the Greek island of Paros. Comments from script readers were generally favourable, but it was never produced – though it did receive a rehearsed reading at the Sheffield Crucible, in 1985, under the direction of the late Clare Venables. This was thanks to her assistant at the time, Jen Coldwell, who noticed and liked the script. With the benefit of Clare's comments, and the perspective of time, I made a few changes to the text in the mid 1990s, and again more recently.

The play makes two main departures from the traditional Garden of Eden story – apart from having God, rather than Adam, name the animals! It reworks a Christian myth into an utterly non-Christian theology. And it changes Eve's role from one of weakness to one of conscious strength.

There are two other obvious differences between the play and the Bible. The tempter is Satan, not the serpent; and the fruit is an apple. But both these, of course, are part of the usual re-telling of the story.

On the theology. The premise is that God and Satan were once a single united being. God, for his own reasons, has decided to split them apart, and create a physical world. Satan comes to see that the fate of living things in that world will hardly be comfortable. But he is prohibited by his separation from seeing love; which may – or may not – change everything.

Incidentally, the language used by Satan, in his pleas to God, will inevitably be interpreted by some as homoerotic. This perhaps says more about our culture than about the play. Satan and God have been closer than brothers; they've been closer than twins; they've been closer than identical twins; they've been closer than conjoined twins. They've been one person. The only language available for Satan's sense of loss was that of family relationships. But in our culture, all such language has become potentially sexualised.

Then there is the role of Eve. In the traditional story, Eve is tempted into eating the fruit of the tree; the temptation being that, if she and Adam eat, they will gain God's wisdom, his knowledge of good and evil. In the play, Eve makes instead the conscious decision to eat the apple, in order to try to help Satan. It is humanity's first moral choice – Eve leads humanity from mythology into morality. In reaching that decision, she has already had to take on the knowledge of good and evil. But, inevitably, she cannot foresee all the consequences.

Some readers criticised the part of Adam as being underwritten. That was a deliberate choice. Much of the play is about the conflict between two strong male characters. I didn't feel able to interpose a third. Instead, Adam's immediate reaction to the world is physical observation and inquiry. He has his own insights into God and Satan, but they don't dominate his thoughts. Thirty-five years later, that may seem like stereotyping, or it may seem a fair reflection of tendencies usual in the formation of the male mind. But there was in any case no intention to generalise; that characterisation for Adam simply matched the needs of the story.

In contrast, almost all scriptreaders recognised the moral strength and significance of Eve. But one, in the mid 1990s, was deeply critical. One of that reader's remarks was that I had turned the crucial encounter between Satan and Eve into a seduction scene. A second, that Eve's very first acts were flirtatious – the water-splashing, and her instigation of the dancing. My mental response to the first was that the encounter between Eve and Satan (or the serpent) is always a seduction scene; the difference in my telling was that I'd made Eve strong enough to take over the seducing, and to turn it into something else. As to the second, I immediately added a new instruction to the script: "N.B.: Throughout this, Eve must not seem in any way coy or flirtatious. She simply has, for the moment – having just been created! – the playful good humour of the young. She will grow up quickly enough."

Whether, another 21 years on, my responses seem adequate, I'm not going to try to judge. It depends in part, no doubt, on whether you see Eve as an individual, or as a representative of all women. One could say that this Eve does indeed begin as the object of the male gaze – but breaks free from that. That she begins that way is almost inevitable, if one is to keep anything of the traditional story – a male God, an already-created male partner, and (in the popular telling) a male depiction of Satan. Her breaking free is not. In any event, the play – and the world in which it was written – are beginning to edge into history. Past writings are inevitably seen through the lens of current culture. Sometimes some allowance is made for past perspectives. Sometimes, in the recognition of common humanity, none is thought necessary.

A third comment from the same reader was that it was a pity that Satan spoke only in quotations, as it would have been interesting to hear him speak in his own voice...

I must admit this rather surprised me. Certainly, Satan does use some actual quotations (as God does too); and – far more often – references to popular sayings and turns of phrase. But on the other hand... "The fire forgets the spark." "There's no game unless you play it." "It's a busy world, between the skull and the sky." "As free as a fish in a frying pan." "A full heart can make wrong seem right." "We can only care about what we care about." "There'll be more sweat than sweetness, in the world." Surely these counted as some kind of voice?

And then a suspicion grew in me, that perhaps I'd done my job too well. That perhaps the above went unnoticed as original because they read so well as quotations? Coin phrases too effectively, and the new minted may just get counted in with the old.

Indeed, I was quite tempted to mark in the script where Satan really does 'speak in quotes'! – words borrowed from others. But in the end didn't (except in a couple of places where the quotation marks are to suggest that Satan uses a 'quoting' tone of voice). Most in any case will be familiar enough. One exception might be "...clothed with the sun"; which is in fact from the Bible, chapter 12 of the Revelation of St. John.

David Heidenstam.
Quy Nhon, Vietnam.
2nd January, 2018.

PRODUCTION NOTES

REQUIREMENTS
Cast: 3M, 1F
Fairly simple set, prop, and costume requirements.
Basic light and sound facilities.
Tapes of bird songs, birds flocking, animals moving,
and animal cries.

ESTIMATED PLAYING TIME
1 hour 45 minutes.

ESTIMATED RUNNING TIME
2 hours 5 minutes.
(Allowing 20 minutes for the interval and time between
scenes – mostly between Act Two, Scenes One and Two.)

SETTING
A part of the Garden of Eden, over 24 hours, on the 5th
and 6th days of Creation.

PARTS
God
Satan (known as 'The Devil')
Adam
Eve
(Skills: Eve - singing voice; Satan - pan pipes.)

SET
A single set used throughout.
Centre stage: a grassy clearing, with rocks to sit on and a
pool of water.
Stage edges: a jumbled mass of foliage from many climes.

For Act Two, Scene Two, rapid scenery and property changes are needed, to mark the switch from a spring-like scene to one resembling late autumn.

COSTUMES

For the first three scenes, God and Satan can be played in any clothes. (God's comment that they "go with the job" simply refers to their wearing clothes at all.) Satan needs pockets for some medium-sized items. God needs a knapsack or bag for some quite bulky ones – and if desired ludicrously large pockets as well. But specific costume changes are needed for Act Two, Scene Two: see pp. 130-131.

Adam and Eve are traditionally naked before they eat the 'apple': i.e. throughout the events of Act Two, Scene One. See the next pages for some thoughts on handling this. Again, a specific change of costume (and makeup) is needed for Act Two, Scene Two: see pp. 128-129.

OTHER NOTES

Handling of the garlic scene, p. 10. A bulb of garlic straight from the soil would be moist and fairly easy to pull apart (and in any case Satan has the knife used for paring the apple). But more conveniently, God could have, apparently, broken apart the bulb before he rises from the soil, so that all he offers are some cloves. In any event, God must pass to Satan everything he is holding, whether plant, bulb, or cloves, or it makes no sense for Satan to offer some back.

OPTIONAL PROLOGUE

This is included here on pp. 146-152, and would add about five minutes to playing/running times. N.B. It is only a possible production device, before curtain up; not part of the text proper of the play.

ADAM AND EVE
THEIR 'CLOTHING' IN ACT TWO, SCENE ONE

Adam and Eve are traditionally naked before they eat the apple. There are some obvious options for handling this.

A proscenium-arch production on a large stage might opt for actual nudity. It's the least likely choice, but, with the distancing provided by such a staging, it might succeed as part of the general tone of irreverence.

Flesh-coloured body stockings or similar are another obvious possibility, again probably best suited to a large stage.

At the other extreme, for a very small-scale production, casual clothes might be preferred, even fake nakedness probably being more distracting than useful.

And in between these extremes, perhaps for a typical mid-scale production, there is the option of Adam and Eve wearing limited clothing, such as swimming costumes.

In the script, these clothing options can be handled in one of two ways – covered by very small changes to just a couple of lines.

The first is Satan's, "Anyway – doesn't he get any clothes?" Which can simply be amended to, "doesn't he get any more clothes?"

And the second is also Satan's: in the scene with Eve, where he says "Smoking? In public? With nothing on?" Which can be changed to, "With nothing much on?"

The original lines would cover nudity and fake nudity. But they would also cover approaches where Adam and Eve are clothed but remain theoretically naked – the audience is just required to suspend disbelief.

The amended lines would, of course, work where Adam and Eve wear limited clothing, such as swimming costumes. They acknowledge this – and so make it just another part of the general rewriting of Genesis.

God's sewing of further clothing would still be appropriate. So would Satan's embarrassment at dancing with Eve, and his line "I should be undressed for the occasion" – as these would just reflect the contrast between the full costume of God and Satan and the relative 'undress' of Adam and Eve.

Satan's comment "Nothing like leather", referring to Eve's skin beneath his hand in the dancing position, would also still work. More realistically if Eve's costume is backless or two-piece, but still well enough even if it is not.

* * *

OPTIONAL PROLOGUE

This prologue may be useful for productions. But it is not part of the actual text of the play.

It should begin as lights go down, and while late-comers settle themselves in. It is played over the sound system by unseen actors to the darkened auditorium. It would very likely be pre-recorded.

It should have the intimate, 'close to microphone' quality of an over-amplified cinema soundtrack, played behind a film's opening credits.

The trite naturalism is deliberate – the whole scene should be played in throwaway, and hardly register. It is simply a frame for what follows. Serving perhaps to heighten, by contrast, the later sense – despite the irreverence – of a doom-laden mythology being played out.

*

HOUSE LIGHTS: *down.*

CURTAINS: *remain closed.*

LIGHTS: *none.*

FOUR VOICES: THREE MALE, ONE FEMALE

(In practice, of course, the actors will be those used in the play proper. So the lines have been allocated accordingly: those

marked G for the actor who plays God, those marked E for Eve, etc. They should not speak as they will in the body of the play. But there is no need for them to disguise their voices.)

Opening SOUNDS: clearing of throats, scraping of chairs, shifting of bodies – the sounds of a committee settling down.

S. So.

E. ..Yes.

G. Let's see.

A. Well..

G. (*clears throat*)

S. Umm..

A. Where do we start?

E. Start at the start.

G. ..Yes.

All right.

(*Silence.*)

A. (*clears throat*)

S. Umm: .."Initially.." ..No.

147

(*Silence.*)

G. ..."In the first place.."?

S. ..No.

A. "Once upon a time.."?

E. No, no.

(*Silence.*)

A. "The first thing.. that happened.."

(*Silence.*)

S. Well...

A. ..(O.k.?)

(*Silence.*)

G. "The first thing that happened."

S. "The first thing that happened.."

E. "Was.."

G. ..No..

S. Yes.

E. "The first thing that happened.."

A. "Was.."

G. ..Well..

E. .."That.."

A. "The.." er..

S. .."Absolute.."

A. "The Absolute.."

E. "Made.."

G. .."Everything.."

E. "Made everything."

S. "He.."

E. Or "she".

G. Or "she".

E. "Made.."

A. "Everything."

Starting with..

G. Starting with?

E. "Starting with.."

G. Oh, 'starting with'.. "Starting with.. The.."

S. Umm

A. (*clears throat*)

G. ..Starting with everything.

(*Silence.*)

S. "At the start of everything, the – everything.. made.. everything.."

E. (*Sigh.*)

(*Silence.*)

G. (*Clears throat.*)

(*Silence.*)

S. "In the beginning.."

A. What?

S. "In the beginning.."

G. Ah.

E. "In the beginning.."

A. "God.."

G. ..No..

S. Yes.

A. "God.."

G. "God"

E. "Created.."

S. "Made"

E. "Made"?

S. "Made"

G. "In the beginning.."

S. "God.."

E. "Made.."

(*Pause.*)

A. "The heaven and the earth."

(*Silence.*)

S. That's it.

G. That's it?

E. Yes, that's it.

(*Silence.*)

S. (*aggrieved*) .....They usually put out biscuits....

(End of Prologue.)

* * *

Also by David Heidenstam

Tales for my dog
80 microfictions from humour to horror

No, not - mostly - tales about dogs
Just stories about human beings
But any intelligent dog would understand
And in the end you will too...

Shortlisted for Self-Publishing Review 2018 Book Awards

"Probably my favorite book of the contest, in terms of heart
and talent... / a hugely enjoyable read - intelligent and ironic
and deftly crafted... / amusing, poetic, evocative, strange..."
SPR Book Awards, judges' reviews

"They are wonderful stories: remind me of shorter versions of
Aesop's *Fables* or the Persian stories of Mullah Nasreddin."
Editor of a long-established UK literary journal

"The cover grabs and the content works... This set [of stories]
are really worth reading."
Peter Finch, UK poet, author, critic

"..highly original.. [The] writing is extraordinary.. I was
staggered by some of the lines..."
Philippa Donovan, founder of Smart Quill

And from members of the reading public:
"really fun to read" (USA)
"some of it reminds me of the very clever Czech and Russian
writers I studied" (UK)
"subtle and intelligent stories" (Germany)
"a work of high imagination" (France)
"I love it" (Serbia)

If you've enjoyed this book – or if you haven't! – you may wish to leave a review on Amazon.

For more about Grey Dolphin Press, and to order copies of this book in paperback and e-book, please visit greydolphinpress.com

For other writings by David Heidenstam, please visit davidheidenstam.com

EARLY ANALYTIC
PHILOSOPHY

Leonard Linsky

EARLY ANALYTIC PHILOSOPHY

FREGE, RUSSELL, WITTGENSTEIN

Essays in Honor of Leonard Linsky

EDITED BY

WILLIAM W. TAIT

OPEN COURT • CHICAGO AND LA SALLE, ILLINOIS

PREFACE

Leonard Linsky retired from the faculty of the Philosophy Department at the University of Chicago at the end of Autumn Quarter 1992. His colleagues and friends, including a large number of students, past and present, who had studied with him, wished to honor him on the occasion. Nothing would have fulfilled the wish so well as a conference centering on the figures of early analytic philosophy he is so fond of: Frege, Russell, Wittgenstein and Carnap. With financial support from the Department of Philosophy and the Chicago Humanities Institute, such a conference was held on April 10–12, 1992. The idea for the present volume grew from a proposal to publish a proceedings of the conference. Indeed, all of the authors of papers in this volume, with the exception of Steve Gerrard, Bernard Linsky, Erich Reck and I, gave talks at the conference. With the exception of Peter Hylton's, all of the papers published here by speakers at the conference were based on or were the basis of their talks. Hylton read a paper, "Functions and propositional functions in *Principia Mathematica*", which was already committed for publication in *Russell and Analytic Philosophy* (ed. A. Irvine and G. Wedeking), Toronto: Toronto University Press, 342–60, and decided to contribute another paper to this volume. Tyler Burge's paper had also been committed for publication to *Mind,* and is now in print in Vol. 101, no. 404 (October 1992), but is reprinted here with the kind permission of *Mind.* Anthony Anderson and Burton Dreben read papers to the conference, "The Axiom of Infinity in Russellian Intensional Logic" and "Frege and Metalogic", respectively, but did not contribute papers to the volume. As for the contributors to this volume who did not speak at the conference, Gerrard and Reck were graduate students at the University of Chicago and worked extensively with Leonard. Bernard Linsky's paper, on a topic central to his father's interests, is reprinted here, with a small amendment, from *Russell: The Journal of the Bertrand Russell Archives,* Vol 10, no. 2 (ed. Kenneth Blackwell), Winter 1990–91. My own contribution to the volume grew out of a presentation I gave in the spring of 1992 in a reading group of which Leonard was also a member. The topic seemed suitable and so I used—or perhaps abused—my position as editor to include it in this volume as a mark of my respect for a long-time friend and colleague.

> . . . *tra filosofica famiglia*
> *Tutti lo miran, tutti onor li fanno*

ACKNOWLEDGMENTS

I thank the Department of Philosophy and the Chicago Humanities Institute of the University of Chicago for their financial support of the original conference in honor of Leonard Linsky, the Division of Humanities for a grant to help with the costs of preparing the manuscript, *Mind* for permission to include the paper by Tyler Burge and, especially, Gregory Fayer for his considerable help with editing the volume.

1

Tyler Burge

FREGE ON KNOWING THE THIRD REALM[1]

Anyone who reads Frege with moderate care is struck by a puzzle about the central objective of his work. His main project is to explain the foundations of arithmetic in such a way as to enable us to understand the nature of our knowledge of arithmetic. But he says very little about our knowledge of the foundations. A full treatment of this and associated puzzles would require more room than I have here.[2] I want to give a short solution to the puzzle, and then discuss one aspect of it that I find interesting.

The short solution is that Frege accepted the traditional rationalist account of knowledge of the relevant primitive truths, truths of logic. This account, which he associated with the Euclidean tradition, maintained that basic truths of geometry and logic are self-evident. Frege says on several occasions that such primitive truths—as well as basic rules of inference and certain relevant definitions—are self-evident. He did not develop these remarks because he thought they admitted little development. The interesting problems for him were finding and understanding the primitive truths, and showing how they, together with inference rules and definitions, could be used to derive the truths of arithmetic.

This short solution seems to me correct—as far as it goes. It does, however, leave out a lot. Frege thought that knowledge of the axioms of geometry required intuition—an imaginative or broadly perceptual capacity [1968, pp. 19–21]. Knowledge of the basic truths of logic simply required reason. He regarded both types of basic truths as self-evident, but the differences between the two types of knowledge are significant. That is one complication. Another is that Frege uses a variety of terms that are translated "self-evident".

---

[1]I am indebted to Tom Ricketts for clarifying his views, discussed in note 16. I have also benefited from remarks from various participants at a conference on early analytical philosophy held at the University of Chicago in honour of Leonard Linsky.
[2]An auxiliary puzzle attends this primary one. Most of Frege's philosophical work is directed at correcting what he regards as the misunderstandings embedded in normal practice and language—misunderstandings that he thought had prevented a correct understanding of the fundamental notions present in his account of the foundations. But he has even less to say about the epistemology of his analysis and elucidation of the notions that interested him than he does about knowledge of the foundations.

His sophisticated understanding of the notion is neither psychologistic nor purely proof-theoretic. He does not mean by it what most contemporary philosophers would mean by it. His uses of it relate in interesting ways to his basic philosophical views. A third complication is that there are complex relations between Frege's appeals to self-evidence and an appeal he makes to pragmatic epistemological considerations. This appeal makes his rationalism original and gives it, I think, special relevance to modern problems. Although these points are worth developing, I will not discuss them here. Instead, I shall discuss an intensification of the puzzle in the light of the short solution that I have just given.

Frege assumes that only truths are self-evident. He also assumes that it is rational to believe what is self-evident, given that it is well understood. Frege believes in other types of purely mathematical justification for arithmetical judgments besides self-evidence and derivation from self-evident truths.[3] But these other types also involve only reason. The key idea in what follows is that Frege assumes that we can know arithmetic and its foundations purely through reason, and that individuals are reasonable and justified in believing basic foundational truths (e.g. [1979a, p. 175], [1983, p. 190]).

Frege held that both the thought contents that constitute the proof-structure of mathematics and the subject matter of these thought contents (extensions, functions) exist. He also thought that these entities are non-spatial, non-temporal, causally inert, and independent for their existence and natures from any person's thinking them or thinking about them. Frege proposed a picturesque metaphor of thought contents as existing in a "third realm". This "realm" counted as "third" because it was comparable to but different from the realm of physical objects and the realm of mental entities. I think that Frege held, in the main body of his career, that not only thought contents, but numbers and functions were members of this third realm.[4] (Cf. [1968, p. viii], [1967a, pp. 15–16], [1962, p. xvii]). Entities in the other realms depended for determinate identities on functions (concepts) in the third realm. Since logic was committed to this realm, and since all sciences contained logic, all sciences were committed to and were partly about elements of this realm. Broadly speaking, Frege was a Platonist about logical objects (like numbers and truth values), functions, and thought contents. I shall say more about Frege's Platonism later, but I think that I have said enough to enable me to introduce the problem that I want to discuss.

---

[3]I distinguish purely mathematical justifications from justifications of mathematics that derive from applications to the empirical world—which he also seems to have believed in, but which I lay aside.
[4]Frege's logic is not committed to thought contents, only to extensions and functions. But this is an artifact not of his views about logic, but of his interests in deriving arithmetic from logic. For that, he did not need to refer to thought contents (*Gedanken*). But he clearly envisioned a logic which was committed to thought contents. In the correspondence with Russell, for example, he indicates the need for special names of senses to avoid the "ambiguity" of indirect discourse or propositional attitude attributions (cf. [1980, p. 153], [1976, p. 236]).

The problem is that of understanding how reason alone could justify one in believing that a thought is true, when the thought has a subject matter that is as independent of anyone's thinking as Frege indicates it is. How could mere reasoning give one any ground for believing that a realm of entities is one way rather than another when that realm is so independent of that reasoning? How could reasoning and understand have any tendency to tell one how things in such a realm really are?

The problem is clearly kin to a problem about the relation between the knowledge and truth of mathematics that is commonly discussed today.[5] The contemporary problem is that of understanding how our beliefs about mathematics could have any tendency to be true, given that we do not appear to bear causal-perceptual relations to the subject matter of mathematics. This may be seen as a problem for Frege. But it is not one that he would have naturally formulated for himself. His attitude toward the point that numbers and thought contents are not causally effective ("wirklich") seems to have been "so what?".[6] He showed no special interest in the causal theory of knowledge, or in cashing out his occasional physical-contact metaphors of "grasping" thoughts. The idea that mathematical or logical knowledge should be judged by reference to the standard of empirical knowledge would have seemed foreign to him.

Like Frege I see no reason to think that mathematical or logical knowledge is questionable because it apparently lacks causal-perceptual relations to its subject matter. But I formulated a problem that made no reference to causal-perceptual relations. This formulation seems not to import assumptions foreign to Frege. A theory of knowledge should not make it puzzling how being reasonable could be conducive to having true beliefs. Frege's rationalist theory of knowledge combines with his Platonism to raise a question at just this point. Why did he not discuss the question?

Some recent interpretations of Frege suggest that it is a question that is somehow precluded by his philosophy, or that it rests on fundamental misreadings of his views. One might question the notion of "subject matter" that the formulation of the problem uses. Or one might claim that Frege's notion of truth or of logic blocks a "meta-standpoint" from which one could raise the question. Or one could doubt whether Frege's Platonism should be understood in the way that the "third realm" metaphor suggests, and maintain that in talking about numbers or thought contents, Frege was really talking about our language or our cognitive

---

[5][Benacerraf, 1983a].

[6]Actually, he does provide an argument: objective sense-perception requires perceptual belief; but perceptual belief requires grasp of thoughts in the third realm—a non-causal relation; so one cannot cite the element of causal interaction in sense perception as providing grounds for thinking that knowledge cannot involve non-causal cognitive relations to abstract entities [1984, pp. 369–370], [1967b, p. 360].

practices in such a way that no gap between our beliefs and the numbers was even formulable. I will not criticize in detail all such lines for short-circuiting our question for Frege, though I will remark on some of them in a general way. I think none provides a good grounds for ignoring the question. In fact, Frege himself gives an answer to it. The reason why he did not discuss it in detail is similar to the reason why he did not discuss knowledge of the foundations in detail. He believed that he had little to add to a traditional answer. I think that his answer is worth understanding.

Let us back up a bit. I want to explain in more detail what I mean by saying that Frege was a Platonist about logical objects, functions, and thought contents.

First, some preliminary disclaimers. Although I think that Frege maintained a metaphysical view about numbers and other such entities, I do not believe that this view dominated his thinking. His is, for the most part, the relaxed Platonism of a mathematician who simply assumes that there are numbers, functions, and so on, and who regards these as an abstract subject matter which can be accepted without special philosophical explanation, which is clearly different from mental or physical subject matters, and which mathematics seeks to characterize correctly. One can see this attitude toward functions very prominently in "On Function and Concept". Frege highlighted the inter-subjective objectivity of scientific theorizing. He believed that standard mathematical practice told one most of what was true about mathematical entities, and he thought that one could know mathematical truths independently of any philosophy. Indeed, he assumes that ordinary mathematical practice yields "certain" knowledge even prior to the execution of his foundationalist program [1977, §13], [1968, §2].

Most of Frege's uses of his metaphysical view are defensive. His metaphysical remarks ward off idealist, physicalistic, psychologistic, reductive, or deflationary positions because he thinks that they prevent clear understanding of the fundamental notions of logic and arithmetic. As I shall later show, he does give his Platonism extra-mathematical work. But he does not think out this side of his philosophy as someone would who was concerned about certainty or who believed that logic and mathematics had no other cognitive underpinning than that provided by philosophy.

Another preliminary point about Frege's Platonism is that, although he uses the Platonic metaphor of vision on occasion, when characterizing our knowledge, he shows no interest in developing the metaphor. He appeals to no faculty other than reason in his account of our mathematical knowledge. Moreover, as I have intimated earlier, his epistemological views are complex, and involve not only Platonic elements, but elements not at all associated with traditional Platonism. The discussion in what immediately follows will be concerned with the Platonic character of Frege's *ontology*. For now, I lay epistemology aside.

As is well-known, Frege thought that extensions—including numbers,—functions—including concepts,—and thought contents are imperceptible, non-spatial, atemporal, and causally inert.[7] He emphasizes that numbers [1968, p. 108], concepts [1968, p. vii], and thought contents [1967a, p. 23], [1962, p. xxiv] are discovered—not created. He sharply distinguishes the act of thinking, which does occur in time, from the thought contents that we "grasp" or think, which are timeless. So in coming to know thought contents that denote numbers, concepts, and the like, one discovers objects, concepts, and relations that are what they are timelessly, independently of any causal influence. One comes to "stand in relation", as Frege says, with non-spatial, atemporal entities [1984, pp. 363, 369], [1967b, pp. 353–4, 360], [1967a, p. 23], [1962, p. xxiv].

Frege calls numbers, concepts, and thought contents "objective". By this he means, partly, that they are not intrinsically borne by a mind, as a pain or an after image is. He says that they are subject to laws. They are common property to different rational beings [1968, p. 26], [1984, pp. 363ff.], [1967b, pp. 355ff.]. Much of Frege's discussion of atemporal entities centres on their objectivity. For many of his purposes, the intersubjectivity and lawfulness of logic are its key properties.

Many of these things might be maintained by someone who was not a Platonist. One might make the remarks about imperceptibility, non-spatiality, atemporality, and causal inertness, if one glossed them as part of a practical recommendation or stipulation for a theoretical framework, having no cognitive import—or as otherwise not being theoretical claims or claims of reason. Carnap might have said at least some of those things, though only given certain background qualifications. Or one might have some other basis for qualifying these remarks, reading them as "non-metaphysical" or as lacking their apparent ontological import. Moreover, certain idealists might say these things. Kant might have said them, given certain background qualifications. He could have seen numbers as just as genuinely existent and discoverable as physical objects are. And he could see their objective status in terms of the possibility of inter-subjective agreement on laws governing them. Platonism has no monopoly on claims to lawlike or inter-subjective objectivity about non-spatial, atemporal entities. So we need to say more in order to distinguish Frege's view from alternatives.

I would not take very seriously a reading of Frege as a Carnapian. Discussing my attitude would require going more into his methodology and episte-

<hr/>

[7]Numbers are counted imperceptible [1968, p. 85], [1979a, p. 265], [1983, p. 284]. Thoughts are termed imperceptible [1984, p. 369], [1967b, p. 360]. Numbers are counted non-spatial [1968, pp. 58, 61, 85, 93]. Thoughts are counted non-spatial [1984, pp. 369–370], [1967b, p. 360]. Concepts or other functions are counted atemporal and by implication imperceptible, non-spatial, and causally inert [1968, p. vii, 37], [1984, p. 133], [1967b, p. 122]. He also suggests these points about concepts indirectly [1967a, p. 23], [1962, p. xxiv], [1984, p. 198], [1967b, pp. 181–182]. Numbers are counted atemporal [1984, p. 230], [1967b, p. 212]. Thoughts are counted atemporal [1984, pp. 369–370], [1967b, p. 360]. Numbers are counted causally inert [1968, p. 85], [1967a, pp. 15–16], [1962, p. xviii]. Thoughts are said to be causally inert [1967a, p. 23], [1962, p. xxiv], [1979a, pp. 137–138], [1983, pp. 149–150], [1984, pp. 230, 371], [1967b, pp. 212, 361–362].

mology than I plan to. I think it clear, however, that Frege was trying to provide a rational foundation for mathematics—in a way that Carnap would have regarded as misguided. Frege saw reason, not practical recommendation, as giving logical objects to us (e.g. [1968, p. 105]). There is nothing remotely akin to Carnap's Principle of Tolerance either in Frege's philosophical pronouncements, or even more emphatically, in his temperament.

What interests me more is the distinction between Frege's Platonism, on the one hand, and certain idealisms or certain vaguer "practice"-oriented anti-Platonisms, on the other. Platonism, as I understand the doctrine, regards some entities (for Frege, some objects and all functions) as existing non-spatially and atemporally. Further, it avoids commenting on them as having special status, including being dependent for their existence or nature (as opposed to their discovery) on practice or mental activity. They are in *no way* derivative, instrumental, fictional, or otherwise second class. The relevant entities are fundamental. It would be incompatible with Platonism to regard them as essentially part of an appearance or perspective for a thinker—as Kant would have—though they may impose constitutive conditions on such appearances or perspectives. Platonism rejects any deeper philosophical commentary that would indicate that the nature or existence of these atemporal entities is to be regarded as in any way dependent on something mental, linguistic, communal, or on anything like a practice or activity that occurs in time. In Kant, we find a non-Platonic explanation of mathematical structures in terms of a mental activity, "synthesis", that underlies the categories and the forms of spatial and temporal intuition. And in Hegel abstract structures are held to be abstractions from spirit in history. Recently, some philosophers have sought to avoid being "metaphysical", contenting themselves with generalized remarks that mathematical objects are grounded in some unspecified way in linguistic or mathematical practice. Such views can admit non–spatio-temporal entities and can grant them objective status. But they are not Platonic in my sense. They regard atemporal entities as derivative from human practices—such as linguistic activity. I see such views as covertly idealist. Idealism regards actual activity or practice as implicated in the nature and existence of non–spatio-temporal structures. Platonism holds that structure is more fundamental than actual activity.

Frege's Platonism shows itself in two ways. One is that he never enters the commentary that an idealist (or a deflationist) would enter on his claims about non–spatio-temporal entities, or about their objectivity or their discoverability. He takes them to be fundamental. The other is that he claims, more than once, that the assumption of the relevant entities explains the inter-subjective objectivity of science and communication. I will discuss these points briefly, in turn.

There is, as far as I can see, no evidence that Frege thought that the existence or nature of these non–spatio-temporal entities was to be explained in terms of human language, human inference, human practices (including the *activity* of

judgement), or other patterns of human activity in time. Frege thought of extensions, functions, and thought contents as genuinely existing entities.[8] He
opposed thinking of such entities as having some derivative status. He inveighs
against any suggestion that they are products of the mind, mere symbols, or otherwise dependent on events in time.[9] Had he maintained that extensions, functions, or thought contents were dependent on human conceptualization or human
language, judgment, or inference (actual or possible), he would have said so, and
thereby qualified the numerous remarks that have traditionally invited the Platonic interpretation of his work. He never does say so. His claims that atemporal
entities are independent of us are unqualified.

On several occasions, Frege compares the objectivity and existence of numbers, concepts, or thought contents with the existence and objectivity of physical
objects. He compares numbers to the North Sea as regards objectivity (1968, p.
34). In doing, so, he very explicitly indicates that the entity that we call "the
North Sea" is what it is completely independently of our imposing the boundaries or making a map that we use to associate that entity with the name "the
North Sea". He elaborates this comparison elsewhere:

> Just as the geographer does not create a sea when he draws boundary lines and says:
> the part of the ocean's surface bounded by these lines I am going to call the Yellow
> Sea, so too the mathematician cannot really create anything by his defining. Nor can
> one by pure definition magically conjure into a thing a property that in fact it does
> not possess—save that of now being called by the name with which one has named
> it. [1967a, p. 11], [1962. p. xiii]

He compares a mathematician's relation to numbers with the astronomer's relation to the sun [1979a, p. 7], [1983, p. 7] and to the planets [1968, p. 37]. He
says that, like geographers, mathematicians cannot create, but can only discover
"what is there and give it a name" [1968, p. 108]; cf. also [1967a, pp. 23–24],
[1962, p. xxiv], [1979a, p. 137], [1983, p. 149]. He compares our epistemic relation to numbers and concepts (and probably thought contents) to our grasping a
pencil:

> The picture of grasping is very well suited to elucidate the matter. If I grasp a pencil,
> many different events take place in my body . . . but the pencil exists independently
> of them. And it is essential for grasping that something be there which is grasped . . .
> In the same way, that which we grasp with the mind also exists independently of this
> activity . . . and it is neither identical with the totality of these events nor created by

---

[8]He quantified over them with quantifiers of different types. He used first-order quantifiers for the
objects, second-order quantifiers for the functions. The quantifiers are appropriately read as involving existential commitments.

[9]For extensions and numbers, cf. [1968, passim], [1967a, pp. 10, 12], [1962, pp. xii, xiv], [1967a, pp.
15–16], [1962, p. xviii], [1984, p. 230], [1967b, p. 212]. For concepts or functions, cf. [1968, p. viii],
[1984, p. 133], [1967b, p. 122]. For thoughts, cf. [1984, pp. 363, 370], [1967b, pp. 353–354,
360–361].

it as part of our own mental life. [1967a, pp. 23–24], [1962, p. xxiv]; cf. [1979a, p. 137], [1983, p. 149]

Thought contents exist independently of thinking *"in the same way"*, he says, that a pencil exists independently of grasping it. (The artifactual character of pencils plays no role in his understanding of the analogy, as other examples indicate.) He says that thought contents are true and bear their relations to one another (and presumably to what they are about) independently of anyone's thinking these thought contents—"just as a planet, even before anyone saw it, was in interaction with other planets" [1984, p. 363], [1967b, p. 354]. And he compares a thought's independence of our grasping it to the star Algol's independence of anyone's being aware of it [1984, p. 369], [1967b, p. 359].

All these comparisons suggest (and those of [1967a, pp. 23–24], [1962, p. xxiv], [1984, pp. 363, 369], [1967b, p. 354, 359] explicitly state) that numbers, functions, and thought contents are independent of thinkers "in the same way" that physical objects are. Frege nowhere asserts or clearly implies that he maintains any sort of idealism—Kantian or otherwise—about the physical objects studied by the physical sciences. He nowhere qualifies the ontological status of physical objects. It is dubious historical methodology to attribute to a philosopher with writings that stretch over decades a large, controversial doctrine if he nowhere clearly states it in his writings. If Frege had believed in any such idealism about physical objects (or any doctrine qualifying their ontological status), he would have surely said he did.[10] Doing so would have been necessary for a philosopher to balance the flat-out statements about mind-independence that Frege makes.[11]

---

[10]Such passages as [1979a, p. 137], [1984, p. 149], or any of the various passages about independence of mind that I discuss below, would require strong qualification, which Frege nowhere makes, to be compatible with any sort of idealism or deflationary reading. For an interpretation of Frege as a Kantian idealist, see [Sluga, 1980] e.g. pp. 59–60, 115–116. Sluga cites mainly considerations that are external to Frege's texts. He also writes, "the central role of the Fregean belief in the primacy of judgments over concepts would seem to be explicable only in the context of a Kantian point of view". Sluga does not explain this remark. I think it misleading. Judgments and inferences are a source of discovery. But logical theory is about the forms of correct judgment and inference—not about judgments and inferences. Frege regards judgment as a form. (Cf. [1984, pp. 383–385], [1967b, pp. 372–374].) I know of no evidence that he saw this form as dependent for its nature or existence on actual activities of judgment, or on anything like Kantian synthesis; there is substantial evidence that he did not.

[11]Some philosophers have suggested that Frege's use of the context principle somehow suggests a qualification on his Platonism. Issues surrounding Frege's context principle(s) are, of course, extremely subtle and complex. But it seems to me that the suggestion must involve some confusion. The context principles govern relations between linguistic expressions and their senses or referents. They do not bear directly on the nature of the senses or referents themselves at all. At most, one of the principles might be coherently thought to rule out certain naive forms of epistemological Platonism (those that require that we have perception-like intuition of mathematical objects). There are many complex issues here, and some of them are not completely independent of ontology. But I think that any simple appeal to the context principles to motivate opposition to my interpretation will confuse language and epistemology with ontology.

Frege thought that to know the physical world, one has to grasp thoughts (which bore for him eternal denotational relations to concepts and extensions) that are eternal and eternally true. Logic is embedded in the content of any knowledge. Since logic is about (denotes) concepts and other functions, relations, and logical objects, all knowledge is at least partly about non–spatio-temporal entities. Moreover, logic concerns the forms of correct judgment and inference; and logical structure is discovered by reflecting on patterns of correct judgment and inference. But Frege does not give the slightest indication that he thought that either the physical world or the non–spatio-temporal entities inevitably appealed to in knowing it depend in any way on any activities of judgment, inference, or linguistic practice.[12]

Frege not only compares non–spatio-temporal entities to physical objects in their independence of us; he makes unqualified statements about the independence of such entities from anything about us. He repeatedly claims that both the truth of thought contents and thought contents themselves are independent of individuals' and groups' thinking the thoughts or recognizing them to be true [1967a, pp. 15, 23], [1962, pp. xvii, xxvi], [1968, p 60], [1984, p. 363], [1967b, p. 354]. He writes: "What we want to assert in using that proposition [that the number three is prime] is something that always was and always will be objectively true, quite independently of our waking or sleeping, life or death, and

---

[12]An interpretation of Frege similar to Sluga's is proposed in [Weiner, 1990]. In interpreting the North Sea comparison [Frege, 1968, p. 34], Weiner notes Frege's remark that if we should happen to draw the boundaries of what we call "the North Sea" differently, what we now call "the North Sea" would still exist, though perhaps unrecognized. But she continues. "It is important to realize, however, that the claim that such unrecognized objects exist need not be a substantive metaphysical claim. For . . . to claim that unrecognized objects exist is simply to claim that it is possible to formulate (heretofore unformulated) concepts under which exactly one object falls" (p. 171). Weiner cites no texts to support this reading. I see no reason to think that existence claims for Frege are "simply" claims about possibility or about formulations: he gives every indication that they are not about possibility, language, or activity at all. Later she correctly claims that Frege believed our knowledge requires language or drawing boundaries. But she moves without argument from this remark about knowledge to one about the world: "Frege's view is that the physical world is not articulated—that we impose structure on it" (p. 184). The language of imposition is not present or implied in Frege. That concepts mark boundaries of the ocean is nowhere said to depend in any way on anything about language or people. (Similarly, with concepts demarcating possible numerations in such cases as packs of cards.) Frege writes: "To bring an object under a concept is merely to recognize a relation that already existed beforehand" [1984, p. 198], [1967b, pp. 181–182]; cf. [1979a, p. 137], [1983, p. 149]. Weiner glosses Frege's claims that mathematical truths are independent of us by *excepting* an alleged presupposed need to impose structure and formulate boundaries linguistically (p. 201ff.). She further writes, "discovering what is 'there' in the 'realm of the abstract' amounts to discovering what meets the descriptions that interest us" (p. 203). Weiner cites no texts to support either of these claims. Frege makes no exceptions or qualifications on his claims of independence; he notes no such presupposition. And it is at best deeply misleading to say that for Frege discovering mathematical structures "amounts to" discovering something associated with words, our interests, or ourselves. When our interests and descriptions happen to accord with mathematical truth, we do, of course, discover things that "meet" those interests and descriptions. But Frege explicitly says that our relation to logical truths and mathematical structures is "inessential" to their nature and existence [1984, p. 371], [1967b, p. 361].

irrespective of whether there were or will be other beings who recognize or fail to recognize this truth" [1984, p. 134], [1967b, p. 123].

The lack of qualification in his claims of independence is especially striking in two passages: one where he writes that someone's thinking a thought has "nothing to do" either with its truth or with the thought content itself [1984, p. 368], [1967b, p. 359]; and another where he writes that thought contents are not only true independently of our recognizing them to be true, but they, the thought contents themselves, are "absolutely independent of our thinking" [1979a, p. 133], [1984, p. 145]. Independence is independence. Frege's repeated remarks about mind-independence of non–spatio-temporal entities would not have been literally true, if they had been backed by a set of unstated qualifications of the sort that an idealist (or deflationary) interpretation of them would require. Ultimately the idealist asserts dependence of the thought contents and timeless objects on some underlying practice or activity that makes possible the framework in which attributions of objectivity are made. No idealist—and no deflationist who thought that non–spatio-temporal entities were dependent on our language, practices, or judgments, or who thought that general philosophical assertions about them were "non-factual"—would have made such statements without careful, explicit qualifications. Frege enters no such qualifications.

Frege repeatedly inveighs against seeing logic (or mathematics) as embedded in language in the way that grammar is.[13] He thought that thought contents, logical objects, and logical functions bore no such essential dependence relation to the actual practice of thinking or language use. For Frege, the subject matter of logic is not the nature or human thinking or practice [1967a, p. 13], [1962, p. xvi], *even when that practice accords with the laws of truth:* "But above all we should be wary of the view that it is the task of logic to investigate actual thinking and judging, insofar as it is in agreement with the laws of truth" [1979a, p. 146], [1983, p. 158]—the published translation is ambiguous in a way that does not match the German. This independence insures, for Frege, no scope for variation in the laws of logic between one group of thinkers and another [1979a, pp. 7, 146], [1967b, pp. 7, 158], [1967a, p. 13], [1962, pp. xv–xvi].

Frege criticizes one Achelis who writes,

> . . . the norms which hold in general for thinking and acting cannot be arrived at by the one-sided exercise of pure deductive abstraction alone; what is required is an

---

[13]Some interpreters of Frege have taken his views to be redescriptions of features of our practices of judgment or of linguistic use. Although Frege does describe logical structures that inform linguistic and cognitive practice, and does think that by reflecting on and reforming such practice, we can discover these structures, I know of no evidence that Frege thought that the theory of judgment is really fundamentally about the activity or practice of judgment, much less linguistic practice. It is important to distinguish Frege's method of discovery (which does focus on language and activities of judgment) from Frege's views about the nature of thought contents and of judgment. It is also crucially important to realize that Frege was interested in judgment as a norm yielding form, not in judgment as a human activity. Frege thought that thought contents and the form of judgment bore no essential relation to either language or activities (practices) of judgment, potential or actual, of human beings.

empirico-critical determination of the objective principles of our psycho-physical organization which are valid at all times for the great consciousness of mankind.

Frege replies:

[It appears that according to Achelis] the laws in accordance with which judgments are made are set up as a norm for how judgments are to be made. But why do we need to do this? . . . Now what is our justification for isolating a part of the entire corpus of laws and setting it up as a norm? . . . Are [the laws of logic] like the grammar of a language which may, of course, change with the passage of time? This is a possibility we really have to face up to if we hold that the laws of logic derive their authority from a source similar to that of the laws of grammar . . . if it is normal to judge in accordance with our laws of logic as it is normal to walk upright [1979a, p. 147], [1983, p. 159].

Frege thought one can discover logic by reflecting on linguistic and mathematical practice. But he makes it very clear that his logical theory is not about practices, and does not take its authority from such practices. They are not what ground the normative structures that logic articulates.[14]

A second way Frege's Platonism shows itself lies in his attempts to explicate the success of the science, the fact of intersubjectively objective cognitive practices, and indeed the authority of logic, in terms of the timelessness of the truths and structures of logic. In *The Basic Laws of Arithmetic* he states that the laws of logic (which he also calls the laws of truth) are authoritative *because* of their timelessness: "[the laws of truth] are boundary stones set in an eternal foundation, which our thought can overflow, but never displace. It is because of this that they have authority for our thought if it would attain to truth." [1967a, p. 13], [1962, p. xvi].

Frege frequently claims that only because individuals are not the bearers of thought contents is scientific communication possible [1967a, p. 17], [1962, p. xix], [1979a, pp. 133, 137–138], [1983, pp. 144, 149–150], [1984, pp. 363, 368], [1967b, pp. 354–359]. But he sometimes goes further. In the logic manuscript of 1897 he indicates that it is the timelessness of the subject matter of logic—the laws' not containing conditions that might be satisfied at some times and not at others—that enables logic to provide completely universal laws of truth [1979, p. 148], [1983, p. 160]. The idea seems to be that all true thoughts are eternally true if they are true at all; but some have temporal subject matters. Some true

---

[14]Frege writes that there is no contradiction between something's being true and everyone's taking it to be false [1967a, p. 13], [1962, pp. xv–xvi], making it clear that he does not believe in some general connection between thought contents (or intentional contents, or what are expressed in language) and actual judgments and practice that would close any possible gap between mind and subject matter. There is more evidence for this fact in his discussion of scepticism in "The Thought". The example he gives in [1967a, p. 13] and [1962, pp. xv–xvi] concerns an empirical truth. As I discuss below, he indicates that some truths—simple truths of arithmetic and basic logical truths—can be denied only through madness, and that any attempt to deny them in a thoroughgoing way will undermine judgment itself.

laws even contain conditions that might be satisfied at certain times but not at others. But the laws of logic cannot be about temporal subject matters and cannot contain such conditions. For if the truth of some thought follows from the truth of others, then it must always follow. So to account for the universal aspect of entailment, one must assume that the subject matter of logic is eternal. (The conclusion of this argument, though not the argument itself is stated in [1967a, p. 13], [1962, p. xvi].)

In "Thoughts" Frege gives two more arguments that scientific objectivity (of communication and of knowledge of the physical world, respectively) is explicable only on the view that thought contents belong to a "third realm" that is neither mental nor physical. In the first argument [1984, p. 363], [1967b, p. 354] he holds that scientific communication cannot be understood on the assumption that thought contents are ideas in particular people's minds. He had previously maintained that thought contents are clearly not perceptible or knowable on the basis of perceptions [1984, pp. 354, 360], [1967b, pp. 345, 351]. He concludes [1984, p. 363], [1967b, p. 354] that in order to understand the objectivity of the communal scientific enterprise, one "must recognize" the third realm. The timelessness of the truths of this realm and the fact that their truth is independent of whether anyone takes them to be true are clearly seen as part of an account of how a "science common to many on which many could work" is possible.[15]

In the second argument [1984, p. 368], [1967b, p. 359], Frege indicates that a "firm foundation of science" must be facts that are independent of men's varying states of consciousness. Facts are, he maintains, true thoughts. True thoughts have the requisite independence: not only are they not part of anyone's "inner" mental world; their truth "Has nothing to do with" someone's thinking them. The work of science consists in the discovery of true thoughts (which provide a "firm foundation" for the science). Moreover, Frege argues that the applicability of mathematical truths to investigations at any time (he cites application of mathematics in an astronomical investigation into events in the distant past) is possible *because* a mathematical thought's truth, and the thought content itself, are timeless. So, he concludes, explicating the objectivity of science and the temporally neutral applicability of mathematics requires that both the thoughts and their truth be timeless.[16]

---

[15]Although this argument is not explicit in his 1968, the attitude behind it is not hard to discern in the introduction [1968, pp. vii–viii]***. I think that the argument is the least interesting of the three arguments I am discussing.

[16]Thomas G. Ricketts [1986] opposes reading Frege as "the archetypical metaphysical platonist" (p. 65), according to which "the mind-independent existence of things is for Frege a presupposition of the representational operation of language: it explains how our statements are determinately true or false apart from our ability to make or understand them". This description of Platonism does not fit the Platonism I attribute. Frege was clearly not trying to give a general explanation of linguistic representation or even of intentionality in judgment. But—in contrast to Ricketts—I think that Frege thought, as the previously cited passages indicate, that assuming the mind-independence of all thought contents, concepts, and logical objects, was necessary to understanding the objectivity of scientific practice and the universal applicability of logic and mathematics. I do not think that he

These arguments take for granted the existence of the objectivity manifested in inter-subjectively accepted norms for communication and the checking and confirming of scientific results. Frege thinks that we need no reassurance about its solidity. He is not concerned with scepticism. He regards ordinary certainties as certain [1977c, §13], [1968, p. 2]. He does not seek foundations, nor does he appeal to his Platonism, to bolster confidence in an otherwise doubtful scientific enterprise. He does not view philosophy in the grand manner, as protecting science against otherwise dangerous philosophical worries. He articulates his Platonism because he finds a refusal to qualify the timelessness of mathematical structures, or to explain them in terms of something more familiar and temporal—such as our minds or practices—provides the best understanding of scientific inter-subjective objectivity. He thinks his view shows why practices that have been found to be firm are in fact firm [1968, p. 2].

Let us turn to Frege's views about how we know this third realm of entities. As I indicated earlier, I am prescinding from complexities in Frege's epistemology. What is important for our purposes is that Frege thought that our knowledge of the primitive logical truths and inference rules, depended on a logical faculty—reason [1968, p. 21], [1980, pp. 37, 57], [1976, 37, 89], [1962 II, §74], [1984, p. 405], [1967b, p. 393], [1979a, pp. 267–273], [1983, pp. 286–292].) The question is: How could Frege believe that reason alone could give one knowledge of an atemporal realm of entities that are completely independent for their existence, nature, and relations to one another, of anyone's reasoning?

Frege is aware that foundational questions about our knowledge of mathematical structures ultimately come down to questions about knowledge of the

---

thought that such objectivity would somehow be in jeopardy in the absence of such an explanation. Logic was for him epistemically prior to philosophy of logic. It is rather that such an explanation accounts for what is involved in judgment, logical inference, and logical truth. Ricketts elaborates: "The crucial feature of this [Platonist] line of interpretation is its taking ontological notions, especially that of an independently existing thing, as prior to and available apart from logical ones, from notions of judgment, assertion, inference, and truth" (p. 66). Ricketts also thinks that Frege's claims about the objectivity associated with judgment are not meant to be factual claims, and that there is therefore no possible explanation for Frege of objectivity. As I indicate in the text, I see no evidence for a relevantly applicable distinction in Frege between factual and non-factual claims. Moreover, Frege's Platonism does not involve any claim about the priority of ontological notions over logical notions. (I do not see even initial plausibility to attributing this assumption to Frege.) Logic and ontology are mutually entangled in Frege. Logic is about what is, as Frege says [1984, p. 351], [1967b, p. 342]; it has an ontology. But logic is the most general science. So no thought about being could be independent of its notions. Moreover, Frege's most fundamental ontological categories (function and object) are logical categories. Nor does Frege's appeal to ontology in his account of the objectivity of science and the universality of logic imply that he thought that ontological notions were prior to logical ones, much less available apart from them. The explanation is not a definition, derivation, or reduction. All the key ontological notions he uses both presuppose and include logical notions. Rather he thought that a full understanding of logic involved appeal to notions like logical object, function, thought content, mind-independence, timelessness, causal inertness, imperceptibility, non-spatiality. Frege thought of himself as describing the ontological features that logic must have. Logical and ontological notions are interrelated for Frege; and all the relevant logical objects and functions are timelessly related to the relevant notions (thought components). Frege sees the whole logical structure, not just objects, in a Platonic fashion.

primitive truths and inference rules. He is admirably clear that logic does not answer these questions: "The question why and with what right we acknowledge a law of logic to be true, logic can answer only by reducing it to another law of logic. Where that is not possible, logic can give no answer" [1967a, p. 15], [1962, p. xvii]; "We justify a judgment either by going back to truths that have been recognized already or without having recourse to other judgments. Only the first case, inference, is the concern of Logic" [1979a, p. 175], [1983, p. 190]. Frege lays fundamental epistemological questions aside in much of his work, especially in *Basic Laws of Arithmetic*. But it would be a serious misunderstanding to think that he thought that the questions were off limits.[17] For he expresses a consistent interest in them.

Of course, he thought that one could not and need not argue for the basic logical truths. But he did see them as a source for the justification of the belief in them by a person who understood them. He thought that they were self-evident. We justify our judgment of the basic truths, as he said, without having recourse to other judgments [1979a, p. 175], [1983, p. 190].

One needs to bear in mind here a three-fold distinction that Frege often carries along in his writings (it is very explicit in "The Thought" [1984, p. 352], [1967b, pp. 342–343]: (*a*) psychological explanation of belief or judgment, including an account of its acquisition, (*b*) justification of our belief or judgment, and (*c*) grounding for logical truth. Frege always lays aside psychological explanation. But he repeatedly discusses the justification of "our" belief or judgment in logical truths as well as the grounding of logical truth. Understanding grounding of truth is a matter of understanding the natural order of truths, which is independent of thinking or practice, and the "same for all men" [1968, p. ii, 17]***, [1967a, pp. 13, 15], [1962, pp. xvi, xvii]. One understands the grounding of truth when one understands the natural order of logical and mathematical proofs, and the primitive truths on which such proofs rest. What grounds logical truths are the primitive logical truths.

One of Frege's primary motivations for understanding logical truth and the proof structure of logic was to understand the nature of justification for our mathematical judgments. In *Foundations of Arithmetic* Frege begins in §§1 and 2 by announcing an interest in the proof structure of mathematics. But he immediately associates this structure with the question of the justification of belief. In §2 he says that the aim of proof is, partly, to place a proposition beyond doubt. In §3 he says that "philosophical motives" underly his inquiry into the foundations of mathematics: The motives turn out to centre on answering the question "Whence do we derive the justification of our assertion [of mathematical truths]?" The

---

[17]Cf. also [1979, pp. 3, 175], [1983, pp. 3, 190]. Contrast [Ricketts, 1986a, p. 81] "There is, as far as Frege is concerned, nothing to be said about the justification for our recognition of those basic laws of logic to be truths"; and [Weiner 1990, pp. 71–72]. Frege says a good bit about the epistemology of belief in the basic laws, scattered through his writings. I shall not discuss these passages in this paper, however.

question of whether arithmetic is analytic turns out to concern the justification for making a judgment. He refines this to read, it concerns "the ultimate ground upon which rests the justification for holding [a proposition] to be true."

What is important about this passage is not only Frege's concentration on justification for judgment, but also his belief that the justification of an arithmetical judgment derives from the mathematical foundation (*Grund*)—from the primitive truths. The problem [of finding the justification for assertion or judgment], he says, is to be solved by "finding the proof of the proposition and following it back to the primitive truths" [1968, p. 4]. One might ask, how can a problem of the justification of our beliefs or judgments be solved by citing primitive truths? How can such truths be primary in an account of justification?

Frege's line is made clearer in "The Thought" where he characterizes laws of truth as general laws which concern not "what happens" but "what is". Speaking of these laws about "what is" in the third realm, Frege says that "from the laws of truth there *follow* ["ergibt sich"—a non-technical term] prescriptions about asserting, thinking, judging, inferring" [1984, p. 351], [1967b, p. 342]. Frege then calls these prescriptive epistemic laws "laws of thought" [1984, p. 351], [1967b, p. 342]. This is a paradigmatic Platonic direction of explanation: from what *is* in an abstract realm to what is reasonable. What could be the nature of this derivation from general laws of truth—which concern logical objects and functions—to prescriptive laws about judgment? Frege writes: "[the laws of truth] are boundary stones set in an eternal foundation, which our thought can overflow, but never displace. It is because of this that they have authority for our thought *if it would attain to truth* [1967a, p. 13], [1962, p. xvi].

Is it contingent that a judging subject "would attain to truth"? Frege is certainly insistent that the laws of truth are independent of their being taken to be true by anyone [1967a, pp. 13, 15], [1962, pp. xvi, xvii]. Moreover, he thinks it not contradictory to suppose something's being true which everyone takes to be false [1967a, p. 13], [1962, pp. xv–xvi]. On the other hand, Frege sees judgment as an advance from thought content to truth value. The function or aim of judgment is to reach truth. So to be a judging subject, one must have this aim or function insofar as one makes judgments. In this sense, the prescriptions of the laws of truth must apply to the judgments of judging subjects.

There is a second way in which Frege thinks that there is a deep, non-contingent relation between the laws of truth and prescriptive laws about judgment. To be rational, he thinks, one must be disposed to acknowledge the simplest logical truths. Judgments in contradiction with the laws of logic would constitute a kind of madness [1967a, p. 14], [1962, p. xvi]. In fact, Frege appears to believe that failure to acknowledge primitive logical laws, like the principle that every object is identical with itself, and even certain truths of arithmetic, would throw thought into confusion and undermine the possibility of genuine judgment and thought [1968, p. 21]. This suggests that he was inclined to believe that a disposition to acknowledge basic logical truths and inferences—and a disposition not to deny non-basic but relatively simple truths of arithmetic—was a condition not only for being rational but for being a judge or thinker at all.

Here it is worth looking very carefully at a famous passage in *Basic Laws*. Frege considers a supposed possibility in which beings had laws of thought (prescriptions for judgment) that contradicted ours. He claims that such beings would exhibit a "hitherto unknown type of madness", and indicates that such beings' procedures for taking things to be true would be in radical disaccord with the laws of truth [1967a, p. 14], [1962, p. xvii]. Shortly afterwards, he writes: .

> If we step away from logic, we may say: we are compelled to make judgments by our own nature and by external circumstances; and if we do so, we cannot reject this law—of Identify, for example; we must acknowledge it unless we wish to reduce our thought to confusion and finally do without all judgment whatever. I shall neither dispute nor support this view: I shall merely remark that what we have here is not a logical consequence. What is given is not a ground (*Grund*) for something's being true, but for our taking it to be true. Not only that: this impossibility of our rejecting the law in question hinders us not at all in supposing beings who do reject it; where it hinders us is in supposing that these beings are right in so doing . . . Anyone who has once acknowledged a law of truth has by the same token acknowledged a law that prescribes the way in which one ought to judge, no matter where, or when, or by whom the judgment is made [1967a, p. 15], [1962, p. xvii].

Frege is taking a hands-off attitude toward the epistemological issues for the purpose of his mathematical treatise. But, given his own beliefs, what does he neither dispute nor support in the view he states? Some have thought that in citing the limits of logic, he is prescinding from any judgment about grounds for our taking something to be true, as opposed to the ground for its being true. Some have even held that grounds for our taking something to be true are thought by Frege to be psychologistic, and of no interest to him. These are serious misreadings of the passage.

Understanding grounds for our *taking* something to be true had long been what motivated his inquiry into the foundations of arithmetic. (Cf. especially [1968, p. 3], where he uses exactly the same German terms as he does in the above-cited passage: grounds for taking [holding] something to be true.) One page earlier in *Basic Laws* Frege characterized the laws of logic in the double way I have described: not only as laws of truth but as laws that "prescribe the way in which one ought to think" [1967a, p. 14], [1962, p. xvi]—as laws of thought. What Frege takes no position on is whether we are compelled to acknowledge the laws by our own nature and by external circumstances.

This is indeed a psychological matter. He thinks that any such psychological law would admit of conceivable exceptions—mad beings that do reject the law. But where he writes, "we must acknowledge it unless we wish to reduce our thought to confusion and finally do without all judgment whatever", he is speaking in his own voice. For he had already indicated that he believes that renouncing the laws of arithmetic (which are less basic for him than the basic laws of logic) would be to reduce thought to confusion and make thinking impossible [1968, p. 21]. Frege thinks that acknowledging these laws, at least implicitly in one's actual thinking, is necessary for having reason and for being a non-degenerate thinking and judging subject. (He apparently believed that although a mad person could reject a law, abiding by such rejection would reduce thought to confusion, and by degrees undermine judgment altogether.) These are normative, not psychological, judgments. Although they are not logical consequences, they are part of Frege's epistemic view.

So let us summarize the view that Frege maintains. He holds that justification for holding logical laws to be true rests on and follows from primitive laws of truth. He spells out this dependence of epistemic justification on the laws of truth in two ways. He thinks that laws of truth indicate how one ought to think "if one would attain to truth". But a judging subject necessarily would attain to truth, insofar as it engages in judgment. So any judgment by a particular person necessarily is subject to the prescriptive laws set out by the primitive laws of logic. One is justified in acknowledging them because doing so is necessary to fulfilling one's aim and function as a judging subject.

Frege's second way is: acknowledgement of certain laws of truth is necessary for having reason and for engaging in non-degenerate thinking and judging. One is rationally entitled to judge the primitive laws of logic to be true because the nature of reason—and even non-degenerate judgment—is partly constituted by the prescription that one acknowledge at least the simple and basic laws of truth. To put it crudely, reason and judgment—indeed mind—are partly defined in terms of acknowledging the basic laws of truth.[18]

Our problem was to explain how, for Frege, mere reason could give grounds to believe that a subject matter is any particular way, given that the subject matter is atemporal, causally inert, and independent of thinking about it. Most current approaches to the substantive problem look for some analog of causal interrelation in our mathematical knowledge. More traditional views—both Platonic and idealist—see the relation as individuative or constitutive.

An idealist line is to make the subject matter constitutively dependent on thinking, synthesis, or practice. Frege's line is to hold that, although the laws of

---

[18]One can see this view alluded to in the passage where Frege claims that logic can, with anti-idealists and anti-psychologistic qualifications, be seen as the study of not minds but Mind (*Geist*) [1984, p. 369], [1967b, p. 359]. One can also see it in his claim: "We might with alteration of a well-known proposition say: the proper object of reason is reason. In arithmetic we are not concerned with objects which we come to know as something alien from without through the medium of the senses, but with objects given directly to reason, which as her most proper objects are completely transparent to her" [1968, p. 115]. Cf. also [1977, §23], [1968, §26]. These quotes are not idealist, as they have sometimes been taken. They are expressions of the view that the basic forms and objects of logic constitutively inform minds, and help define what it is to be mind or reason.

truth are independent of judging subjects, judging subjects are in two ways not independent of the laws of truth. First, to be a judging subject is to be subject to the prescriptions of reason, which in turn are provided by the laws of truth (logic). For judgment has the function of attaining truth; and the laws of logic— which are constituted by atemporal thoughts and atemporal subject matter—provide universal prescriptions of how one ought to think, given that one's thinking has the function of attaining truth. Second, being a judging subject is to have or have had some degree of reason. Having or having had some degree of reason requires acknowledging, at least implicitly in one's thinking, the simplest, most basic logical truths and inferences; and doing so commits one to an atemporal subject matter. Questions of "access" to the third realm are on reflection seen to be misconceived. For, to reverse somewhat Gertrude Stein's dictum about Oakland, there is no there there.

Why was this line not more prominent in Frege's philosophy? He thought that his primary contribution lay in identifying primitive truths and inference rules, and in deriving arithmetic from them. He accepted the traditional rationalist–Platonist line about the relation between reason and primitive truths. He did not think it needed substantial elaboration. Like Frege, I think that this neglected line is not to be dismissed. Unlike Frege, I think it may be worth developing.

2

Michael Friedman

CARNAP AND WITTGENSTEIN'S
TRACTATUS

In his "Intellectual Autobiography" Carnap makes it clear that Wittgenstein—
that is, the Wittgenstein of the *Tractatus*—was the philosopher who, after
Frege and Russell, had the greatest influence on Carnap's own philosophical
thinking. For it was from Wittgenstein's *Tractatus* that he derived his characteristic conception of logical and analytic truth:

> For me personally, Wittgenstein was perhaps the philosopher who, besides Russell
> and Frege, had the greatest influence on my thinking. The most important insight I
> gained from his work was the conception that the truth of logical statements is based
> only on their logical structure and the meaning of the terms. Logical statements are
> true under all conceivable circumstances; thus their truth is independent of the con-
> tingent facts of the world. On the other hand, it follows that these statements do not
> say anything about the world and thus have no factual content. [Carnap, 1963, p. 25]

Whereas Frege and Russell had shown that all mathematical truth is logical—
and therefore, for those who accept the view that all logical truth is analytic, that
mathematical truth is also analytic—Wittgenstein was the first to articulate the
true nature of logical truth itself: the truths of logic are tautologies that necessarily hold in all possible circumstances and hence say nothing about the world.[1]

This conception of the tautologous character of logical and mathematical
truth represents, for Carnap, the most important point of agreement between his

---

[1]Carnap explains Wittgenstein's distinctive contribution to the articulation of the concept of analytic
truth as follows: "I had learned from Frege that all mathematical concepts can be defined on the
basis of the concepts of logic and that the theorems of mathematics can be deduced from the principles of logic. Thus the truths of mathematics are analytic in the general sense of truth based on logic
alone. The mathematician Hans Hahn, one of the leading members of the [Vienna] Circle, had
accepted the same conception under the influence of Whitehead and Russell's work, *Principia
Mathematica*. Furthermore, Schlick, in his book *Allgemeine Erkenntnislehre* (1918), had clarified
and emphasized the view that logical deduction cannot lead to new knowledge but only to an explication or transformation of the knowledge contained in the premises. Wittgenstein formulated this
view in the more radical form that all logical truths are tautological, that is, that they hold necessarily in every possible case, therefore do not exclude any case, and do not say anything about the facts
of the world" [1963, p. 46].

philosophy and that of the *Tractatus*. But there is also an equally important point of fundamental disagreement. Whereas the *Tractatus* associates its distinctive conception of logical truth with a radical division between what can be said and what can only be shown but not said—a division according to which logic itself is not properly an object of theoretical science at all—Carnap associates his conception of logical truth with the idea that logical analysis, what he calls "logical syntax," is a theoretical science in the strictest possible sense:

> Furthermore, there is a divergence on a more specific point which, however, was of great importance for our way of thinking in the Circle. We read in Wittgenstein's book that certain things show themselves but cannot be said; for example the logical structure of sentences and the relation between the language and the world. In opposition to this view, first tentatively, then more and more clearly, our conception developed that it is possible to talk meaningfully about language and about the relation between a sentence and the fact described. . . . [I] pointed out that only the structural pattern, not the physical properties of the ink marks, were relevant for the function of language. Thus it is possible to construct a theory about language, namely the geometry of the written pattern. This idea led later to the theory which I called "logical syntax" of language. [Carnap, 1963, p. 29]

Indeed, in *The Logical Syntax of Language* Carnap states his divergence from Wittgenstein here in particularly sharp and striking terms:

> Wittgenstein considers that the only difference between the sentences of the speculative metaphysician and those of his own and other researches into the logic of science is that the sentences of the logic of science—which he calls philosophical elucidations—in spite of their theoretical lack of sense, exert, practically, an important psychological influence upon the philosophical investigator, which the properly metaphysical sentences do not, or, at least, not in the same way. Thus there is only a difference of degree, and that a very vague one. The fact that Wittgenstein does not believe in the possibility of the exact formulation of the sentences of the logic of science has as its consequence that he does not demand any scientific exactitude in his own formulations, and that he draws no sharp line of demarcation between the formulations of the logic of science and those of metaphysics. [Carnap, 1934, §73]

Carnap's divergence from Wittgenstein here is thus absolutely central to his own attempt to articulate a radically new conception of *scientific* and therefore non-metaphysical philosophy.[2]

Finally, Carnap also explains that his conception of logical syntax—which enables him to break with Wittgenstein over the say/show distinction and the inexpressibility of logical analysis—is itself principally derived from metamathematical investigations of Hilbert, Tarski, and Gödel:

---

[2]It is not sufficiently appreciated, for example, that it is precisely through the conception of philosophy as exactly formulable logical syntax that Carnap replies to the standard objection according to which the theses of logical positivism are themselves unverifiable in terms of experience: see especially [Carnap, 1935, pp. 36–38].

My way of thinking was influenced chiefly by the investigations of Hilbert and Tarski in metamathematics, which I mentioned previously. I often talked with Gödel about these problems. In August 1930 he explained to me his new method of correlating numbers with signs and expressions. Thus a theory of the forms of expressions could be formulated with the help of concepts of arithmetic. He told me that, with the help of this method of arithmetization, he had proved that any formal system of arithmetic is incomplete and incompletable. When he published this result in 1931, it marked a turning point in the development of the foundation of mathematics.

After thinking about these problems for several years, the whole theory of language structure and its possible applications in philosophy came to me like a vision during a sleepless night in January 1931, when I was ill. [Carnap, 1963, p. 53]

What Carnap came to see in his fevered state was, as it were, that Wittgenstein's doctrine of analytic truth plus the metamathematical work of Hilbert, Tarski, and Gödel equals his own distinctive conception of the philosophical enterprise.

Wittgenstein's *Tractatus* therefore exerted a deep and basically two-pronged influence on Carnap's philosophy. On the positive side, Carnap derives the idea of the essentially non-factual character of analytic—that is, logical-mathematical—truth directly from the *Tractatus*. On the negative side, by reacting against the *Tractarian* conception of the ineffability of logic Carnap develops perhaps his most important philosophical contribution: the idea of philosophy as logical syntax of language and thus as itself an exact science. Finally, by putting these two sides together Carnap arrives at the idea that philosophy, too, is essentially non-factual and says nothing about the world:

The chief motivation for my development of the syntactical method, however, was the following. In our discussions in the Vienna Circle it had turned out that any attempt at formulating more precisely the philosophical problems in which we were interested ended up with problems of the logical analysis of language. Since in our view the issue in philosophical problems concerned the language, not the world, these problems should be formulated, not in the object language, but in the metalanguage. Therefore it seemed to me that the development of a suitable metalanguage would essentially contribute toward greater clarity in the formulation of philosophical problems and greater fruitfulness in their discussions. [1963, p. 55][3]

In one way or another, then, virtually all of Carnap's most characteristic philosophical ideas and distinctions result from the influence—both positive and negative—of Wittgenstein's *Tractatus*.

---

[3]Compare p. 64: "The distinction between logical and factual truth leads also to a sharp boundary line between syntax as the theory of form alone, and semantics as the theory of meaning, and thus to the distinction between uninterpreted formal systems and their interpretations. These distinctions are meant not as assertions, but rather as proposals for the construction of a metalanguage for the analysis of the language of science. In this way we obtain also a clear distinction between questions about contingent facts and questions about meaning relations. This difference seems to me philosophically important; answering questions of the first kind is not part of the philosopher's task, though he may be interested in analyzing them; but questions of the second kind lie often within the field of philosophy or applied logic."

I

In the *Aufbau* Carnap's conception of logic is that of *Principia Mathematica,* and the influence of Wittgenstein's *Tractatus* here appears to be very slight. To be sure, Carnap uses the term "tautology":

> *Logic (including mathematics) consists only of conventional stipulations* about the use of signs *and of tautologies* on the basis of these stipulations. The signs of logic (and mathematics) therefore do not designate objects, but rather serve only for the symbolic fixing of these stipulations. [Carnap, 1928, §107]

But Carnap does not in any way engage the issues actually involved in Wittgenstein's doctine of tautology. For example, he raises no questions about the axioms of infinity, reducibility, and choice and simply takes it completely for granted that all the objects of classical mathematics are in fact generated by his "tautologies."[4]

Carnap's first serious engagement with the Wittgensteinian concept of tautology occurs in his *Abriss der Logistik* [Carnap, 1929]. He introduces the notion of a truth-function in §3 along with an explicit reference to 4.442 of the *Tractatus*. The concept of tautology is then introduced via an example of one, described as follows:

> This function therefore has the peculiarity that it is *always true* no matter what truth values [*Aussagewerte*] pertain to the arguments. Such a function is called a *"tautology"*. If p and q are determinate statements in a tautology, then the validity of the tautology is independent of whether p or q are true. The tautology therefore communicates nothing about the obtaining or not obtaining of the states of affairs designated through p and q; it is *contentless* [*inhaltsleer*] (but not senseless [*sinnlos*]). [Carnap, 1929, §4b]

Carnap emphasizes the crucial point that tautologies cannot be conceived simply as maximally or completely general truths but are rather true solely in virtue of their logical form:

> The essential character of logical propositions, in contrast to empirical [propositions], does not lie in the circumstance that they are general assertions but rather in the circumstance that they are tautologies: they are necessarily true on the basis of their mere form, but also contentless. [1929, §4d]

Accordingly, Carnap here counts neither the axiom of choice [§24b] nor the axiom of infinity [§24e] as logical principles. Moreover, following Ramsey, Carnap obviates the need for the axiom of reducibility by adopting the *simple* theory of types [§9b].

---

[4]As Carnap himself intimates in [1963, p. 24], then, it seems that he did not really attempt to come to terms with the doctrines of the *Tractatus* until he moved to Vienna and participated in the discussions of the *Tractatus* within the Vienna Circle.

Carnap provides a somewhat fuller discussion of the three problematic axioms of *Principia* in "Die Mathematik als Zweig der Logik" [Carnap, 1930]. He introduces "the attempts at criticism and development" of logicism of Wittgenstein and Ramsey in §4. The key idea, once again, is that the problematic axioms fail to be tautologies:

> The tautologies are therefore always true, solely on the basis of their form, independently of whether the argument propositions are true or false. Every proposition of logic is a tautology, thus according to the conception of logicism also every proposition of mathematics. But the *axiom of infinity* is not valid on the basis of its form alone; it is valid, if at all, as it were accidentally. For many individual domains it is valid, for others not. Whether one can speak of an absolute individual domain appears problematic. The *axiom of choice* likewise does not hold on the basis of its form alone, in so far as under the "existence" of the choice class one does not understand the consistency of this assumption but rather its constructive exhibition; its validity depends on what propositional functions are taken to be given in the thought domain in question and which principles of construction for the derivation of further propositional functions (and thereby classes) are set up. The *axiom of reducibility* can be shown not to be tautological. [1930, §4]

So what is the status of these axioms? As above, the axiom of reducibility is dispensable within the simple theory of types on the basis of Ramsey's work. For the other two axioms, however, we must adopt Russell's expedient: they are not logical principles but special assumptions upon which certain key theorems of mathematics must be viewed as conditional. Strictly speaking, therefore, such theorems can no longer be viewed as parts of logic at all.

In this period Carnap's conception of the tautologousness of logical truth thus corresponds rather well to that of the *Tractatus*. For Wittgenstein, like Carnap, begins by rejecting what he takes to be the conception of logical truth of Frege and Russell—namely, the conception of logical truths as completely universal or maximally general truths containing only variables and logical constants:

> The mark of the logical proposition is *not* general validity.
>
> For to be generally valid means *only:* to be accidentally valid for all things. An ungeneralized proposition can be just as tautologous as a generalized [proposition]. [1922, 6.1231]

And the crucial point, I take it, is that on the conception of logical truths as maximally general it is not at all clear that logical truths say nothing about the world. Indeed, on this conception it appears that logical truths are simply the most abstract and general truths about the world—as Russell famously and colorfully puts it: "logic is concerned with the real world just as truly as zoology, though with its more abstract and general features" [Russell, 1919, Ch. 16]. If, however, to make a claim about the world is to assert some particular distributions of truth values to elementary propositions, and if tautologies are true for all possible such distributions of truth values, then it is manifest—and for the first time—that logical truths make no claim whatsoever about the world. It is in *this* sense that logical truths are analytic [1922, 6.11].

It follows that the problematic axioms of *Principia Mathematica*—despite their maximally general form—cannot themselves be tautologies:

> One could call logical general validity essential, in contrast with accidental [general validity], for example, that of the proposition "all men are mortal". Propositions like Russell's "axiom of reducibility" are not logical proposition, and this explains our feeling that they, if true, could only be true through a happy accident. [1922, 6.1232]
>
> A world can be thought in which the axiom of reducibility is not valid. But it is clear that logic has nothing to do with the question whether our world is actually so or not. [1922, 6.1233]

At least to this extent, then, Carnap appears to be in close agreement with the conception of the *Tractatus*.[5]

Yet Carnap, unlike Wittgenstein, could not long remain satisfied with a conception of logical-mathematical truth according to which most of the truths of classical mathematics are not analytic after all. In this sense, Carnap attempts to remain faithful to Frege's and Russell's logicism nonetheless. Carnap describes the evolution of his position within the Vienna Circle as follows:

> [T]he purely logical character of some of the axioms used in the system of *Principia Mathematica* seemed problematic, namely, that of the axiom of reducibility, the axiom of infinity, and the axiom of choice. We were gratified to learn from the studies on the foundations of mathematics made by F. P. Ramsey that the so-called ramified theory of types used in the *Principia* is unnecessary, that a simple system of types is sufficient, and that therefore the axiom of reducibility can be dispensed with. With respect to the other two axioms we realized that either a way of interpreting them as analytic must be found or, if they are interpreted as non-analytic, they cannot be regarded as principles of mathematics. I was inclined towards analytic interpretations; but during my time in Vienna we did not achieve complete clarity on these questions. Later I came to the conviction that the axiom of choice is analytic, if we accept the concept of class which is used in classical mathematics in contrast to a narrower constructivist concept. Furthermore, I found several possible interpretations for the axiom of infinity, different from Russell's interpretation, of such a kind

----

[5]With respect to the axiom of infinity, however, it appears that Carnap's and Wittgenstein's views are not in fact in agreement. It appears that Wittgenstein himself does subscribe to the "absolute individual domain" Carnap finds problematic; for Wittgenstein's notion of tautology—arrived at by considering all possible truth value assignments to a *given* set of elementary propositions—does not involve the consideration of variable "individual domains." Nevertheless, it appears that for Wittgenstein the axiom of infinity could nonetheless not be a tautology: if true it would rather show itself in language through the existence of an infinite number of distinct names—5.535. Wittgenstein does not explicitly discuss the axiom of choice, but it appears that he would be even more reluctant to count it as a truth of logical-mathematical truth than is Carnap: "The theory of classes is entirely superflous in mathematics. This hangs together with the circumstance that the generality we need in mathematics is not *accidental* [generality]"—6.031.

that they make this axiom analytic. The result is achieved, e.g., if not things but positions are taken as individuals. [1963, pp. 47–48]

As Carnap indicates, his new understanding of the analyticity of such axioms as infinity and choice was only achieved after he left Vienna for Prague in 1931; it therefore belongs to his logical syntax period.

The key move of *Logical Syntax* is the rejection of the "logical absolutism" of the *Tractatus*. There is no longer a single language in which all meaningful sentences are formulated, and there is no longer a single set of privileged logical sentences (such as the tautologies of the *Tractatus*). Instead, there is an indefinite multiplicity of distinct formal languages or linguistic frameworks, each with its own characteristic set of logical truths or analytic sentences. Thus linguistic frameworks answering to a constructivist conception in which the axiom of choice, say, is not acceptable are perfectly permissible, but so too are linguistic frameworks answering to the classical conception of set—in which, therefore, the axiom of choice is a logical principle after all. The point is that there is simply no notion of logical "correctness" independent of a given formal language or linguistic framework; there is only the purely *internal* notion of correctness or validity relative to the specified logical rules of one or another such framework. Thus, for example, whether or not the axiom of infinity is derivable from some set of antecedently designated logical principles—as it is in Frege's original system—there can be no objection whatsoever to a formal language or linguistic framework in which the axiom of infinity is rather laid down as a primitive logical principle. For there is again simply no question—independently of one or another linguistic framework—whether the axiom of choice is or is not a "correct" logical principle.

More specifically, both of the languages considered in *Logical Syntax* are "coordinate languages" in which the individual objects are designated by numerals and the individual quantifiers thus range over the natural numbers. These numerical coordinates are then viewed as possible "positions" for empirical objects. Sentences asserting the existence of (any number of) empirical objects are then formulated by introducing empirical descriptive function signs that take appropriate (empirically determined) values on some class of numerical coordinates or "positions." The axiom of infinity therefore asserts that there are an infinity of possible "positions" for empirical objects but leaves the number of empirical objects actually occupying these "positions" entirely undetermined: *this* number can be determined only by synthetic propositions. Yet it is an analytic proposition that there are an infinity of numerical coordinates or possible "positions" simply because this proposition is now taken as a primitive logical truth of the formal languages or linguistic frameworks in question.

At this point one might feel that all connection with *Wittgenstein's* notion of tautology and analyticity has been lost. How, in particular, can we continue to maintain that the axiom of infinity is true in all possible circumstances and thus says nothing about the facts of the world? The answer is that, in the linguistic frameworks under consideration, the axiom of infinity is true for all possible interpretations—more precisely, for all possible substitutions—of the primitive non-logical or descriptive signs of the language. And, within each formal language or linguistic framework, the logical signs or logical constants are sharply distinguished from the non-logical or descriptive signs. Of course, there is no longer a single privileged set of logical constants—the primitive logical constants of *Principia Mathematica,* for example—but rather a distinct class of logical signs or logical constants characterizing each distinct formal language or linguistic framework. Finally, in the two formal languages considered in *Logical Syntax,* all the numerals happen to be logical signs (more precisely, zero and successor are designated by primitive logical constants). It follows that the axiom of infinity contains only logical signs or logical constants, and, since it is a primitive proposition in both formal languages in question, it is a theorem of these languages invariant under all substitutions of non-logical or descriptive signs. Hence it is a logical or analytic truth in Carnap's sense within both linguistic frameworks.

II

Wittgenstein's doctrine of tautology is also based on a sharp distinction between all other meaningful signs and the so-called logical constants. I say "so-called" because the essence of Wittgenstein's view is that the logical constants are not meaningful signs at all—strictly speaking there are *no* logical constants:

> Here it is manifest that there do not exist "logical objects," "logical constants" (in Frege's and Russell's sense). [5.4]

Putting what I take to be the same point in a somewhat different way, Wittgenstein states as his "fundamental thought" that the so-called logical constants are not representative of, do not go proxy for, objects:

> The possibility of the proposition rests on the principle of the representation of objects by means of signs.

> My fundamental thought is that the "logical constants" are not representative. That the *logic* of the facts can not be represented. [4.0312]

Thus Wittgenstein's conception of the logical constants is intimately connected with his picture theory of meaning, on the one hand ("the principle of the representation of objects by means of signs"), and his idea that logical form is itself inexpressible, on the other ("the *logic* of the facts can not be represented").

Without attempting to enter into the manifold interpretive difficulties here, I will now try simply to touch on those aspects of Wittgenstein's conception most relevant to a comparison with Carnap. I will thus sketch, if you will, a Carnapian reading of the *Tractatus.*

All meaningful linguistic expression, in the *Tractatus,* rests on the elementary propositions. Elementary propositions consist of names, which, I assume, come in different logical categories—corresponding to individual signs, predicate and relation signs, function signs of higher logical types, and so on. Each such logical category is associated with a class of grammatically intersubstitutable signs. Elementary propositions—grammatically acceptable concatenations of names—then have two essential features: first, they themselves contain no logical constants (no quantifier-signs or propositional connectives); second, they are all logically independent of one another. It follows that any arbitrary assignment of truth values to the elementary propositions depicts a possible complete description of a "world" delimited by these propositions and that any such complete description of a "world" is generated by an assignment of truth values to the elementary propositions. Thus, anything one might want to say about such a "world" can be said by picking out a set of truth value assignments to elementary propositions.

All other propositions—all other meaningful claims about the world—are therefore truth-functions of the elementary propositions: all other propositions are determined by picking out some subset of "rows" of the truth-table whose arguments are the elementary propositions. The so-called logical constants are then simply expedients for expressing in practice how particular complex propositions—corresponding to particular subsets of truth value assignments to elementary propositions (particular subsets of "rows" of the truth-table whose arguments are the elementary propositions)—are iteratively generated from the elementary propositions via truth functional operations. The propositional connectives generate complex propositions from finite classes of basis propositions; the quantifiers generate complex propositions from (potentially) infinite classes of basis propositions specified by permitting some particular constituent in a given proposition—some particular name—to vary arbitrarily within its grammatically admissible substitution class.

Strictly speaking, then, the so-called logical constants are entirely unnecessary for meaningful representation of the world: elementary propositions and truth value assignments to elementary propositions completely exhaust the function of meaningful representation. This is why the 5.4's, which articulate Wittgenstein's new conception of the logical constants, are a commentary on 5—"The proposition is a truth function of the elementary propositions"—and follow 5.3:

> All propositions are results of truth-operations on the elementary propositions.
>
> The truth-operation is the mode and manner in which the truth-function arises out of the elementary proposition. . . .
>
> Every proposition is the result of truth-operations on elementary propositions. [5.3]

Accordingly, the "vanishing" of the so-called logical constants depends on the privileged and exhaustive role of the elementary propositions:

> This vanishing of the apparent logical constants also appears when "$\sim (\exists x) . \sim fx$" says the same as "$(x) . fx$", or when "$(\exists x) . fx . x = a$" says the same as "$fa$". [5.441]

> Indeed all logical operations are already contained in the elementary propositions. For "fa" says the same as "$(\exists x) . fx . x = a$".

> Where there is compositeness, there is argument and function, and where there are the latter, there are already all the logical constants.

> One could say: *The one* logical constant is that which *all* propositions, according to their nature, have in common.

> But this is the general form of the proposition. [5.47]

In this sense, therefore, there are no such things as the logical constants: there is only the general form of the proposition, that is, the general form of a truth-function [6], that is, the general circumstance that all meaningful assertions correspond to sets of truth-value assignments to elementary propositions.

Two consequences of fundamental importance now follow for the nature of logic. First, logic and logical form cannot themselves be the subject of meaningful representation, for logical forms are not objects that can be represented by signs at all. All meaningful representation is of the various truth possibilities of the elementary propositions, and, strictly speaking, there simply are no logical signs—no signs, as it were, representing logical form. Second, the so-called logical truths are tautologies: propositions which as truth-functions come out true for all possible assignments of truth values to elementary propositions. Such tautological propositions therefore say nothing: they make no claim about the world for they leave *all* truth possibilities for the elementary propositions entirely open. Nevertheless, tautological propositions *show* something—namely, how various truth possibilities and truth-operations (truth-possibilities and truth-operations corresponding to genuinely meaningful, factual propostions, for example) are formally related. On this reading, then, the doctrine of tautology, the conception of the logical constants, the picture theory of meaning, and the say/show distinction are indeed intimately connected. They are all parts of an overarching conception based on the priority and exhaustiveness of the elementary propositions.

On this reading, finally, the fundamental technical problem with the Tractarian doctrine of tautology does not involve a limitation to truth-functional logic or the assumption that first-order quantificational logic is decidable. For, on the one hand, quantificational propositions are intended precisely to depict truth-possibilities for (possibly) infinite sets of basis propositions, generated by varying via substitution some particular component name in a given basis proposition [5.2's]; and, on the other hand, once one sees that quantification is thereby accommodated, there is no particular reason to impose a requirement of decidability: tautologies say nothing because they are consistent with *all* possible truth value assignments to elementary propositions, not because they (supposedly) can be effectively calculated. The fundamental technical problem—from our Carnapian point of view—is rather that quantification is explained purely substitutionally. We are therefore unable to accommodate quantificational logic where a substitutional interpretation is inappropriate, and, in particular, we are unable to accommodate higher-order quantification.

Carnap himself explains this last problem as follows:

> Wittgenstein demonstrated this theses [that all logical truths are tautologies] for molecular sentences (i.e., those without variables) and for those with individual variables. It was not clear whether he thought that the logically valid sentences with variables of higher levels, e.g., variables for classes, for classes of classes, etc., have the same tautological character. At any rate, he did not count the theorems of arithmetic, algebra, etc., among the tautologies. But to the members of the Circle there did not seem to be a fundamental difference between elementary logic and higher logic, including mathematics. Thus we arrived at the conception that all valid statements of mathematics are analytic in the specific sense that they hold in all possible cases and therefore do not have any factual content. [1963, p. 47]

In *Logical Syntax,* as we know, Carnap uses "coordinate languages" in which the first-order variables range over the natural numbers. Therefore, a purely substitutional interpretation of the individual quantifiers is perfectly admissible here. However, in evaluating the higher-order quantifiers of Language II—a type-theoretical language sufficient for all of classical mathematics—Carnap came to see under Gödel's influence that a substitutional interpretation is inadequate (due to indefinable sets of numbers [§34c]). The definition of analyticity for such a higher-order language can thus by no means proceed substitutionally: what we require, in effect, is a standard Traskian ("referential" or "objectual") truth-definition for all of classical mathematics.[6]

Once again, therefore, Carnap's problem with the strict Tractarian conception of tautology rests on its inability to comprehend full classical mathematics. And it is for this reason that Carnap repeatedly insists that his own conception of logical or analytic truth, although it is self-consciously modelled on that of the *Tractatus,* has nevertheless successfully captured the notion in question *for the first time.*

> In this way [i.e., through Carnap's own work in *Logical Syntax* and *Studies in Semantics*], the distinction between logical and factual truth, which had always been regarded in our discussions in the Vienna Circle as important and fundamental, was at last vindicated. In this distinction we had seen the way out of the difficulty which had prevented the older empiricism from giving a satisfactory account of the nature of logic and mathematics. . . . Our solution, based on Wittgenstein's conception, consisted in asserting the thesis of empiricism only for factual truth. By contrast, the truths in logic and mathematics are not in need of confirmation by observations,

---

[6]For a discussion of this point see [Coffa, 1987, pp. 547–572].

because they do not state anything about the world of facts, they hold for any possible combination of facts. [1963, p. 64]

By extending Wittgenstein's conception of tautology in the manner of *Logical Syntax*—that is, by defining the logical truths as, in effect, those truths valid for all interpretations of the non-logical or descriptive vocabulary, and, crucially, by allowing the numerals and the signs for ("referential" or "objectual") higher-order quantification to count as logical constants in an appropriate formal language—Carnap has, for the first time, explained why all the propositions of classical logic *and mathematics* are tautologous and say nothing about the world.

III

It is clear, however, that, by thus extending the notion of tautology, Carnap has also transformed this conception into something that would be completely unacceptable from the standpoint of the *Tractatus*. This can be seen most clearly by considering the radical differences between the two conceptions with respect to precisely the issue of the nature of the logical constants.

In the *Tractatus* there is a single privileged set of so-called logical constants: namely, the classical truth-functional connectives together with (substitutionally interpreted) classical quantifiers. This is because, once again, meaningful propositions are conceived initially as corresponding to subsets of truth possibilities for the elementary propositions, and logic is exhausted by the formal relations— basically relations of containment—between different such subsets of truth possibilities. Hence classical truth-functional logic, including (substitutionally interpreted) classical quantificational logic, is the only conceivable logical possibility. For Carnap, by contrast, there is no such thing as the unique "correct" logic and therefore no single privileged set of logical constants. To be sure, classical truth-functional logic—including classical first-order quantificational logic—is one possibility; and for this language Wittgenstein's list of the logical constants is indeed appropriate. But the important point, for Carnap, is that this is only one possibility among many others. Formal languages with other sets of logical constants are equally admissible and equally "correct." In particular, there can be no objection to extending the classical logical constants to include the identity sign, the numerals, and ("referential" or "objectual") higher-order quantification; and this, as we have seen, is how Carnap is able to hold that all of classical mathematics is analytic.

It follows that, when one considers a language suitable for classical mathematics, the essence of Carnap's position lies in a fundamental extension of the notion of logical constant far beyond the scope this notion had in Frege, in Russell, or, especially, in Wittgenstein. Indeed, in *Logical Syntax* Carnap holds that the narrower notion of logical constant is not even well-defined:

Whether, in the construction of a system of the kind described, only logical symbols in the narrower sense are to be included amongst the primitive symbols (as by both Frege and Russell) or also the mathematical symbols (as by Hilbert), and whether only logical primitive sentences in the narrower sense are to be taken as [logically]-primitive sentences, or also mathematical sentences, is not a question of philosophical significance, but only one of technical expedience. In the construction of Languages I and II we have followed Hilbert and selected the second method. Incidentally, the question is not even accurately formulated; we have in general syntax made a formal distinction between logical and descriptive symbols, but a precise classification of the logical symbols in our sense into logical symbols in the narrower sense and mathematical symbols has so far not been given by anyone. [1934, §84]

As we have seen, Carnap is perhaps a bit too casual here. For the only way in which he can continue to maintain that full classical mathematics is analytic is precisely by considering "Hilbertian" languages in which certain primitive mathematical symbols are now declared to be logical constants.

Yet in the *Tractatus,* of course, there can be absolutely no question of extending the class of logical constants to include primitive mathematical symbols. Indeed, as is well known, even the identity sign creates serious problems there, for identity cannot be conceived as a truth operation on elementary propositions (see 5.3's). The essence of the Tractarian conception lies rather in a contraction of the notion of logical constant that self-consciously assimilates this notion to that of "auxiliary" symbols such as brackets [5.461] and punctuation marks [5.4611]—that is, to signs that *manifestly* have no independent meaning. Carnap's tendency, on the contrary, is to move in precisely the opposite direction:

Examples of signs which are regarded as **logical** are the sentential connectives ('~', '∨', etc.), the sign of the universal operator ('for every'), the sign of the element-class relation ('∈', 'is a'), auxiliary signs (e.g., parentheses and commas as ordinarily used in symbolic logic, punctuation marks in the written word languages), the sign of logical necessity in a (non-extensional) system of modalities ('N'). Further, all those signs are regarded as logical which are definable by those mentioned; hence e.g. the sign of the existential operator ('∃', or 'for some'), signs for universal and null classes of all types, the sign of identity ('=', 'the same as'), all signs of the system of [*Princ. Math.*] by Whitehead and Russell and of nearly all other systems of symbolic logic, all signs of mathematics . . . with the meaning they have when applied in science, all logical modalities (e.g. Lewis' 'strict implication'). [1943, §13]

And Carnap elsewhere explains that parentheses, brackets, and the like are *mere* auxiliaries.[7] Thus, if we divide the putative candidates for logical constants into,

---

[7]See [Carnap, 1958, §3a]: "Among the logical signs are the parentheses '(' and ')' and the comma ',' as in e.g. '$F(a,b)$'. However, these signs have only a subordinate role, analogous to that of punctuation marks."

first, brackets and other auxiliaries, second, logical signs in the traditional narrower sense, and third, primitive mathematical signs, the tendency of the *Tractatus* is to assimilate all logical constants to the first class, whereas Carnap's tendency is to assimilate them to the third class.

Accordingly, in *Logical Syntax* the logical constants are initially completely
on a par with all other primitive symbols. All expressions are introduced purely
syntactically, and no expression has any independently specified meaning. We
begin simply with primitive expressions and strings thereof, and the logical
expressions, in particular, are simply a syntactically specified subclass of expressions. Purely syntactic formation rules delimit the class of grammatical strings
of expressions or sentences of the language in question; purely syntactic transformation rules delimit the class of theorems—that is, consequences of the null-
class of sentences—of the language in question. In what Carnap calls general
syntax these transformation rules then induce a purely syntactic distinction
between logical and descriptive signs [§50] and thus a purely syntactic distinction between logical and physical theorems [§51], analytic and synthetic truths
[§52]. All these notions are therefore entirely relative to the transformation rules
of a given formal language or linguistic framework, a circumstance that Carnap
explicitly contrasts with Wittgenstein's "absolutism":

> Later, Wittgenstein made the same view [that analytic propositions are true solely on
> the basis of their formal structure] the basis of his whole philosophy. "It is the char-
> acteristic mark of logical sentences that one can recognize from the symbol alone
> that they are true; and this fact contains in itself the whole philosophy of logic"
> ([*Tractatus*] p. 156 [6.113]). Wittgenstein continues: "And so also it is one of the
> most important facts that the truth or falsehood of non-logical sentences can *not* be
> recognized from the sentences alone." This statement, expressive of Wittgenstein's
> absolutist conception of language, which leaves out the conventional factor in lan-
> guage-construction, is not correct. It is certainly possible to recognize from its form
> alone that a sentence is analytic; but only if the syntactical rules of the language are
> given. If these rules are given, however, then the truth or falsity of certain synthetic
> sentences—namely, the determinate ones—can also be recognized from their form
> alone. It is a matter of convention whether we formulate only [logical]-rules, or
> include [physical]-rules as well; and the [physical]-rules can be formulated in just as
> strictly formal a way as the [logical]-rules. [1934, §52]

Needless to say, a language in which certain primitive laws of physics are built
into its logical syntax at the outset would be completely anathema from the point
of view of the *Tractatus*.

In sum, we might express the essential difference between the two conceptions as follows. The *Tractatus* begins with a philosophical picture of the nature
of meaningful representation. All meaningful claims correspond to subsets of
truth possibilities for a given set of elementary propositions; and, since the elementary propositions are entirely independent of one another, arbitrary distribu-

tions of truth value assignments are possible. Furthermore, although the elementary propositions are composite—they consist of names which can be independently varied within given substitution classes—they nonetheless contain no logical constants. The conception of the logical constants as truth operations on the elementary propositions and of analytic propositions or tautologies as holding for every possible distribution of truth values to the elementary propositions then follow directly from this initial philosophical picture of meaningful representation. Carnap, by contrast, begins with no such philosophical picture. He begins simply with the idea of a syntactically specified formal language given by formation rules and transformations rules. There is no independent notion, in particular, of what it means for a sign to represent an object in the world or for a sentence to make an assertion or claim about the world. Carnap instead exploits syntactic features of the transformation rules to define a distinction between logical and descriptive signs; and this distinction then induces a distinction between analytic and synthetic sentence—which, as it were, *syntactically represents* the notion of meaningful claim about the world. Carnap's assertion that analytic sentences are empty of factual content and make no real claim about the world has therefore an entirely different sense and force from Wittgenstein's similar-sounding assertion.

IV

By the same token, Carnap's assertion that logical form and logical syntax are perfectly capable of exact expression has very little to do with the Tractarian denial of a similar-sounding proposition. What Carnap means is that if we view language purely syntactically (as consisting simply of arbitary expressions and strings thereof), then we can perfectly well describe the logical syntax of such a language—that is, its formation and transformation rules—in a syntactic metalanguage. For example, from the perspective of a syntactic metalanguage, the grammatical sentences are a certain subset of the set of all possible strings of primitive symbols, and the transformation rules depict certain relations between such strings of symbols. Further, and what is of most relevance to our central theme, the logical constants are simply a syntactically specified subclass of expressions defined in a particular way from the transformation rules. Logical syntax is thus simply the theory of a certain class of formal structures—combinatorial structures generated by strings of symbols—and it is in this sense that Carnap asserts that *"syntax is exactly formulable in the same way as geometry is"* [1934, §73].

When the *Tractatus* denies that logical syntax is expressible, by contrast, it of course does not intend to deny that one can formulate a combinatorial theory of strings of symbols. But, from the point of view of the *Tractatus,* this would

simply be a particular theory formulated within a more comprehensive language—a language that embodies and presupposes logical form and logical syntax in precisely the sense of the *Tractatus*. The symbol in Carnap's syntactic
metalanguage designating the negation sign in the object language, for example,
has nothing to do with the truth operation associated with negation in the sense
of the *Tractatus*. On the contrary, Carnap's symbol is simply a *name* for a particular object—of the negation symbol in the object language. The truth operation
associated with negation is therefore not represented by this symbol—indeed,
according to the *Tractatus* it is of course not *represented* at all—it is rather
shown by the use of whatever symbol expresses negation in the metalanguage.
And Carnap's syntactic metalanguage now becomes *the* language in Wittgenstein's sense—that is, *the* language in which all logical relations are expressed:

> The proposition can present the whole of reality, but it cannot present what it must
> have in common with reality in order to be able to present it—logical form.
>
> In order to be able to present logical form we would have to be able to set ourselves
> up outside of logic with the proposition, and this means outside the world. [4.12]

Language in the *Tractatus*—that is, *the* language—is that system of symbols
through which all truth possibilities for the elementary propositions are presented; and logical form—that is, the general form of the proposition—cannot
itself be presented because truth operations on elementary propositions are not
in *this* language a possible object of representation via names. A mere combinatorial structure of strings of expressions is not a *language* in the sense of the
Tractatus.

Now Carnap, in *Logical Syntax*, is sensitive to the circumstance that in the
Tractatus there is only a single language and that, accordingly, the idea that the
logical syntax of *this* language could be expressed in a syntactic metalanguage is
completely unacceptable from the Tractarian point of view. And it is precisely
here, in fact, that Carnap brings to bear the method of arithmetization introduced
by Gödel:

> Up to the present, we have differentiated between the object-language and the syn-
> tax-language in which the syntax of the object-language is formulated. Are these
> necessarily two separate languages? If this question is answered in the affirmative
> (as it is by Herbrand in connection with metamathematics), then a third language
> will be necessary for the formulation of the syntax of the syntax-language, and so on
> to infinity. According to another opinion (that of Wittgenstein), there exists only one
> language, and what we call syntax cannot be expressed at all—it can only "be
> shown". As opposed to these views, we intend to show that, actually, it is possible to
> manage with one language only; not, however, by renouncing syntax, but by demon-
> strating that without the emergence of any contradictions the syntax of this language
> can be formulated within this language itself. In every language S, the syntax of any
> language whatsoever—whether of an entirely different kind of language, or of a sub-
> language, or even of S itself—can be formulated to an extent which is limited only
> by the richness of the means of expression of the language S. [1934, §18]

Carnap outlines Gödel's arithmetization of syntax in the following section [§19]. Carnap's idea, then, is that one can respond to the Tractarian doctrine that there is only a single language by, first, conceiving this language as itself a purely syntactic object, and, second, using Gödel's method of arithmetization to correlate numbers with symbols. The syntactic metalanguage is thereby embedded in the object language (provided that the object language includes elementary arithmetic), and, in this precise sense, the object language can express its own syntax.

Yet it is clear once again, I think, that this ingenious suggestion does not in fact address the concerns of the *Tractatus* at all. For, once again, the *Tractatus* would emphatically reject Carnap's very first step: the conception of language as a purely combinatorial syntactic object. Thus, just as the *Tractatus* would insist that the expression designating the object language symbol for negation in a syntactic metalanguage has nothing to do with real negation (that is, with that particular truth operation on elementary propositions), it would for the same reason insist that the number correlated with the negation symbol (in Carnap's arithmetization the number 21) has nothing to do with real negation either. Real negation can be expressed neither by a metalinguistic name nor by a numeral; it is rather *shown* by the use of whatever symbol is associated with that particular truth operation on elementary propositions.

Carnap, characteristically, has transformed an originally philosophical point into a purely technical question—in this case, the technical question of what formal theories can or cannot be embedded in a given object language. Considered purely as a technical question, however, the situation turn out to be far more complicated than it initially appears; and this circumstance is, I think, not without interest from the point of view of our present concerns. For it turns out, again as a consequence of Gödel's researches, that it is as a matter of fact not possible in most cases of interest to express the logical syntax of a language in Carnap's sense in the language itself. Indeed, the problem arises precisely in connection with syntactically representing the crucial distinction between logical and descriptive constants.

I mentioned several times above that, in *Logical Syntax,* a distinction between logical and descriptive signs is induced by the transformation rules of the language in question [§50]. Given this distinction, a division of all theorems of the language into logical and physical, analytic and synthetic, then follows easily: logical or analytic theorems remain theorems under all substitutions of descriptive expressions [§§51, 52].[8] How then are logical signs distinguished from descriptive signs? The idea is that the logical signs are those signs such that *all* the sentences containing only these signs are determinate in the language—

---

[8] In [Carnap, 1942] this same idea is given a semantical reading: the logical or analytic truths remain true for all *interpretations* of the descriptive predicates—§16, 2a. As Carnap states, this change accommodates Tarski's work, and, in particular, the existence of indefinable properties.

that is, either they or their negations are theorems of the language. For sentences essentially containing descriptive signs, by contrast, although *some* such sentences may by theorems of the language as well (that is, physical-theorems such as general laws of physics) this will not be the case for *all* such sentences (for sentences ascribing particular values at particular space-time coordinates to various physical fields, for example). In this way Carnap accommodates the pre-theoretical idea that the meaning and application of logical signs is entirely determined by the syntactical rules of the language in question.

It is immediate from Gödel's work, however (and Carnap himself is completely clear about this point), that, for a language containing classical arithmetic, the distinction between logical and descriptive signs—and thus the distinction between analytic and synthetic sentences—can only be correctly drawn if the transformation rules of the language are non-recursive. Indeed, it immediately follows that the notion of theoremhood for such a language must be non-arithmetical and thus not definable in the language itself. The distinction between logical and descriptive signs and the corresponding notion of analytic sentence can only be defined in a language containing classical mathematics plus a (Tarskian) truth definition for classical mathematics and thus in a language essentially richer than the language with which we began. Thus, the logical syntax in Carnap's sense for a language for classical mathematics can only be expressed in a distinct and essentially richer metalanguage; the logical syntax for this metalanguage can itself only be expressed in a distinct and essentially richer meta-metalanguage; and so on. And it is precisely this situation that Carnap has in mind when he qualifies his introduction of the method of arithmetization in §18 (cited above) by the phrase *"to an extent which is limited only by the richness of the means of expression of the language S."*

In commenting upon this consequence of Gödel's incompleteness theorem— namely, the circumstance that an infinite sequence of richer and richer metalanguages is thus necessary after all—Carnap remarks:

> This is the kernel of truth in the assertion made by Brouwer [*Sprache*], and, following him, by Heyting [*Logik*], p. 3, that mathematics cannot be completely formalized. In other words, *everything mathematical can be formalized, but mathematics cannot be exhausted by one system;* it requires an infinite series of ever richer languages. [1934, §60d]

Does this same situation not represent the kernel of truth—from Carnap's point of view, of course—in Wittgenstein's doctrine of the inexpressibility of logical syntax?

3

Steve Gerrard

DESIRE AND DESIRABILITY: BRADLEY, RUSSELL AND MOORE VERSUS MILL

I

John Stuart Mill's *Utilitarianism* contains one of the most notorious paragraphs in the history of philosophy. It begins:

> The only proof capable of being given that an object is visible is that people actually see it. The only proof that a sound is audible is that people actually hear it; and so of the other sources of our experience. In like manner, I apprehend, the sole evidence it is possible to produce that anything is desirable is that people do actually desire it.[1]

The English founders of analytic philosophy, Bertrand Russell and G. E. Moore, treated this passage with contempt, and its 20th-century notoriety is due to them. Russell writes in *A History of Western Philosophy:*

> John Stuart Mill, in his *Utilitarianism,* offers an argument which is so fallacious that it is hard to understand how he can have thought it valid. He says: Pleasure is the only thing desired; therefore pleasure is the only thing desirable. He argues that the only things visible are things seen, the only things desirable are things desired. He does not notice that a thing is "visible" if it *can* be seen, but "desirable" if it *ought* to be desired. Thus "desirable" is a word presupposing an ethical theory; we cannot infer what is desirable from what is desired.[2]

---

[1] [Mill, 1861, Chapter IV, paragraph 3].

[2] [Russell, 1945, p. 778]. It is the target, not the contemptuous phrasing, that should surprise here. Russell's *History,* after all, is practically characterized by its clever scorn. He writes, for example, that Kant "is generally considered the greatest of modern philosophers. I cannot myself agree with this estimate [. . .]" (p. 704), and concludes his chapter on Hegel with: "[t]his illustrates an important truth, namely, that the worse your logic, the more interesting the consequences to which it gives rise" (p. 746). (As we shall see, however, in Part IV, not even Russell could touch the nasty tone of F. H. Bradley. As a preview, he says of John Stuart Mill's father, that he is "a man whose courage rose higher as facts grew more opposite [. . .]") [Bradley, 1935, p. 271].

The reason the target might be surprising is that John Stuart Mill was Russell's godfather and Russell expressed great early admiration for him (he even refers to Mill as "my former Pope" [Russell, 1946, p. 10]); See [Schilpp, 1946, p. 3], and [Clark, 1976, p. 23] for the details of the godfather arrangements. Russell's final assessment of Mill is in [Russell, 1956a, pp. 122 and 143]:

> What [Mill] achieved depended more upon his moral elevation and his just estimate of the ends of life than upon any purely intellectual merits. [. . .] Mill deserved the eminence which he enjoyed in his own day, not by his intellect but by his intellectual virtues.

Russell's accusation of fallacy in *A History* derives from his fellow rebel G. E. Moore's attack on Mill 42 years earlier in *Principia Ethica*. Moore, was, by most accounts, the most amiable of men. Yet after quoting Mill's notorious paragraph he writes: "[t]here, that is enough. That is my first point. Mill has made as naive and artless a use of the naturalistic fallacy as anybody could desire."[3] A paragraph later Moore writes one of the most scornful sentences in his usually mild-mannered corpus: "[w]ell, the fallacy in this step is so obvious, that it is quite wonderful how Mill failed to see it."[4] Moore continues:

> The fact is that 'desirable' does not mean 'able to be desired' as 'visible' means 'able to be seen'. The desirable means simply what *ought* to be desired or *deserves* to be desired; just as the detestable means not what can be but what ought to be detested and the damnable what deserves to be damned. Mill has, then, smuggled in, under cover of the word 'desirable,' the very notion about which he ought to be quite clear.[5]

This article has two chief issues. The first is whether Mill, in fact, committed a fallacy in the notorious passage. I shall argue that he does not,[6] and, instead, that Russell and Moore have made the mistake. The second chief issue concerns

---

[3][Moore, 1903, p. 66].

[4]Another especially nasty sentence is reserved for another Millian view: "[p]ray consider what this contemptible nonsense really means" [Moore, 1903, p. 72].

[5][Moore, 1903, p. 67].

[6]Others, of course, have argued that Mill did not commit a fallacy. The most important articles in the literature are: [Seth, 1908], [Hall, 1949], and [Mandelbaum, 1969]. See also [Berger, 1984], especially Chapter 2; and [Ryan, 1970], especially Chapter XI. Most defenders place great weight on Mill's claim in Chapter I of *Utilitarianism* that "[i]t is evident that this cannot be proof in the ordinary and popular meaning of the term. Questions of ultimate ends are not amenable to direct proof." My defense does not emphasize this and instead takes a different approach. No matter how many times the defense is made, however, it doesn't seem to penetrate the field. For example, in an otherwise excellent textbook, *With Good Reason: An Introduction to Informal Fallacies*, [Engel, 1990], S. Morris Engel writes:

> A particularly striking example of the direct influence of language on thinking is the famous fallacy committed by the English philosopher John Stuart Mill in one of his works on ethics. Mill is here dealing with the question of what is the most *desirable* end or aim of human conduct and argues that it is happiness, as utilitarianism teaches. But how can we prove that happiness is indeed the one true ideal that we should desire? To this Mill replies: [here Engel quotes the notorious paragraph from *Utilitarianism*]. But critics of Mill have pointed out that he had been deceived by his manner of expressing himself. Though the words *desirable, visible,* and *audible* are structurally similar, they are not semantically the same. *Desirable* is not related to *desired* in the same way that *visible* and *audible* are related to *seen* and *heard,* for the first involves a moral distinction that the other two do not. *Visible* means simply that something is "capable of being seen" (and *audible* means something "capable of being heard"), but *desirable* implies that something is "worthy of being desired," that it "ought" to be desired. This being so, it may be quite true that a thing's being seen or heard proves that it is visible or audible, but it does not follow that, because a thing is desired, it is for that reason desirable. Many people desire drugs, but that does not prove that drugs are therefore desirable. [p. 102]

the sources of their misreading of Mill; that will lead us to examine the origins of analytic philosophy in England and to challenge the traditional historical account of the subject.

Returning to the first issue, Russell and Moore have accused Mill of fallacy, but which fallacy is he supposed to have committed? There are three likely candidates. The first two are traditional: (1) the is/ought fallacy (this seems to be the force of Russell's and Moore's analysis of "desirable" as "*ought* to be desired" as opposed to what "is desired" or "can be desired"), and (2) a *petitio principii* or begging the question (this seems to be the force of Russell's "presupposing an ethical theory" and Moore's "smuggled in"). (3) The third fallacy is Moore's contribution in *Principia:* the "naturalistic fallacy". In Part II of this article I will argue that Mill did not commit the is/ought fallacy; in Part III I will argue that he did not commit a *petitio principii*. Those two parts will constitute my defense of Mill, and involve contending that Mill's argument is best taken as having both a normative premise and conclusion, and interpreting Mill's claims along Aristotelian lines. One form Russell's and Moore's (and others') misreading took was not to read Mill's paragraph in context: in the context of both *Utilitarianism* itself and the rest of Mill's corpus. Part of my defense will consist of supplying the missing textual context, and thus I will be quoting more than is perhaps usual.

The naturalistic fallacy dominated the discussion of ethics in the English-speaking philosophical world for most of this century. What has not been sufficiently noticed is how much the original formulation of the fallacy was tied in with the peculiar metaphysics of Moore's *Principia* and Russell's *Principles of Mathematics*. I thus postpone my discussion of the naturalistic fallacy until we examine that metaphysics in Part VIII.

If my defense of Mill in Parts II and III is successful, then new questions naturally arise: why did Russell and Moore misread Mill so badly; why did they treat him with such scorn? Frege said, "Error and superstition have causes just as much as correct cognition",[7] and, we can add: some causes of error are more interesting than others. Not all mistakes have deep explanations, but I think this one does; we can say more than merely that Russell and Moore misread Mill. (Misreading other philosophers is, after all, practically an occupational disease.) Their misreading had a pattern and a history—a pattern and a history that helps shed light on analytic philosophy's creation myth.

1903 was the official revolutionary year: with the publication of both Moore's *Principia Ethica* and Russell's *Principles of Mathematics,* analytic philosophy was born in England. All of us raised in the analytic tradition know (or should know) Russell's celebration of that break from Idealism:

---

[7][Frege, 1977b, p. 2]. Although the broad subject of this article is the birth of analytic philosophy in England, Frege, the continental founder of analytic philosophy, will play a prominent comparative role.

> [Moore] took the lead in rebellion, and I followed, with a sense of emancipation. Bradley argued that everything common sense believes in is mere appearance; we reverted to the opposite extreme, and thought that *everything* is real that common sense, uninfluenced by philosophy or theology, supposes real. With a sense of escaping from prison, we allowed ourselves to think that grass is green, that the sun and stars would exist if no one was aware of them, and also that there is a pluralistic timeless world of Platonic ideas. The world, which had been thin and logical, suddenly became rich and varied and solid.[8]

That is the creation myth of analytic philosophy. The second half of this article examines the myth's veracity in the light of our investigation of Russell's and Moore's accusations against Mill. John Maynard Keynes, in "My Early Beliefs", writes "Russell's *Principles of Mathematics* came out in the same year as *Principia Ethica;* and the former, in spirit, furnished a method for handling the material provided by the latter".[9] One of the chief targets of this new method was, strangely enough (from the point of view of the myth), not Idealism, but the Empiricist Mill's little argument, and Moore's attack is one of the most powerful set pieces in *Principia.*

The core of the myth (which has its origins in Russell's memories) is that with philosophical argument aided by the new logic, Russell and Moore slew the dragon of British Idealism, whose chief representatives were J. M. E. McTaggart, T. H. Green, and, of course, F. H. Bradley. An additional aspect is that the war was mainly fought over two related doctrines of British Idealism (or, as it is sometimes called, Absolute Idealism). The first doctrine is an extreme form of holism: abstraction is always falsification. Truth can be fully predicated of the Absolute alone, not of any of Its constituents. The new method of analysis could not be more opposed to this, and Moore is said to have defeated this view in *Principia.* That book's motto, taken from Bishop Butler's *Sermons,*[10] "[e]verything is what it is, and not another thing" (including, Moore might add: and not part of the Absolute), is the battle cry which announces the strategy. The second Idealist doctrine is that external relations are not real. "[W]riters strongly influenced by Hegel", Moore writes in Baldwin's 1901 *Dictionary of Philosophy and Psychology,* "[. . .] hold[. . .] the doctrine that no relation is purely 'external,' i.e. fails to affect the essence of the things related [. . .]".[11] Russell is said to have defeated the Idealist claim about relations in *Principles of Mathematics.*[12]

---

[8][Russell, 1946, p. 12].
[9][Keynes, 1972: pp. 438–439]. Keynes, piling on phrases in order to portray undergraduate enthusiasm, also says of Moore's influence and the revolutionary year: "it was exciting, exhilarating, the beginning of a renaissance, the opening of a new heaven on a new earth, we were the forerunners of a new dispensation, we were not afraid of anything" [p. 435].
[10][Butler, 1983, Preface, paragraph 39].
[11][Moore, 1901] in [Baldwin, 1960, p. 446].
[12]See, for example, p. 221: "We are now in a position to meet the philosophic dislike of relations. The whole account of order given above, and the present argument concerning abstraction, will be

The picture is of a clean and clear transition: one philosophical system refuted and overthrew another. (The very title of Moore's classic essay "The Refutation of Idealism", published in *Mind* in the revolutionary year, becomes part of the myth.) We recognize that both Russell and Moore had their youthful Idealist periods, but according to the myth their Idealist season was brief and no residue of it remained once the break was made.[13]

The real picture is, as real pictures always are, much more complicated.[14] My first step in showing this will be, in Part V, to trace the history of the analytic condemnation of Mill's little argument. There we will find, much, I believe, to our surprise, that the origin of Moore's assault is to be found in the Idealist camp—and F. H. Bradley! We will see that the roots, the point, and even the form of *Principia*'s objections to Mill lie in Idealism: the supposedly revolutionary document of 1903 appropriates from Idealism as much as it rejects. Part VI locates Bradley's, Russell's, and Moore's attacks on Mill in the context of all three's anti-psychologism and anti-empiricism. A major point will be that Bradley, Russell, and Moore were all anti-psychologistic in both ethical and nonethical philosophy. In Part VI I also argue that the origin of the analytic philosophers' anti-psychologism, which played such a crucial role in the development of the discipline, is to be found in Idealism and, above all, once again in Bradley. In Part VII I show that Moore's 1899 article, "The Nature of Judgment", is *both* a reaction against and an appropriation of Bradley's arguments. This, in turn, leads to the metaphysics of *Principia Ethica* and *Principles of Mathematics,* which I discuss in Part VIII. There we will at last be in a position to examine the naturalistic fallacy in its proper metaphysical environment.

My investigation, then, begins with Mill's notorious argument and the analytic reaction to it, traces the history of that reaction back to Bradley and Idealism, shows how that reaction develops into the revolutionary metaphysics of 1903, and finishes, once again with the analytic attack of Mill, this time set in its proper background. Through the investigation of Russell's and Moore's

---

necessarily objected to by those philosophers—and they are, I fear, the major part—who hold that no relations can possess absolute and metaphysical validity".

[13]Moore, however, tended to hide the view that he even had a brief Idealist period. In his autobiography he reports of an undergraduate tea in Russell's rooms with the Idealist professor McTaggart. "McTaggart", Moore says, "in the course of conversation had been led to express his well-known view that Time is unreal. This must have seemed to me then (as it still does) a perfectly monstrous proposition, and I did my best to argue against it" [Moore, 1968, pp. 13–14]. This makes it seem as if there is a seamless web between Moore's nineteenth century undergraduate enthusiasm and his 1925 "The Defense of Common Sense". What Moore ignores is his own Idealist early essays, where he held a view commensurate with McTaggart's. (Gilbert Ryle also makes this point in "G. E. Moore's 'The Nature of Judgment' " [Ryle, 1970, pp. 90–91].)

[14]Peter Hylton's superb *Russell, Idealism, and the Emergence of Analytic Philosophy* [Hylton, 1990] has, more than any other book, contributed to showing the genuine complications behind the myth. In this article I am greatly indebted to that book, as well as, above all, to Leonard Linsky's teachings.

responses to one argument by Mill, I hope to help write a revisionist history of the birth of analytic philosophy.

II

If Mill's paragraph that begins this article is one of the most notorious in the history of philosophy, then Hume's paragraph where he introduces the is/ought fallacy is one of the most famous:

> I cannot forbear adding to these reasonings an observation, which may, perhaps, be found of some importance. In every system of morality, which I have hitherto met with, I have always remark'd, that the author proceeds for some time in the ordinary way of reasoning, and establishes the being of a God, or makes observations concerning human affairs; when of a sudden I am surpriz'd to find, that instead of the usual copulations of propositions, *is,* and *is not,* I meet with no proposition that is not connected with an *ought,* or an *ought not.* This change is imperceptible; but is, however, of the last consequence. For as this *ought,* or *ought not,* expresses some new relation or affirmation, 'tis necessary that it shou'd be observ'd and explain'd; and at the same time that a reason should be given, for what seems altogether inconceivable, how this new relation can be a deduction from others, which are entirely different from it. But as authors do not commonly use this precaution, I shall presume to recommend it to the readers; and am persuaded, that this small attention wou'd subvert all the vulgar systems of morality [. . .].[15]

Is there evidence that Mill recognized and was concerned with the is/ought fallacy? Let us begin with the very book Moore and Russell criticized.

In Chapter II of *Utilitarianism,* Mill is explaining utilitarianism by attempting to refute various objections. One objection is that "men can do *without* happiness" (par. 11), that renunciation is noble and "the beginning and necessary condition of all virtue". To this religious objection Mill replies that "self-sacrifice must be for some end" (par. 15), and that end must be

> to increase the amount of happiness in the world; but he who does it [renounces his personal happiness] or professes to do it for any other purpose is no more deserving of admiration than the ascetic mounted on his pillar.[16]

---

[15][Hume, 1988, Book III, Part I, Sect. I; pp. 469–70]. As influential as it has been, Hume's paragraph should not necessarily be taken as Hume's final view; it has been argued that the paragraph is a stage in a dialectical development. See [MacIntyre, 1959], and [Rorty, 1993].

[16]Both the tone and point are similar to what the originator of the is/ought distinction has to say in Section IX, Part I of *An Enquiry Concerning the Principles of Morals* [Hume, 1983, pp. 73–74]:

> Celibacy, fasting, penance, mortification, self-denial, humility, silence, solitude, and the whole train of monkish virtues; for what reason are they every where rejected by men of sense, but because they serve to no manner of purpose [. . .] We justly, therefore, transfer them to the opposite column, and place them in the catalogue of vices [. . .].

Mill concludes his anti-ascetic argument with this clear use of the distinction he is supposed not to be aware of: "[the ascetic] may be an inspiriting proof of what men *can* do, but assuredly not an example of what they *should*".[17]

Changing the manner, but not the subject, the first paragraph of Frege's *Begriffsschrift* draws a distinction which is crucial to the anti-psychologism of early analytic philosophy:

> we can inquire, on the one hand, how we have gradually arrived at a given proposition and, on the other, how we can finally provide it with the most secure foundation. The first question may have to be answered differently for different persons; the second is more definite [. . .].[18]

Logical Positivists labelled this distinction the context of discovery versus the context of justification, and it is related to an older distinction called the genetic fallacy.[19] While not identical to the is/ought fallacy, Frege's distinction has a similar structure. It involves, first, a clear separation of categories [is/ought: descriptive/evaluative; Frege: origin/justification], and second, the characteristic that the first category is factual, whereas the second is normative. (It is *not* part of Frege's distinction that the second category not be empirical, as some kinds of justification are empirical: "we divide all truths that require justification into two kinds, those for which the proof can be carried out purely by means of logic and those for which it must be supported by facts of experience".[20]) One way of putting this distinction is that when we ask "What is the reason to believe *x*?" we have so far asked an ambiguous question.[21] We can disambiguate by asking either for the cause, the motive, or the justification or ground for the belief. (In some discussions the cause and motive are not distinguished, but lumped together; Frege, in the *Begriffsschrift,* is primarily concerned with the psychological logicians' confusion of causes with justifications.) The cause and motive will be subjective in a way the justification or ground are not.[22]

---

[17]*Emphasis* in original; note also the use of "proof".

[18][van Heijenoort, 1967b, p. 5].

[19]This in turn is related to a point Hobbes makes in his objections to Descartes' Meditation IV [Descartes, 1971, p. 145]:

> This phrase, *a great illumination of the understanding,* is metaphorical, and thus no ground for argument. Anybody who feels no doubt claims such an 'illumination' and has an inclination of the will to assert what he has no doubt about, no less than one who really knows. So this 'illumination' may be the reason why a man obstinately defends or holds an opinion; but cannot be ground for knowledge of its truth.

[20]Frege, p. 5 in [van Heijenoort, 1967b].

[21]See also [Moore, 1903, p. 143]: "That [a self-evident proposition] appears true to us may indeed be the *cause* of our asserting it, or the reason why we think and say that it is true: but a reason in this sense is something utterly different from a logical reason, or reason why something is true."

[22]Frege's distinction is *one* way, among many, of drawing the subjective/objective line.

The structure of *Utilitarianism* shows that Mill is aware of the point behind Frege's distinction (although there he is mainly concerned with motive, not cause). After explaining utilitarianism in Chapter II, Mill divides the question "Why should I believe or obey it?" into two, strictly consistent with the Fregean lines. Chapter III, titled "Of the Ultimate Sanction of the Principle of Utility", asks in the first paragraph, "what are the motives to obey?", and Mill's answers clearly recognize the subjective element of motives. Chapter IV (which contains our famous paragraph), however, titled "Of What Sort of Proof the Principle of Utility is Susceptible", concerns the justification or ground of the principle. If that is not enough, Chapter V ("On the Connection between Justice and Utility"), shows an obvious recognition of the genetic fallacy. Mill is arguing that considerations of justice do not serve as counterexamples to utility (the classic problem for any version of utilitarianism; in Rawls' modern version the criticism is that utilitarianism cannot account for the separateness of persons), and he begins by recognizing how strong the sentiment of justice seems to be in people's minds. But then Mill writes:

> In the case of this, as of our other moral sentiments, there is no necessary connection between the question of its origin and that of its binding force. That a feeling is bestowed on us by nature does not necessarily legitimate all its promptings.[23]

Thus, we see that Moore and Russell should have noticed that Mill recognized the is/ought fallacy (and its cousins) even if their reading of Mill was confined to the book they criticized.

If we turn to Mill's *A System of Logic*, which Russell, at least, certainly read,[24] the evidence is even clearer. *A System of Logic* is a massive work which dominated the reading list in England's universities until the Hegelian revolution.[25] Its final chapter is titled "Of the Logic of Practice, or Art; Including Morality and Policy". There Mill draws the following distinction between a science and an art:

> It is customary [. . .] to include under the term moral knowledge [. . .] an inquiry the results of which do not express themselves in the indicative, but in the imperative

---

[23][Mill, 1861, Ch. V, par. 2].
[24]See [Russell, 1967, p. 90], where Russell says:

> I had already been interested in philosophy before I went to Cambridge, but I had not read much except Mill. What I most desired was to find some reason for supposing mathematics true. The arguments in Mill's *Logic* on this subject already struck me as very inadequate. I read them at the age of eighteen.

[25]If *Utilitarianism* suffered the wrath of the English founders of analytic philosophy, then *A System of Logic* suffered the wrath of the Continental founder. Frege, in *The Foundations of Arithmetic*, even exceeds the contempt with which Moore and Russell treat Mill, calling Mill's Empiricist view, for example, "gingerbread or pebble arithmetic!" [Frege, 1884, p. vii]. For excellent discussions of Frege's attack of Mill, see [Weiner, 1990, pp. 36–39], and [Resnik, 1980, Chapter 4].

mood, or in periphrases equivalent to it; what is called the knowledge of duties, practical ethics, or morality.

Now, the imperative mood is the characteristic of art, as distinguished from science. Whatever speaks in rules, or precepts, not in assertions respecting matters of fact, is art: and ethics, or morality, is properly a portion of the art corresponding to the sciences of human nature and society.[26]

Russell, in his emotivist phase, could not have agreed more.[27]

A few pages later comes the passage which clinches the evidence:

Propositions of science assert a matter of fact: an existence, a coexistence, a succession, or a resemblance. The propositions now spoken of do not assert that anything is, but enjoin or recommend that something should be. They are a class by themselves. A proposition of which the predicate is expressed by the words *ought* or *should be,* is generically different from one which is expressed by the words *is,* or *will be.*[28]

Thus, the evidence, both in *Utilitarianism* itself and in Mill's other works, is conclusive that Mill both recognized and was attentive to the is/ought fallacy. However, the fact that Mill was aware of the fallacy is not sufficient evidence that he did not commit it; better logicians than Mill have occasionally fumbled. What we need is a plausible interpretation of the offending passage that is safe from fallacy—plausible both from a textual point of view, locating the passage in Mill's corpus, and from a philosophical point of view, giving a reasonable (if not necessarily correct) view of ethics.

If Mill is not committing the is/ought fallacy, then what is he doing in the notorious passage?

The key to my interpretation is that in moving from "desire" to "desirable" Mill is not committing the is/ought or correlate fallacies because *the "desire" of Mill's premise is already normative.* Contra Moore and Russell, there really is an analogy between desired/desirable and seen/visible. We do not count a pink elephant as *visible* because it *is seen* by a drunkard, and analogously, Mill would not count living like a pig as *desirable* because it *is desired* by the same drunkard. The *desire* of Mill's premise does *not* mean what any drunken peasant would desire; it means what an educated person under proper conditions would desire. The analogy *is* helpful: what *is seen* is evidence for what *is visible* only

---

[26][Mill, 1974a, Book VI, Chapter xii, sec. 1; p. 943]. In a footnote Mill remarks that he is using "Art" in a sense "older and I hope, not yet obsolete" than that used "to denote the poetical department or aspect of things in general, in contradistinction to the scientific".

[27]See, for example, [Russell, 1935, p. 237]: "Ethics [. . .] contains no statements, whether true or false, but consists of desires of a certain general kind [. . .]. Science can discuss the causes of desires, and the means for realizing them, but it cannot contain any genuinely ethical sentences, because it is concerned with what is true or false." This is far different from Russell's Moore-like views in his 1908–1910 "The Elements of Ethics" [Russell, 1966].

[28][Mill, 1974a, Book VI, ch. xii, sec. 6; p. 949].

under certain conditions, conditions that mirror the evidential relationship between *desired* and *desirable*. *Seen* and *visible* are connected by, among other things, proper lighting conditions (a property of the environment) and lack of color blindness (a property of the agent). *Desire* and *desirable* are connected by proper political surroundings (the environment) and proper character (the agent).

Whether the "proper" is Moore's "smuggling"[29] will be examined more carefully in Part III (on the *petitio*); for now, however, let us note that it would be smuggling only if Mill had hidden it (it is a little hard, if not, perhaps, actually contradictory, to *openly* smuggle). Similarly, Russell *is* right when he says that "'desirable' is a word presupposing an ethical theory"[30] but what he should have noticed is that Mill's use of "desire" also presupposes an ethical theory—an ethical theory, however, which far from being hidden is a main subject of Mill's life work.

One deep difference between Mill's version of utilitarianism and his father's and Bentham's, is that Mill maintains that pleasures differ not only in quantity, but also in quality. (We will see that Moore also objects to this.) As is well known, Mill is reacting to Bentham's claim that "prejudice apart, the game of pushpin is of equal value with the arts and sciences of music and poetry". The first objection Mill considers to utilitarianism is that the teaching that life should be devoted to pleasure is "a doctrine worthy only of swine".[31] Mill responds that "pleasure" does not mean "mere sensation". "It is quite compatible with the principle of utility", Mill writes, "to recognize the fact that some kinds of pleasure are more desirable and more valuable than others".[32] The question naturally arises, what is the criterion of differentiation between pleasures? Mill explains: "[o]f two pleasures, if there be one to which all or almost all who have experience of both give a decided preference, irrespective of any feeling of moral obligation to prefer it, that is the most desirable pleasure."[33] The test is "by those who are *competently acquainted* with both" pleasures.[34] Mill summarizes this discussion with a famous comparison:

> It is better to be a human being dissatisfied than a pig satisfied; better to be Socrates dissatisfied than a fool satisfied. And if the fool, or the pig, are of a different opinion, it is because they only know their own side of the question.[35]

---

[29][Moore, 1903, p. 67].
[30][Russell, 1945, p. 778].
[31][Mill, 1861, Ch. II, par. 3]. It is possible that Mill had Aristotle in mind here. In *The Nicomachean Ethics* [Aristotle, 1980, I.5], Aristotle writes that "to judge from the lives that men lead, most men, and men of the most vulgar type, seem (not without some ground) to identify the good, or happiness, with pleasure [. . .]". After listing two other kinds of life (the political and the contemplative), Aristotle continues "[n]ow the mass of mankind are evidently quite slavish in their tastes, preferring a life suitable to beasts [. . .]".
[32]Ch. II, par. 4.
[33]Ch. II, par. 5. Moore quotes this in [Moore, 1903, p. 77].
[34]Ch. II, par. 5; *emphasis added.*
[35]Ch. II, par. 6.

Thus, in the proof it is Socrates' desires which count for what is desirable, not the fool's.[36]

Mill's discussion of the criterion by which to distinguish qualities of pleasure might serve as a sketch of how he conceives the transition between what is desired and what is desirable. To use Aristotle's terminology, the desirable is what the *phronimos*, the man[37] of practical wisdom, desires.

We will shortly return to that Aristotelian point. But first, four paragraphs earlier I delineated two conditions that connect the desired with the desirable: proper character and proper politics. In *An Examination of Sir William Hamilton's Philosophy*, Mill emphasizes the aspect of character:

> The difference between a bad and a good man is not that the latter acts in opposition to his strongest desires; it is that his desire to do right, and his aversion to doing wrong, are strong enough to overcome, and in the case of perfect virtue, to silence, any other desire or aversion which may conflict with them. It is because this state of mind is possible to human nature, that human beings are capable of moral government: and moral education consists in subjecting them to the discipline which has most tendency to bring them to this state. The object of moral education is to educate the will: but the will can only be educated through the desires and aversions; by eradicating or weakening such of them as are likeliest to lead to evil; exalting to the highest pitch the desire of right conduct and the aversion to wrong; cultivating all other desires and aversions of which the ordinary operation is auxiliary to right [. . .][38]

Mill's *desire* is an *educated desire* (and much of his philosophy should be taken as philosophy of education in that sense).

In *On Liberty,* not surprisingly, Mill emphasizes the aspect of politics. "The object of this essay," Mill writes, "is to assert one very simple principle [. . .] that the sole end for which mankind are warranted, individually or collectively, in interfering with the liberty of action of any of their number is self-protection."[39] But in the next paragraph Mill gives an essential qualification

---

[36]I will allow myself this nasty remark only in a note: in order to understand the proof of Chapter IV, one must first read Chapter II. I do not want to pretend, however, that Mill's division of pleasures is not problematic; it was attacked from the very beginning; some of the literature in note 6 discusses this. I can only give here the barest of sketches of a response. Mill's argument is sometimes taken to be unfalsifiable in the following way: (1) All people who have experienced both prefer Pushkin to pushpin; (2) Francis has experienced both, but prefers pushpin; (3) Therefore, Francis did not *really* experience both. That argument, of course, *is* a fallacy, and is of the same form as typical racist arguments. But, there is an independent test for whether someone is competently acquainted with the quality of pleasures and thus is an expert: whether she thrives. There is an analogy to aesthetic theory; we can identify someone as having good taste even if we don't share her tastes. This brings up a new problem, however: all accounts of thriving are partially infected by ethical theory. At this point we have reached a problem for all ethical theory, not just Mill's (and perhaps even for all theory). (I am grateful to Amelie Rorty for suggestions which led to this note.)

[37]Mill would say "person". In later editions of his *System of Logic* Mill usually used "person" and "people" instead of "man" and "men".

[38]*An Examination of Sir William Hamilton's Philosophy,* [Mill, 1974b, p. 453].

[39]*On Liberty,* [Mill, 1974c, p. 68].

which, in effect, classifies the "desire" of his notorious argument's premise as normative:

> It is, perhaps, hardly necessary to say that this doctrine is meant to apply only to human beings in the maturity of their faculties. [. . .] we may leave out of consideration those backward states of society in which the race itself may be considered as in its nonage. [. . .] Despotism is a legitimate mode of government in dealing with barbarians [. . .] Liberty, as a principle, has no application to any state of things anterior to the time when mankind have become capable of being improved by free and equal discussion [. . .][40]

My separation of the aspects of politics and character in an educated desire is for exposition purposes. It is part of Mill's philosophy that no complete and actual separation is possible. (This is true not just for Mill's philosophy; remember, he served as a member of parliament.) In other words: for Mill, ethics is a branch of politics.

The allusion to Aristotle[41] is no accident. In effect, I am reading Mill as much more of an Aristotelian than he is usually understood to be, both by himself and by his commentators. The Aristotelian notion of the *phronimos* ties together the various strands of my interpretation and defense of Mill. On Aristotle's view, the man of practical wisdom provides the standard. "Regarding *practical wisdom*", Aristotle writes in *The Nicomachean Ethics*, "we shall get at the truth by considering who are the persons we credit with it".[42] By observing what they desire, we learn what is desirable. Again, the *desire* of Mill's proof is not what the drunken peasant desires, it is what the *phronimos* desires, and what the *phronimos* actually does desire *is* evidence for what is desirable. Mill and Aristotle do not differ on the criterial role of experts or *phronimoi;* they differ on what is to be expected from mass education.[43]

Moore completely misses Mill's Aristotelianism and the function of experts in Mill's proof. In section 47 of *Principia,* Moore disputes that sense can be made of Mill's effort to distinguish pleasures not only by quantity but also by quality. Moore argues that such a distinction is inconsistent with Mill's hedonism. "Can one pleasure", Moore asks rhetorically, "be pleasanter than another, except in the sense that it gives *more* pleasure?"[44] Moore then comments, in a sentence that his pupil Wittgenstein might well later have remembered,[45]

---

[40][Mill, 1974c, p. 69]. As the dots and brackets indicate, I have heavily abridged Mill's paragraph.
[41][Aristotle, 1980, I.2].
[42][Aristotle, 1980, VI.5], where the example of the *phronimos* is Pericles. Aristotle goes on to say that "[p]ractical wisdom, then, must be a reasoned and true state of capacity to act with regard to human goods."
[43]For much here I am indebted to conversations with Amelie Rorty, but this point in particular I especially owe to her.
[44][Moore, 1903, p. 78].
[45]Other places in the *Philosophical Investigations* [Wittgenstein, 1958] where Wittgenstein might have been directly commenting on *Principia* are: Section 77, where in a discussion of family resemblances, vagueness, and the false desideratum of sharp boundaries, Wittgenstein writes "[a]nd this is the position you are in if you look for definitions corresponding to our concepts in aesthetics or

"'Pleasant' must, if words are to have any meaning at all, denote some one quality common to all the things that are pleasant; and, if so, then one thing can only be more pleasant than another, according as it has more or less of this one quality". After discussing the preference of experts, Moore writes: "[. . .] the basis of Mill's Hedonism collapses, for he is admitting that one thing may be preferred over another, and thus proved more desirable, although it is not more desired".[46] As happens so often in the history of philosophy, one person's *reductio* is another's credo. Because it is the *phronimoi*'s desires that count, Mill consistently and repeatedly holds—not "is admitting"—one thing may be preferred over another, and thus proved more desirable, although it is not more desired (by the nonexpert).

III

My argument has been that Mill's proof has a normative premise and a normative conclusion, and is thus hardly a candidate for the is/ought fallacy. But have I saved Mill from one fallacy only to force the interpretation that he committed another, even more pernicious, one? Don't a normative premise and a normative conclusion lead simply to a *petitio principii*?[47] Isn't this the force of Russell's "presupposing an ethical theory" and Moore's "smuggled in"?[48] Let us see.

---

ethics", and Section 182, in a discussion pointing out the extremely complicated roles of words in language, Wittgenstein writes "[a]nd hence definitions usually fail to resolve [philosophical paradoxes]; and so, *a fortiori* does the assertion that a word is 'indefinable'". For a very late reference, see *Remarks on the Philosophy of Psychology,* Vol. I [Wittgenstein, 1980a] Section 160, where Wittgenstein writes of the word "specific" in the context of a discussion of copies of impressions: "[I]t is as little of a resource as the word 'indefinable' when one says that the word 'good' is indefinable".

[46][Moore, 1903, p. 79].

[47]It is worth quoting, if only in a note, most of a paragraph from [Mill, 1974a, Book V, Chapter vii, Section 2; p. 824], where Mill analyzes the fallacy of *Petitio Principii* with an ethical example:

Many more of the arguments of the ancient moralists, and especially of the Stoics, fall within the definition of Petitio Principii. [Consider Cato's claim] That if virtue were not happiness, it could not be a thing to *boast* of: That if death or pain were evils, it would be impossible not to fear them, and it could not, therefore, be laudable to despise them, &c. In one way of viewing these arguments, they may be regarded as appeals to the authority of the general sentiment of mankind which had stamped its approval upon certain actions and characters by the phrases referred to; but that such could have been the meaning intended is very unlikely, considering the contempt of the ancient philosophers for vulgar opinion. In any other sense they are clear cases of Petitio Principii, since the word laudable, and the idea of boasting, imply principles of conduct; and practical maxims can only be proved from speculative truths, namely from the properties of the subject matter, and cannot, therefore, be employed to prove those properties. As well might it be argued that a government is good because we ought to support it, or that there is a God because it is our duty to pray to him.

[48][Russell, 1945, p. 778], [Moore, 1903, p. 67].

The premise of Mill's proof, what he uses in order to conclude what is *desirable,* is what a *phronimos* actually does desire. The premise, thus, has both a normative element (the *phronimos*) and an empirical one (the actual desire).[49] So far, in order to combat the charge of an is/ought fallacy, I have been emphasizing the normative element. To combat the charge of a *petitio* we have to see the importance Mill puts on the empirical element, and in order to understand that we need to see what he is opposing.[50] Let us turn, once more, to the rest of Mill's corpus, in particular, to Mill's *Autobiography,* the book that Russell once wrote to his first wife "is at the bottom of a great deal in me".[51]

In his *Autobiography,* Mill says that as an alternative to "[t]he German, or *a priori* view of human knowledge [. . .]",[52] his "'System of Logic' supplies what was much wanted, a text-book of the opposite doctrine—that which derives all knowledge from experience [. . .]".[53] Mill's reason for combatting this *a priori* school is primarily practical:

> The notion that truths external to the mind may be known by intuition or consciousness, independently of observation and experience, is, I am persuaded, in these times, the great intellectual support of false doctrines and bad institutions. By the aid of this theory, every inveterate belief and every intense feeling, of which the origin is not remembered, is enabled to dispense with the obligation of justifying itself by reason, and is erected into its own all-sufficient voucher and justification. There was never such an instrument devised for consecrating all deep-seated prejudices.[54]

In a later chapter Mill calls his own school "that of Experience and Association"; this time the enemy is labelled "that of Intuition", but the reasoning is the same, even if the rhetoric is more heated still:

> [the difference between the schools] is full of practical consequences, and lies at the foundation of all the greatest differences of practical opinion in an age of progress.

---

[49]This mirrors Hume's own ideal observer solution to his is/ought problem.

[50]Just as to understand Moore and Russell we have to examine what *they* were opposing (see Hylton) or to understand the later Wittgenstein, we have to see how he understood Frege and Russell (see [Goldfarb, 1983] and his paper in this volume).

[51]"I am *very* glad thee has read Mill's *Autobiography* at last. It is at the bottom of a great deal in me" [Russell, 1992, pp. 95–96].

[52][Mill, 1924, p. 157].

[53][Mill, 1924, p. 158].

[54]Fairness to Frege requires that I continue the quotation:

> And the chief strength of this false philosophy in morals, politics, and religion, lies in the appeal which it is accustomed to make to the evidence of mathematics and of the cognate branches of physical science. [. . .] In attempting to clear up the real nature of the evidence of mathematical and physical truths, the "System of Logic" met the intuitive philosophers on ground on which they had previously been deemed unassailable; and gave its own explanation, from experience and association, of that peculiar character of what are called necessary truths, which is adduced as proof that their evidence must come from a deeper source than experience. [Mill, 1924, p. 157–158]

The practical reformer has continually to demand that changes be made in things which are supported by powerful and widely-spread feelings, or to question the apparent necessity and indefeasibleness of established facts; and it is often an indispensable part of his argument to show, how those powerful feelings had their origin, and how those facts came to seem necessary and indefensible. There is therefore a natural hostility between him and a philosophy which discourages the explanation of feelings and moral facts by circumstances and association, and prefers to treat them as ultimate elements of human nature; a philosophy which is addicted to holding up favourite doctrines as intuitive truths, and deems intuition to be the voice of Nature and of God, speaking with an authority higher than that of our reason. In particular, I have long felt that the prevailing tendency to regard all the marked distinctions of human character as innate, and in the main indelible, and to ignore the irresistible proofs that by far the greater part of those differences, whether between individuals, races, or sexes, are such as not only might but naturally would be produced by differences in circumstances, is one of the chief hindrances to the rational treatment of great social questions, and one of the greatest stumbling blocks to human improvement. This tendency has its source in the intuitional metaphysics which characterized the reaction of the nineteenth century against the eighteenth, and it is a tendency agreeable to human indolence, as well as to conservative interests generally [. . .].[55]

No wonder, as Alan Ryan remarks, Mill's "attacks on intuitionism [had] the aspect of a crusade".[56]

Mill is clearest (and most forceful) about his enemies in the *Autobiography*, but even in *Utilitarianism* he attacks the *a priori* and intuitionist or natural faculty schools.[57] Mandelbaum points out that although Mill tends to conflate them, the rationalist (*a priori*) and moral sense (intuitionist) schools are distinct. "The connection between these two dissimilar doctrines," Mandelbaum writes, "and the sense in which they may be said to form a single philosophical school, is that both are 'nativistic': both appeal to some sort of native, inborn capacity to distinguish moral truths, whereas utilitarianism holds that moral discriminations are to be accounted for through the effects of experience."[58]

Mill's conception of his present enemy, then, is that the nativists have, in the service of prejudice, conveniently distanced themselves from human desires. In distinguishing pleasures by quality as well as quantity, Mill was fighting the piggish possibility (or inclination?) of previous utilitarians (such as his father and Bentham). The effect of the *phronimos* is to liberate desire from the pig and the peasant. But the nativists go too far: they disengage what is desirable from *any* human desire, not just from that of the *phronimos*. Thus, the empirical element, the actual desiring, is crucial to Mill's proof. There is no *petitio* because the premise contains both normative and empirical elements, and because both

---

[55][Mill, 1924, pp. 191–192].
[56][Ryan, 1970, p. xii].
[57]See Chapter I, par. 3 and Chapter III, pars. 7–8.
[58][Mandelbaum, 1969, p. 223]. We might add that the moral sense and intuitionist schools are also distinct.

elements are necessary to avoid piggishness, on the one hand, and fantasy, on the other.

Summarizing my interpretation, we can partially reword Mill's notorious paragraph as follows (with comments in parentheses): *The only proof capable of being given that an object is visible to a human being is that a properly constituted and situated person actually sees it.* (This eliminates hallucinations and color blindness.) *The only proof that a sound is audible to a human being is that a properly constituted and situated person actually hears it; and so of the other sources of our experience.* (Mill is emphasizing the empirical nature of morals in opposition to the nativists; notice how Aristotle, *The Nicomachean Ethics* I.4–5 also takes the actual desiring to be crucial to what is the good for man.) *In like manner, I apprehend, the sole evidence it is possible to produce that anything is desirable to human beings is that properly educated citizens* (notice the plural) *of properly governed states actually do desire it over time.* (If such people do not desire it, then, no matter how much a theory might recommend it, it is a dangerous mirage, not a genuine part of human happiness. Both the plural and "over time" clauses are due to *On Liberty,* where Mill adopts an experimental pluralism.)

There certainly might be objections to this formulation. Kant and Kantians[59] come immediately to mind, but these objections involve deep conflicts between empirical and nonempirical ways of doing ethics, between competing views of human good, and between different conceptions of human nature; they do not involve fallacies we learned "at our mother's knee".[60]

IV

So ends my defense of Mill, but one charge of fallacy remains. "Mill", Moore writes, "has made as naive and artless a use of the naturalistic fallacy as anybody could desire".[61] What is this naturalistic fallacy that Moore thinks the accusation of is such a devastating weapon? As generations of commentators have discov-

---

[59]But not Rawls: see the Aristotelian Principle [Rawls, 1971, p. 426]: "other things equal, human beings enjoy the exercise of their realized capacities (their innate or trained abilities), and this enjoyment increases the more the capacity is realized, or the greater its complexity". Towards the end of a long footnote to this sentence, Rawls writes that "Mill comes very close to stating [the Aristotelian Principle] in *Utilitarianism,* ch. II, pars. 4–8". Close to the Aristotelian Principle is the following remark from Wilhelm von Humboldt's *The Sphere and Duties of Government* [von Humboldt, 1969, p. 16]: "The true end of man, or that which is prescribed by the eternal or immutable dictates of reason, and not suggested by *vague and transient desires,* is the highest and most harmonious development of his powers to a complete and consistent whole" (*emphasis added*). Mill enthusiastically quotes this passage on p. 121 of *On Liberty* (remember, as well, that the motto of that book is from von Humboldt). The emphasized clause about transient desires gives additional support to my interpretation of Mill.

[60]C.D. Broad says this of Mill's alleged fallacy in [Broad, 1930, p. 174].

[61][Moore, 1903, p. 66].

ered, the answer is not clear; at different places in *Principia* Moore describes it differently.

One of the simplest definitions Moore gives is: "[t]hat fallacy, I explained, consists in the contention that good *means* nothing but some simple or complex notion, that can be defined in terms of natural qualities".[62] The immediate context is a further criticism of Mill: "[i]n Mill's case", Moore continues, "good is thus supposed to *mean* simply what is desired; and what is desired is something which can thus be defined in natural terms". That version makes the naturalistic fallacy look like the is/ought fallacy or one of its factual/normative cousins discussed in Part II. However, Moore sometimes drops from the formulation anything to do with naturalism: "in other words, [. . .] we are all aware of a certain simple quality, which (and not anything else) is what we mainly mean by the term 'good' [. . .]".[63] A page later Moore says that even metaphysical definitions of *good* which identify *good* with explicitly nonnatural properties should still be called the "naturalistic fallacy": "[i]t should be observed that the fallacy, by reference to which I define 'Metaphysical Ethics,' is the same in kind; and I give it but one name, the naturalistic fallacy".[64] Leading to even more confusion about his fallacy and its name, Moore also says "[e]ven if [good] were a natural object, that would not alter the nature of the fallacy nor diminish its importance one whit".[65] The purest form of the fallacy (and the one to which we will return in Part VIII) is given at the end of Chapter II: "the fallacy which consists in identifying the simple notion which we mean by 'good' with some other notion".[66]

Not all abstraction might be falsification, but it is impossible to see through the confusion as long as the naturalistic fallacy is abstracted from its natural home: the shared metaphysics of *Principia* and *Principles of Mathematics*.[67] We

---

[62][Moore, 1903, p. 73].

[63][Moore, 1903, p. 38].

[64][Moore, 1903, p. 39].

[65][Moore, 1903, p. 14].

[66][Moore, 1903, p. 58]. See [Baldwin, 1990, pp. 70–71], where Baldwin uses some of the same quotations to show that "Moore's discussion is hopelessly confused on this matter". Baldwin's Chapter III, titled "The naturalistic fallacy," is helpful, even though in a brief discussion he gets Mill wrong. The literature on the naturalistic fallacy is massive; the most important article is W. K. Frankena's deflationary "The Naturalistic Fallacy" [Frankena, 1939] reprinted in [Foot, 1967]. Frankena's article is justly considered a classic, but for our broader purposes it should be noted that Frankena holds that:

> [. . .] Mill certainly did commit a fallacy in drawing an analogy between visibility and desirability in his argument for hedonism; and perhaps his committing *this* fallacy, which, as Mr. Broad has said, we all learn about at our mothers' knees, is chiefly responsible for the notion of a naturalistic *fallacy*. [Foot, 1967, p. 54]

See also [Lewy, 1964] for evidence that Moore anticipated and even agreed with some of Frankena's objections.

[67]Frankena gets some of this, but certainly not all.

will thus postpone our direct discussion of the alleged fallacy until Part VIII; the purest form of the naturalistic fallacy, I will argue there, is completely entwined with that metaphysics. As a way of introducing that metaphysics (and, especially its history), let us first turn to the sources of Moore's and Russell's attack on Mill.

V

Henry Sidgwick, a teacher of both Moore and Russell, held an ethical philosophy in which the basic principles were utilitarian but their derivation was through *a priori* intuitions. Sidgwick published his major work, the *Methods of Ethics,* in 1874, and continually revised it in several later editions.

Although Moore reports that Sidgwick's "personality did not attract me, and I found his lectures rather dull",[68] it is to Sidgwick that Moore gives a rare and gracious credit in *Principia.* Moore introduces his attack on Mill this way:

> [. . .] I propose to take first Mill's doctrine, as set forth in his book called *Utilitarianism:* we shall find in Mill a conception of Hedonism, and arguments in its favour, which fairly represent those of a large class of hedonistic writers. To these representative conceptions and arguments *grave objections, objections which appear to me to be conclusive, have been urged by Professor Sidgwick. These I shall try to give in my own words;* and shall then proceed to consider and refute Professor Sidgwick's own much more precise conceptions and arguments.[69]

Accordingly, when we turn to the *Methods of Ethics* we expect to find, in Sidgwick's other words, criticisms of Mill, prominent among them the desire/desirable confusion, that "naive and artless a use of the naturalistic fallacy as anybody could desire". And we do find numerous criticisms of Mill, including a criticism of the notorious paragraph which begins this article. Curiously enough, however, Sidgwick's criticism is of the *second half* of that paragraph, not the first, where we find the seen/visible / desire/desirable transition.[70] After quoting the notorious paragraph, Sidgwick, in the first edition of *Methods,* writes:

---

[68][Moore, 1968, p. 16].

[69][Moore, 1903, pp. 63–64 *emphasis added*].

[70]For completeness, here is the second half of Mill's paragraph [Mill, 1861, Chap. IV, par. 3]:

> If the end which the utilitarian doctrine proposes to itself were not, in theory and in practice, acknowledged to be an end, nothing could ever convince any person that it was so. No reason can be given why the general happiness is desirable, except that each person, so far as he believes it to be attainable, desires his own happiness. This, however, being a fact, we have not only all the proof which the case admits of, but all which it is possible to require, that happiness is a good, that each person's happiness is a good to that person, and the general happiness, therefore, a good to the aggregate of all persons. Happiness has made out its title as *one* of the ends of conduct and, consequently, one of the criteria of morality.

Now it must be borne in mind that is as a "standard of right and wrong," or "directive rule of conduct," that the utilitarian principle is put forward by Mill. Hence, in giving as a statement of this principle that "the general happiness is *desirable,*" he must be understood to mean (and his whole treatise shews that he does mean) that it is what each individual *ought* to desire, or at least to aim at realizing in action.[71]

The criticism that Sidgwick goes on to make is, in effect, that each man may desire his own happiness, but it does not follow that each desires the happiness of all. (Sidgwick puts it that this "argument leads primarily to the principle of Egoistic instead of Universalistic Hedonism".) Other critics have labelled this the fallacy of composition; illegitimately inferring that what is true of the part is thereby also true of the whole.[72] Moore echoes this criticism on pp. 104–105 of *Principia,* but it is of minor concern to him.

By the 6th edition of *Methods,* Sidgwick introduces his criticism with a slightly different wording:

Now, as we have seen, it is as a "standard of right and wrong" or "directive rule of conduct," that the utilitarian principle is put forward by Mill: hence, in giving as a statement of this principle that "the general happiness is *desirable,*" he must be understood to mean (and his whole treatise shows that he does mean) that it is what each individual *ought* to desire, or at least—in the stricter sense of 'ought'—to aim at realizing in action.[73]

This time Sidgwick adds the following footnote:

It has been suggested that I have overlooked a confusion in Mill's mind between two possible meanings of the term 'desirable,' (1) what can be desired and (2) what ought to be desired. I intended to show by the two first sentences of this paragraph that I was aware of this confusion, but thought it unnecessary for my present purpose to discuss it.

Thus, instead of finding a refutation of the desire/desirable argument in a prominent place in Sidgwick, we find a hint of it only in a footnote to a later

---

[71][Sidgwick, 1874, p. 365].

[72]Many of the defenses of Mill given in note 6 attempt, successfully I believe, to meet this charge as well. Since neither Moore nor Russell make much of this, it is not my concern here. I will, however, include Bradley's formulation of this criticism in *Ethical Studies* [Bradley, 1927; p. 113], both because it is clear and because the nastiness of his objection is too good to miss. (The reader should recall that Mill was especially concerned that utilitarianism not be a philosophy for pigs.)

Whether our 'great modern logician' thought that by this he had proved that the happiness of all was desirable for each, I will not undertake to say. [. . .] If many pigs are fed at one trough, each desires his own food, and somehow as a consequence does seem to desire the food of all; and by parity of reasoning it should follow that each pig, desiring his own pleasure, desires also the pleasure of all. But as this scarcely seems conformable to experience, I suppose there must be something wrong with the argument, and so likewise with the argument of our philosopher.

A page later Bradley writes: "[t]his is not a good theoretical deduction, but it is the generation of the Utilitarian monster, and of that we must say that its heart is in the right place, but the brain is wanting".

[73][Sidgwick, 1981, p. 388].

edition. Indeed, if we want to find the origin of the suggestion that will play such a prominent role in *Principia,* we have to turn to the philosopher who, according to Russell's official version of the myth, is the leader of the enemy camp: F. H. Bradley!

In 1877 (three years after the first edition of Sidgwick's book) Bradley published a pamphlet titled *Mr. Sidgwick's Hedonism: An examination of the main argument of* The Methods of Ethics. The pamphlet is more notable for its sharp tone than for its accurate reading of the *Methods,*[74] but here we find what I conjecture must have been the real origin of the "suggestion" to Sidgwick. Section 2 asks what is surely the chief question in the analysis of Mill's argument: "What is the relation of desire to the desirable?"[75] On the next page Bradley indicts Sidgwick for the very fallacy of which Moore accused Mill:

> The audacious *petitio principii* which commended itself to Mr. Mill (365) is perhaps more veiled in our author's pages, but through its thin disguise we recognize the old cause of our errors, the unconscious equivocation by which desirable means indifferently, What I like, or, What I ought to like, just as the conclusion suggests.[76]

Here Bradley appends the following footnote, which must have further annoyed Mr. Sidgwick:

> It is interesting to see that, in his remarks on Mr. Mill's proof of Utilitarianism, our author calls attention to the fact that in this 'desirable' = what one *'ought* to desire' (365), and instructive to notice that he seems unaware of Mr. Mill's equivocation.

Thus, the history of Moore's attack can be traced back into the Idealist camp. The charge of fallacy did not originate with Moore's teacher—rather, the chief of the Idealists accused Sidgwick himself of committing the fallacy.

Indeed, the earliest formulation of Moore's criticism that I can find[77] is in a work by John Grote, whom Passmore calls "a home-grown Idealis[t]"[78] (The

---

[74]See [Schneewind, 1977, pp. 392–401] for an excellent discussion of Bradley's pamphlet. F. H. Hayward [Hayward, 1901, p. 184] labels the pamphlet "an elaborate and violent attack upon Sidgwick's leading principles". In the Preface to the second edition of the *Methods* Sidgwick acknowledges the pamphlet but does not deign to mention Bradley's name: "a third [reviewer] has gone to the length of a pamphlet under the impression (apparently) that the 'main argument' of my treatise is a demonstration of Universalistic Hedonism". (p. xii)

[75][Bradley, 1935, p. 78].

[76][Bradley, 1935, pp. 79–80]. The page numbers in parentheses in this and the next quotation are in Bradley's original, and refer to the first edition of *Methods*.

[77][Schneewind, 1977, p. 184] reports that "[t]he writer of the anonymous book [*Utilitarianism Explained and Exemplified*] against Mill of 1864 points out—for what seems to be the first time in print—the failure of the analogy between 'visible' and 'desirable', and suggests, not very clearly, that there is a 'fallacy of speech' involved in the argument". I have been unable to check Schneewind's source.

[78][Passmore, 1968, p. 53].

usual dating of the Continental invasion and the birth of British Idealism is 1865, with the publication of J. H. Stirling's *The Secret of Hegel.*) Mill's *Utilitarianism* was published in three issues of *Fraser's Magazine* in 1861, and in book form in 1863. John Grote died in 1866, but in 1870 his very critical *An Examination of the Utilitarian Philosophy,* edited by Joseph Bickersteth Mayor, was published. The subject of Grote's Chapter IV is Mill's Chapter IV. Grote writes: "I come now to Mr. Mill's proof of utilitarianism, or rather of that particular form of utilitarianism of which he is the author".[79] Later on in the chapter Mayor appends to one of Grote's footnotes the following comment: "[t]he analogy by which Mr. Mill supports his argument here deserves attention though it has not been noticed by Prof. Grote." Mayor quotes the offending passage from Mill, then writes:

> But by *visible* and *audible* we mean capable of being seen and heard, and in this case the argument holds good; if an object is seen, it must have the capacity of being seen; the latter proposition is merely a restatement of a part of the former. But the word *desirable* does not mean capable of being desired, but deserving to be desired, and in the argument, 'an object is desired therefore it is desirable,' the latter proposition gives a new statement quite independent of that which was contained in the former.[80]

We are now certainly very close to Moore's own formulation of the objection— 33 years earlier, and by an Idealist!

There is still another piece of evidence of the Idealist background of Moore's objection. In *Principia* (pp. 114 and 120), Moore accuses John S. MacKenzie of committing the metaphysical version of the naturalistic fallacy in MacKenzie's *A Manual of Ethics.* MacKenzie was a professor of philosophy in South Wales, and a former Fellow, like Moore, of Trinity College, Cambridge. In his Preface he writes, "[i]t is perhaps hardly necessary to say", giving an indication of the atmosphere in British universities at the end of the 19th century, "that the metaphysical point of view adopted in this Manual is that of the school of Idealism [. . .]".[81] In the very book that Moore attacks for committing the naturalistic fallacy, MacKenzie accuses Mill of our familiar error. If the reader can stand one more formulation of the objection, I will include it, especially considering that the wording is so close to Moore's. After quoting our infamous passage, MacKenzie writes:

> It is here assumed that the meaning of the word "desirable" is analogous to that of "visible" and "audible." But "visible" means "able to be seen," and "audible" means "able to be heard"; whereas "desirable" does not usually mean "able to be desired."

---

[79][Grote, 1870, p. 58].
[80][Grote, 1870, p. 65, fn.].
[81][Mackenzie, 1897, p. vii].

There is scarcely anything that is not able to be desired. What we mean is rather that it is *reasonably to be desired,* or that it *ought* to be desired.[82]

Within the decade Moore will repeat this attack, almost in the same form, and before the new century is very old it will be forgotten that the charge originated before Moore.

As interesting as (I hope) this history of the desire/ desirable argument has been, it is of little *philosophical* interest unless the relationship between the analytic philosophers' and the Idealists' uses of the argument is more than a simple shared misreading of Mill. Otherwise, Moore's appropriation of the argument would be no more significant than his appropriation of the form of his title from Newton (it sets the tone—that is all). There is, however, such a deep relationship: anti-psychologism, which, in the British Idealist assault on Mill, was a species of their anti-empiricism.

The Idealists' objections to Mill's notorious paragraph should be seen in the context of the previous revolution in British philosophy. The movement that Moore and Russell overthrew was itself a revolutionary doctrine. "What we want at present", one of our title characters writes, "is to clear the ground, so that English philosophy, if it rises, may not be choked by prejudice". The author is not Moore or Russell, but Bradley in his Preface to the first edition of *The Principles of Logic.*[83] British Empiricism dominated English philosophy until the last half of the nineteenth century. Mill was the last of the important British Empiricists, and when the Idealists' Continental invasion arrived, Mill was the target of most of the criticisms. A Cambridge man's comment in his 1901 book reveals the atmosphere:

> Economists, logicians, moralists, theologians, and sociologists are united in the execution of one task—the criticism of Mill. No feeling of compunction animates the breasts even of those who owe him the most for providing them with much easy and excellent "copy," and with many a text for a lengthy and triumphant discussion.[84]

(In Bradley's case the opposition was not simply philosophical; it was also political. "In political matters", Wollheim writes, Bradley "was deeply conservative or reactionary [. . . and] was the implacable enemy of all utilitarian or liberal teaching [. . .]".[85]) Russell and Moore, as the next Parts will show more clearly,

---

[82][Mackenzie, 1897, p. 213]. MacKenzie adds this note: "[t]he fallacy here involved is that known to writers on Logic as the 'Fallacy of Figure of Speech'" [p. 214, n. 1]. Later Mackenzie says of Mill's paragraph, "[n]ow it would be difficult to collect in a short space so many fallacies as are here committed" [p. 219].

[83][Bradley, 1883, p. vi]. The texts of the first and second editions of Bradley's *Logic* are identical; however, the pagination is different, and the second edition has additional notes and some closing material titled "Terminal Essays". Future references to Bradley's *Logic* will be to the second edition, London, Oxford University Press, 1922.

[84][Hayward, 1901, p. 18]. Hayward describes himself sympathetic with idealism [p. vi].

[85][Wollheim, 1959, p. 14].

did rebel against Bradley and the Idealists, but they kept the previous revolution's rejection of, at least, Mill and the tradition of British Empiricism.[86]

VI

Anti-psychologism played a crucial role in the substance of both the English and Continental origins of analytic philosophy, although Frege's anti-psychologism was far more visible. The founders' polemical positions were quite different.[87] Frege considered his chief opponent to be naturalism; idealism, he thought, was only a minor annoyance that could be dismissed with a few quick arguments. Thus, the importance he places on anti-psychologism is no mystery, and it plays a large polemical role in his works. Moore and Russell, however, conceived their chief opponent to be Idealism. Their work was as deeply anti-psychologistic as Frege's, but they saw no need to trumpet it on every page. In fact, if I am right about the Idealist origin of their anti-psychologism, to advertise it would be to undermine their own self-image as revolutionaries.

Let us turn to the sources of Moore's and Russell's anti-psychologism. Their teacher Sidgwick barely (but carefully) skirted psychologism. In his *Outlines of the History of Ethics,* Sidgwick discusses the importance of human desires to ethics, and concludes that

> in various ways ethical questions lead inevitably to psychological discussions; in fact, we may say that all important ethical notions are also psychological; except perhaps the fundamental antitheses of "good" and "bad," "right" and "wrong," with which psychology, as it treats of what is and not of what ought to be, is not directly concerned.[88]

This was not nearly strong enough for Moore and Russell. Their anti-psychologism was not only full-fledged, but, to use a Freudian term, *overdetermined;* they could have gotten it from either Kant or, once again, Bradley. And from either one they would have the example of anti-psychologism in both ethics, on the one hand, *and* logic, epistemology, or metaphysics on the other (although in Kant's case the concern was much more with transcendental than with formal logic).

Even though Moore's teacher was Sidgwick, a kind of utilitarian, his entry into moral philosophy was through Kant. The first sentence of one of Moore's earliest publications, "Freedom", reads: "[t]he present paper is selected from a

---

[86]Hylton writes: "Moore and Russell, in their early work, seem to assume that Empiricism is false—they do not take it seriously enough to argue against it in any detail. They both explicitly accept that the Idealists have refuted Empiricism" [Hylton, 1990, p. 22]. Baldwin concurs [Baldwin, 1990, pp. 39–40]: "[Moore's] early philosophy also incorporates the rejection of empiricism which he took over from the idealist philosophy he rejected".

[87]Warren Goldfarb raised this point in conversation with me.

[88][Sidgwick, 1902, pp. 5–6].

much longer essay on Kant's notion of Freedom, which I hope in future to rearrange and enlarge into a treatise on the whole of his Ethical Philosophy".[89] The much longer essay was his prize fellowship dissertation, "The Metaphysical Basis of Ethics".[90]

Kant, of course, would have opposed Mill's ethics in almost every possible way; he argued strenuously against both consequentalism and hedonism, and Mill certainly held both (if *hedonism* is glossed appropriately). For our present purposes, however, Kant's most relevant objection is that ethics cannot be built on an empirical foundation. Kant's anti-psychologism in ethics is a species of his ethical anti-empiricism. In the *Groundwork* he argues that since moral laws are both universal and necessary they can only be established *a priori*.[91] Kant specifically excludes "the nature of man", "the circumstances of the world", and precepts "founded on principles of mere experience" from being relevant to the moral law.[92] Part of "the nature of man" is human psychology, and part of that is what humans (even wise ones) actually desire. One of the chief points of separating a categorical imperative from hypothetical ones is to exclude desires; if desires were included, then the imperative would apply only to those who have the appropriate desire, and that would destroy the moral law's universality and necessity. Mill's transition from what is desired to the desirable would thus be, on Kant's view, triply bad: it is empirical[93]; it is not only empirical, it is psychological; it is not only psychological, it is based on desires.

Bradley's anti-psychologism was prominent in both ethics and logic. In his *Ethical Studies,* for example, in a discussion of punishment (where, typically, the main enemy is Mill) he writes:

> We must be careful here not to suffer ourselves to be led astray. The empirical origin in history, or in the individual, of the notions of justice and desert is for us altogether beside the point. For we are concerned with the *'What',* and not here at all with the question, 'How comes it to be?' *And though often (I do not say, always) for a complete result we must consider both,* yet to run them into one, and confuse them together, is an error as common as it is utterly ruinous.[94]

---

[89][Moore, 1898, p. 179].

[90]There are actually two dissertations with the same title; the second (submitted in 1898) was a revision of the first (submitted in 1897).

[91]This is the same form of argument that Leibniz used against Locke in the *New Essays* to show that arithmetic could not have an empirical foundation. The connection between the ethical and the mathematical point is important here.

[92][Kant, 1785, Preface, p. 389 Ak]. There is a similar argument in the Second Section, p. 408 Ak.

[93]The fact that on my interpretation Mill's premise is only partly empirical would not matter to Kant; on Kant's view *any* empirical infection was deadly.

[94][Bradley, 1927, p. 29, *second emphasis added*]. The first edition was published in 1876; the second edition has additional notes. Future references will be to the second edition. For another typical attack on Mill, see p. 316 n. 1, where Bradley quotes Mill and then writes: "[a]nything in the way of shallow reflection on the psychological form, anything rather than the effort to grasp the content".

What should be striking to readers with analytic backgrounds is that (with the exception of the emphasized phrase, to which we will return later) this passage about ethics is astonishingly similar to the passage from Frege's *Begriffsschrift* quoted in Part II. (*Ethical Studies* and the *Begriffsschrift* were published within three years of each other.)

Leaving ethics for logic, Bradley repeats the point. In the second edition of *The Principles of Logic,* Bradley writes:

> Both logic and psychology, if they are to exist at all, must remain each in principle independent. The undistinguished use of both at once must, even where instructive, remain in principle confusion. And the subordination of one to the other, whenever seriously attempted, will never, I think, fail to make manifest in its result the absurdity of its leading idea.[95]

Frege was not very concerned about protecting the purity of psychology from the infection of logic,[96] but with the exception of that nuance, he would have found an ally here.[97] In fact, there are passages in Bradley like the following from the first edition of the *Principles,* published one year before Frege's *Foundations of Arithmetic,* which, with a change of country, could have come straight from Frege:

> In England at all events we have lived too long in the psychological attitude. We take it for granted and as a matter of course that, like sensations and emotions, ideas are phenomena. And, considering these phenomena as psychical facts, we have tried (with what success I will not ask) to distinguish between ideas and sensations. But, intent on this, we have as good as forgotten the way in which logic uses ideas.[98]

(We will shortly return to that last sentence.)

We have this situation. Kant, Bradley, Russell, and Moore are anti-psychologistic in both ethics, on the one hand, and logic, epistemology, and metaphysics on the other. In both kinds of case Mill or Mill-like positions are seen as the chief examples of psychologism. Mill's alleged move in logic is to take what is *a priori* and reduce it to empirical generalizations. Mill's notorious paragraph

---

[95][Bradley, 1922, p. 613].

[96]As close as he gets is: "[i]t may, of course, serve some purpose to investigate the ideas and changes of ideas which occur during the course of mathematical thinking; but psychology should not imagine that it can contribute anything whatever to the foundation of arithmetic" [Frege, 1884, p. vi].

[97]See, for example, this paragraph from [Frege, 1977b, p. 25], published in 1918, only four years before the second edition of Bradley's *Principles:*

> Not everything is an idea. Otherwise psychology would contain all the sciences within it, or at least it would be the supreme judge over all the sciences. Otherwise psychology would rule even over logic and mathematics. But nothing would be a greater misunderstanding of mathematics than making it subordinate to psychology. Neither logic nor mathematics has the task of investigating minds and contents of consciousness owned by individual men. Their task could perhaps be represented rather as the investigation of *the* mind; of *the* mind, not of minds.

[98][Bradley, 1883, p. 2].

allegedly makes the same move in ethics: it takes what is to our four other philosophers *a priori* (what is desirable or good or in conformity with the moral law) and reduces it to empirical generalizations about what people desire. The cost, so the accusation goes, is the same in each case: psychologism everywhere, it is claimed, leads to the loss of objectivity. Thus, Mill's notorious little argument would have been to Kant, and was, to Bradley, Russell and Moore, a prime example of an empirical and subjective infection of the *a priori* and objective. It is what literary theorists call a *synecdoche*—the part which stands for the whole— helping to account for the intensity of the condemnation of the argument.

There are different ways of arguing from psychologism to the loss of objectivity. *Some* of the variation depends on the differing ways the opponent is supposedly being psychologistic. Resnik, in a discussion of Frege's anti-psychologism, has usefully delineated four psychologistic positions in logic, which, *mutatis mutandis,* would apply to ethics as well:

> (1) the use of mental entities in place of abstract ones, (2) the preference for descriptions of the genesis of mathematical and logical notions over reductive definitions, (3) the treatment of logic as the science of human thinking, and (4) the reduction of truth to acceptance.[99]

Bradley's complaint in ethics about those who seek the "empirical origin in history" of justice (quoted above), and Frege's distinction in logic concerning "how we have gradually arrived at a given proposition" (quoted above in Part II) are directed at the second kind of psychologism.

Bradley gives an argument for psychologism's loss of objectivity (an instance of Resnik's type (1)), that, for our purposes, is crucial.[100] Let us return, as promised, to our sentence from *The Principles of Logic*—"[. . .] we have as good as forgotten the way in which logic uses ideas"—and see in which way, according to Bradley, logic does use ideas. The next paragraph (and section) begins: "[f]or logical purposes ideas are symbols, and they are nothing but symbols".[101] Everything, whether an idea of a horse or Belesarius itself, on Bradley's view, has two sides: (1) existence and (2) content. But symbols[102] have an additional aspect: they have (3) *meaning,* and it is this meaning that is logic's concern.

The relevant point here is that with the additional aspect of *meaning* the term "idea" becomes ambiguous. The first sense of "idea" is psychological, and includes

---

[99][Resnik, 1980, p. 26]. For one of the best discussions of Frege's anti-psychologism, see [Ricketts, 1986a, pp. 65–95].

[100]Hylton discusses parts of the same argument on pp. 59–61, Wollheim on pp. 27–31, and Baldwin on p. 13.

[101][Bradley, 1922, pp. 2–3].

[102]What turns something into a symbol is the way it is used. (Comparisons to the *Tractatus* are intriguing.) Something need not be an idea in order to be used as a symbol—Bradley gives the examples of flowers being used as symbols for hope or love [Bradley, 1922, p. 3]. For the purposes of the argument against psychologism, however, the only relevant symbols are ideas.

only the aspects of existence and content. The second sense is logical, and includes only the aspects of content and meaning, dropping existence.[103] (I agree with Hylton that "[e]xactly what connection [Bradley] sees between [a symbol's] content and signification is hard to ascertain [. . .]"[104], but the crucial point here is that psychological ideas have the aspect of existence and not that of meaning, whereas logical ideas have the aspect of meaning and not that of existence. The aspect of content is not important for our present purposes.)

We can now be more precise about Bradley's account of this form of psychologism in logic: this form is characterized by substituting the psychological sense of "idea" for the logical sense.

Bradley objects to this that the latter sense requires ideas to be universal, whereas the former sense requires them to be particular. Words (whether on paper or in speech)[105] and psychological ideas are, to Bradley, all particulars. The distinction between ideas and sensations might be fundamental in psychology, but from the point of view of logic, Bradley says, no such distinction is relevant: "both are facts and neither is a meaning". In purple prose Bradley emphasizes their particularity:

> Neither [i.e. sensations and psychological, as opposed to logical, ideas] is indifferent to its place in the stream of psychical events, its time and relations to the presented congeries. [. . .] The lives of both are so entangled with their environment, so one with their setting of sensuous particulars, that their fleeting character is destroyed if but one thread is broken.[106]

In other words, every psychological idea is what it is, and not another thing.

The particularity of psychological ideas, which is a function of their existence, makes them unsuitable for logic. A logical idea, on the other hand, is a universal[107], and "can not as such exist. It can not ever be an event, with a place in the series of time or space. It can be a fact no more inside our heads than it can outside them."[108] It is, in other words, part of Frege's third realm.[109]

---

[103]Compare [Frege, 1884, p. 37, n. 1]: "An idea in the subjective sense is what is governed by the psychological laws of association; it is of a sensible, pictorial character. An idea in the objective sense belongs to logic and in principle non-sensible, although the word which means an objective idea is often accompanied by a subjective idea, which nevertheless is not its meaning."

[104][Hylton, 1990, p. 60 n. 19].

[105][Bradley, 1922, p. 4].

[106][Bradley, 1922, p. 7].

[107][Bradley, 1922, p. 168].

[108][Bradley, 1922, p. 7].

[109]See [Frege, 1977b, p. 17]: "A third realm must be recognized. Anything belonging to this realm has it in common with ideas that it cannot be perceived by the senses, but has it in common with things that it does not need an owner so as to belong to the contents of his consciousness". Anthony Manser, in "Bradley and Frege" [Manser, 1984, p. 313], writes: "[. . .] it would seem that what Frege meant by 'the thought' was virtually identical to what Bradley meant by 'meaning'. We can see how the attempt to eschew psychologism forces both into similar positions. Logic is concerned with meanings, not with what is private and peculiar to individuals".

One facet of a psychological idea's particularity that especially interested Bradley (and might interest contemporary readers) is its privacy. Bradley argues that a psychological idea is "my private psychical event"[110] and, as such, cannot be part of a judgment. He gives as an example the judgment (or what we would now call a proposition) "The whale is a mammal". As long as we take the idea of *a mammal* as psychological, and therefore, private, we cannot predicate it of real whales, "[f]or [the psychological idea] belongs to me, and is an event in my history; and, unless I am Jonah, it can not enter into an actual whale". Thus, the psychological interpretation of ideas makes judgment impossible; since truth and falsehood are properties of judgments,[111] this form of psychologism makes it nonsensical to say something is true or false. Psychologism, on Bradley's argument, destroys objectivity in logic.

Psychological ideas are "so entangled with their environment", so particular, that my present idea of white is not only necessarily *mine,* it is also not the same as my idea of white a moment ago. Psychological logicians may investigate the settings and histories and nuances of psychological ideas all they want; but that investigation will not be of objects that are suitable components of judgment, and thus their investigations will reveal nothing about truth and objectivity.

Going against the myth, we find that Russell gives an early argument against psychologism which depends on the very distinctions we just saw Bradley make. (What goes against the myth is not that Russell was, in his youth, influenced by Bradley; what goes against it is that the influence survived the revolution.)

Russell wrote an undergraduate paper around 1894 titled "On the Distinction between the Psychological and Metaphysical Points of View". Russell later says of 1894: "I read Bradley at this time with avidity, and admired him more than any other recent philosopher".[112] The paper is thoroughly Bradlyian, including a moment of Bradlyian phenomenology:

> If I lie in a field on a hot day with my eyes shut, and feel sleepily the heat of the sun, the buzz of the flies, the slight tickling of a few blades of grass, it is possible to get into a frame of mind which seems to belong to a much earlier stage of evolution; at such times there is only what Bradley would call "a vague mass of the felt" [. . .][113]

More significantly, not only is the conclusion of Russell's argument the same as Bradley's, but the premises explicitly invoke *The Principles of Logic*'s threefold

---

[110][Bradley, 1922, p. 8].

[111]To Bradley truth and falsehood are only matters of degree. I am here emphasizing the similarities between Bradley and Russell and Moore; if I were emphasizing the differences I would focus on that point, which the analytic philosophers strongly objected to. That objection is part of the genuine revolution.

[112][Russell, 1946, p. 10].

[113][Russell, 1983, p. 196].

distinction: "[w]e have thus seen how a psychosis [*mental event* in the jargon of the day] has three aspects under which it may be viewed: (1) Its existence (2) Its content (3) Its *meaning*."[114] Here, however, either misreading or reinterpreting Bradley, Russell claims that "Psychology deals with the second [content] alone".[115] Russell is thus going against Bradley by ignoring the existence aspect of psychological ideas. Since, as we have just seen, Bradley uses that very aspect in his argument against psychologism (a psychological idea's particularity depended on its existence), Russell, obviously, has to use a different technique. He gives an infinite regress argument:

> Any particular act of belief exists, and it has meaning; the meaning, indeed, is here evidently of overwhelming importance; but, in accordance with the principle of Psychology, we abstract from these two sides of belief, leaving it merely as a psychical phenomenon. It follows that we can no longer be concerned with the logical grounds for any belief, since these have references to its meaning, but only to the psychological causes. But every result we obtain as to these causes is itself a proposition demanding our belief, and if we subject it to a similar criticism to that which produced it, we only get a fresh proposition, and so on *ad infinitum,* so that our procedure is circular.[116]

Significantly, for our purposes, Russell explicitly compares this case with desire: "[t]he same criticism applies (though less obviously) to a psychological treatment of desire", and through desire to ethics:

> Of course I do not mean that Psychology is not a valuable study, full of important results; I only mean, that, *being from the first one-sided, its results throughout are necessarily one-sided;* and that its criticism [. . .] can have no direct bearing on our view as to the correctness of beliefs or the morality of desires [. . .][117]

In a later (1897) address to the Apostles, "Is Ethics a Branch of Empirical Psychology", Russell seems to challenge the analogy between belief and desire. In this fascinating (and troubling) paper Russell argues there is a disanalogy between the foundations of ethics and the foundations of epistemology. He thus answers the title question with a purely psychologistic "yes". If ethics is a branch of psychology, then "[a]t present," Russell writes, "I see no way of distinguishing between the good and the desired." Russell is thus forced to conclude that "I regard the good, therefore, as totally devoid of objectivity, and

---

[114][Russell, 1983, p. 197].
[115][Russell, 1983, p. 197].
[116][Russell, 1983, p. 197].
[117][Russell, 1983, p. 198; *emphasis added*]. The italicized clauses are particularly Bradlyian elements, and we will examine Bradley's view on the one-sided nature of logic and psychology in Part VII.
[118][Russell, 1983, p. 104].

as a matter for purely psychological investigation".[118] I take this essay as a thought-experiment of the consequences of denying the anti-psychologistic analogy between epistemology and ethics, and thus reducing ethics to psychology and the desired; the result is the expulsion of objectivity. Evidence that this is a thought-experiment and not Russell's considered view is Russell's admission "[t]hat my conclusion is satisfactory, I do not pretend", and the plea, in Apostleian language, for "our brother Moore" to set him straight.[119]

In 1895, a year after his Bradlyian undergraduate paper, Russell's first published work, a review of a book by G. Heymans, appeared. Russell quotes from the author's preface that "'my conviction [is] that the empirical method of investigation and proof, which I wish to advocate towards my fellow-philosophers, is precisely the method of presentation best fitted for introducing men of scientific culture to philosophy'".[120] Russell's criticisms are thoroughly anti-empiricist and anti-psychologistic; he argues that Heymans has illegitimately conflated the causes of belief with the grounds of correct belief. This is two years before *An Essay on the Foundations of Geometry;* Russell is still deeply in his Idealist period.

All this evidence shows: Moore and Russell were anti-psychologistic in both ethical and nonethical philosophy; Moore's anti-psychologism was likely taken from Kant; Russell's was almost certainly taken from Bradley; and both Moore and Russell's anti-psychologistic positions, which played such a prominent role in their post-revolution philosophies, were a product of their Idealist periods.

We saw the Kantian influence on Moore's personal history (i.e. his fellowship dissertations) and his philosophy, but even early in his career Moore was never an uncritical follower of Kant; he certainly, for example, did not share Kant's rejection of consequentialism. He never, however, rescinded Kant's anti-psychologism, either in ethics or in other philosophy; in fact, Moore's complaint was not that Kant and the Idealists were anti-psychologistic; it was that, in his eyes, they were not anti-psychologistic enough.[121] It was this complaint, not any quarrel about relations or abstraction, that induced Moore to lead the revolt and Russell to follow. To see this, we need to return to Bradley and the Magna Charta of English analytic philosophy: Moore's 1899 article "The Nature of Judgment".[122]

---

[119][Russell, 1983, p. 104].

[120]"Review of Heymans, *Die Gesetze und Elemente des wissenschaftlichen Denkens* [Russell, 1983, p. 251].

[121]See, for instance, [Moore, 1903, p. 133], where Moore finds Kant insufficiently anti-psychologistic in epistemology.

[122][Moore, 1899]. It is reprinted in [Moore, 1986]. The latter edition helpfully includes the original pagination. "The Nature of Judgment" is discussed in [Hylton, 1990, Chapter 4, section 1], [Baldwin, 1990, Chapter II, section 4], and in [Ryle, 1970].

VII

Moore begins that article by agreeing with Bradley that the constituents of judgments, and thus what is essential for there to be truth and falsehood, must be *meanings,* universals, or logical ideas (Moore accurately treats these terms as synonyms for Bradley), not psychological ideas. He writes on the second page:

> Now to Mr. Bradley's argument that "the idea in judgment is the universal meaning" I have nothing to add. It appears to me conclusive, as against those, of whom there have been too many, who have treated the idea as a mental state.[123]

But, Moore claims, Bradley's logical idea or universal meaning, while certainly a necessary step in the right direction, is insufficiently anti-psychologistic.

Moore's interpretation of *The Principles of Logic* is that Bradley's logical ideas are abstracted from his psychological ideas, and thus, a psychological element is necessary; a psychological element that will infect judgment and destroy objectivity. There *is* some evidence for Moore's interpretation; Bradley, after all, does say, and Moore (accurately) quotes him, that a "meaning consists of a part of the content (original or acquired) cut off, fixed by the mind, and considered apart from the existence of the sign".[124] But Bradley later claimed this was simply rhetorical excess, and that the psychological element was not needed *here.*[125]

Moore would have been much better served appealing to an aspect of Bradley that *was* an essential part of his theory; namely, the incompleteness of logic:

> Truth necessarily (if I am right) implies an aspect of psychical existence. In order to be, truth itself must happen and occur, and must exist as what we call a mental event. Hence, to completely realize itself as truth, truth would have to include this essential aspect of its own being. And yet from this aspect logic, if it means to exist, is compelled to abstract.[126]

This is the strain in Bradley's thought I earlier italicized when quoting him, and noted that this distinguished him from Frege. Recall that in discussing ethics, for example, Bradley wrote that "for a complete result we must consider both" the empirical origins and the nature of punishment. (See n. 94.) Bradley's logic and anti-psychologism are more complicated than we have so far acknowledged; he held what might be called a staged anti-psychologism. At one stage or level (the level Russell and Moore inherited), the anti-psychologism was complete: no infection of any psychological kind allowed. But on the next level (the level that Moore should have been rejecting in "The Nature of Judgment", and certainly

---

[123][Moore, 1899, p. 177].
[124][Moore, 1899, p. 177], [Bradley, 1922, p. 8].
[125]See Bradley's letter to Moore quoted in [Baldwin, 1990, p. 14], and Baldwin's discussion.
[126][Bradley, 1922, p. 612].

did reject later), both logic and psychology are incomplete, and need each other. This must have been at least partly what Russell had in mind with the sentence that immediately followed his version of the myth in "My Mental Development" (quoted above in Part I): "[m]athematics could be *quite* true, and not merely a stage in dialectic."[127]

But nevertheless, rightly or wrongly, or rightly for the wrong reasons, Moore interprets Bradley as being psychologistic, and thus, dangerously susceptible to the same attacks that Bradley marshalled against Mill and the other Empiricists.[128]

Moore has a solution to all this psychologism. He begins by announcing, "I shall in future use the term 'concept' for what Mr. Bradley calls a 'universal meaning' [. . .]".[129] These *concepts,* which are specifically designed to battle Bradley's alleged psychologism, are the direct descendants of Bradley's *meanings* in *The Principles of Logic,* the immediate predecessors of Russell's *terms* in the *Principles of Mathematics,* and the ancestors of Wittgenstein's *objects* in the *Tractatus.*[130] (In the following crucial quotation, where Moore explains his use of *concepts* I have added numbers in brackets for a comparison with Russell's *terms* in *Principles of Mathematics.*) "With this, then" Moore writes,

> we have approached the nature of a proposition or judgment. [1] A proposition is composed not of words, nor yet of thoughts, but of concepts. [2] Concepts are possible objects of thought; but that is no definition of them. [3] It merely states that they may come into relation with a thinker; and in order that they *may* do anything, they must already *be* something. It is indifferent to their nature whether anybody thinks them or not. [4] They are incapable of change; and the relation into which they enter with the knowing subject implies no action or reaction.[131]

At this precise moment, with this precise philosophical conception, Platonic Atomism is born.[132] It will develop into analytic philosophy by way of the metaphysics of *Principia Ethica* and the *Principles of Mathematics.* When united with the new logic of Frege and Russell, its descendants will dominate English-speaking philosophy for the rest of the century.

---

[127][Russell, 1946, p. 12].

[128]Moore's argument here is reminiscent of (but certainly not identical to) Russell's undergraduate infinite regress argument discussed above in Part VI. See [Moore, 1899, pp. 177–178] and also [Hylton, 1990, p. 132].

[129][Moore, 1899, p. 177].

[130]See [Linsky, 1988, p. 628].

[131][Moore, 1899, p. 179].

[132]*Platonic Atomism* is Hylton's name for the early metaphysics of Moore and Russell; Moore's description above fully justifies the adjective in Hylton's phrase "*Platonic* Atomism". See [Hylton, 1990, p. 112, n. 7].

VIII

Let us now examine how all of the chief features (numbered in brackets) of the just quoted paragraph from "The Nature of Judgment" reappear in Russell's *Principles of Mathematics.*

In the Preface of the *Principles of Mathematics* (p. xviii), Russell writes that "[o]n fundamental questions of philosophy, my position, in all its chief features, is derived from Mr G. E. Moore". In a later footnote Russell acknowledges his friend with a more specific reference: "[t]he notion of a term here set forth is a modification of Mr G. E. Moore's notion of a *concept* in his article 'On the Nature of Judgment' [. . .]".[133] Indeed, Russell's *terms* have all the characteristics that Moore attributed to his *concepts* in the last passage quoted from "The Nature of Judgment"—and all these characteristics are important in the break from Idealism. A *term* is Russell's chief ontological category, and the way he introduces that expression is almost identical to Moore's feature [2]: "[w]hatever may be an object of thought, or may occur in any true or false proposition, or can be counted as *one,* I call a *term*".[134]

Feature [3] is, in reaction to Bradley (or, more accurately, Moore's reading of Bradley), a direct statement of Moore's full-fledged anti-psychologism. In a well known passage, but a little more poetically and in the context of arithmetic, Russell echoes the point:

> Arithmetic must be discovered in just the same sense in which Columbus discovered the West Indies, and we no more create numbers than he created the Indians. The number 2 is not purely mental, but is an entity which may be thought *of.* Whatever can be thought of has being, and its being is a precondition, not a result, of its being thought of.[135]

This complete mind-independence is guaranteed by Moore's feature [4] and Russell's parallel: "every term is immutable and indestructible. What a term is, it

---

[133][Russell, 1903, p. 44 n]. Russell continues, however, that his notion "differs in some important respects" from Moore's. Russell divides terms into *things* and, confusingly enough: *concepts* (Russell's and Moore's *concepts* are not related). Things can only occur as the subject of a proposition, whereas concepts can occur either as the subject or not. Thus, Russell's concepts have dual roles, whereas things do not: there is no such thing as *socratizing.* (See sec. 48, pp. 44–45) Moore makes no such differentiation. Moore was not a logician, and throughout his career was not sensitive to the internal structures of sentences. This Russellian refinement of Moore, however, is not relevant to the present discussion.

[134][Russell, 1903, p. 43].

[135][Russell, 1903, p. 451]. This helps explain why after his acknowledgment to Moore in his Preface, Russell writes: "[b]efore learning these views from him, I found myself completely unable to construct any philosophy of arithmetic, whereas their acceptance brought about an immediate liberation from a large number of difficulties [. . .]". (p. xviii)

is, and no change can be conceived in it which would not destroy its identity and make another term".[136] (Bishop Butler is smiling.)

In the context of our present discussion, however, the most striking parallel between Russell and Moore concerns Moore's feature [1]: "[a] proposition is composed not of words, nor yet of thoughts, but of concepts [. . .]". Not everything in "The Nature of Judgment" survives in *Principia*—for one thing, Moore no longer uses the term "concept" in the technical way he does in "The Nature of Judgment"—but the point of this feature is very much alive, indeed, in *Principia*. Analytic philosophy is often equated with the linguistic turn; Dummett, for instance, writes that "[t]he fundamental principle of analytical philosophy is the priority, in the order explanation, of language over thought [. . .]".[137] As we will see, however, this claim does not conform with the history (if *Principia* and *Principles of Mathematics* are not works of analytic philosophy, then nothing is).

In *Principia,* Moore defines ethics as "the general inquiry into what is good".[138] This, then, in Section 2 leads to "our first question: What is good?"[139] The question, Moore recognizes, is ambiguous, and as no one else can, he proceeds to differentiate the senses and eliminate those which do not concern him. By Section 6 he has refined the question to read "[h]ow is good to be defined?"[140] Here Moore gives an answer which directly contradicts Dummett:

> Now, it may be thought that this is a verbal question. A definition does indeed often mean the expressing of one word's meaning in other words. But this is not the sort of definition I am asking for. [. . .] My business is solely with that object or idea, which I hold, rightly or wrongly, that the word is generally used to stand for. What I want to discover is the nature of that object or idea [. . .][141]

"Object or idea" is the nontechnical substitute for "The Nature of Judgment"'s "concepts"; we must however, never take "idea" in *Principia* to mean "psychological idea", and Moore's rejection of a linguistic philosophy can only be correctly understood in the light of "The Nature of Judgment"'s rejection of Bradley. Moore thought of verbal definitions as simply reports of how people used words,[142] and consequently no more significant to metaphysics than Mill's reports of what people desired were for ethics. To rely on either report would be

---

[136][Russell, 1903, p. 44]. See the *Tractatus* 2.027: "[o]bjects, the unalterable, and the subsistent are one and the same", and, once again, [Linsky, 1988].

[137][Dummett, 1991a, p. 17]. He adds "the only route to a philosophical account of thought is through an analysis of its expression in words or symbols, that is, a theory of meaning".

[138][Moore, 1903, p. 2].

[139][Moore, 1903, p. 3].

[140][Moore, 1903, p. 6].

[141][Moore, 1903, p. 6].

[142]See also [Moore, 1903, p. 2]: "for verbal questions are properly left to the writers of dictionaries and other persons interested in literature; philosophy, as we shall see, has no concern with them".

to allow psychologism to return; thus, in Moore's eyes, to expel objectivity.[143] What is good can depend no more on what people say than on what they think. In both *Principia* and *Principles of Mathematics* ontology is the first philosophy: English analytic philosophy begins with the rejection of a linguistic turn.[144]

Russell explicitly relates an ill-designed linguistic turn to, once again, of all people: F. H. Bradley! Examining this argument will lead us back to the naturalistic fallacy. Section 51 of *Principles of Mathematics* parallels *Principia's* section 6 and "The Nature of Judgment"'s feature [1]. It attempts a proof that language is irrelevant to logic. The proof involves reading (or rather, misreading) Bradley in precisely the same way Moore did in "The Nature of Judgment"; the accusation is that Bradley's *meanings* are psychologistic even at stage one.[145] Russell begins by remarking that unlike his own view, "[i]t is customary to regard all propositions as having a subject and a predicate [. . .]"[146] He makes a bow to fairness by acknowledging "[t]his is, of course, an account of the theory in question which will strike its adherents as extremely crude; but it will serve for a general indication of the view to be discussed". Unmentioned is that Bradley himself criticizes traditional logic for forcing all propositions into subject-predicate form, writing that "[i]n their ordinary acceptation the traditional subject, predicate, and copula are mere superstitions".[147] Nevertheless, Russell believes that "Mr Bradley's Logic" itself is committed to that superstition,[148] and that this leads to the doctrine that "all words stand for ideas having what [Bradley] calls *meaning* [. . .]". Russell finds, with Moore, that Bradley's notion of *meaning* is dangerously psychologistic; it "is a notion confusedly compounded of logical and psychological elements". (Recall that the whole point of

---

[143]Ryle makes the following intriguing suggestion: "[t]he vehemence of [Moore's] attack on the naturalistic fallacy in *Principia Ethica* [. . .] suggests that the notion of *Good,* together with those of *ought, right* and perhaps *End,* had been for him, all along, of quite special importance. So it may be that his epistemological anti-empiricisms and anti-psychologisms got their heat from his ethical anti-relativism" [Ryle, 1970, p. 100].

[144][Linsky, 1988, pp. 624–625] dates the beginning of the analytic linguistic turn as 1905, with Russell's "On Denoting".

[145]Russell does not seem to recognize, however, that there are different stages in Bradley's account.

[146][Russell, 1903, p. 47].

[147][Bradley, 1922, p. 21]; see also pp. 11 and 13.

[148]Whether Russell is right depends on which level or stage Bradley is talking about. On one level, to Bradley, forcing every judgment into the subject-predicate mold results in error; on another level *reality* is the subject of every judgment. The first level is more prominent in Bradley's *Principles of Logic,* the second is more prominent in his other works. See, for instance, Chapter III of *Essays on Truth and Reality* [Bradley, 1914, pp. 28–29]:

Every idea essentially qualifies reality, but no idea on the other hand does this simply and bodily. Every idea has its own existence as a fact, and with this side of its being it, as an idea and so far, does not qualify reality. Its essence, we may say, lies in ignoring or in discounting this side of itself. And thus everywhere truth and ideas have a double aspect.

The real debate here between Russell and Bradley is whether truth admits of degree.

Bradley's *meanings* was to *save* logic from Mill's psychologism; this criticism must have greatly bothered Bradley.) Russell continues: "[w]ords all have meaning, in the simple sense that they are symbols which stand for something other than themselves." He then paraphrases Moore's feature [1]: "[b]ut a proposition, unless it happens to be linguistic, does not itself contain words: it contains the entities indicated by words". Russell makes the same point in a famous letter to Frege, dated 12 December 1904:

> I believe that in spite of all its snowfields Mont Blanc itself is a component part of what is actually asserted in the proposition 'Mont Blanc is more than 4000 metres high'. We do not assert the thought, for this is a private psychological matter [. . .][149]

Returning to *Principles of Mathematics,* after making this point Russell finishes his proof: "[t]hus meaning, in the sense in which words have meaning, is irrelevant to logic". So much for the linguistic turn.

(But not so much for Bradley. The last sentence in the Mont Blanc quotation copies Bradley's own argument against psychologizing logical ideas, which we discussed above in Part VII. Russell and Moore have turned Bradley's own arguments against him.)

The universe of *Principia* and *Principles of Mathematics* is a universe of robust ontology: *"[b]eing",* Russell writes, "is that which belongs to every conceivable term, to every possible object of thought [. . .] Numbers, the Homeric gods, relations, chimeras and four-dimensional spaces all have being [. . .]".[150] It is a pluralistic universe of discrete objects. In his acknowledgment to Moore in his Preface, Russell declares that

> I have accepted from him [. . . propositions'] independence of any knowing mind; also that pluralism which regards the world, both that of existents and that of entities, as composed of an infinite number of mutually independent entities [. . .][151]

Regardless of whether the simple object is ethical or logical, it is both independent of the mind and, if known, cognized the same way. The purpose of analysis at the beginning of Analytic Philosophy is to break down and define complex objects; once we have reached the simple objects, we have reached the level of indefinables, and then the analogy is always with perception. "The discussion of indefinables", Russell writes, in this context meaning by "indefinables" what we would now call logical constants, "—which forms the chief part of philosophical logic—is the endeavour to see clearly, and to make others see clearly, the entities

---

[149][Frege, 1980, p. 169]. I discuss this in the context of the *Tractatus* in "Two Ways of Grounding Meaning" [Gerrard, 1991a, p. 106 and n. 13]. See also [Linsky, 1988].
[150][Russell, 1903, p. 449].
[151][Russell, 1903, p. xviii].

concerned, in order that the mind may have that kind of acquaintance with them which it has with redness or the taste of a pineapple".[152] In a later chapter Russell writes about indefinables that "[a]ll depends, in the end, upon immediate perception; and philosophical argument, strictly speaking, consists mainly of an endeavour to cause the reader to perceive what has been perceived by the author."[153] (We should emphasize that here the context is strictly local: Both Moore's and Russell's views of philosophical argument were even then far broader; Russell's present discussion is restricted to argument about indefinables.) Moore concurs: "[m]y point is that 'good' is a simple notion, just as 'yellow' is a simple notion; that, just as you cannot, by any manner of means, explain to any one who does not already know it, what yellow is, so you cannot explain what good is".[154]

In this metaphysical universe of *Principles of Mathematics* and *Principia* there could be no more basic mistake than to confuse one simple object with another (simple or complex) object. This, at long last, leads us straight to what I claimed in Part IV was Moore's purest formulation of the naturalistic fallacy: "the fallacy which consists in identifying the simple notion which we mean by 'good' with some other notion".[155] In its native environment of the metaphysics of Platonic Atomism, there could be no *greater* mistake, to Moore, because there could be no more *basic* mistake.

In Part III I argued that Mill did not commit the is/ought fallacy. The power of the naturalistic fallacy to convince might be due to its apparent closeness to the is/ought fallacy, but the naturalistic fallacy is *not* Hume's.[156] In Part IV I argued that Mill did not commit a *petitio principii*. We can now see that Mill *did* violate Moore's principles; however doing so is not a fallacy (naturalistic or otherwise), it is simply going against the metaphysics of Platonic Atomism. Mill's mistake was historical, not logical. He got caught in a metaphysical and

---

[152][Russell, 1903, p. xv]. There is a certain irony (perhaps even self-conscious) in the example. Locke, in arguing for his empiricism, claimed that "if a Child were kept in a place, where he never saw any other but Black and White, till he were a Man, he would have no more *Ideas* of Scarlet or Green, than he that from his Childhood never tasted an Oyster, or a Pine-Apple, has of those particular Relishes" [Locke, 1690, Book I, Chapter I, Sec. 6]. Both *Principles* and *Principia* are deeply anti-empiricist. In attacking an argument from Mach, Russell writes that "[t]his argument contains the very essence of empiricism, in a sense in which empiricism is radically opposed to the philosophy advocated in the present work" [p. 493]. Russell footnotes the article "Nativism" in [Baldwin, 1960]. The article turns out to be written by Moore.

[153][Russell, 1903, p. 130].

[154][Moore, 1903, p. 7].

[155][Moore, 1903, p. 58].

[156]This article also explains the mystery of why there is no mention of Hume in *Principia,* (Philippa Foot alludes to this mystery in her Introduction to her *Theories of Ethics* [Foot, 1967, p. 1].) Moore and Russell would have read Hume as being thoroughly psychologistic; thus he would have been the last person they would have appealed to. The naturalistic fallacy arose from the metaphysics of Platonic Atomism, not from Hume.

polemical cross fire. Bradley's objections' to Mill's alleged psychologism (in both ethics and logic) created *meanings;* Moore's "The Nature of Judgment" accusations of psychologism against Bradley led to *concepts;* these, in turn gave rise to Russell's *terms* and the metaphysics of both *Principia* and *Principles of Mathematics.* Each step of this path was partly designed to exclude what Mill thought was central to ethics and epistemology: human desires and psychological ideas.

Regardless of whether there are internal or external relations, there are no simple relations. Bradley, Moore, and Russell all rejected Mill's Empiricism in both ethical and nonethical philosophy. Moore and Russell built on Bradley's foundations at the same time (and often in the same way) they were trying to destroy those foundations. Analytic Philosophy began with Russell's and Moore's rejection of the residue of Mill's Empiricism that they thought remained in Idealism.[157]

---

[157]Fairness (and a sense of irony) require that I close this essay by pointing out that Mill himself was extremely fond of charging his philosophical predecessors with fallacy. Book V of *A System of Logic,* titled "On Fallacies" accuses, among others: Plato [pp. 815, 825], Aristotle [pp. 761–762, 815], Cicero [pp. 812–813], Descartes [pp. 751–752, 771, 813], Leibniz [p. 755], Bacon [p. 801], and Berkeley [pp. 815–816]. If I have committed any fallacies in this article, it is obviously not due to the generous help I have received. Conversations with Amelie Rorty first led me to believe that Mill had a case; Jenny Gerrard and Lydia Goehr made very helpful suggestions on earlier drafts; Hilary Putnam, Samuel Fleischacker, Sally Sedgwick, Amelie Rorty, and Alan White did the same for a later draft; and Deborah Wilkes of Hackett Publishing Company cheerfully sent me an essential book at a crucial time; I am grateful to them all.

4

Warren Goldfarb

WITTGENSTEIN ON FIXITY OF MEANING

Leonard Linsky has long urged that Wittgenstein's *Investigations* be read against the backdrop of Frege, Russell, and the early Wittgenstein, and that scrutiny of the interplay between later Wittgenstein and early analytic philosophy is important for our understanding of both. This advice is particularly apt with respect to the first hundred-odd sections of the *Investigations,* for here Wittgenstein most directly engages themes from the earlier writers. In this paper, I shall discuss one portion of those opening sections, namely, §§65–88. This swatch of text begins with Wittgenstein's introduction of the notion of family resemblance, and contains the well-known "Moses" section in which Wittgenstein criticizes Russell's analysis of ordinary proper names. In it Wittgenstein is treating questions about language and meaning that are far from fully explicit. Nor, I think, is his *procedure* at all well understood. This has led to a view of his criticisms of the early analytic tradition that, although not grossly inaccurate, is certainly simplistic. My aim below is to try to gain a more nuanced and, I hope, deeper understanding of both the objects of Wittgenstein's attack and the nature of his moves against them.

I. FAMILY RESEMBLANCE

The notion of family likeness is introduced by Wittgenstein in the *Blue Book* to counter what he sees as a basic philosophical misstep, "The tendency to look for something in common to all the entities we commonly subsume under a general term" (p. 17).[1] Wittgenstein depicts this tendency as an important component of the "craving for generality" that is the source of much philosophical error. He goes on in the *Blue Book* to characterize numerous concepts as family likenesses: ability, expectation, understanding, being guided, as well as the illustrative example of games.

---

[1]Works by Wittgenstein are cited by name in the text. Editions used are cited in the bibliography. Citations by section number alone are to the *Investigations.*

In *Philosophical Investigations* Wittgenstein introduces the notion of family resemblance in §65, in response to an interlocutory challenge to specify what is common to all languages. He once again illustrates the notion with the term "games". However, it is not often remarked that in the *Investigations* there is little further discussion except with respect to this example, and, more important, he invokes the notion of family resemblance or likeness far more rarely than in the writing of a few years earlier. I suspect, in fact, that the notion of family resemblance by itself plays a less important role in the *Investigations* than the *Blue Book* might lead us to think. Rather than an antidote to a particular isolatable sort of philosophical error, it is used as just one part of a sustained attack on a more general, and deeper, target.

To see this, it is helpful to start with the obvious question, namely, what work the introduction of "family resemblance" is meant to do at all. The brevity of Wittgenstein's discussion leaves much room for interpretation, but the following description should be uncontroversial. Family resemblances are nests of properties, similarities, and relations that the things falling under a general term have and have to each other. They are elaborate and not summarizable networks of features that are exhibited across the range of items to which the term applies. The example of games illustrates how many different categories of features may enter: overall structure, function, stakes, individual physical practices, and so on. This motley of features is not readily surveyable, and in it one sees much crisscrossing. It cannot be done justice by a disjunction of properties, or similarity-circles, or the like. Also noncontroversial, if put vaguely enough, is Wittgenstein's intention in introducing the notion. He means it to work against some idea of common property, essence, attribute, concept, Platonic form, etc., that is, that which all objects falling under the general term share.

The first question, then, is: How does the notion do this work? Suppose we accept Wittgenstein's point about games. (I certainly find it convincing; the occasional attempts in the literature to provide a definition of "game" seem hopelessly inadequate.) Suppose we accept too that there are other examples of the same phenomenon. At first blush, the conclusion is that, for at least some general terms, there is nothing characterizable or definable in simpler terms that is common to all items falling under the term. Thus, if talk of a common property, essence, attribute, or the like is taken as committing one to the existence of such characterizations or definitions, the mere adducing of family resemblance terms is effective.

Yet then the position against which this "first blush" conclusion works is rather special. It is the position that all general terms—except, presumably, a few that are the most basic—must be explicitly definable from more basic ones. No doubt this is a position that Wittgenstein opposes; but equally clearly he intends his considerations to be more broadly applicable. The first blush conclusion does not carry much weight even against the search for the "essence of language." It merely presents the possibility that the search will fail, because there is no definable common feature, but it gives us no positive reason to abandon the search. Similarly, if the point is taken this way, nothing much is done in characterizing "to be able to" as a family term, as Wittgenstein does in the *Brown Book* (p. 117), since few would assert that this concept is definable in a simpler vocabulary.

The "first blush" conclusion boils down merely to this: some of our concepts possess readily statable necessary and sufficient conditions (like "rectangle" and, perhaps, "arthroprod"); but others do not. One might well react: Is it surprising that some general terms have no readily statable equivalents? Indeed, *that* is why we need the general term. No other manageable expression does the work it does; it is indispensable.

To be sure, a position that maintains there *is* something in common among all the instances of a general term, but it need not be characterizable in independent terms, may easily collapse into triviality. The triviality I have in mind is this: what all games have in common is that they're properly called "games". Here, of course, having the "common property" is just a restatement of the fact that the items do fall under the general term. To see what philosophical views Wittgenstein is moving against, we should consider what makes the position more than a triviality. Something is meant to be added in moving from the general term to a notion of common property, essence, attribute, form, or the like. The idea, I would propose, is that there must be something that *underlies* the application of general terms to instances. Here we need to get clearer about what is at stake. To do this, it is helpful to ask what is not satisfactory, what seems not to be answered, if we rest with the triviality that all that games have in common is that they are games.

We apply a general term to new instances, and deny it of other items. The questions left unanswered by the triviality are the natural ones: what do we rely on in such ascriptions and denials; what does a new ascription communicate? The common property, essence, attribute, or the like, is to give the locus for the answer to these questions. Since it is what the instance has, partakes of, or possesses, in virtue of which it is an instance, and hence in virtue of which we ascribe the general term, it has the roles of guiding us in ascribing and of giving content to new ascriptions. The common property, attribute, etc., thus figures both in our knowledge when we understand the general term and as the standard of correctness for ascription of the term, the basis for distinguishing correct ascriptions from incorrect ones.

Wittgenstein believes, on my view, that such an inchoate conception of common property, essence, attribute, or the like tends to be adopted as a first step. The sorts of considerations I outlined can make it look as though there *must* be some such thing at an underlying level, on pain of our ascriptions seeming arbitrary or irrational. Once (and only once) the step to this inchoate conception is taken, an agenda of further questions is then established. A developed philosophical view goes on to refine the conception, to provide the particular characteristics of the items. One view might wind up differentiating the various roles, addressing them via separate intensional and extensional aspects (as Frege does), and another may not (like Russell); views of their ontological status, of the nature of grasping them, of whether there are basic ones in terms of which all are to be analyzed, and so on, may also differ. Wittgenstein is not concerned with these developed theories. Rather, he is trying to expose what I call the "proto-philosophical level": the way of looking at things that we tend to adopt at the start, without noticing that a step has been taken, which then functions to establish what questions are to be asked and answered by philosophical theorizing.[2]

How, then, does Wittgenstein's adducing of family resemblance concepts work against this demand for a property, essence, or attribute which underlies our ascriptions of a general term? One way is this: adducing family resemblances points up a disparity between the role that the property or essence or attribute is meant to play and our actual proceedings. With respect to general terms of a family-likeness sort, we have difficulty saying anything correct of a uniform and general nature about the items that fall under the term—for example, about all games. In contrast, in particular cases there are richly textured explanations we would give of why such-and-such a practice is correctly deemed a game or not. The emphasis here is not on indefinability, but rather on the wealth of considerations we bring to bear in individual cases. This already suggests that the "common property of being a game" is not playing the role I described. Indeed, the content of what can be said generally seems to be entirely parasitic on what we say in particular cases; no content is added at the general level.

The upshot is that framing matters in terms of common properties simply does not reflect the actual abilities we have in using general terms in new cases, nor the ways in which such use communicates. We cannot say that there is this otherwise ineffable thing that guides us, given the tension between the uniformity of that depiction and what we actually say to justify ourselves in particular cases of ascribing or denying the term. Any appropriate account will have to look different.

This, then, is the "second blush" point of introducing family resemblances. Everything that could be thought to go on in general with respect to the use of such a general term is parasitic on the highly variegated features of individual

---

[2]The idea of the proto-philosophical is elaborated in my "I Want You to Bring Me A Slab: Remarks on the Opening Sections of the *Philosophical Investigations*" [Goldfarb, 1983].

cases. The general level adds nothing, and in that sense it is empty. This speaks against the ideas that knowledge of the common property or essence or attribute *informs* ascriptions in new instances.

II. FIXITY OF MEANING

However, this still does not go far enough, it seems to me. For one could respond: all that has been shown is that the account of general terms needs to be made more complicated. It may not be a simple common property that is at stake in how we make new ascriptions of a general term and in what those new ascriptions communicate. It may be something more complex. Grasping such a general term is not a single, simple feat, but rather a multitudinous and multilayered one, involving all sorts of explicit and tacit knowledge. There is, nonetheless, *something* to be grasped that underlies our use of the general term; it is a complex thing, which comprehends or is a summation of all the particular cases.

In this response, family resemblance is a replacement for the common property; it is meant to play the same role. Now a question arises as to what is left of that role. The first blush has impelled us to give up characterizability in simpler terms. The second blush showed there would be no informative general account of what guides us in ascription, except that which emerges in the particular cases. What is left is that which is implicit in thinking of a level underlying the use of a general term at all. It is the insistence that, whether it come from common property or family resemblance, there must be a certain kind of fixity. There must be some final arbiter of correctness; something unconditioned with reference to which the correctness or incorrectness of any potential ascription is made out. Only given this fixity could there be a principled ground for distinguishing a revision in our use of "game" from the discovery of a new game; only given it, could it be definite what we stake ourselves to in making a new ascription or denial, and could it be definite what counts as a justification of any such ascription or denial. Its fixity provides us with what we are staking ourselves to, in making a new ascription or a new denial.[3] The response to the second blush retains the idea that such fixity must be secured; it simply complicates the structure of what secures it.

Consequently, I would propose, Wittgenstein is concerned to undercut this response. I believe he takes the demand for fixity to embody an incorrect picture of rationality. Moreover, the response also leads naturally to just the sort of ana-

---

[3]Frege says, "If everything were in continual flux, and nothing maintained itself fixed for all time, there would no longer be any possibility of getting to know anything about the world and everything would be plunged in confusion"—and from there he immediately goes on to talk of the immutability of concepts [Frege, 1884, p. VII].

lytic projects Wittgenstein is concerned to block, where analysis is conceived as getting at the structure of the underlying level (analysis as like chemical analysis). In particular, it leads to the project of analyzing the understanding of a general term as a complex of explicit and tacit knowledge that covers all the potential particular cases.

I read Wittgenstein's concern with this response in his discussion of the lack of "sharp boundaries" of our concepts, starting in §68. Again and again, he reminds us that we do ordinarily, in fact, use vague and open-ended terms, with no hint that they are substandard or deviant. These reminders are meant to elicit what, despite these features of ordinary language, can nonetheless drive us to say, with Frege, "concepts must have sharp boundaries" or with the early Wittgenstein, "It seems clear that what we MEAN must always be *'sharp'*."[4] In §68 Wittgenstein has his interlocutor respond to "Can you give the boundary [of the concept game]? No." with "But then the use of the word is unregulated". Shortly afterward, the interlocutor continues, "But if the concept 'game' is uncircumscribed like that, you don't really know what you mean by 'game'" (§70). The issue is not mere vagueness, but rather regulatedness. The notion that the use of the term must be completely regulated, from beforehand, is another expression of what I have called the demand for fixity. Now, Wittgenstein belittles the notion of complete regulatedness, and mocks the call for complete circumscription; he asks, "Is it senseless to say: 'Stand roughly there?'" (§71) Rejoinders like this are best viewed as meant to get us to make explicit the sources of such a notion of regulatedness, that is, the conception of how language operates, and of what must be included in *real* knowledge of what a term means, that lies in back of the demand for fixity.

Thus there is a "third blush" reading of Wittgenstein's aims in these sections, as concerning the notion of the fixity of meaning. This is a more general issue than that of common properties or essences; correspondingly, family resemblance plays only a supporting part in the considerations. Wittgenstein's tactics are several. There are the continual reminders of how we actually operate with language. There is a short discussion of "seeing what is common" among various items, which aims at showing that this is not a general notion that evidences the fixed underlying level of properties. (Here, it should be noted, he treats color-words, not family likeness notions.)

One important, and characteristically Wittgensteinian, argument addresses the notion that the underlying level provides in an unconditioned and self-sufficient way the full story about the use of the general term in particular cases. In §§73–74 Wittgenstein discusses samples, for example, of a color or a shape. Among the lessons of these sections are that nothing intrinsic about the sample determines that it is a sample of one rather than the other general term it instanti-

---

[4][Frege, 1903, §56], [Wittgenstein, 1979a, p. 68].

ates, and that it is possible to take the item as a sample in many different ways. To understand the item as a sample of a particular concept is a matter of how it is used; it's a question of the role of the item in our practices. This argument should sound familiar. Elsewhere in the *Investigations,* Wittgenstein makes essentially the same point about signposts, mental pictures, and (most widely discussed, nowadays) rules: the signpost does not determine its application, the mental picture does not determine its projection onto the world, and the rule does not supply its own interpretation. Application, projection, interpretation are practices; they are not further signposts, additional mental images, or rule-like additions to rules.

The conception of a level underlying the use of general terms which satisfies the demand for fixity requires an absolute notion of determination. For what lies at that level is conceived as comprehending everything relevant to each individual case of ascription or denial of the term; it is meant to explain, or at least to encompass, our practices fully. Hence it cannot presuppose any practices, any knowing how something is to be taken. Wittgenstein's argument is meant to show that we have no model for that sort of determination. I do not think it correct to describe the argument as showing outright that such a notion of determination is incoherent. Rather, our coming to use the notion in the conception shows a confusion. For we wish to imagine the underlying level on the model of external standards, like samples or signposts, but at the same time the demand for fixity forces us to avoid presupposing just those surroundings, those practices, that make the standards into standards.

Thus, on this reading, Wittgenstein is suggesting that the conception of the underlying level, that unconditionedly determines everything about the use of the general term in particular cases, is misguided. The argument emphasizes the role of our practices, and particularly the need to rely on our going on to employ items (samples, signposts, words) in various ways. This then raises a contrast with one aspect of the demand for fixity, namely, its requirement that the underlying level operate absolutely: independently of anything about us, and in particular, independently of our practices, and the ways we characteristically operate.

This contrast is also exhibited in Wittgenstein's discussion of explaining and knowing the meaning of "game". An explanation of the term, plausibly enough, would use examples of games. Its success is a matter of getting the learner to employ those examples in a certain way. On the conception of the underlying level, this has to be a matter of the learner surmising something that the explainer (in principle) cannot explicitly formulate. Then, what is surmised is what determines, in an absolute way, that the learner will employ the examples in the right way. The family nature of "games" by itself makes this picture look strained; the argument above about the need for practices undercuts it further. Again, Wittgenstein emphasizes that we have no model for what would have to occur given the conception. "Here giving examples is not an *indirect* means of

explaining—in default of a better. For any general definition can be misunderstood too." (§71) The difficulties in the conception arise from the notion that the
underlying level must be self-sufficient, and so must prescind from reliance on
our practices.

In contrast, Wittgenstein asks (§75):

> Isn't my knowledge, my concept of game, completely expressed in the explanations
> that I could give? That is, in my describing examples of various kinds of game;
> showing how all sorts of other games can be constructed on the analogy of these;
> saying that I should scarcely include this or this among games; and so on.

Wittgenstein does mean "completely expressed". But then the reliance on us and
our practices is obvious. For it is only given facts about us—that anyone who
understands my explanations will take the examples in a particular way, that
anyone who uses the same explanations as I do in fact will have the same concept of game—that knowledge of the meaning of "game" can be claimed to be
fully contained in those explanations. Of course those explanations do not *logically* yield just my concept of game; they do not *insure* that my knowledge
extends in the standard way to new cases. The demand for fixity of meaning
stems from the desire for something to give just this assurance, in the absence of
any reliance on facts of our common experience. Wittgenstein is concerned to
point out that the search for such a thing is a search for a phantasm—"any general definition can be misunderstood"—but also, that there is no need to embark
on this search.

Wittgenstein makes a similar point in *Remarks on the Foundations of Mathematics* (p. 320):

> I can train someone in a *uniform* activity. E.g. in drawing a line like this with a
> pencil on paper:
>
> _··_··_··_··_··_··_
>
> Now I ask myself, what is it that I want him to do, then? The answer is: He is always
> to go on as I have shown him. And what do I really mean by: he is always to go on
> in that way? The best answer to this that I can give myself, is an example like the
> one I have just given.
> I would use this example to show him, but also to show myself, what I mean by
> uniform.
> We talk and act. That is already presupposed in everything that I am saying.

Cora Diamond gives a helpful gloss on this passage: "If I need to explain something to another person, it is true that *certain* possibilities may need to be ruled
out . . . But the idea of a philosophical account of what I really mean by 'he is
always to go on in that way' is of an account addressed to someone on whose
uptake, on whose responses, we are not at all depending"; Wittgenstein is noting
that the philosophical error is to "take it that a specification of what I really

mean picks it out, not as might be for another human being, but in a sense absolutely, from *the* possibilities."[5]

So far I've been suggesting that Wittgenstein sees the demand for fixity of meaning as arising out of a vain attempt to avoid relying on facts about us, and the way we normally operate. There is another sense in which it is only granted a reliance on normality that the explanations we can give fully express our knowledge of the concept. What I have in mind here is a normality about the world. Just as agreement in those explanations will not "insure" agreement in concept, if normal human practices are not assumed—if, for example, some person acts like the wayward child of §185 who just doesn't get it about adding 2 to numbers larger than 1000—so too those explanations will not "insure" agreement if the world cannot be relied upon to act in its normal ways. We may well agree on everything we would ordinarily say about a concept, and every way we could think to explain it; but if a truly bizarre and out-of-this-world item were to come along as a candidate for inclusion under the concept, we might well disagree. The philosophical desire to preclude this is another basis for the demand for fixity of meaning: again, it's the idea that what is meant has to be picked out from *all* the possibilities, not just the ones that actually, from time to time, arise.

III. NAMES AND DESCRIPTIONS

Wittgenstein's point can be elucidated by a close look at §79. Here the particular focus has shifted from general terms to singular terms, but his easy segue into the section supports the view that the topic has been and continues to be fixity of meaning. On the surface the section is a relatively straightforward attack on the theory of descriptions. Wittgenstein points out that, when we use a proper name, there often is no one description that we would be willing to equate with the name: we may have in mind several descriptions, different ones may come up at different times, and so on. Indeed, Wittgenstein has sometimes been taken to be suggesting that proper names operate by means of a "cluster" of descriptions.

It should be noted that a Russellian (or a Fregean, since for the purposes at hand the differences between Frege's analysis of proper names and Russell's is irrelevant) can still think that in everyday language we often do not assign fixed meanings to names. On those views, that is just to say that in everyday language we often speak ambiguously. Frege said, "So long as the thing meant remains the same, such variations of sense may be tolerated although they are to be avoided in the theoretical structure of demonstrative science."[6] The theory of descriptions or of sense tells us how names can function at all, but there may

---

[5]Cora Diamond, "Realism and the Realistic Spirit", in [Diamond, 1991, p. 68].
[6][Frege, 1892a, p. 27].

well be slack in our ordinary uses, in how our utterances connect with the descriptions or senses that determine reference. The theories tell us how objects can be singled out at all, and establish the standards for rational language use. They then give us the standpoint from which to describe failings of everyday language and to devise improvements. (Wittgenstein remarks on this blend of themes several times; see §81, §98, §101.) In particular, what a speaker consciously has in mind at the moment of uttering a proper name is not a decisive factor. These theories cannot be undercut simply by pointing out that speakers often do not have in mind any specific description, or even any definite cluster of descriptions.

To my eye, rather than offering a somewhat jejune criticism of Frege and Russell, Wittgenstein is operating at a deeper level. He is trying to examine what leads one at the very start to think that proper names have a fixed meaning, which determines what is named and endows assertions containing those names with content. To do this, he wants to elicit the plain facts that seem to point in the direction of these theories. What I mean by "plain facts" are the practices we have regarding names and explanations, clarifications of names, and justifications of assertions containing names when challenges to those assertions arise. These practices, Wittgenstein believes, are construed so as to fuel a picture of how individuals are picked out by language.

An important plain fact is this: if I am called upon to explain the use of a name in a particular case, I shall usually supply a description. It is, after all, the natural way—except in cases when ostension suffices—of answering the question, "Whom do you mean by X?" Indeed, if an assertion I make using a name is challenged in certain ways, I may be *required* to provide a description. When certain matters of fact are put into question, then such an amplification is mandatory if I am to support my statement, indeed, if I am to be deemed as "knowing what I'm talking about." That is how I am held to account for my assertion; for the provision of a description is what makes it clear what would count, in the face of the challenge, as a justification for my assertion. In that sense, it is a precondition for the possibility of there being a justification for the assertion. Thus, if certain facts are in question, if the world is recalcitrant in various relevant respects, it seems that in order for me to have been staking myself to a claim in making the assertion, there has to be some description that clarifies what claim that was, by elaborating what the name is contributing.

Now one can go on: the world *might* be recalcitrant in all sorts of ways; there is always the possibility that *any* fact may be in question. And then it seems inevitable to conclude that, if I am staking myself to a definite claim in making an assertion containing a name, there has to be something that tells what the name is doing no matter how the world is—that is, without taking for granted *any* facts. It has to be definite what, given any way the world is, would count for the assertion and what against it; only thus could the question of justifying the assertion even make sense. This then requires a fixed content to the name, which picks out, in a definitive and unconditioned way, from all possible circumstances precisely those under which the name refers. In Frege's and Russell's hands, this becomes the requirement that one description be taken as definitional.

I take it, then, that Wittgenstein is depicting a movement, or, better, a slide, from the plain fact that in particular circumstances, should certain relevant facts come into question, we are obligated to supply a description, to the general demand that if we are to be genuinely accountable for our claims, a description has to be fixed so that no matter what the facts are, it is determinate what our claims require of the world. The commonplace that we have to be responsible for our words in the face of challenges that actually arise becomes the demand that it has to be given, in advance of any particularities or information which would tell us what the actual challenges might be, what counts as meeting any possible challenge. The picture is that language must operate no matter how the world is, in a vacuum of fact. It must be presuppositionless.

Now Wittgenstein is no stranger to this picture, for it is central to his early work. In the "argument" for simples of the *Tractatus* (2.0211, 2.0212), he speaks of the eventuality that "whether a proposition had sense would depend on whether another proposition were true" and concludes, "In that case we could not sketch out any picture of the world (true or false)." In 4.061 he says, "It must not be overlooked that a proposition has a sense that is independent of the facts." The theme was sounded early in his *Notebooks,* when he says, "The method of portrayal [of the world by language] must be completely determinate before we can compare reality with propositions at all to see whether they are true or false . . . Whether a proposition is true or false is something that has to appear. We must however, know in advance *how* it will appear" (p. 23). In the *Investigations,* Wittgenstein is trying to show how the picture of presuppositionlessness is constituted, and he is imputing to it a key role not just in his own earlier work but also—less explicitly and presumably in more inchoate form—in the ways Frege and Russell frame their thinking about meaning.

To undercut the demand for fixity of meaning, in §79 Wittgenstein's tactic is to examine more closely the crucial "plain fact", the obligation we have to supply descriptions in the face of appropriate challenges or calls for clarification. He suggests that our practices are not as simple and uniform as the philosophical construction put on them. Indeed, the practices point in a direction away from that construction, not towards it. We don't simply supply a description to which we are subsequently committed; our practices are far more variegated. Often, more than one description will be involved, and they may have different sorts of relations to each other and to the original name. In the face of a yet further challenge, we may revise the characterization of who is meant—and there are circumstances in we would be justified in that. There are circumstances too in which we would not be justified, such a revision *would* be considered to be reneging on the original claim. We may start out with many descriptions, subsequently allowing some to be false while maintaining our original claim; in other contexts, the claim would have to be abandoned rather sooner. *What* we do will differ in different circumstances. All that can be said generally about our practices is that if the need arises, there ordinarily would have to be some number of descriptions that we could bring in, and any, some, or most of them might be at stake depending on the particular circumstances. As a *theory,* of course, this is little more than: when we use a name, we ought to have something to say about it, but what we have to say, and with what tenacity, depend on the case at hand and the nature of the calls for clarification; and that is not much of a theory. Wittgenstein's point, of course, is not to present a theory; it is, rather, to unravel what leads to one.

IV. PRESUPPOSITIONLESSNESS

Wittgenstein's next tactic, in §80, is to challenge directly the picture of the presuppositionlessness of language, in particular the notion that our claims have a content that fits them out for work no matter how the world is. He presents the scenario of a repeatedly disappearing and reappearing chair, and asks:

> Have you rules ready for such cases—rules saying whether one may use the word "chair" to include this kind of thing? But do we miss them when we use the word "chair"; and are we to say that we do not really attach any meaning to this word, because we are not equipped with rules for every possible application of it?

The word "chair" is humdrum; to question our understanding of it would be mad. Yet (assuming the example is convincing) we find circumstances in which our understanding of the word does not tell us what to do, what verdict to give on the applicability of the word. We simply do not know in the imagined case how to use the word. Yet that does not force us to think of our language as insufficient. The lesson is that if enough about the world goes awry, our words may fail. Nothing about the words as we have them now tells us how to go on with them in extraordinary circumstances like those. This, of course, goes directly against the picture of presuppositionlessness, that the method of portrayal of the world by language must be independent of all facts. And hence it goes against that which greases the slide from the plain facts about our practices with names to the demand for fixity of meaning.

The point that words may fail if the world goes too much awry was also made by John Austin, using more picturesque examples.

> If we have made sure that it is a goldfinch, and a real goldfinch, and then in the future it does something outrageous (explodes, quotes Mrs. Woolf, or what not), we

don't say we were wrong to say that it was a goldfinch. *We don't know what to say.* Words literally fail us.[7]

Suppose that I live in harmony and friendship for four years with a cat: and then, it delivers a philippic. We ask ourselves, perhaps, 'Is it a real cat? or is it *not* a real cat?' 'Either it *is*, or it is *not*, but we cannot tell which.' Actually, that is not so: *neither* 'It is a real cat' *nor* 'It is not a real cat' fits the facts . . . each is designed for other situations than this one: you could not say the former of something which delivers philippics, nor yet the latter of something which has behaved as this has for four years . . . Ordinary language breaks down in extraordinary cases.[8]

Austin continues, "Now no doubt an *ideal* language would *not* break down, whatever happens. In doing physics for example, . . . our language is tightened up." Here Wittgenstein would disagree, I think correctly. His implicit suggestion is that we have *no* examples of a presuppositionless language; it is a philosophical chimera. None of our language games contain rules which determine verdicts about usage in every conceivable case; so, in the end, we have no idea of what this would be. Ordinary communication relies on the world's proceeding ordinarily. This is an important part of the background to Wittgenstein's saying that language includes agreement in judgments as well as in definitions (§242).

Finally, a general issue Wittgenstein must consider, in connection with the notion of fixity of meaning, concerns the nature of justification. Wittgenstein sees that justification, if taken on a natural and standard philosophical model, is an important support for the picture of language as presuppositionless. I suggested before that the very possibility of there being such a thing as justifying our assertions can seem to rely on those assertions' making a definite claim on reality, no matter how the world is. Evidently, the notion of justification at work here is that of complete justification, one in which nothing is implicit, any fact relied upon is given its due place in the structure of the justification. This view of justification crops up repeatedly in the *Investigations;* it is the justification that provides guarantees against any conceivable counterpossibility, or any conceivable doubt. That such justifications must be (in principle, at least) obtainable is an outcropping of a picture of rationality that Wittgenstein wishes to oppose.

There is an analogous view of explanations of meaning that has been at issue throughout the material I've discussed. This is the idea of complete explanations, which address any conceivable unclarity or confusion and preclude any possible misunderstanding. Now an explanation of the meaning of a sentence, on this model, would have to include an account of any presuppositions the sentence has; but once these presuppositions are made explicit they are no longer presuppositions, but rather part of the content of the sentence. Hence the possibility of such explanations implies that language is presuppositionless.

---

[7]"Other Minds", in [Austin, 1979, p. 88]. Austin uses the example to illustrate his denial that language is "predictive."

[8]"The Meaning of a Word", in [Austin, 1979, p. 67].

Clearly, then, Wittgenstein must go against these views of justification of knowledge and explanation of meaning. In particular, he must forestall any idea that the justifications and explanations that we actually employ have features that would lead to or require the philosophical construals. He takes up this challenge in §§82ff. He argues that the burdens the philosophical models impose on explanations or justifications are the products of confusion, that there are no guarantors of the sort envisaged. He emphasizes that for something to function as an explanation requires surroundings provided by the particular circumstances, the interests of the parties concerned, what those parties have in common and what not, and so on. It is these surroundings that give explanations their function and their point. Similar remarks apply to justifications. The philosophical construal, in contrast, envisages context-independent notions. Wittgenstein urges that such notions would be so different from those we actually employ that it is unclear what their value would be, or why we should want them. In an extremely important remark (§87), he says:

> An explanation may indeed rest on another one that has been given, but none stands in need of another—unless *we* require it to prevent a misunderstanding. One might say: an explanation serves to remove or to avert a misunderstanding—one, that is, that would occur but for the explanation; not every one that I can imagine.
>
> It may easily look as if every doubt merely *revealed* an existing gap in the foundations; so that secure understanding is only possible if we first doubt everything that *can* be doubted, and then remove all these doubts.
>
> The sign-post is in order—if, under normal circumstances, it fulfills its purpose.

In going against the philosophical construals of explanation and justification, Wittgenstein is attacking central features of a picture of what rationality comes to. Early analytic philosophy gave concrete form to that picture by its various workings-out of the structure and nature of logic. Wittgenstein says, after admitting that language includes agreement in judgments, not just definitions, "This seems to abolish logic, but does not do so." (§242) It certainly abolishes logic in the sense of Frege, Russell, or the early Wittgenstein; for logic in their sense requires the presuppositionlessness that "agreement in judgments" denies. The question is whether logic in any sense that supports a notion of rationality is abolished too. Wittgenstein asserts that it isn't; but how the appropriate distinctions between rationality and inclination are then to be sustained—which is just the question of what "appropriate" means here—has not yet, to my mind, been sufficiently elaborated.

Whether or not they can be sustained, and indeed whether or not we find the sort of view Wittgenstein is urging the least bit congenial, I think it undeniable that what he focuses our attention on, considerations that may be wellsprings of notions of fixity of meaning, determinateness of sense, means of portrayal of the world by language, and may be implicit factors in the way these notions are framed, is exceptionally important in understanding the views he is opposing.

One may wind up rejecting what Wittgenstein is urging; but one cannot deny that his procedures are extraordinarily and importantly illuminating about the nature of the positions developed in early analytic philosophy and still very much with us today.[9]

[9]I am grateful to Burton Dreben, Sean Greenberg, Joseph McDonald, Edward Minar, and Thomas Ricketts for helpful comments and suggestions.

5

Peter Hylton

FUNCTIONS, OPERATIONS, AND SENSE IN WITTGENSTEIN'S *TRACTATUS*

The notion of an *operation* plays a crucial role in the *Tractatus*.[1] The account of representation which that book gives—the so-called 'Picture Theory of meaning'—applies directly only to what Wittgenstein calls elementary propositions.[2] It is clear, however, that none or almost none of the propositions which we utter or write or enquire about satisfy the conditions for being an elementary proposition. We therefore need an explanation of non-elementary propositions, and of their relation to elementary propositions. Such an explanation must have the consequence that the fundamental account of representation which does not apply directly to non-elementary propositions nonetheless does apply to them indirectly—so the explanation must show that all the real work of representation is done at the level of elementary propositions, and that what goes on in non-elementary propositions requires nothing new in principle. Wittgenstein's explanation is, as is well known, that all propositions are truth-functions of elementary propositions (5). So for Wittgenstein an explanation of the truth-functional compounding of simpler propositions into more complex propositions is required not simply for an account of logic but rather for an account of the possibility of representing the world (indeed it is a crucial doctrine of the *Tractatus* that in a sense *nothing* is required for logic—nothing, that is, that is not already implicit in any kind of method of representing the world in any way at all). To say that non-

---

[1] Ludwig Wittgenstein, *Tractatus Logico-Philosophicus* [Wittgenstein, 1922]. References and citations to this work are made by section numbers standing alone. I have generally followed the Pears and McGuiness translation, but have occasionally made minor changes.

[2] It might be said, further, that the account applies directly only to *fully analysed* elementary propositions. I think this is correct, and I take it to be Wittgenstein's view that thought is, so to speak, a fully analysed language. Note that the notion of a thought is introduced before that of a proposition (at 3), and the notion of a proposition introduced in terms of a thought and its expression (at 3.1). Wittgenstein, I think, does not attribute 'magical' properties to thought—does not make it do what could not be done by any language; but I think he does take it to be a fully analysed language. Since we are clearly not aware of the complete analysis of the things we say, this position commits Wittgenstein to the view that we are in some sense not fully aware of our thoughts—that the mind is not transparent to itself. But this is a view that he explicitly accepts; see note 18 below.

elementary propositions are truth-functions of elementary propositions is not enough. On a Fregean or Russellian account of truth-functional compounding, it introduces new elements—the truth-functions—which are not required for elementary (i.e. non-compound) propositions (it is for this reason that logic, on the accounts of Frege and Russell, sometimes seems to be a subject with a distinct subject-matter of its own—as opposed to Wittgenstein's account of logic as made up of tautologies). As I hope our quick sketch indicates, Wittgenstein must avoid any such new elements; he must, therefore, give an explanation of truth-functional compounding which does not, in the relevant sense, require new elements. The notion of an operation is central to this explanation.[3]

There is, however, a major interpretive problem surrounding the passages in which the notion of an operation is introduced and explained (the 5.2s, i.e. 5.2–5.254). The problem, moreover, comes at a crucial juncture, for it arises from Wittgenstein's insistence, in 5.25, that "Operation and function must not be confused with each another." Here, it seems plausible to suppose, Wittgenstein is recording his disagreement with the Fregean and Russellian treatments of truth-functional compounding, and is claiming that his account is crucially different. Let us look briefly at the Fregean and Russellian accounts. Frege's account of negation and the conditional—which he takes as primitive in the *Grundgesetze*[4]—is that they are functions. He introduces the notion of a function by mathematical examples (section 1). He introduces truth-values as the denotations (*Bedeutungen*) of indicative sentences (section 2). This then enables him to give an account of predicates as a special case of functional expressions: they denote a special case of functions, called *concepts* (*Begriffe*), defined as those functions whose values for any argument are always truth-values (section 3). This in turn enables Frege to introduce negation as a concept, in this sense. It is, he says, "a function whose value is always a truth-value; it is a concept under which falls every object with the sole exception of the True" (section 6). The conditional is introduced in similar fashion, as a two-place function whose values are always truth-values (section 12; note that here, as in the case of negation, Frege does not stipulate that the *arguments* of such functions are always truth-values: it is his consistent view that any function must be defined for all arguments). Russell introduces his primitives, negation and disjunction, very sketchily in the main body of the text of *Principia Mathematica*[5] (see p. 93). The

---

[3]This is not to say that this is the only role that the notion of an operation plays in the *Tractatus*. It is crucial also for the notion of a formal series, and hence for Wittgenstein's account of mathematics. But the role that I have emphasised—as part of the account of truth-functional compounding—is, I think, the central one.

[4][Frege, 1893].

[5][Whitehead and Russell, 1910]. All my references are to the first volume [Russell, 1903]. I take Russell alone to be responsible for the more fundamental parts of the work, which are my concern in what follows.

Introduction contains a somewhat more discursive, though perhaps confusing, discussion. Russell first introduces the general notion of a function of propositions (meaning a function which takes propositions as arguments and as values), by saying: "An aggregation of propositions . . . into a single proposition more complex than its constituents, is a function *with propositions as arguments*" (p. 6; emphasis in the original). He then introduces four special cases of such functions, negation, disjunction, conjunction, and material implication, and says that only two of these need be taken as primitive. (We shall return to Russell's confusing statement.)

For both Frege and Russell, then, it might seem that ways of truth-functionally compounding sentences are functions. So, it is natural to assume, in insisting that operations are not functions, Wittgenstein is insisting that his treatment of such ways of compounding is different from theirs. But what are the differences? It appears, as Max Black points out,[6] that everything, or almost everything, that Wittgenstein says about operations could with equal correctness be said about functions. Thus, for example, the statement that function and operation must not be confused is immediately preceded by the statement that "an operation does not assert anything; only its result does, and this depends on the bases of the operation" (5.25). But, as Black says, what is said here of operations could equally be said of a function, such as the function "x^2"; it too does not assert anything or say anything. Again, Wittgenstein says: "A function cannot be its own argument, whereas the result of an operation can be its own basis." (5.251). Here too it seems that Wittgenstein takes himself to be marking a difference between functions and operations, but it is quite unclear that he has in fact done so, for what he says would seem also to be true of operations. An operation itself (as opposed to the result of an operation) cannot be the argument or basis of an operation; and surely the *result* of applying a function to an argument can, at least in some cases, in turn be an argument for that function (as Black says: "a *value* of a function can sometimes be an argument of that function—3^2 can itself be squared", p. 261).

The interpretive difficulty is thus that, on the one hand, Wittgenstein is clearly concerned to emphasise the difference between functions and operations; yet, on the other hand, what he says about operations does not seem in fact to introduce a notion which is significantly different from that of a function. Now a first step towards resolving this difficulty is to reconsider exactly what Wittgenstein's target is. When he insists that the truth-operations—such as negation, or disjunction, or his own symbol "N", a generalised version of the Sheffer stroke— are not functions, what is he primarily concerned to deny? Black assumes that his target is the idea that such operations can be assimilated to mathematical

---

[6][Black, 1964, p. 258]. I discuss Black's view because it does, I think, represent a natural response to the passages I am chiefly concerned with. Most subsequent commentators do not consider the issues I am concerned with in any detail.

functions, such as "square of".[7] This idea, it might be assumed, is common to
Frege and Russell, and is thus a natural target for Wittgenstein. I shall argue,
however, that these natural assumptions about Wittgenstein's target are mistaken.
As I see the matter, Russell employs a notion of a propositional function which
is in fact quite distinct from that of an ordinary mathematical function (whereas
Frege explicitly employs a generalised and clarified version of the mathematical
notion). And we can make clear sense of Wittgenstein's remarks in the 5.2s if we
see them as directed in the first instance against Russell's view that the truth-
operations are propositional functions in something like Russell's sense of that
expression. (I say that we should see Wittgenstein's remarks as directed *in the
first instance* against Russell, but I take them to be anti-Fregean as well as anti-
Russellian. Our discussion will put us in a position to return to the idea of truth-
operations as functions in the Fregean sense.)

It is crucial to our discussion of this issue that what Wittgenstein is opposing
is the idea that truth-functional compounding takes place by means of propositional functions *in Russell's sense,* and that that sense is not Frege's. Before we
examine that issue, however, it is worth noting that if there is such a difference
between Russellian propositional functions on the one hand and Fregean (or
mathematical) functions on the other hand, then it is plausible that Wittgenstein
is discussing propositional functions, rather than functions in the mathematical
sense. We know that Wittgenstein studied the fundamental portions of *Principia
Mathematica,*[8] and in that book Russell uses "function" always to mean "propositional function", referring to non-propositional functions as "descriptive functions",[9] and it is not unreasonable to suppose that Wittgenstein would have followed him in this usage. At least some of the uses of the word "function"
(*funktion*) in the *Tractatus,* moreover, must be taken to mean "propositional
function", if we are to make even *prima facie* sense of them. Thus 5.501 states,
as a method of describing a number of propositions, the following: "Giving a
function *fx,* whose values for all values of *x* are the propositions to be
described." And, again, 5.5301 speaks of an object as *satisfying* a function (the

---

[7]There is a question here about how we are to understand ordinary mathematical functions. I shall
assume that they are to be understood extensionally—i.e. that functions which for every argument
have the same value (i.e. are co-extensive) are not distinct. This is the sort of view of functions that
leads some to identify them with sets of ordered pairs. Although Frege does not adopt a set-theoretic
account, I think that he presupposes an extensional view of functions. The question of Frege's views
here is complicated by the fact that he does not think that the notion of identity applies to functions;
he does, however, take co-extensiveness to play the same role among functions as identity does
among objects.

[8]Apart from the external evidence, which is clear, Wittgenstein twice refers to "Russell and Whitehead"—at 5.252 and 5.452. Along with Frege, Mauthner, and Russell standing by himself, they are
the only authors explicitly referred to in the *Tractatus.*

[9]Thus the footnote to p. 39 of *Principia Mathematica* says: "When the word 'function' is used in the
sequel, 'propositional function' is always meant." Russell first introduces non-propositional functions in §30, which is entitled "Descriptive Functions": unlike propositional functions, descriptive or
non-propositional functions thus play no part in the fundamental portions of the work.

German is *genügen*), which hardly makes sense unless it is a propositional function that Wittgenstein has in mind.

If propositional functions are, as is perhaps natural to assume, simply a kind of function, then it can make little difference whether Wittgenstein is speaking, in the 5.2s and elsewhere, about functions or about propositional functions. If propositional functions are simply a special case of functions—those functions whose values happen to be propositions—then to interpret Wittgenstein as speaking about propositional functions, rather than about functions *tout court* is simply to interpret him as speaking about the special case rather than the more general notion. In some cases this might seem to be an unduly restrictive interpretation. In the present case, however, it seems as if it could make no difference at all. If ways of compounding propositions truth-functionally are to be thought of as functions at all, then surely they should be thought of as propositional functions,[10] for the upshot of any such compounding is always a proposition, never a number, say, or some other object. So one might think: perhaps in denying that operations are functions Wittgenstein is to be construed, if we are really concerned with accuracy, as denying that they are propositional functions—but what difference does it make? The answer is that it makes a great deal of difference, because propositional functions, as Russell conceives of them, are *not* special cases of a more general notion of a function, but have some crucial features which distinguish them from functions in the general sense. This matter is crucial for our purposes, and must be explained at some length.[11]

In *Principia Mathematica*, as already noted, Russell does not take the general notion of a function for granted and introduce propositional functions as a special case, picked out by the fact that propositional functions have propositions as values (as Frege does take the general notion of a function for granted, and picks out concepts as a special case of functions, namely those whose values for any argument are truth-values). Rather he takes propositional functions for granted, and defines other functions (descriptive functions) as needed. By means of the definite description operator (which is, of course, defined in its turn) we may define a one-place function $f(x)$ from a two-place propositional function, xRy, by saying that $f(x) =$ the object y such that xRy (this only succeeds in defining a function if R obeys the right uniqueness conditions: for any given object a, there must be at most one object y such that xRy). Russell gives the general form of this kind of definition at §30.01 of *Principia Mathematica*. Obviously the technique can be generalised: from any $n+1$ place propositional function (which satisfies the relevant uniqueness condition) we can define an n-place function.

---

[10]Here I am, of course, thinking of matters in Russellian rather than Fregean terms. For Frege such a function is a concept (*Begriff*), i.e. a function whose value for any argument is a truth-value. For the moment I shall continue to take this Russellian framework for granted; we shall return to the contrast between Wittgenstein's view and Frege's.

[11]The next three paragraphs draw heavily on my essay "Functions and Propositional Functions in *Principia Mathematica*" [Hylton, 1994].

So far the point is merely technical: rather than taking for granted the general notion of function, as Frege does, and distinguishing propositional functions as special cases, Russell rather takes the notion of a propositional function as fundamental, and introduces descriptive (i.e. non-propositional) functions as needed. Lying behind the technique is the fact that for Russell propositional functions have characteristics which one cannot suppose functions (if taken as primitive, rather than defined) to have. Both propositions and propositional functions, on Russell's account, are structured entities, which contain parts. Propositional functions bear a particular structural relation to the propositions which are their values: a proposition shares the structure of any propositional function of which it is the value. (Similarly, a proposition which is the value of a given propositional function for a given object as argument *contains* that object.) Two propositions which are both values of a given propositional function, for different arguments, have some aspect of their structure in common, and that structure is also shared by the propositional function. (Conversely, I think it is also true that if two propositions have some aspect of their structure in common, then they are values, for different arguments, of some one propositional function.) It is worth emphasising the contrast that this makes between propositional functions and functions in the ordinary sense, mathematical functions, for example. A mathematical function is not naturally thought of as a structured entity (if it were, then the set-theoretic representation of a function as a set of ordered pairs would be grossly inadequate). And there is no plausible sense of "structure" in which a mathematical function, and an object which is the value of that function for some argument, shares a structure.

On Russell's conception of propositional functions, however, the propositional function *x is wise* does share a structure with the proposition that Socrates is wise: the propositional function is not mere mapping of objects onto propositions. Thus it makes sense to say of a propositional function—and not merely of the words which express a propositional function—that it contains a variable ranging over certain entities—e.g. over all propositional functions of a certain type.[12] This point also enables us to make sense of the curious way in which Russell introduced the idea of a function whose arguments are propositions. He describes such a function, as we saw, as "An aggregation of propositions . . . into a single proposition more complex than its constituents" (see p. 93, where this phrase is quoted in context). Now this would be a very puzzling description if he had in mind the notion of a function in something like the mathematical sense. No one would describe a mathematical function, say, as being or resulting in "an aggregation of numbers into a single number more complex than its constituents". On the contrary, it is characteristic of a function in the ordinary sense that the result of applying a function to an object or to a number of objects is in

---

[12]This point is crucial to an understanding of the fact that *Principia Mathematica* puts forward a *ramified* theory of types. Besides the essay referred to in the previous note, see also [Goldfarb, 1989].

no sense an "aggregation" of those objects, or more complex than they. Thus twelve results from applying the two-place plus function to five and seven, but it is in no clear sense an aggregation of them, or more complex than either.

Even more clearly, if we take a non-mathematical function such as "father of," there is no sense at all in which Philip of Macedonia is an aggregation of his son Alexander, and no relevant sense in which the former is more complex than the latter. But Russell's phrase is not simply a piece of nonsense: it is, rather, a reflection of the fact that he is presupposing a notion of a propositional function which cannot be assimilated to the ordinary or mathematical notion of a function. The value of a propositional function for a number of arguments can be described as an aggregation of them, and more complex than them, for it contains them. It is this Russellian notion of a propositional function, I wish to claim, that is Wittgenstein's immediate target in the 5.2s.

Let us, then, return to the vexed passages in the 5.2s and see how we can interpret them if we take Wittgenstein to be arguing against Russell's view that truth-functional ways of compounding propositions are propositional functions in the sense indicated. Wittgenstein insists in 5.25 that "The occurrence of an operation does not characterize the sense of a proposition." This seems to me the crucial point. The remarks of the previous paragraph indicate that it *is* a characteristic of a proposition, in Russell's sense, that it can be obtained as the value of a certain propositional function: two propositions which are values of some one propositional function have something in common with each other (and indeed with the propositional function).[13] Thus on Russell's account a proposition which is obtained by application of the propositional function disjunction to two propositions p and q is a disjunctive proposition—it contains a constituent corresponding to disjunction. It must thus be a different proposition from that which we obtain if we first apply to each of p and q the propositional function corresponding to negation, then take the resulting propositions as arguments to the propositional function corresponding to conjunction, and then take the resulting proposition as argument to the propositional function corresponding to negation. In short: for Russell "p v q" must represent a different proposition from that represented by "$\sim(\sim p$. $\sim q)$". But this is precisely the result that Wittgenstein wants to avoid. His view is that the above sentences express the same proposition, and hence that the occurrence of e.g. disjunction does not characterise the sense of a proposition.[14]

---

[13] I do not speak here of a propositional function *occurring* in a proposition, for it is Russell's view in *Principia Mathematica* that propositional functions are not themselves constituents of propositions, i.e. do not occur in propositions. See pp. 54–55 of *Principia Mathematica*. The reasons for this view have to do with the theory of types; see [Hylton, 1990, pp. 300–301].

[14] Robert J. Fogelin speaks of Wittgenstein's "*disappearance* theory of logical constants", and compares it with Russell's analysis of the apparent referring expressions which are definite descriptions (see [Fogelin, 1976, p. 36]). This comparison, however, seriously understates the point. On Russell's theory of descriptions, two propositions each of which is naturally expressed by a sentence containing the phrase "the King of France" have something in common—the result of the theory is that what they have in common is not the occurrence of a certain object, referred to by that phrase, but is rather

5.25 continues: "Indeed, no statement is made by an operation (*Die Opera-tion sagt ja nichts aus*), only by its result, and this depends on the bases of the operation." Here again there is a contrast with Russellian propositional functions. A propositional function, such as *x is wise*, it might be said, *does* make a statement, in a loose sense—only as yet an incomplete statement: it says of some as yet unspecified object that it is wise. For Russell, it is worth noting, this idea that we can think of a propositional function as making a statement, in a certain sense, is elevated to an important point of doctrine. He speaks of asserting a propositional function, as distinct both from asserting a particular value of the propositional function, and from asserting all values of the propositional function. This is at the basis of his idea of typical ambiguity, by which he hopes to resolve some of the problems created by the restrictions of type theory. Thus he says: "When we assert something containing a real [i.e. free] variable, we cannot strictly be said to be asserting a *proposition,* for we only obtain a definite proposition by assigning a value to the variable, and then our assertion only applies to one definite case, so that it has not at all the same force as before. When what we assert contains a real variable, we are asserting a wholly undetermined one of all the propositions that result from giving various values to the variable. It will be convenient to speak of such assertions as *asserting a propositional function*." (*Principia Mathematica,* p. 18).[15] The point of the sentence from 5.25 which we are discussing is surely that even in the loose sense in which a propositional function can be thought of as saying something—as making at least an incomplete statement—an operation does not say anything. This point is very closely connected with the idea that operations, unlike Russellian propositional functions, do not characterise the sense of a proposition. In a loose or incomplete sense a propositional function can be said to say something, and the value of that propositional function is a proposition that says the same thing about a particular object. That, of course, is why two propositions that are values of the same propositional function have an aspect of their sense in common: although they may be about different objects, what the one says about the one object is the same thing that the other says about the other object. Whatever else operations are, Wittgenstein is here saying that are not like *that.*

The final article in which Wittgenstein makes the contrast between functions and operations is 5.251: "A function cannot be its own argument, whereas the result of an operation can be its own basis." The interpretive difficulty which this poses is, as we saw, that Wittgenstein seems to be marking a difference between

---

that they share a certain structural property, and that each contains certain predicates. Wittgenstein's view, however, is that two propositions each of which is naturally expressed using disjunction, say, have *nothing* in common in virtue of that fact: the occurrence of the operation does not characterize the sense of the proposition.

[15]It is perhaps this that Wittgenstein is criticising when he insists, as early as 1912, that the propositions of logic contain only apparent, i.e. bound, variables. See the letter to Russell, dated 22/6/12, in *Letters to Russell, Keynes and Moore* [Wittgenstein, 1974b, p. 10].

objects and functions, yet if we take "function" in the Fregean or mathematical sense, then what he says would seem to hold equally if we interchange the words "operation" and "function". If, on the other hand, we take "function" in the first half of this sentence to be referring to propositional functions, then the difficulty is at least partly solved. The result of applying a propositional function to an object is, of course, a proposition. And this proposition cannot in turn be taken as an argument for that propositional function. Where F(a) is a proposition which is the value of the propositional function F(x) for the argument a, F(F(a)) is nonsense. Such an expression is banned by Russell's theory of types, and it is clear that while Wittgenstein rejected the idea of *theory* of types, he largely accepted the restrictions that Russell imposed.[16] This appears to be only a partial solution to the interpretive problem, for it does not seem to explain the first half of the sentence: "A function cannot be its own argument". While this is clearly something that Wittgenstein believed, for it is stated also at 3.333, it cannot be taken as marking a difference between propositional functions and operations, for an operation (as distinct from the result of an operation) is surely also something that cannot be taken as its own argument. The solution here, I think, is that for Wittgenstein the point that a propositional function cannot be its own argument, and the point that it cannot be applied to one of its own values, are very similar. The reason that Wittgenstein gives for the former point is "because the function sign already contains the prototype of its own argument, and it cannot contain itself" (3.333). Whether we attempt to apply a propositional function to itself, or to one of its values, the fundamental point is the same: we are giving the propositional function arguments which presuppose, or contain, the propositional function itself. I take it that Wittgenstein is here relying on his earlier discussion of these matters, in the 3.33s; the first half of the sentence serves to remind us of that discussion.

To this point I have argued that the contrast that Wittgenstein draws in the 5.2s is between operations and *propositional* functions in Russell's sense, and that this enables us to make clear sense of passages which are other wise quite baffling. The crucial point of this contrast, as we have seen, is that the occurrence of an operation does not characterise the sense of a proposition. Hence, as Wittgenstein says in 5.254, "Operations can vanish [*verschwinden*] (e.g. negation in '~~p' . ~~$p = p$)." This point is of course directly connected with what Wittgenstein himself calls his "fundamental thought": that the logical constants do not name anything, are not the representatives of entities (4.0312; see also 5.4). Put a little differently, the point is that the logical constants do not introduce new elements into the senses of the sentences in which they occur. The fun-

---

[16]Wittgenstein's objection to the theory of types is that the restrictions cannot be stated, and that a correct understanding of language would make it clear that there is nothing that needs to be stated: "The rules of logical syntax must go without saying, once we know how each individual sign signifies." (3.334). The discussion of the theory of types, especially in 3.333, suggests that Wittgenstein thought that all of Russell's restrictions were correct—only their status was misunderstood.

damental connection between language and the world is set up simply at the level of elementary propositions, and our ways of compounding elementary propositions into non-elementary propositions do not require any further connections of this sort.

At this point it may seem as if the point that Wittgenstein makes by means of the notion of an operation could have been made more simply and perspicuously if he had said: truth-functional symbols do not stand for Russellian propositional functions; rather they stand for Fregean functions. Many of the points that we have made about operations *do* seem to apply equally to functions in the ordinary mathematical sense, which Frege generalises. So what is the point of the notion of an operation? This sort of criticism of Wittgenstein seems to overlook the most fundamental element in Frege's view of language. For Frege all linguistic expressions—including, in particular, functional expressions, and expressions containing them—have two aspects: *Sinn* and *Bedeutung*. It is only if we focus on functions themselves—i.e. on the *Bedeutungen* of functional expressions—that we have something which appears to play the same role as Wittgenstein's operations. In particular, functions do *vanish* in the sense that Wittgenstein requires of operations: three squared divided by three, say, is just three over again—the number bears no trace of the fact that it is obtained by the application of two functions. But the 'vanishing' of functions in this sense is just a special case of a more general phenomenon, which makes it clear that a Fregean account which deals only with Fregean *Bedeutungen* will not be adequate for Wittgenstein's purposes. At the level of Fregean *Bedeutungen* too much vanishes. Wittgenstein's concern here is with propositions, sentences. And for Frege the *Bedeutungen* of a sentence is simply its truth-value—*everything* vanishes, everything, that is, that distinguishes one sentence from another with the same truth-value.

The issue, let us remember, is what explanation we can give of non-elementary propositions, i.e. to put the matter roughly in Fregean terms, of the senses of compound sentences. Wittgenstein has (we are assuming) an account of how elementary propositions represent atomic facts; the explanation of non-elementary propositions is then supposed to show, or to have as a consequence, that no new elements are required to extend this account to propositions which are truth-functions of elementary propositions. Clearly, it will not do simply to equate such propositions with what Frege called the *Bedeutungen* of the corresponding sentences. That has the consequence that there are only two non-elementary propositions—clearly not a view that Wittgenstein can accept. Nor, on the other hand, will it do to equate non-elementary propositions with what Frege called the senses (*Sinne*) of the corresponding sentences. There is at least a strong strain in Frege's thought which suggests that the sense of a complex expression is made up of the senses of the parts of that expression.[17] The *Sinn* of the double

---

[17]Thus Frege says, for example, "thoughts have parts out of which they are built up . . . as we take a thought to be the sense of a sentence, so we may call a part of a thought the sense of that part of the

negation of a sentence is thus different from the *Sinn* of the sentence itself, because the first does, as the second does not, contain the *Sinn* of the negation symbol. Therefore, Frege's account has the same drawback as Russell's, from Wittgenstein's point of view: the (*Sinne* of the) logical constants do *not* vanish.

At this point one might think that Wittgenstein's view can be described as a sort of hybrid. Elementary propositions are to be treated as Russell treated them, or to be thought of as having senses like Frege's *Sinne*. Logical constants, on the other hand, are to be thought of as Fregean functions, only without *Sinne*. This idea has the merit of capturing a crucial point of Wittgenstein's view: that the logical constants are not like ordinary, fully meaningful, words—that they do not contribute to the senses of sentences in which they occur in anything like the same way as other expressions. But what account is there, on this view, of the sense of the non-elementary sentence? On Frege's own account, the sense of the non-elementary sentence is presumably that of the sense of the elementary sentence[s] combined with the sense of the logical constant. But if the logical constant has no sense, what then? A logical constant, on this account, is presumably a function which maps one or more senses (those of elementary, or relatively simple sentences) onto other senses—but there is not, in this account, any suggestion that there must be an internal relation between the argument sense and the value sense, still less that the latter contain the former. An object which is the value of a function for a given argument does not, except in odd cases, contain the object which is the argument. But it is crucial to Wittgenstein's account that the sense of a proposition which is a truth-function of a number of other propositions is made up out of the senses of those other propositions. In other words, it is characteristic of a function, in the Fregean sense, that not only does it vanish but also its arguments vanish: there is no internal connection that two entities must have if the first is the value for some function with the second as argument. But this is not so in the case of Wittgenstein's operations: the operations themselves vanish, but the propositions which are their arguments do not.

I go into the relation between Wittgenstein's operations and Frege's functions because it indicates how hard it is to make sense of what Wittgenstein says from within a Fregean framework, and it suggests why this should be so: because Wittgenstein's notion of an operation is integral to a re-conceiving of the idea of the sense of a sentence. Wittgenstein's conception of an operation cannot easily be captured in Fregean or Russellian terms because it is part of a conception of the sense of a sentence—i.e. a conception of a proposition— which also cannot easily be captured in those terms. To go further into these matters we need to go beyond the distinctness of the notion of an operation from that of a function, and consider more positively the role that operations play for Wittgenstein. And here there are two points, each of which is crucial, and which

sentence which corresponds to it" [Frege, 1979b, p. 225]. For some qualifications to the attribution of this view to Frege, see [Baker and Hacker, 1984, pp. 325, 380–385].

may seem to contradict one another. On the one hand, as we have seen, an operation does not characterise the sense of a proposition. No proposition is intrinsically disjunctive rather than conjunctive or negative: any proposition can be expressed in a way that uses any one of these operations (even an elementary proposition—see e.g. 5.441). This is fundamental to Wittgenstein's conception of sense, which individuates senses or propositions far more coarsely than does that of Frege or of Russell: any two logically equivalent sentences, for Wittgenstein, have the same sense, or express the same proposition.[18] On the other hand, clearly the occurrence of an operation in a sentence contributes to its sense. The disjunction of two sentences yields a sentence with a sense different from that obtained if we conjoin those same sentences. So although operations vanish—they do not occur as part of the proposition—still they do affect which proposition it is that a given sentence expresses.

How is it possible that both of these things can be true of operations?—It seems almost to demand that operations be something and yet nothing!—In a way this is right. An operation is not itself part of, or an element in, the sense of a proposition. It is, rather, the expression of a relation (an internal relation, in Wittgenstein's sense) between one proposition and another. As Wittgenstein says at 5.22: "An operation is the expression of a relation between the structures of its results and of its bases." (The relation is internal precisely because it concerns the structures of propositions in this way.) Similarly, perhaps more explicitly, at 5.241 we have: "An operation is not the mark of a form, but only of a difference in forms." Conjunction expresses a different difference, so to speak, from that expressed by disjunction: hence the proposition which is a conjunction of two others is not the same as that which is a disjunction of those same two others. Given two sentences, conjoining them expresses a proposition that differs from them in a determinate way—by being their conjunction. But this proposition is not intrinsically conjunctive: it is, for example, also expressed by a sentence which negates the disjunction of the negations of two propositions, or by one that uses only the Sheffer stroke. The conjunction symbol serves only to express the difference between the propositions that you start with and the proposition that you end with: it does not also characterise the proposition that you end with.

All of this may, however, seem simply to assert that both of the two apparently conflicting points apply to operations, without doing anything to dispel the apparent conflict. But I think there is progress. The crucial point of the above discussion is this: that an operation may express the difference between two senses,

---

[18]Such a conception of sense is possible because Wittgenstein does not accept that our thoughts are, so to speak, transparent to us. He does not accept, that is to say, that if I have a thought I must know what thought it is, that if I have two thoughts I must know whether they are the same, and so on. This is, I think, implicit almost from the start. It becomes explicit at such moments as these: "every possible proposition is legitimately constructed, and if it has no sense this can only be because we have given no meaning to some of its constituent parts. (Even if we believe that we have done so.)" (5.4733). This view is, I think, crucial for the doctrine of the *Tractatus* as a whole.

without at the same time characterising either sense. Why should these two points be thought to conflict? Surely because we assume that the only way to express the difference between two senses is by being part of one of them (and, presumably, by *not* being part of the other, or at least not being part of it in quite the same way). If this seems to be an obvious principle, it is perhaps because we think of senses of sentences, or of propositions, in a Fregean way. We assume a principle of compositionality about sense: that the sense of the sentence (or indeed of any complex piece of language) is made up of the senses of its parts—and made up of them almost in the way that a wall is made of bricks (I call this way of thinking of sense *Fregean;* as we have seen, however, some qualifications may be necessary in ascribing this view to Frege himself. See note 17 above). Now Wittgenstein does not simply reject this view, he rejects the assumptions implicit in it. For Wittgenstein the constituent parts of a fully analysed sentence—*names,* in his sense—do not have *Sinn* at all: this is implicit in various remarks in the 3.1s and 3.2s, and is made explicit at 3.3, which says "Only propositions have sense". Names have *Bedeutung* (3.203), a name stands for (*vertritt*) an object (3.22), but only propositions have sense. Thus on Wittgenstein's view there is not even a sensible question to be asked, whether the sense of a sentence is made up of the senses of the parts of the sentence. A fully analysed sentence is made up of names (3.2), and names have no senses. Sense, for Wittgenstein, is not an attribute of the simplest linguistic expressions, and we cannot see the senses of sentences as made up from the senses of their simpler parts. Sense is, rather, a phenomenon that first arises when names are combined into meaningful sentences. Although Wittgenstein uses the Fregean terminology of *Sinn* and *Bedeutung,* he is clearly putting forward a radically different conception from that of Frege.

The fact that only propositions have *Sinn*—that Wittgenstein does not use the expression at all in connection with sub-sentential units of language—may make it seem all the more mysterious that the logical constants have no *Bedeutung.* If logical constants have neither *Sinn* nor *Bedeutung,* does it not follow that they are simply meaningless marks, marks which play no role at all in the language? But that conclusion is intolerable: the negation of a proposition has a different sense from that proposition itself, and the conjunction of two propositions has a sense different from the disjunction of the same two propositions. The force of these can perhaps be diffused by a comparison which Wittgenstein himself makes in the 5.46s. Parentheses, or other ways of marking distinctions of scope, are crucial to the sense of logical schemata in many systems. A string of symbols such as "$p \supset q \ \& \ r$" can be punctuated in either one of two ways, as "$p \supset (q \ \& \ r)$" or as "$(p \supset q) \ \& \ r$".[19] In some systems, that is to say, parentheses or brackets

---

[19]Rather than parentheses, or other explicit signs of grouping, and conventions governing their use, we can, of course, adopt conventions which make such use of parentheses unnecessary—e.g. that "$\supset$" is always to mark a larger break than "&". Or we may adopt Polish notation, which removes such ambiguities with no conventions beyond those of the basic semantics. But these alternative possibilities are not to the present point.

or some other explicit sign of grouping are essential to the sense of what is expressed. Yet, as Wittgenstein himself says, "surely no one is going to believe that brackets have an independent meaning" (5.461). Yet the same questions that we asked about logical constants can be asked about brackets: if they have neither a *Sinn* nor a *Bedeutung,* how can they be more then meaningless marks? How can they be crucial for the sense of what is expressed? This question does not seem pressing. In some cases, at least, we seem to have no trouble accepting that symbols may affect the sense of what is expressed without themselves having sense.[20] But if we can accept this of brackets, parentheses, and other signs of punctuation, why not of logical constants? This, I take it, is the point that Wittgenstein is making at 5.4611 where he says: "Signs for logical operations are punctuation-marks."

Now an example of a phenomenon is, of course, not an explanation of that phenomenon. If we wished to know how logical constants can affect the sense of a proposition without themselves having sense, it is not an answer to be told: in the same way that brackets do. What the example may do, however, is to lead us to see that the question is based on certain assumptions about sense, assumptions that are not inevitable. In particular, it comes naturally to us to think of the sense of a sentence as a sort of entity (subject, as noted above, to a principle of compositionality), and to think that this entity has a structure or complexity which corresponds to that of the sentence itself (or would do so if the sentence were in ideal form—a fully analysed sentence of a logically perfect language). Both Frege's conception of the *Sinn* of a sentence, and Russell's conception of a proposition, at least approximate this view, and it has great appeal for those who have followed Frege and Russell. Thus Carnap, for example, in *Meaning and Necessity,*[21] introduces a distinction between intension and extension as a modification of Frege's distinction between *Sinn* and *Bedeutung.* He introduces the term "proposition" to mean the intension of a sentence (p. 27), which he takes to be a complex entity: "Any proposition must be regarded as a complex entity, consisting of component entities, which, in their turn, may be simple or again complex . . ." (p. 30). This Fregean conception of sense leads inevitably to the problematic questions about the logical constants (and, indeed, about parentheses): how can they affect the senses of the sentences in which they occur if they do not themselves have sense?

---

[20]Church classifies brackets among what he calls "improper symbols": "in addition to proper symbols there must also occur symbols which are *improper* . . . i.e. which [have] no meaning in isolation but which combine with proper symbols (one or more) to form expressions that do have meaning in isolation" [Church, 1944, p. 32]. (I owe this reference to Leonard Linsky). Carnap, however, takes the distinction to be a matter of degree, and also to be "highly subjective". See *Meaning and Necessity* [Carnap, 1947, p. 7]. Neither author says anything about the present issue, however.
[21]See [Carnap, 1947].

Wittgenstein, however, opposes this Fregean conception of sense in the *Tractatus*. The sense of a proposition is simply that things are a certain way: "A proposition *shows* its sense. It *shows* how things stand *if* it is true. And it *says that* they do so stand." (4.022; emphasis in the original). The sense of a non-elementary proposition, in particular, is that one of a number of combinations of elementary propositions obtains, while all of the other combinations do not obtain. "The sense of a proposition is its agreement and disagreement with possibilities of holding and non-holding of atomic facts." (4.2), where we are immediately told that an elementary proposition asserts that an atomic fact obtains (4.21). To revert to the case of parentheses: one might wish to say that parentheses function not by having a sense themselves, but rather by indicating how other senses should be combined. In Wittgenstein's view, I think, something similar can be said of operations. An operation, as its name perhaps suggests, is less like an entity, that might be a constituent of more complex entity, than it is like something we *do*. We can use the senses of one or more elementary propositions to say that such-and-such a sense does *not* obtain—this is how things are: *not* like this; or that one or other of these senses obtains—this is how things are: either like this or like that. To reify the notion of sense and then inquire into the composition of the sense of this or that sentence, as if we were chemists enquiring into the composition of some substance—that, I take it, is exactly the view that Wittgenstein opposes.[22]

---

[22]This is not the paper that I gave at the "Early Analytic Philosophy"conference in April 1992 in honor of Leonard Linsky, but is an extension or application of the fundamental idea of that paper (which is referred to in note 11, above). I hope that this paper is also an appropriate tribute in another way: it arises out of a seminar I gave at the University of Illinois at Chicago in the Spring of 1993, and Leonard was an active participant (to put it mildly) in that seminar. As well as Leonard, I thank the other members of the seminar. Jim Harrington, in particular, may recognise some ideas from an interchange between us.

6

Bernard Linsky

WAS THE AXIOM OF REDUCIBILITY A PRINCIPLE OF LOGIC?

The title of this paper is in the past tense to indicate that the question it will address is whether the Axiom of Reducibility is a principle of logic according to the view of logic that Russell had when writing the first edition of *Principia Mathematica*.[1] It is often said that Logicism was a failure because when it avoided the Scylla of contradiction in Frege's system, it fell into the Charybdis of requiring obviously non-logical principles at Russell's hands. The axiom of reducibility is cited along with the Axiom of Infinity as a non-logical principle which Russell had to add to his system in order to be able to develop mathematics.

I want to consider this criticism of the axiom from several points of view. Why is it thought that the axiom of reducibility is not a principle of logic? What reasons does Russell actually give for doubting its logical status? Are they good reasons?

1. OBJECTIONS TO THE AXIOM

The Ramified Theory of Types of the first edition of *Principia* goes beyond the divisions of the "simple" theory between individuals, first-order propositional functions which apply to individuals, second-order propositional functions which apply to first-order functions, etc. It further subdivides each of these groups according to the range of the bound variables used in the definition of each propositional function. Russell often used the example of the predicate "*x* has all of the properties of a great general" which will itself be a property of great generals, but not one within the range of that particular quantifier "all". It will thus define a propositional function of a higher type than any of the vari-

---

[1] Page references will be to A.N. Whitehead and B. Russell, *Principia Mathematica to *56* (Cambridge: Cambridge University Press, 1962)

ables bound by that quantifier. Similarly, a difference of type would have to be marked in the theory of real numbers between the property "belonging to the set X" and "being the least upper bound of the set X", as the latter is defined in terms of a quantifier ranging over *all* members of X. The consequent division of numbers, and types generally, into different orders makes much ordinary reasoning seemingly invalid. The axiom of reducibility eases this difficulty. It asserts that for any propositional function, of whatever type, there is a *coextensive* propositional function of the lowest type compatible with its arguments, called a "predicative" propositional function.[2] Thus there will be a propositional function true of just those individuals with all the properties of a great general, which itself is of the same type as those properties quantified by "all". There will be a propositional function true of the least upper bound of a set X of the same type as the function "is a member of X" and so on. The ready availability of predicative propositional functions, guaranteed by the axiom of reducibility, allows them to substitute for classes in Russell's famous "no-class" theory of classes.[3] Sentences seemingly about "the class of Φ s" are to be analyzed as existential sentences asserting that some predicative propositional function coextensive with ϕ has the given properties. The axiom of reducibility thus both avoids some of the stringency of the ramified theory of types and guarantees the existence of the predicative propositional functions that replace classes. It is these very virtues that have been the source of doubt about the axiom.

Objections to the axiom of reducibility often combine several related points, in particular, that it makes an existence claim that is not purely logical, that it

---

[2]Strictly speaking there is an infinite number of axioms of which the following applies to one place propositional functions; *12.1 $(\exists f)$: $\phi x. \equiv_x f!x$. Thus for every propositional function f there is a materially equivalent *predicative* function f of the lowest order compatible with arguments of the same type. I follow the formulation of the ramified theory of types of Alonzo Church, "Comparison of Russell's Resolution of the Semantical Antinomies with That of Tarski", *Journal of Symbolic Logic*, 41 (1976): 747–60. The following brief sketch will be enough for what follows. Variables and constants are assigned *(r-) types*, i for individuals and $(\beta_1, \ldots, \beta_m)_{/n}$ for m-ary propositional functions of level n with arguments of types $\beta_1, \ldots, \beta_m$. (Propositional variables will have the $r - $ type $( )_{/n}$.). $n \geq 1$ is the level of the expression. (When $n = 1$ it is predicative). $(\alpha_1, \ldots, \alpha_m)_{/k}$ is directly lower than $(\beta_1, \ldots, \beta_m)_{/n}$ if $\alpha_1 = \beta_1, \ldots, \alpha_m = \beta_m$ and $k < n$. The order of an individual variable (type i) is 0, the order of a variable of type $(\beta_1, \ldots, \beta_m)_{/n}$ is $N + n$ where N is the maximum of the orders of $\beta_1, \ldots, \beta_m$. The force of the division of types is felt in the restriction on well-formed formulas: $f(x_1, \ldots x_m)$ is a *wff* if f is a variable or constant of type $(\beta_1, \ldots, \beta_m)_{/n}$, x_1 is a variable or constant of type β_1 or directly lower, $\ldots$, and x_m is a variable or constant of type β_m or directly lower. That propositional functions defined with quantifiers will have a raised type is made explicit by the comprehension schemas including: $\exists f^{(\beta 1, \ldots, \beta m/n)} f(x_1, \ldots, x_m) \equiv x_1, \ldots, x_m P$ where the bound variables of P are of order less than the order of f and the free variables and constants are greater. The axiom of reducibility is very similar:
$(\Phi^{(\beta 1, \ldots, \beta m)/n)}(\exists f^{(\beta 1, \ldots, \beta m)/1)} \Phi(x_1, \ldots, x_m) \equiv x_1, \ldots, x_m. f(x_1, \ldots, x_m)$
[3]The "theory" is stated as an axiom schema very much like the contextual definition of definite descriptions:
*20.1 $f\{\hat{z} (\phi z)\}. = : (\exists \phi): \phi!x. \equiv_x .\psi x : f \{\phi! \hat{z}\}$ *Df*

seems ad hoc and so lacks the obviousness of genuine logical principles, that the whole ramified theory of types of which it is a part is itself not purely logical, and, indeed, borders on incoherence since it seems to take back with the axiom of reducibility all of the ramification of types which is its hallmark. I consider these objections in turn.

It is often suggested that the axiom of reducibility is like the axiom of infinity in making an existence claim and as such is not a principle of logic. Viewed as a comprehension schema, or perhaps like the axiom of separation, the axiom would look like the axioms of Zermelo-Fraenkel set theory, which is seen as a rival to logicism as a foundational scheme.[4] Set theory is viewed as having given up the project of reducing mathematics to logic, and instead as having resorted to just postulating the existence of those distinctively mathematical entities that are needed to develop the rest of mathematics. The axiom of reducibility also seems to postulate the existence of peculiarly mathematical entities, predicative propositional functions, and so would seem to be of a piece with set theory.

Russell himself was suspicious of a priori existence proofs. He often claimed that logic cannot prove the existence of certain things, such as God, or how many things there are in the world.[5] But this is not a very good reason to say that logicism with the axiom of reducibility is a failure. One could have known that no logicist program could work if the problem lies in proving existence claims. In arithmetic we can prove many existence claims, for example, that there is an even number between 4 and 8. Since we could prove an existence claim, if logicism were correct, then logic could prove an existence claim, which is impossible, Q.E.D. There is no need to find the particular source of the existence claim to disqualify the logicist program; we know it must be there from the start. (One might provide an analysis of mathematical existence claims that gives them some other logical form, just as Russell's theory of descriptions analyzes descriptions as not really singular terms. For Frege and Russell, however, there were legitimately *logical* objects, whether courses of values or propositional functions, and quantification over mathematical objects was to be reduced to quantification over them.) Surely then, it is no objection to the status of the axiom of reducibility as part of a logicist program that it asserts an existence claim. The objection must rely on the nature of the existence claim which is made. One might argue that logic should make no assumptions about the number of *individuals,* or lowest level

---

[4]Gödel says that in the realist, simple theory which ought to replace the ramified theory of types, ". . . the place of the axiom of reducibility is now taken by the axiom of classes, Zermelo's *Aussonderungsaxiom* . . ." in [Gödel, 1944, pp. 140–141].
[5]See *Introduction to Mathematical Philosophy* (London: Allen and Unwin, 1919), p. 141.

entities, that there are. While one might want to avoid a free logic, and assume that there is at least one, the assumption of a countable infinity of objects, as made by the axiom of infinity, might lie outside of purely logical principles. As merely a claim about the existence of certain propositional functions, however, this restriction does not bar the axiom of reducibility from logic.

Another, related objection is that the axiom of reducibility simply undoes the construction of the hierarchy of propositional functions that is the very purpose of ramifying the theory of types.[6] If the higher type propositional functions of a given order are seen as constructed from those of lower type, then adopting the axiom of reducibility would be self-defeating. If all the classes there are have already been constructed at the first level, then all the convoluted ways of producing defining conditions for classes out of simpler classes do not really accomplish anything. Doesn't this make the constructions pointless? Quine has argued that the axiom of reducibility is a platonistic existence assertion and so violates the constructivist motivation for the ramification of the theory of types. Quine's objection thus combines the two lines of criticism I am discussing. He charges that the axiom both undoes the effect of the ramification and commits the theory to a platonistic view of propositional functions (which, when its use/mention confusions are cleared up, amounts to a theory of sets.)

Criticism of the axiom of reducibility is sometimes more indirect. Following Ramsey, it is often charged that the ramified theory of types involves an unnecessary complication of the simple theory of types, one introduced in order to deal with the semantic paradoxes that are not properly logical paradoxes.[7] The axiom of reducibility then inherits the non-logical character of the system to which it belongs. Accordingly, a defence of the axiom will require a defence of the ramified theory of types as itself a system of logic. The answer to these questions comes in seeing the ramified theory of types as a system of intensional logic which includes the "no-class" account of sets, and indeed the whole development of mathematics, as just a part. A defence of the axiom of reducibility, then, leads to a defence of the whole ramified theory of types and the logicist project to which it belongs.

---

[6]Quine presents this objection in [Quine, 1969, pp. 249–258]. See also Myhill cited in note 12 for a response.

[7]F.P. Ramsey, "The Foundations of Mathematics (1925)", in *The Foundations of Mathematics and Other Logical Essays* (London: Routledge and Kegan Paul, 1931), pp. 1–61. Quine makes this objection as well. On his account, the set-theoretic nature of the axiom is hidden by its quantification over propositonal functions which are creatures of the confusion of use and mention, of semantics and ontology.

2. THE ORIGIN OF THE AXIOM

Although this paper is concerned with the justification of the axiom of reducibility within Russell's views at the time of writing *PM,* a look at the earlier history of the principle will help to explain its role in his thinking. One stereotype of the evolution of Russell's thought is that he first had a simple theory of types, designed to handle his original paradox of sets, later adding the "ramification" in order to handle the semantic paradoxes and, then, realizing that the ramification made impossible the project of reducing mathematics to logic, introduced the axiom of reducibility, undoing the effect of the ramification.

This account is quite wrong. It may follow the natural ordering of topics in a presentation of the theory of types, which Russell himself uses, but it does not present the historical development of the theory. To begin with, type theory was effectively ramified from its earliest formulations around 1906–1907.[8] The distinctive feature of ramification is to distinguish propositional functions which take arguments of the same type by the ranges of the bound or "apparent" variables that occur in them. Russell's early attempts at solving the paradoxes deliberately avoided any division of types. This was in part due to his desire to see all quantifiers as unrestricted, which was in turn due to a belief in the universal character of logic.[9] But once Russell accepted Poincaré's analysis of the paradoxes as due to a vicious circle, he immediately saw that the range of the universal quantifiers in propositional functions needs to be restricted to a specific totality, in other words, the need for ramification.

Just before finally accepting the need for types, Russell held his "substitutional" theory according to which all quantifiers are unrestricted but the (seeming) quantifiers over propositional functions *are* restricted. This is not a real restriction of quantifiers, however, because expressions for propositional functions are "incomplete symbols" which can be eliminated by contextual definitions. The real range of quantifiers is all objects and all propositions. The next stage of development for Russell was to see the need for type distinctions among propositions. In the paper "On 'Insolubilia' and Their Solution by Symbolic Logic",[10] Russell adopts the vicious circle principle as the analysis of the para-

---

[8](Note added for this volume.) Leonard Linsky has persuaded me that my attempt at revisionist history is itself misleading. He has long maintained that the essence of the simple theory of types is present in Appendix B to *Principles of Mathematics,* (New York: Norton, n.d.) that the *intensional,* but not *semantic,* paradox of propositions in the last paragraph of that appendix requires ramification of the simple theory, although Russell only recognized the force of that paradox in his letter to Frege of 29 September 1902. (See *Gottlob Frege: Philosophical and Mathematical Correspondence.* G. Gabriel et.al., editors, Chicago: University of Chicago Press, 1980, pp. 147–148.) Still, on this account, the theory of types did not remain unramified for long, and the ramification was justified by what seem to be logical rather than semantic paradoxes.

[9]See Peter Hylton, "Russell's Substitutional Theory", *Synthese,* 45 (1980): 1–31.

doxes and the consequent need for at least type distinctions among propositions, while still denying the reality of propositional functions with his "substitutional" view. Yet he immediately acknowledges that "every statement containing x and an apparent variable is equivalent, for all values of x, to some statement ϕx containing no apparent variable" (p. 212). Thus, for example, propositions about *all* propositions of a given sort, say all those asserted by Epimenides, must be (materially) equivalent to some proposition which does not include such quantification. This claim amounts to an axiom of reducibility.

What reason did Russell give for believing such a claim? This passage appears in response to the criticisms of the logicists' account of induction that Poincaré based on the vicious circle principle. For a logicist, the principle of induction says that *all* properties possessed by 0 and hereditary with respect to the successor relation are possessed by all numbers. The vicious-circle principle requires that the quantification over "all" properties must be restricted to avoid reference to any impredicative properties defined with apparent variables ranging over all numbers.[11] As this is required in so many uses of the induction principle, adopting the vicious-circle principle seems to "destroy many pieces of ordinary mathematical reasoning" (p. 211). Thus Russell saw that the adoption of type theory with the consequent restriction of bound variables to ranges of significance undercuts those principles that seem to rely on unrestricted quantification (even when the real quantifiers are only those ranging over objects and propositions, as in the "substitutional" account). The definition of identity, that x and y are identical if and only if they share *all* properties, is another such example, which will be discussed more below.

This simultaneous appearance of types and the axiom of reducibility is all the more remarkable for the fact that at the time Russell did not even see the hierarchy of types as one of properties or propositional functions, but rather simply of propositions. In the "Insolubilia . . ." paper he was still in the grip of the "substitutional" theory that attempted to define away propositional functions with contextual definitions and the primitive notion of replacing one object by another in a proposition. The axiom of reducibility, then, did not make its appearance as a view about the existence of propositional functions, but rather as a necessity given the need to restrict quantifiers to types. Given that restriction, generalizations over all properties must be replaceable by quantifiers ranging over only a certain type of properties.

The axiom of reducibility guarantees that restricting attention to properties of only one type will not invalidate standard patterns of reasoning about *all* properties because if any property does not apply to an object, one of that chosen

---

[10]Reprinted in *Essays in Analysis,* ed. Douglas Lackey (New York: Braziller, 1972), pp. 190–214.
[11]Poincaré would seemingly ban all impredicative properties, while Russell would restrict them to a distinct type.

type will not. Thus induction says that any property possessed by 0 and heredi-tary with respect to the successor relation will be possessed by all numbers. The axiom of reducibility says that any property of numbers will be coextensive with a predicative property. If a number lacks a property, it will lack a coextensive predicative property, and if it has a property, it will have a coextensive predica-tive property. Consequently, Russell is able to use as his definition of identity the weaker claim that $x = y$ if and only if x and y have all the same predicative prop-erties (*13.01 $x = y$. = : (ϕ) : ϕx: $\supset$. $\phi!$ y Df). The axiom of reducibility allows one to restrict attention to the predicative properties of x and y. A justifi-cation of the axiom of reducibility, then, must consist of a reason to believe that one can so restrict attention to the properties of one preferred type, the predica-tive functions.

In what follows I wish to explain the role of the axiom of reducibility in Rus-sell's thinking at the time of *Principia Mathematica* when his ontology was con-siderably different. In fact, I believe, the ontology he had in the background of *PM* is what provided the justification for the axiom at that time. What can be learned from its earlier appearance, however, is that the axiom was an integral part of the notion of a theory of types, not some afterthought used to patch up a defect resulting from the addition of ramification to an earlier, simpler theory of types. It is the whole ramified theory of types with reducibility that needs justifi-cation, not the axiom on its own.

3. RUSSELL'S DOUBTS ABOUT THE AXIOM

Let us turn, then, to Russell's views in *Principia Mathematica*. To evaluate those it is instructive to look at his reasons for the later *abandonment* of the axiom of reducibility which is one of the characteristic differences between the systems of the first and second editions of *PM*. What reasons did Russell himself give for doubting that the axiom is logical? There is very little about it in the Introduc-tion to the second edition. All he says is:

> One point in regard to which improvement is obviously desirable is the axiom of reducibility (*12.1.11). This axiom has a purely pragmatic justification: it leads to the desired results, and to no others. But clearly it is not the sort of axiom with which we can rest content. (p. xiv)

Russell's objection is hardly explicit. We know that the objection doesn't amount to by looking at the argument *for* the axiom in the Introduction to the first edition:

> That the axiom of reducibility is self-evident is a proposition which can hardly be maintained. But in fact self-evidence is never more than a part of the reason for accepting an axiom, and is never indispensible. The reason for accepting an axiom,

as for accepting any other propositions, is always largely inductive, namely that
many propositions which are nearly indubitable can be deduced from it, and that no
equally plausible way is known by which these propositions could be true if the
axiom were false, and nothing which is probably false can be deduced from it.
(p. 59)

He goes on to say that the inductive evidence for the axiom of reducibility is
good so the real problem is that:

... although it seems very improbable that the axiom should turn out to be false, it is
by no means improbable that it should be found to be deducible from some other
more fundamental and more evident axiom. It is possible that the use of the vicious-
circle principle, as embodied in the above hierarchy of types, is more drastic than it
need be, and that by a less drastic use the necessity for the axiom might be avoided.
(pp. 59–60)

In the second edition Russell says that by following Wittgenstein's example
in making the logic extensional one can avoid the axiom of reducibility but still
prove many useful theorems.[12] So this objection to the axiom of reducibility was
that it should be proved from more self-evident axioms, or avoided in the proof
of the desired theorems by adopting a different axiom. Russell then does not
require that the axiom be self-evident, and does not express any doubt about its
truth; rather he thinks it is redundant. (It is important to note that Russell
includes *logical* axioms among those that need not be self-evident, as long as
they have the right deductive strength.) At the time of the first edition he thought
that the axiom might be redundant because an excessively strong form of the
vicious-circle principle had introduced too many types which then had to be
integrated with the axiom of reducibility. The vicious-circle principle forbids the
existence of any entity such as a totality, or propositional function, which
depends on itself in the wrong way. If a propositional function depends on a
totality, then it cannot be a member of that totality, and hence belongs to a new
type, thus ramifying type theory. But with the principle of extensionality anything true of one propositional function will be true of every coextensive one, so
the *only* thing on which a propositional function can depend is its extension, and
so the type theory cannot be ramified. Extensionality thus weakens the force of
the vicious-circle principle by limiting what a propositional function can depend
on, and thus what it could depend on viciously. Other principles limiting the
dependence of propositional functions by identifying some which are distinguished in the full ramified theory would have the same effect. It is clear that
even at the time of writing the Introduction to the second edition of *PM* that

---

[12]Russell even claims this about the ramified theory of types in the first edition. This claim is shown
incorrect in John Myhill, "The Undefinability of the Set of Natural Numbers in the Ramified *Principia*", in George Nakhnikian, ed., *Bertrand Russell's Philosophy* (London: Duckworth, 1974).

Russell thought the principle of extensionality was too strong. Thus this doubt about the axiom of reducibility was a doubt about the vicious-circle principle and the number of type distinctions it introduces, rather than a doubt about the existence claim made by the axiom.

A richer guide to Russell's thinking about the axiom of reducibility is in the *Introduction to Mathematical Philosophy,* written in 1918 between the two editions of *PM.* There he expresses doubts about whether the axiom has the character of a regular principle of logic. One worry is that the axiom is not general or widely enough applicable. Thus: "This axiom, like the multiplicative axiom and the axiom of infinity, is necessary for certain results, but not for the bare existence of logical reasoning" (p. 191). He goes on to explain that it does not have the universal applicability of, for example, the quantifier laws, and so could be just added as a special hypothesis whenever it is used. Here, obviously, Russell is concentrating on the use of the axiom of reducibility in the construction of the natural and real numbers. It is not so clear that the axiom would seldom be used outside the theory of classes and mathematics, as can be seen from its role in proofs about identity. The need for impredicative definitions in mathematics, in particular for the notion of the *least upper bound* of a set of real numbers, has led many to see the "certain results" to which Russell alludes, to be only a limited part of higher mathematics. Indeed, the appeal of developing a "predicative" analysis has suggested that the axiom is in fact debatable. But of course Russell's project was to develop mathematics, and so his attention was precisely on the role of impredicative definitions in mathematics. Attention to the identity of indiscernibles should remind us of the frequency of talk of *all* properties of a thing within metaphysics. Since without the axiom of reducibility such talk is banned, we see that the axiom is not just needed for the development of higher mathematics.

Russell goes on to question the *necessary* truth of the axiom of reducibility, demanding that a logical truth be true in "all possible worlds" and not just in this "higgledy-piggledy job-lot of a world in which chance has imprisoned us" (p. 192). So Russell has qualms about both the generality of the axiom and its necessary truth, features he took to be characteristic of logical truths. It is these remarks that are most likely the source of many claims that the axiom of reducibility is not a principle of logic because it is not intuitively obvious enough, or a general enough principle of reasoning.

Russell's objections here are a mixed lot. He has a theoretician's concern that the axiom is ad hoc and could be replaced by more basic principles. He is also concerned that the axiom is not a *necessary* truth, another feature which does not distinguish logic from a very general metaphysical theory of the world. Russell's concern that the axiom is only of use in mathematics, and not a general principle of reasoning shares this character. Given Russell's earlier remarks that axioms need not be directly evident, it is hard to attribute to him a view of the nature of

logic which marks it off from a more substantive metaphysical theory, other than
by differences of degree.

These, then, were Russell's various qualms about the axiom of reducibility.
What can be said in defence of the axiom? Should Russell have had such qualms
about it, given its role in his logic?

4. Principia Mathematica as Intensional Logic

I wish to argue that in fact the axiom of reducibility plays a crucial role in the
logic of *PM* because of the distinctive role of predicative propositional functions. It is a realist view about propositional functions, in particular, a view about
predicative propositional functions as encapsulating the real features of objects,
which serves as a justification for the axiom within the philosophical system of
PM.

First it is important to get clear about the role of the axiom of reducibility in
Russell's theory of classes. It does not just undo the effects of the ramification as
the "constructivist" reading suggests. Here I rely on the recent work of Alonzo
Church and Leonard Linsky on what might be called the "intensional interpretation" of *Principia Mathematica*.[13] They have argued that despite the central project in *PM* of developing mathematics, which is an extensional subject, the logic
of *PM* is fundamentally intensional. The intensional nature of the logic explains
many otherwise puzzling features of its presentation. One example is the role of
scope in the theory of definite descriptions. In extensional contexts the scope
differences do not have any logical effect, as long as the descriptions are proper.
Why, then, are they introduced with such care? Likewise, several features of the
"no-class" theory also depend on the intensionality of propositional functions. In
particular, the significance of the axiom of reducibility depends on the logic
being intensional. Linsky's argument goes like this. Russell's contextual analysis
of classes, the "no-class" theory, is very similar to the analysis of definite
descriptions, including the possibility of scope distinctions. Just as it is true (and
proved in *PM**14.3) that scope distinctions for definite descriptions make no difference in extensional contexts, it is true that scope distinctions make no difference in extensional contexts for sets. That this is not proved, Linsky argues,
shows that Russell had in mind the application of *PM* to mathematical contexts
where extensionality rules. That it *could be* expressed and proved shows that the

---

[13]See Alonzo Church, *op.cit.*, note 2, and Leonard Linsky, *Oblique Contexts* (Chicago: University of
Chicago Press, 1983), Appendix, as well as Warren Goldfarb's "Russell's Reasons for Ramification",
in C.W. Savage and C.A. Anderson, eds., *Rereading Russell: Essays on Bertrand Russell's Metaphysics and Epistemology*, Minnesota Studies in the Philosophy of Science, Vol. XII (Minneapolis:
University of Minnesota Press, 1989).

logic was set up to handle intensional contexts. Furthermore, there are two conditions to be met for descriptions such as "the *F*" to behave like names with regard to scope and substitution. It is not only necessary that one restrict oneself to extensional contexts, but also the description must be proper (i.e. there must be one and only one *F*). A similar requirement that class abstracts behave like names is that, in addition to occurring in extensional contexts, the requisite predicative propositional function must exist. But the latter is precisely what the axiom of reducibility guarantees. It is, as Gödel remarked, a comprehension principle, but this is in the context of an intensional logic, one capable of expressing much more than just the extensional sentences of mathematics. So, Linsky's argument goes, Russell's ignoring of scope distinctions for class abstracts, unlike his use of them with descriptions, shows that he saw himself as restricting his talk of classes to talk of extensional mathematical contexts, but not so restricting the logic of *PM*.

My interest is not in establishing the intensional nature of the logic of *PM* but rather in the axiom of reducibility. The axiom clearly plays a crucial role in the theory of classes, given the particular contextual definition of classes that Russell presents. While having the force of a comprehension principle, it does not assert the existence of some new, non-logical category of entity, but rather just of a *predicative* propositional function coextensive with an arbitrary propositional function. Because the extensional theory of classes is only part of the whole logic, the axiom of reducibility does not just undo the ramification of the theory of types. It is crucial in the reduction of classes to logic, and unless one assumes that logicism is false and so automatically any talk of classes is not part of logic, it seems to be a quite legitimate logical notion for Russell—provided, of course, that a claim about the existence of a *predicative* propositional function with a given extension can be seen as a logical principle.

What of the charge that the axiom of reducibility undoes the whole point of the hierarchy of types of propositional functions? That assumes that the only point of the hierarchy of types is to represent the possible constructions of propositional functions and hence of classes. What view could hold, rather, that all the classes have been constructed at the level of predicative functions? The answer is that propositional functions of higher types are needed to capture intensional phenomena. The predicative functions are needed to reconstruct the extensional part of logic, that part which deals with the extensions of predicates, or classes. The higher types are needed for intensional phenomena, cases where the same class is picked out by distinct intensions, i.e. propositional functions. This view requires seeing the ramified hierarchy of *PM* not as a constructivist hierarchy of classes but rather as a theory of propositional functions which includes as a part the theory of classes, but which does much more. Of course, predicative propositional functions are not extensional. They can be distinct yet coextensive. Rather, all extensional talk about classes is analyzed as a general (existential) claim about predicative propositional functions.

What then is so special about predicative propositional functions that one can adopt a "comprehension" principle asserting the existence of a coextensive predicative propositional function for every arbitrary propositional function?

5. THE AXIOM OF REDUCIBILITY AND THE IDENTITY OF INDISCERNIBLES

The distinctive character of predicative propositional functions can be seen in the details of Russell's charge that the axiom of reducibility is not a necessary truth. Russell says that

> The axiom, we may observe, is a generalized form of Leibniz's identity of indiscernibles. Leibniz assumed, as a logical principle, that two different subjects must differ as to predicates. Now predicates are only some among what we call "predicative functions", which will include also relations to given terms, and various properties not to be reckoned as predicates. Thus Leibniz's assumption is a much stricter and narrower one than ours. (*Introduction to Mathematical Philosophy,* p.192)

Russell goes on to say that the axiom *seems* to hold of the actual world, for

> . . . there seems to be no way of doubting its empirical truth as regards particulars, owing to spatio-temporal differentiations: no two particulars have exactly the same spatial and temporal relations to all other particulars. But this is, as it were, an accident, a fact about the world in which we happen to find ourselves. (*ibid.*)

How is the axiom of reducibility a "form" of the identity of indiscernibles? The principle of the identity of indiscernibles says that $x = y$ just in case all the same predicates (propositional functions) apply to x and y. The axiom of reducibility allows one to strengthen the principle by only requiring the sharing of all the same *predicative* propositional functions. For suppose that ψx but not ψy where ψ is not predicative. Then there is a predicative propositional function ϕ coextensive with ψ, and thus true of x, which distinguishes x from y with predicative functions alone. Accordingly, Russell's definition of identity at *13.01 is this "restricted" form of the identity of indiscernibles, and the above reasoning is equivalent to the proof of theorem *13.101 ($\vdash : x = y. \supset.\psi x \supset \psi y$), one "half" of the more familiar identity of indiscernibles. (The more controversial half of the principle, that if x and y have all the same properties, then $x = y$, follows immediately from the fact that if they share all properties, they share all predicative properties, and, by definition *13.01, are identical.) The axiom of reducibility is possibly a stronger principle than is needed to prove the identity of indiscernibles from the definition of identity, for the proof only requires that objects sharing all predicative properties share all properties of any type, whereas the axiom of reducibility accomplishes this by providing a predicative property which is coextensive with each arbitrary property. This may have been one of the points where Russell suspected that the axiom of reducibility might be replaced by a simpler principle. Still, however, he accepts the axiom to the extent of calling it a "generalized form" of the identity of indiscernibles. Reasons for accepting that generalized principle would then, for Russell at least, provide a justification for the axiom of reducibility.

What then is the reason for accepting the axiom of reducibility and its accompanying definition of identity? I believe that for Russell it was not just a matter of stipulation that made classes coincide with predicative propositional functions. Rather, he thought that predicative propositional functions really characterize the genuine properties which individuate things in the world. Objects do not always differ in their monadic properties, as Russell argued against Leibniz. It was a distinctive feature of Russell's philosophy that he argued for the reality of relations and hence the irreducibility of some relational properties. Thus "being two miles from x" is a perfectly good relational property, not reducible to any monadic properties of x. It is the original stock of one-place properties, then added to it all the possible relational properties, and Boolean combinations of them, which constitute the predicative propositional functions. It is because Russell saw predicative propositional functions as expressing more than just monadic qualities that he speaks of the axiom as a "generalized" version of Leibniz's principle. Leibniz, according to Russell's account, would presumably endorse an even stronger "axiom of reducibility" to the effect that every propositional function is equivalent (by analysis and not just coextensiveness) with some conjunction of monadic qualities.

Russell feared that it might be a matter of arbitrary postulation, or at least contingently true, that the predicative propositional functions should suffice to distinguish all objects. Why shouldn't some higher type property allow us to distinguish objects? Russell considers examples like "having all the qualities of a great general" and "being a typical F" (where the latter seems to mean something like having all the properties shared by *most Fs*). The answer can be seen in the very nature of these examples. Higher type propositional functions do not really introduce new properties of things. They may characterize new ways of thinking of or classifying them, but they don't introduce any new real properties. Russell himself did not keep clear enough the distinction between propositional functions and these real properties of things, universals. That he sometimes made such a distinction is clear. It is certainly necessary to make such a distinction for him to be able to argue, as he does in the Introduction to the first edition of *PM,* both that propositional functions depend on their values, propositions, in a way that makes the vicious-circle principle applicable, and that propositions are to be analyzed according to the "multiple relation" theory into universals and particulars which are the basic furniture of the world. Thus propositional functions are separated from each other by propositions in the hierarchy of depen-

dence which the vicious-circle principle enjoins us to observe. A simpler way of
seeing that Russell was committed to such a distinction is to observe that it is of
the essence of propositional functions that they allow compounding by logical
connectives; thus "being red or blue" is a perfectly acceptable propositional
function (*PM*, p. 56). Yet universals are only discovered as the end result of
analysis—they can be objects of acquaintance, but are simple. They correspond
with the primitive predicates of a fully analyzed language, not with the arbitrarily complex propositional functions. This distinction is not very clear in *Principia*, however, especially as Russell did not ever explicitly mark it or even
observe it at all times.[14]

If one grants that Russell had in mind some distinction between propositional functions and universals that have a metaphysically important role as that
which underlies the real qualities of things, then it is clear that predicative
propositional functions inherit some of the character of universals. One need not
argue that any two objects will be distinguished by some universal that one has
and the other lacks. That would be to claim that all objects have a unique *nature,*
an implausible metaphysical assumption. But one might hold that *something*
accounts for the particularity of objects, if not their qualities or natures, then perhaps their locations. If one holds a relational view of space, then the view that it
is spatio-temporal location which individuates particulars is one which allows a
relation to individuate.[15] If one were only interested in individuating objects two
at a time, then universals or relational properties might be sufficient. One could
say of objects with different natures that one has *F* and the other does not, where
F is one universal in the nature of the one object. For objects with the same
nature one could use relational properties as one does with spatio-temporal relations of concrete particulars. When whole classes of objects are involved, one
may require Boolean combinations of universals as well as relational properties.
Some of the objects may be distinguished by being *F,* others by being *G,* others
by *not* being *H,* and so on, so that the *predicative* propositional function "being
F and *G* but not *H* . . ." is needed to mark off the class. Russell's qualms about
the axiom of reducibility being contingent amount, then, to the worry that such a
scheme of spatio-temporal relations and properties is merely a contingent characteristic of the world.

As I have presented it, the axiom of reducibility marks out the special role of
predicative propositional functions, which coincide with classes, and indicates
the properties which individuate things in the world. One still needs the whole

---

[14]See my "Propositional Functions and Universals in *Principia Mathematica*", *Australasian Journal
of Philosophy,* 66 (December 1988): 447–460, for a discussion of this point. See, however, Nino
Cocchiarella, "Russell's Theory of Logical Types and the Atomistic Hierarchy of Sentences", in
Rereading Russell, pp. 41–62, for an explicit argument that Russell *identified* propositional functions and universals.
[15]See D.M.Armstrong's *Universals and Scientific Realism* (Cambridge: Cambridge University Press,
1980), chap.11, for a discussion of spatio-temporal location and particularity.

hierarchy of ramified propositional functions to handle all the things that can be said of the world, or thought of it, the whole realm of intensional phenomena. This makes the axiom of reducibility out to be a metaphysical principle. It is one of great generality, however, certainly unlike any principle about numbers as abstract entities or of the sort that might occur in any special science. Still, this accounts for Russell's qualms about it. While the axiom states a very general principle of metaphysics, does it really have the necessity required of a principle of logic? Is it *logically* necessary? Russell was not sure. Ultimately, it was the lure of doing without the ramified theory by adopting the principle of extensionality that made him give up the axiom. But giving up on intensional phenomena was an extreme solution. It undid the whole relation between classes and propositional functions that was at the heart of the first edition of *PM*.

The axiom of reducibility was an integral part of the theory of types. From the beginning it was clear that if a theory of types requires restricting the ranges of bound variables to a given range of significance, or type, then those principles which seem to require quantifying over all properties must be stronger than necessary. Identity, while seeming to require the sharing of all properties, really only requires the sharing of properties of the lowest, predicative order, and the existence of sets, which should allow a set for all predicates, really only requires sets for all predicative properties. As well, all numbers and properties of numbers to which the induction principle will apply are clearly represented at the lowest type. Some criticisms of the axiom and its role seem to require forgetting the intensional nature of the logic, and hence the use for all those additional, non-predicative propositional functions. Russell was aware of the need for an independent justification for the principle, one that showed how conclusions about numbers, classes, and identity could be settled by only considering predicative propositional functions. That predicative propositional functions are all that is needed for the theory of classes and numbers follows directly from the "no-class" theory and the definition of numbers as classes. The adequacy of predicative propositional functions for the definition of identity and other more "metaphysical" or non-mathematical applications of the logic of *PM,* comes from the distinction between propositional functions and universals, and the proximity of predicative propositoinal functions to universals. Predicative propositional functions mark the real kinds in the world. That this is so is a fairly substantive metaphysical claim about the world, and so not obviously of the same generality or as clearly "necessary" as the other principles of Russell's logic. It was however, also not obviously out of place in the logic of *Principia Mathematica.*[16]

---

[16]This paper was written at the Center for the Study of Language and Information at Stanford University. I would like to thank the Center for the use of its facilities, and those at the Center for discussions which led to this paper.

7

Erich Reck

FREGE'S INFLUENCE ON WITTGENSTEIN: REVERSING METAPHYSICS VIA THE CONTEXT PRINCIPLE*

INTRODUCTION AND OVERVIEW

Gottlob Frege and Ludwig Wittgenstein (the later Wittgenstein) are often seen as polar opposites with respect to their fundamental philosophical outlooks: Frege as a paradigmatic "realist", Wittgenstein as a paradigmatic "anti-realist". This opposition is supposed to find its clearest expression with respect to mathematics: Frege is seen as the "arch-platonist", Wittgenstein as some sort of "radical anti-platonist". Furthermore, seeing them as such fits nicely with a widely shared view about their relation: the later Wittgenstein is supposed to have developed his ideas in direct opposition to Frege. The purpose of this paper is to challenge these standard assumptions. I will argue that Frege's and Wittgenstein's basic outlooks have something crucial *in common;* and I will argue that this is the result of the positive *influence* Frege had on Wittgenstein.

*I know very few people who are as dedicated to and enthusiastic about philosophy as Leonard Linsky. As one of his former students I have also come to admire the penetrating clarity of his teaching and writing. And I am deeply grateful for his continuing support of my work. Consequently, I am very happy, and feel honored, to be able to contribute part of my work to a *Festschrift* for him.— This paper has grown out of my dissertation *Frege, Wittgenstein, and Platonism in Mathematics* (University of Chicago, 1992), written under the supervision and with the advice of W. W. Tait, Leonard Linsky, and Michael Forster. A short, rough version of it was presented as a talk at the University of Minnesota, Minneapolis, in March 1993. At that occasion (and during a whole year at the Minnesota Center for Philosophy of Science, as a postdoctoral research fellow) I received valuable feedback from a number of people, including C. Anthony Anderson, Geoffrey Hellman, and Delbert Reed. Finally, countless discussions with Steve Awodey, Andre Carus, Robin Jeshion, and, in particular, Stuart Glennan, Christoph Lankers, Mike Price, and Gisbert W. Selke have helped me clarify my views on the issues involved. — Altogether, I owe a lot to these critics and friends, including many of the ideas presented here; and usually I cannot tell any more which ones to whom (but compare fn. 1 ff. for references to the literature). However, and strangely enough, none of them agrees with everything I say in this paper. Thus all the remaining mistakes should be attributed to me.

It would be absurd to claim that there are no important differences between Frege and Wittgenstein. Likewise, it would be absurd to claim that the later Wittgenstein was not critical of some of Frege's ideas. What, then, is the common element I see? My suggestion is that the two thinkers agree on what I call a *reversal of metaphysics* (relative to a standard kind of metaphysics attacked by both). This is not an agreement on one particular thesis or on one argument. Rather, it has to do with what is *prior* and what is *posterior* when it comes to certain fundamental explanations in metaphysics (also, relatedly, in semantics and epistemology). Furthermore, this explanatory reversal is intimately connected with Frege's *context principle:* "Only in the context of a sentence do words have meaning". As we will see, Wittgenstein takes over this principle and modifies it to: "Only in the practice of a language can a word have meaning".

The context principle has not gone unnoticed in the literature; indeed it has received a number of different interpretations. However, none of them does justice to Frege's and Wittgenstein's understanding of it; and this is, it seems to me, directly connected with the standard ways of categorizing Frege and Wittgenstein: as realist and anti-realist. According to the reading to be developed here, the context principle (in Frege *and* Wittgenstein) *cuts across* the usual realism-vs.-antirealism distinction. What is more, the reversal of metaphysical explanations with which the principle is tied up calls into question this very distinction. Now, this fact also makes it harder to explain my new perspective on Frege and Wittgenstein—since it is at odds with certain widespread (though often only implicit) assumptions in contemporary metaphysics, philosophy of language, and philosophy of mathematics. Some of these assumptions will, then, also have to be subjected to critical scrutiny in the course of this paper.

At the same time, my approach may at first glance not appear to diverge very far from the mainstream, particularly with respect to Frege. For instance, it will turn out that my Frege is a *platonist,* that is to say: he does view mathematical judgments as objective; he does hold that in the corresponding statements our number terms refer to numbers; and he does maintain that these numbers are non-mental, non-physical, self-subsistent objects. In other words, I do not want to deny at all that Frege makes such statements, not even that he means them seriously. Instead, I want to re-interpret *what he means by them,* i.e., *what kind of platonist* he is. I will argue that Frege is a *contextual platonist,* not a *metaphysical platonist*—a crucial difference which should be clear by the end of the paper. In addition, if my new reading of Frege is correct, it becomes possible to see that his platonism is less in opposition to Wittgenstein's anti-platonism than is usually assumed. I will substantiate this conclusion by re-considering Wittgenstein's position, too, both with respect to his critical and his constructive views.

The Fregean and Wittgensteinian ideas considered here are, in my opinion, fascinating and powerful in themselves. But I will not explicitly argue for such a claim in this paper. Instead, my principal goal is *exegetical:* to re-interpret Frege's writings, Wittgenstein's writings, and Frege's influence on Wittgenstein. Since my new interpretations are reactions against certain received views (and against hidden assumptions behind them) I will proceed as follows: First, in *Section I,* I will present what I take to be the standard understanding of Frege's platonism, based on a first look at the most relevant remarks from his writings. In *Section II* I will then indicate how some of Wittgenstein's later views can, in fact, be seen as directed against the corresponding position, although I do not think it is really Frege's. Next, in *Section III,* a close examination of Frege's context principle, both in its critical and its constructive use, will lead us towards a reinterpretation of his views. In *Section IV* I will further explain this new interpretation, as well as the kind of platonism it leads to. Finally, *Section V* will bring us back to Wittgenstein. We will then be in a position to understand his deep sympathies for Frege's context principle; but we will also be able to identify more clearly some remaining differences between the two thinkers.[1]

I. FREGE AND METAPHYSICAL PLATONISM

Throughout his life Frege's main goal was to put arithmetic on a firm foundation. For him this amounted to analyzing and clarifying its logical structure, thus revealing both what it is based on and what it is about. In other words, Frege's logical investigations led him to certain epistemological and metaphysical conclusions: about the basis of arithmetic judgments and the nature of numbers (and functions). As is well-known, Frege's conclusions amount to a kind of *logicism;* that is, for him arithmetic judgments find their foundation in basic logical laws and numbers turn out to be logical entities. This much of the standard reading I do not want to question. More problematic for me—i.e., more in need of clarification—is that Frege's position is usually also characterized as a kind of *platonism.*

---

[1]With respect to my whole perspective (on Frege, Wittgenstein, and platonism) I have been guided by W.W. Tait's "Truth and Proof: The Platonism of Mathematics" [Tait, 1986a]. My interpretation of Frege has, in addition, been influenced by Michael Dummett's "Nominalism" in [Dummett, 1978], by Thomas Ricketts' "Objectivity and Objecthood: Frege's Metaphysics of Judgment" [Ricketts, 1986a), and by the first few chapters of Cora Diamond's *The Realistic Spirit* [Diamond, 1991]. Similarly, my interpretation of Wittgenstein has also been influenced by W.W. Tait's "Wittgenstein and the 'Skeptical Paradoxes' " [Tait, 1986b] and by Steve Gerrard's dissertation *Wittgenstein in Transition. The Philosophy of Mathematics* (University of Chicago, 1986), published in part as "Wittgenstein's Philosophies of Mathematics" [Gerrard, 1991b].

Frege's Platonism (*Vaguely and Naively*). What exactly it means to say that
Frege is a "platonist"—or what could be meant by "platonism" in the first
place—is a central question in this paper. I do not think there is only one possible answer. But let us first look at some *typical characterizations* of "platonism".
For instance, in the *Encyclopedia of Philosophy* we can read:

> By platonism is understood the realistic view, akin to that of Plato himself, that
> abstract entities exist in their own right, independently of human thinking. Accord-
> ing to this view number theory is to be regarded as the description of a realm of
> objective, self-subsistent mathematical objects that are timeless, non-spatial, and
> non-mental. Platonism conceives it to be the task of the mathematician to explore
> this and other realms of being. Among modern philosophers of mathematics Frege is
> a pre-eminent representative of platonism, distinguished by his penetrating lucidity
> and his intransigence. [Barker, 1967, p. 529]

This passage contains the main elements of the understanding of "platonism"
dominant in much of recent metaphysics, philosophy of language, and philosophy of mathematics. It focuses on the following three claims: (*i*) numbers and
other mathematical entities are "abstract objects" which exist "in their own
right"; (*ii*) in mathematics we "describe" these objects, i.e., we talk about them
as members of a "mathematical realm"; and (*iii*) the task of the mathematician is
to "explore" this realm, i.e., to find out what is "objectively the case" in it. At the
same time, an understanding of platonism which just cites these three claims
(without further explication) is still very vague and naive. In fact, it will turn out
to be *ambiguous,* i.e., allow for two rather different interpretations.

It is hard to deny, though, that Frege is a platonist in this vague and naive
sense. He is most explicit about his views in this connection in *Foundations of
Arithmetic* [Frege, 1884]. There he says about numbers as objects:[2]

> [S]urely the number one looks like a definite object, with properties that can be
> specified, for example that of remaining unchanged when multiplied by itself. [p. II]

> But it will perhaps be objected, even if the earth is really not imaginable, it is at any
> rate an external thing, occupying a definite place; but where is the number 4? It is

---

[2]I will quote from Frege's writings using the following editions:

The Basic Laws of Arithmetic (selections), ed. and tr. by M. Furth (University of California
Press: Berkeley, 1967). [Frege, 1967a]
Collected Papers, ed. by Brian McGuinness, tr. by M. Black, V.H. Dudman, P. Geach, et al.
(Basil Blackwell: Oxford, 1984). [Frege, 1984]
Foundations of Arithmetic, bilingual edition, tr. by J.L. Austin (Northwestern University Press:
Evanston, 1968). [Frege, 1884]
Posthumous Writings, ed. by Hans Hermes et al., tr. by Peter Long and Roger White (University
of Chicago Press: Chicago, 1979). [Frege, 1979a]

Notice, however, that in a number of cases I have found it necessary to *amend the usual translations.*
(Whenever these amendments seem crucial, I will also quote the corresponding passages in German.)

> neither outside us nor within us. And, taking those words in their spatial sense, that is quite correct. . . . Yet the only conclusion to be drawn from that is that 4 is not a spatial object, not that it is not an object at all. Not every object has a place. [p. 72]

And about the nature of numbers and the objectivity of arithmetic:

> For number is no whit more an object of psychology or a product of mental processes than, let us say, the North Sea. [p. 34]

> But arithmetic is no more psychological than, say, astronomy. Astronomy is concerned, not with ideas of the planets, but with the planets themselves, and by the same token the objects of arithmetic are not ideas either. [p. 37]

> Even the mathematician cannot create things at will, any more than the geographer can; he too can only discover what is there and give it a name. [pp. 107–108]

Clearly all the three main ingredients of platonism mentioned above are contained in these remarks. (Note, however, that Frege does not use the term 'abstract object' for numbers; he prefers 'logical object', for reasons which will become clear later.)

Another work often cited in connection with Frege's platonism is his late article "Thoughts" (1918–19). As the title suggests, in this article Frege is mostly concerned with the nature of "thoughts", not with numbers. Thoughts in his sense are the contents of judgments—they are what can be asserted, believed, questioned, etc. And they, too, turn out to exist as non-mental and non-physical objects; or as Frege puts it now, they exist in a special "intellectual realm" (which also contains numbers). Thus he writes:

> A third realm must be recognized. Anything belonging to this realm has it in common with ideas that it cannot be perceived by the senses, but has it in common with things that it does not need an owner so as to belong to the contents of his consciousness. Thus for example the thought we have expressed in the Pythagorean theorem is timelessly true, true independently of whether anyone takes it to be true. It needs no owner. It is not true only from the time when it is discovered; just as a planet, even before anyone saw it, was in interaction with other planets. [1984, p. 363]

Our relation to such thoughts is clarified further in a footnote:

> A person sees a thing, has an idea, grasps or thinks a thought. When he grasps or thinks a thought he does not create it but only comes to stand in a certain relation to what already existed—a different relation from seeing a thing or having an idea. (*ibid*)

For Frege the "first realm" is the universe of physical objects, existing in space-time; to it we have access through sense perception. The "second realm" is our psychological world (or worlds), i.e., each person's subjective world of ideas, feelings, and thinking processes; our access here is through direct awareness and introspection. Finally, there is a "third realm", to be contrasted with the earlier two; it contains thoughts and numbers (maybe more). This third realm is, presumably, analogous to Plato's realm of forms; thus the use of the term 'platonism' (in the secondary literature, not by Frege himself).

The Metaphysical Platonist Picture. Unfortunately, many debates about platonism—and thus also about Frege—remain content with vague, general characterizations of it, such as that quoted above.[3] In other words, they rely on rather brief descriptions of platonism, mostly in terms of a few metaphors. Typically, the following kinds of phrases are used in these debates: that "abstract objects", in particular numbers, "really exist", "independently from us", "out there"; that they are not just "created" by us, but "discovered"; that the mathematician is an "explorer", not an "inventor"; etc. Such descriptions are usually followed by rejections (often mere dismissals) of "platonism", and then by proposals of alternative, "anti-platonist" positions.

Now, for my purposes it is necessary to be more careful here, i.e., to pause and ask: Which intuitions underlie these descriptions of platonism, and what exactly is implied by the corresponding metaphors? These questions lead to a first, somewhat more specific and explicit, version of platonism. Since it will be useful to have a concise way of referring to it, let me give it a name; let me call it *metaphysical platonism* ("metaphysical" used here in the pejorative sense of "hard to pin down" and "possibly incoherent"). The core of this view is a simple *picture*—a picture which is supposed to capture what we do in mathematics, in particular when we use mathematical language. More precisely, it is supposed to explain three related phenomena: the *nature* of arithmetic entities, the *meaningfulness* of arithmetic expressions, and the *objectivity* of arithmetic judgments.

Here is the metaphysical platonist picture:

Imagine two realms, namely our mathematical language, proofs, etc. on the one hand, and a world of abstract, mathematical objects on the other. These abstract objects are assumed to exist in themselves, i.e., independently of whether we think about them or not, also independently of what we do and what happens in the physical world; in other words, they exist in a separate realm. Thus on one side we have our term 'the number two', on the other the number 2 itself; and the latter is neither a mental nor a physical entity. Now what happens when we use a mathematical term, for example, 'the number two'? Well, we use it to refer to the number 2. That is to say, somehow we establish a connection between the two sides, a reference relation. Thus, in '2+3=5', '2 is even', etc., the term '2' stands in for the number two; likewise with respect to the other expressions. Furthermore, the truth of arithmetic sentences is characterized as

---

[3]One of the few exceptions, i.e., an attempt to characterize and discuss platonism in a more careful way, is provided by Richard Grandy, in his "A Defense of Weak Platonism" [Grandy, 1977, pp. 359–369]. What he calls "weak platonism" (and defends) is similar to what I will later discuss as "contextual platonism" (see Section III). I should add that I discovered Grandy's article only after I had developed my own views. Nevertheless, it did provide welcome positive reinforcement for me.

follows: '2 is even' is true if and only if the number two (referred to by '2') really falls under the concept "is even" (referred to by 'is even'). Or as it is often put: the sentence is true just in case it corresponds to an actual fact, that is, if and only if the mathematical realm is actually built that way. Finally, our mathematical judgments are objective insofar as they are either true or false, in the sense just explained, i.e., as measured against the initially postulated mathematical realm.

It is important to observe the following three aspects of such a picture: (*a*) In spite of the fact that it tries to be precise and explicit, the characterization of platonism it provides is still more suggestive than definite, i.e., it still relies heavily on metaphors. (*b*) Nevertheless, the picture is presented as an *explanation,* i.e., it is supposed to do some work. In particular, certain metaphysical and semantic notions, namely "existence", "object", and "reference", are supposed to allow for an explanation of other such notions, namely "meaning", "truth", and "objectivity". (*c*) In addition, their explanation is supposed to be completely *independent* of epistemological considerations. That is to say, questions about how we know about the postulated abstract objects are left aside initially; they are to be treated later, after we have talked about metaphysical and semantic issues. (It is, then, with respect to aspects (*b*) and (*c*) that we have gone beyond the "naive" view introduced above.)

Metaphysical Platonism and its Order of Explanation. The way I have just characterized metaphysical platonism highlights questions of conceptual priority, i.e., questions about what, logically speaking, comes first and what comes later. Let me be even more explicit and manifest the *order of explanation* that is implicit in this characterization of platonism:

1. We start by assuming the *existence* of a realm of mathematical entities; one might speak here of the assumption of a "Model-in-the-Sky". This is a realm of abstract *objects.*
2. Then we explain the *meaning* of mathematical expressions and thus their descriptive *use* in terms of *reference.* The reference relation used here is assumed to be some kind of "direct connection" between words and objects.
3. Next, we explain the *truth and falsity* of mathematical statements in terms of such meaning. And we explain the *objectivity* of mathematics in terms of truth/falsity.[5]

But what, then, about mathematical knowledge? This question leads to a fourth step:

---

[4]It is usually assumed to contain functions, too. For simplicity's sake I ignore them here.

[5]What is suggested is, thus, an "adjudication" of our judgments by the assumed "Model-in-the-Sky". The term 'Model-in-the-Sky' is from W.W. Tait's "Truth and Proof: the Platonism of Mathematics"; for a further discussion of such "adjudication," see Steve Gerrard's "Wittgenstein's Philosophies of Mathematics".

4. We postulate some special form of *perception* (or an *intellectual sense*) by means of which we obtain mathematical *knowledge*. Indeed, it seems we have to do so to account for our "access" to the Model-in-the-Sky, since how else could we know about it?

Notice that an explanation along the lines of these four steps—in that order—is what is supposed to give *bite* to metaphysical platonism. That is to say, it is supposed to turn it into a philosophical *position,* as opposed to remaining an innocent picture.

In some of the literature on Frege, in particular in Michael Dummett's writings, special attention is paid to step 2 above: the platonist explanation of "meaning" in terms of "reference". According to Dummett, Frege gives us a *truth-conditional* account of meaning; also, this account is supposed to be *compositional.*[6] What do these two claims amount to? Briefly, the basic intuition seems to be the following: First, take the simple example of '17 is prime'. This sentence says that an object, the number referred to by '17', has a certain property, that referred to by 'is prime'. So the meaning of the sentence is explained in terms of its structure (displaying a relation between '17' and 'is prime'), its constituents (the expressions '17' and 'is prime'), and what they stand for (the number 17 and the concept "is prime"). In other words, the meaning of the sentence is explained by means of an appeal to the conditions under which it is true. (It is true if the number 17 really falls under the concept "is even".) It is this direct connection which makes the account of meaning "truth-conditional". Relatedly, the meaning of the sentence is explained in terms of the meaning of its constituents (at least partly). It is this fact that makes the account "compositional". (Both of these ideas have, of course, to be extended to cover also more complex sentences, i.e., sentences involving logical connectives and quantifiers.[7])

If Frege is a metaphysical platonist, it is easy to see that his position involves a semantics that is both truth-conditional and compositional. In fact, the way I have just described metaphysical platonism displays clearly how both aspects are built right into step 2, i.e., into the explanation of the meaning of a sentence in terms of some basic kind of reference. But notice also the following special feature: In this explanation the "building blocks", i.e., the words and what they stand for, are *prior* to the whole with respect to the explanation; that is, the construction is "bottom-up". In particular, it is thus assumed that the meaning of a word (and, more basically, the identity of its referent) is completely independent from its use. As we will see later, a truth-conditional and compositional account of meaning does not have to have this feature.

To come back to our main discussion, what is most important about metaphysical platonism is its particular order of explanation. The three general

---

[6]See Dummett's "Truth", "The Philosophical Basis of Intuitionistic Logic", and other papers in [Dummett, 1978] as well as [Dummett, 1981]. Compare also, say, [Devitt & Sterelney, 1987].
[7]Of course, "oblique contexts" provide a special problem; see [Linsky, 1983] for a discussion of Frege's solution to it.

aspects of this order to be kept in mind for later are the following: (*a*) According to metaphysical platonism we simply take for granted notions of "existence", "object", and "reference". In other words, these are *primitive* concepts with respect to the explanation. Presumably we can understand them independently of our use of mathematical terms, our mathematical practice, etc. And this independence is essential, since it is exactly the meaningful use of our terms and the objectivity of our practice which we want to *explain*. Furthermore, (*b*) the first two notions in the explanation, "existence" and "object", are considered to be purely *metaphysical*. And the next, "reference", is thought to be purely *semantic*. Using these three, we then explain "meaning", "truth", and "objectivity"; thus, according to the point of view under discussion these latter concepts need, and are susceptible to, an explanation. (*c*) It is only at the end that we throw in an *epistemological* notion: "knowledge". The metaphysical platonist picture suggests, thus, a clean separation of metaphysics, semantics, and epistemology. And this separation is sometimes assumed to be an advantage—it is held that by not separating metaphysics, semantics, and epistemology, confusion is bound to arise.

At the same time, it is this very separation which, according to many critics, also leads metaphysical platonism into immediate trouble. Namely, it leads to the *access problem,* i.e., to the following kinds of questions: How can we know anything about the postulated mathematical realm, i.e., is there really a special mathematical perception? And if so, how should we think about it: how does it work; does everybody have it; is it always reliable; etc.? It turns out that it is not even clear how to begin answering such questions. The above exposition makes clear, I think, what the source of the problem is: we have separated our metaphysics and semantics (the notions of "existence", "object", and "reference") so thoroughly from our epistemology (the notion of "knowledge") that the very possibility of mathematical knowledge appears dubious. Put differently, we have made the *gap* between the two sides from which we start too big. As a consequence it looks impossible, almost by definition, to bridge that gap.[8]

II. WITTGENSTEIN AND THE AUGUSTINIAN PICTURE

If we look at Wittgenstein's writings on mathematics, it is clear that he is opposed to the kind of platonism discussed so far. Both in *Lectures on the Foundations of Mathematics* (1939) and *Remarks on the Foundations of Mathematics* (1937–44) metaphysical platonism comes under explicit and repeated attack. In these writings most of Wittgenstein's criticisms are based on the observation that

---

[8]Paul Benacerraf has brought the access problem into the center of attention in recent philosophy of mathematics; compare [Benacerraf, 1983a] & [Benacerraf, 1983b]. Some people think the access problem is either a pseudo-problem or not a big obstacle; for references see [Maddy, 1984, pp. 46–55]. For a critical discussion of the whole debate see [Tait, 1986a].

metaphysical platonism is guided by a misleading analogy between mathematics and physics. As he argues, this analogy distorts our understanding of the role of proof in mathematics; more generally, it distorts our understanding of the criteria by which mathematical propositions are "adjudicated" in usual mathematical practice. However, these arguments always remain exploratory and tentative in *Lectures* and *Remarks*. And even later Wittgenstein never manages to bring them into a completely satisfying and definite form.[9]

On the other hand, *Philosophical Investigations* (1945–49) contains a different—a subtler and more implicit—critique of platonism, one Wittgenstein also considered more definitive. This critique, or the general discussion it is part of, has implicitly guided my exposition so far. I am, of course, referring to Wittgenstein's discussion of the *Augustinian picture of language*. But before reviewing it let me return briefly to *Lectures* and *Remarks,* for a preliminary consideration of some puzzles about mathematical objects.

The Mysterious Nature of Mathematical Objects. How exactly should we understand the nature of mathematical objects, say that of numbers? And what precisely does it mean to say that they exist in a "special realm"? Such questions suggest themselves in connection with metaphysical platonism, i.e., the metaphysical platonist picture leaves us wondering about them. And Wittgenstein, too, is well aware of them; thus he says in his *Remarks* [1978]:[10]

> Here what is before our minds in a vague way is that this reality is something very abstract, very general, and very rigid. [I, 8]

> [It is a realm of] intangible, i.e. shadowy, objects, side by side with what we all can grasp. [III, 76.]

---

[9]All of this is examined in more detail in Chapter 4 of my dissertation *Frege, Wittgenstein, and Platonism in Mathematics.* For a discussion of how Wittgenstein's arguments change from the 1930s to the 40s, compare also [Gerrard, 1991b].

[10]I will quote from Wittgenstein's writings using the following editions:

The Blue and Brown Books. Preliminary Studies for the Philosophical Investigations, ed. by Rush Rhees (Basil Blackwell: Oxford, 1960); references are to page numbers. [Wittgenstein, 1960]

Lectures on the Foundations of Mathematics, ed. by Cora Diamond (Chicago University Press: Chicago, 1975); references are to page numbers. [Wittgenstein, 1975]

Last Writings on the Philosophy of Psychology, Vol. I, ed. by G.H. v. Wright et al., tr. by C.J. Luckhardt and M.A.E. Aue (Basil Blackwell: Oxford, 1982); references are to remark numbers. [Wittgenstein, 1982]

Philosophical Grammar, ed. by Rush Rhees, tr. by Anthony Kenny (Basil Blackwell: Oxford, 1974), references are to page numbers. [Wittgenstein, 1974a]

Philosophical Investigations, ed. by Rush Rhees et al., tr. by G.E.M. Anscombe (Basil Blackwell: Oxford, 1958); references are to remark numbers for Part I and to page numbers for Part II. [Wittgenstein, 1958]

Remarks on the Foundations of Mathematics, ed. by G.H. von Wright et al., tr. by G.E.M. Anscombe (Basil Blackwell: Oxford, 1978); references are to part numbers and remark numbers. [Wittgenstein, 1978]

Tractatus Logico-Philosophicus, tr. by C.K. Ogden (revised by the author) (Routledge & Kegan Paul: London, 1922); references are to remark numbers. [Wittgenstein, 1922]

Notice, once more, that I have occasionally found it necessary to *amend the standard translations.*

Similarly in his *Lectures* [1975]:

> Take '20+15=35'. One might say it is a statement about numbers. . . . This gives the impression that it's not about some coarse things like scratches, but about something very thin and gaseous. [p. 112]

His general response is:

> A reality corresponds to the word 'two'. . . . Should we say this? It might mean almost anything. [p. 248]

Wittgenstein's first reaction to metaphysical platonism is, thus, to note that it is not really clear what has been suggested; in particular, what does postulating a "realm of abstract objects" amount to? As we saw above, usually all we are given is ambiguous formulas and appeals to vague intuitions.

Now, in itself this is, of course, not yet a strong counter-argument against metaphysical platonism; but at least a suspicion has been raised. We can take this suspicion a step further if we look again at the characterization of metaphysical platonism above. As I pointed out already, the metaphysical-platonist order of explanation starts with primitive notions of *object* and *existence*. The assumption seems to be: it is clear what objects are and what it means to say that they exist—isn't it? Well, yes and no. We all know some *examples* of objects: tables and chairs, rocks, marbles, etc.; and we also know, in some sense, what it means to say that *such* objects exist. But a metaphysical platonist wants to go beyond that and suggest: numbers are objects *like* these, and they exist *like* them. The problem is, then, how to make sense of the "like" here.

If we look closely, a metaphysical platonist tries to do two things at once. First, the claim is that abstract objects (in particular numbers) are objects which exist "in the same sense" in which, say, chairs exist. But what does it mean to say that a particular chair is an object which exists? Well, it seems important that we can see it, touch it, sit on it, trip over it, etc.; more generally, our paradigmatic objects (middle-sized physical objects) occupy a certain spatio-temporal location and they interact causally with their environment (including our senses). However, and secondly, a metaphysical platonist also claims that numbers are *non*-physical (and non-mental); in particular, they are supposed *not* to exist in space-time and *not* to interact with anything causally. But then any initial sense of clarity begins to dissolve; since what are we left with—numbers exist like chairs, yet they do not exist like chairs? It is as if we are given something and then it is taken away again.

Actually, the root of the problems goes deeper here. As we have seen, a metaphysical platonist starts from certain simple and apparently innocent intuitions about middle-sized objects, i.e., intuitions about their nature and existence. But underlying these intuitions are equally simple, and perhaps more forceful, intuitions about *reference* and *truth*. In *Lectures* Wittgenstein captures the two kinds of intuitions together succinctly as follows:

> What is 'reality'? We think of 'reality' as something we can *point* to. It is *this, that*. [1975, p. 240]

And:

> Sometimes what is meant by agreement with reality is quite clear. . . . Collating the
> people in this room.—I may have a list, and I may look at each person in turn and
> tick off his name on the list. "So-and-so, so-and-so, ... The following people are in
> this room." Or "The following people are sitting, the following standing", with a pic-
> ture of standing and sitting, etc. This is the kind of case from which we get our pic-
> ture. [1975, p. 69]

Let me point out, again, that in our context such ideas are supposed to serve as
the basis for an *explanation*—an explanation of what it means for an object to
"exist", for a name to "refer", and for a sentence to be "true". Also, at first
glance this explanation may seem to have some force (at least in the case of middle-sized physical objects). However, when we look more carefully, it becomes
clear that all these intuitions and ideas merely form a misleading *picture;* and
this picture is *inadequate across the board* (as the basis for such an explanation).
But this leads us directly to the core of *Philosophical Investigations.*

The Augustinian Picture of Language. Wittgenstein's *Investigations* starts with a
long quotation from Augustine's *Confessions.* In it Augustine describes how he
learned to speak and understand language as a child, namely as follows: he
observed his parents and other grown-ups naming various objects; thus, he gradually learned to associate names with objects; and then, or after he had learned
to pronounce the names, he used them himself to refer to the corresponding
objects. This is, supposedly, all there is to learning and understanding a language. Wittgenstein comments:

> [Augustine's] words, it seems to me, give us a certain picture of the essence of
> human language. It is this: the individual words in language name objects—sen-
> tences are combinations of names.—In this picture of language we find the roots of
> the following idea: Every word has a meaning. This meaning is correlated with the
> word. It is the object for which the word stands. [1958, § 1]

Later he adds:

> One thinks that learning language consists in giving names to objects. That is, to
> human beings, to shapes, to colors, to pains, to moods, to numbers, etc. To repeat—
> naming is something like attaching a label to a thing. [1958, §26]

Note that Wittgenstein's first reaction is, thus: Augustine's remarks do not
amount to a theory, i.e., a detailed, systematic position, thought through in all its
details and consequences; instead they only suggest a "picture"—the *Augustinian picture of language.*

Basic for the Augustinian picture are the intuitions of *labeling* and of using
the labels as *names.* Augustine conjures up these intuitions by appealing to the
way children (supposedly) learn language. Similarly, the picture may make us
think of language learning as an adult; all we need to learn in that case is (supposedly again) to pick up the labels of a new language, i.e., new name tags cor-

responding to the ones we already know in our old language. However, it goes well beyond a view about language learning—the picture may be taken to contain an *explanation of how language works,* i.e., how it is that we manage to use words to talk about the world.

Seen as such, the Augustinian picture operates on four distinct, but related levels:

(A) The pedagogical and psychological level: On this first level the picture explains (supposedly) *language learning* and *understanding;* and it does so by appealing to how children pick up on word-object relations, namely by "direct observation".

(B) The semantic level: More basically, the picture explains (supposedly) the *meaning of words.* Such meaning consists simply of word-object relations; in other words, the meaning of a word just is the object it stands for.

(C) The metaphysical level: Even more fundamentally, on the first two levels it is presupposed that there is a *world that is in itself divided into objects, simply to be labeled;* that is, there is a world of "self-identifying" objects (and kinds of objects) "out there", and we merely have to put "name tags" on them so as to be able to talk about them. (In other words, we can "fit" language onto a predetermined "structure of the world".)

(D) The epistemological level: Finally, it is presupposed in steps (A), (B), and (C) that we have *direct access* to this world, i.e., that we can "know" the objects in it independently of anything else, through some kind of "direct perception".

Analyzed as such, this explanation of how language works should obviously strike us as familiar (after our discussion of metaphysical platonism above).[11]

The Augustinian picture suggests a rather *general* point of view about language. For me what is crucial about this point of view is, again, the *order of explanation* it embodies:

1. We simply assume the *existence* of a realm of self-identifying *objects* (thus "object" and "existence" are primitive notions). And we take tables and chairs, or people, to be paradigmatic examples.

2. The *meaning* of words is then explained in terms of some form of direct *reference* to such objects (so "reference" is primitive, too). The simple paradigm for how to establish such reference relations is pointing and labeling, as in the baptism of babies and ships.

---

[11]It is debatable, I think, whether we do justice to Augustine himself if we read all of these claims into the short passage quoted (and taken out of context) by Wittgenstein. Then again, notice that Augustine's words bring the metaphysics (and semantics) of the Bible to mind. Compare especially the early parts of Genesis (2:19–20) in which all the animals, having just been created by God, parade before Adam's eyes and simply get *labeled:* "tiger", "eagle", "whale", etc.

3. Next, the *descriptive use* of our words, and the *truth/falsity* of the sentences involving them, is explained in terms of such meaning, thus in terms of reference; and the *objectivity* of our judgments is explained in terms of such truth/falsity.
4. Finally, some kind of *knowledge,* complementing steps 1–3, is implicitly assumed or explicitly postulated. Here the paradigm is "directly observing" things, animals, and people (and thus "knowing" them), as they parade before our eyes.

As should be clear by now, most of my discussion so far has been intended to illustrate the following claim: if we apply the Augustinian picture to mathematics, we arrive exactly at a metaphysical-platonist explanation of how mathematical language is used. In other words, *the Augustinian picture is a generalization of the metaphysical platonist picture.*

One of Wittgenstein's main goals in *Philosophical Investigations* is to discredit the Augustinian picture of language (and various related ideas). And he proceeds roughly as follow: first he argues that it cannot really explain our use of language in general; then he considers the special case of psychological language in order to point out how the picture quickly leads into traditional philosophical problems there; and at the very end of the *Investigations* he adds:

> An investigation is possible in connection with mathematics which is entirely analogous to our investigation of psychology. It is just as little a *mathematical* investigation as the other is a psychological one. It will *not* contain calculations, so it is not, e.g., logistic. It might deserve the name of an investigation of the 'foundations of mathematics'. [1958, p. 232]

As this passage shows, Wittgenstein thinks of his investigations into psychology and into mathematics as parallel case studies. In order to understand better what is involved in this parallel—and thus what a Wittgensteinian "investigation of the foundations of mathematics" would look like—let us now consider his general critique of the Augustinian picture, as well as its application in the case of psychology.[12]

Wittgenstein's Critique of the Augustinian Picture. The core of Wittgenstein's general critique of the Augustinian picture is contained in the following remark:

> "We name things and then we can talk about them: can refer to them in talk."—As if what we did next were given with the mere act of naming. As if there were only one thing called "talking about a thing". Whereas we do the most various things with our sentences. [1958, §27]

---

[12]Gordon Baker and Peter Hacker have also pointed out that Wittgenstein's criticism of the Augustinian picture is meant to apply both to the case of psychological and mathematical language (they speak of "two fruits upon one tree"); compare [Baker and Hacker, 1985]. I agree with parts of their interpretation of Wittgenstein but I strongly disagree with their reading of Frege (as will become clearer in Sections III and IV).

How are we supposed to understand this cryptic passage? The main question introduced in it is the following: Suppose we have put a label (a name tag) on a thing—can that act, in itself, determine the way in which the label is to be used as a name (i.e., the way it is to fit into sentences and the role these sentences are to play in our practices)? In other words, can it determine the *grammar* of the word (in Wittgenstein's sense)? More particularly, can such an act of labeling, in itself, determine that the word is to function as an object name, as opposed to a predicate? And if it is to function as such, how can it determine which predicates can be meaningfully applied to it? etc. Wittgenstein's suggestion is, of course: the labeling of a thing simply cannot, in itself, do all of that.

To be sure, Wittgenstein does not maintain that we, as speakers of English, are not able to point to, say, ships and name them (likewise for properties, e.g., colors). Rather, his claim is that the *mere* act of labeling does not, indeed cannot, bring the label "to life", i.e., make it into a name. In other words, the labeled thing—in itself—does not tell us how to use the label in a language; or as Wittgenstein himself puts it at one point briefly:

> Don't think that you read off what you say from reality. [1958, §292]

To make a long story short, Wittgenstein's most basic criticism of the Augustinian picture consists, thus, in exposing an assumption implicit in it. The assumption is this: by putting a label on it, a "piece of reality" is, in itself, supposed to determine how the label is to be used as a word. Now, having made this assumption more explicit, a more reasonable alternative suggests itself, namely: it is only against an elaborate *background* that naming can work, namely the background of a *language game,* i.e., a whole language and various practices connected with using it.

Early on in *Philosophical Investigations* Wittgenstein gives a simple, artificial example of a language game: that of his famous "builders" [1958, §2 ff.]. The role of this example is to highlight the centrality of *practices* behind any use of words—it is only in connection with such practices that words acquire a determinate use, and thus meaning. More particularly, Wittgenstein remarks (with respect to 'slab' and 'pillar' as used by the builders):

> Now what do the words of this language *signify?* — What is supposed to show what they signify, if not the kind of use they have? [1958, §10]

And later:

> We may say: *nothing* has so far been done, when a thing has been named. It has not even *got* a name except in the language game. [1958, §49]

In other words, without the background of a language game it can hardly be clear what a word means, not even what it *names* (if it functions as a name at all), even after it has been put on something as a "label".

In the later parts of the *Investigations* Wittgenstein considers in more detail the special case of psychological language. In connection with it he uses (amongst others) exactly the same argument we have just looked at (supplemented by some considerations tailored to the peculiarities of the case).[13] Now his main target is the application of the Augustinian picture to words such as 'pain' and 'headache', also to 'thinking', 'believing', 'intending', etc. With respect to these words, we encounter the same pattern of explanation as earlier: (1) Particular instances of pain, and of certain kinds of pain, are supposed to be just "there", determinate in themselves. 2) Thus we can label them, supposedly by some sort of "inner pointing"; for example, we can label one instance with 'headache'. 3) On this basis we can then talk about headaches; that is, we can refer to them and make true and false statements about them. 4) And we have access to headaches directly, since we seem to be immediately aware of them.

Notice that in this case, as in general, Wittgenstein does not deny that we can in some sense point—here point "inside"—, say to a headache. However, he emphasizes:

> When one says "He gave a name to his sensation" one forgets that a great deal of stage-setting in the language is presupposed if the mere act of naming is to make sense. And when we speak of someone's having given a name to his pain, what is presupposed is the existence of the grammar of the word 'pain'; it shows where the new word is stationed. [1958, §257]

And the mistake he wants us to avoid is, once more: to suppose that there is some *primitive* kind of pointing and labeling—*prior* to our ordinary use of language, of self-identifying entities, etc.—on the basis of which we can then give an *explanation* of the meaning and use of our words, and of the truth and falsity of our sentences.

In addition, if we adopt the perspective of the Augustinian picture, i.e., if we grant its basic assumptions, a mystery about the psychological world arises immediately—like in the case of the mathematical world. In this case the problem is not so much how to think about objects, but how to think about *states* and *processes*. That is to say, the following questions arise: What is the nature of psychological states? And in which sense do psychological processes occur? As in the mathematical case, the temptation is now to rely on vague, simplistic analogies to the physical world. Thus, we may try to think of the pain of a person as being "just like" the state of a middle-sized physical object, say its temperature. We may even be tempted to assume that pain *is* a physical state, e.g., a brain state. Similarly for processes. However, this leads quickly to many further questions, since psychological states and processes seem also *different* in crucial respects from physical states and processes. But then the presumed analogy

---

[13]W.W. Tait makes this same observation in [Tait, 1986b].

begins to dissolve again—and we are left with seemingly deep philosophical problems about psychological phenomena.

Wittgenstein is especially interested in the case of psychology because of these problems, i.e., because here reliance on the Augustinian picture leads right into some old philosophical conundrums (parallel to the case of mathematics). Most prominent amongst them are the "problem of other minds" and the "problem of the inverted spectrum". They arise as follows: what is (supposedly) special in the case of psychological language is that the meaning-giving act of "inner pointing" is completely private. That is to say, if I point inside myself and label a feeling 'pain', nobody else has access to what it is I am pointing to (it seems), since it is only me who is aware of it. Conversely, I know what 'pain' refers to only from my own case. But then, as Wittgenstein observes:

> If I say of myself that it is only from my own case that I know what the word "pain" means—must I not say the same of other people, too? And how can I generalize the *one* case so irresponsibly? [1958, §293]

In other words, the problem is now: how do I know that another person means the same thing by 'pain' as me? It seems possible that he or she calls a pleasurable feeling "pain", doesn't it? Even worse, is it not possible that other people do not feel pain at all? Similarly, may other people's use of color terms not be different, for instance "inverted"? Wittgenstein illustrates these questions, and the corresponding philosophical puzzles, in the following graphic and memorable comparison:

> Suppose everyone had a box with something in it: we call it a "beetle". No one can ever look into anyone else's box, and everyone says he knows what a beetle is only by looking at *his* beetle.—Here it would be quite possible for everyone to have something different in his box. One might even imagine such a thing constantly changing. . . . The box might even be empty. (*ibid*)

The "beetle" here corresponds obviously to "private pain", to the "private sensation" of a color, and to similar feelings or sensations.

For the purposes of this paper there is no need to go into more details with respect to these problems. But note what Wittgenstein's general comment about them is:

> How does the philosophical problem about mental processes and states . . . arise? — The first step is the one that altogether escapes notice. We talk of processes and states and leave their nature undecided! Sometime perhaps we shall know more about them—we think. But that is just what commits us to a particular way of looking at the matter. For we have a definite concept of what it means to learn to know a process better. (The decisive movement in the conjuring trick has been made, and it was the one that we thought quite innocent.) [1958, §308]

According to my reading, the "first step", and thus the "decisive movement in the conjuring trick", is to assume the perspective of the Augustinian picture.

According to Wittgenstein, this perspective is fundamentally inadequate (for understanding how language works). And his critique of it applies equally in the case of psychological and of mathematical language. In fact, it applies even in the case of our everyday language for physical objects, states, and processes—since at its core there is a general, very basic argument.[14]

III. FREGE'S USE OF THE CONTEXT PRINCIPLE

If Frege were a metaphysical platonist, all of Wittgenstein's arguments considered so far could be seen as undermining his position. And the two thinkers would be diametrically opposed, as is often assumed. Also, the access problem would be a serious challenge for Frege. However, I do not think that he is a metaphysical platonist—he is *some other kind of platonist*. In order to explain what kind, I will have to direct attention to his so-called *context principle*. Frege uses this principle both *critically* and *constructively;* I will look at each use in turn. But let us begin with the principle itself.

Frege's Formulations of the Context Principle. Frege states the context principle explicitly at four points in *Foundations of Arithmetic* [1884]. First in the introduction:

> One must ask for the meaning of words in the context of a sentence, not in isolation. [p. X]

Then twice in the main body of the text:

> Only in [a complete sentence] do words really have a meaning. [p. 71]

> Only in the context of a sentence do words have meaning. [p. 73]

Finally in its conclusion:

> We adopted the principle that the meaning of a word is to be explained not in isolation, but in the context of a sentence. [p. 116][15]

---

[14]There are, of course, also important differences between psychology and the other two cases. Thus, a form of inner awareness seems to play *some* role with respect to the meaning of psychological words, even if not in the form suggested by the Augustinian picture. Correspondingly, some of Wittgenstein's more detailed arguments in this case (details of his "private language argument") are not transferable to, say, mathematics. I cannot discuss these differences further in this paper.

[15]In the original German: "Nach der Bedeutung der Wörter muss im Satzzusammenhang, nicht in der Vereinzelung gefragt werden." [1884, p. X] "Nur in [einem vollständigen Satz] haben die Wörter eigentlich eine Bedeutung." (p. 71) "Nur im Zusammenhang eines Satzes bedeuten die Wörter etwas." (p. 73) "Wir stellten nun den Grundsatz auf, dass die Bedeutung eines Wortes nicht vereinzelt, sondern im Zusammenhang eines Satzes zu erklären sei." (p. 116) (Notice that I have consistently translated "Satz" as "sentence", not as "proposition" like Austin; my main reason is that for Frege a "Satz" is clearly made up of "Wörter".)

Unfortunately, Frege never elaborates much on how exactly he wants these cryptic pronouncements to be understood. Consequently, it is no big surprise that different interpreters have come up with rather different interpretations. (I will discuss and criticize several of them towards the end of this section.) Given this situation, I suggest that the only way to gain more clarity about the context principle is to look at how Frege actually *uses* it. In other words, I want to look at the *context* of the *context principle* in his writings.

To begin with, notice that *Foundations of Arithmetic* is Frege's most explicitly philosophical work. Its aim is to present his main philosophical ideas (concerning arithmetic, his main object of study). In the introduction to *Foundations* Frege formulates three basic principles which are supposed to guide his whole approach. The context principle is the second of them; the first and third read as follows:

> One must separate sharply the psychological from the logical, the subjective from the objective. [p. X]

> One must keep in mind the distinction between concept and object. (*ibid*)

It is clear, and usually acknowledged in the literature, that these two guiding principles bear directly on Frege's platonism. They obviously have to do with his thesis that numbers are *logical objects* (since they are concerned about what is "logical" and about the notion of "object"). Curiously, the second—the context principle—has received much less attention, especially in connection with the issue of platonism. Yet, in my view this principle, if understood properly, is as crucial for understanding his platonism as the other two.

Frege's Critical Use of the Context Principle. In *Foundations* Frege criticizes a number of other, in his view inadequate, views. One of them, indeed in many ways his main target, is *psychologism;* more precisely, his target is psychologism *as applied to logic and arithmetic.* (Two other important targets are empiricism and formalism.) As Frege understands it, such psychologism comes in two variants; that is, its proponents are committed to one or both of the following two claims: (*i*) Logical and arithmetic entities, in particular numbers, are simply ideas in the minds of people; thus, it is such mental entities we talk about in logic and arithmetic. (*ii*) Logical and arithmetic laws are just psychological laws, i.e., they are laws to be studied in empirical psychology; and as such they are open to empirical verification or falsification. (These two claims have often been held together, but it is not hard to see that they are logically independent from each other.)

What, according to Frege, is wrong with these two claims? Roughly, his two main observations are: (*a*) they misrepresent what our logical and arithmetic terms *mean;* (*b*) they make logic and arithmetic *subjective.* These two mistakes are not unrelated; often the first leads people to the second. Now, Frege thinks

that the first, the more fundamental mistake, can be avoided by paying attention
to the context principle. He even claims in the introduction to *Foundations*
(shortly after introducing his three guiding principles):

> If [the context principle] is not observed, one is *almost forced* to take as the meaning
> of words mental pictures or acts of the individual mind, and so to offend against the
> first principle as well [i.e., the sharp separation between the psychological and the
> logical, the subjective and the objective]. [p. X, my emphasis]

Similarly in his conclusion:

> [O]nly by adhering to [the context principle] can, as I believe, a physical view of
> number be avoided without slipping into a psychological view. [p. 116]

But, one may ask, how does ignoring the context principle lead to "taking as the
meaning of words mental pictures or acts of the individual mind", thus to "slip-
ping into a psychological view"? And how does that make arithmetic subjective?

I suggest that in these two passages Frege has the following in mind: Many
proponents of psychologism look at individual expressions (say 'the number
two') in order to ask, without further ado, what they could possibly mean.
Looked at that way, "in isolation", "one is almost forced" to come up with something like a mental idea or a mental act as its meaning (say the mental image of
two strokes or the mental act of dividing one thing into two)—since what else
could fill the bill? But if one says that such an idea or act is what 'the number
two' means, one has made what arithmetic is about into something mental, and
thus subjective. In addition, one may then jump to the further conclusion that
arithmetic and logic are part of the study of mental processes and states, i.e., part
of psychology.[16]

Frege reacts with the following advice: Do not just look at single, individual
words if you want to understand their meaning (in particular in connection with

---

[16]A clarification about the use of "meaning" in this context: Frege's use of the context principle in
Foundations occurs at a time when he has not yet made explicit the distinction between what he will
later call *meaning* (Bedeutung) and *sense* (Sinn), i.e., between what an expression *refers to*, or stands
for, on the one hand, and what it *expresses*, or says, on the other. Thus, in his discussion of psychologism it is not always made clear what a mental picture or act is supposed to be: the sense or the reference of 'the number two'? — Is Frege himself confused about this distinction in *Foundations?* And
does that create a problem with respect to his use of the context principle? I do not think so. Notice,
first of all, that the blame for the original ambiguity should be put on the psychologistic (even more
the idealist) views under attack. It is they who have obscured the difference between sense and reference, and it is Frege who now clears up the mess. Second, already in *Foundations* it is not hard to
discern where Frege has sense in mind and where reference. For example, in his discussion of formalist views he rejects both the proposal that arithmetic is an empty game, i.e., that no sense is
expressed in it, and the proposal that numbers are just numerals, i.e., that numerals refer to themselves; similarly for his discussion of psychologist views. Finally, as I read the context principle it
applies *both* to sense *and* reference (in *Foundations* and in Frege's later writings). Notice here later
Fregean remarks such as the following: "[I]t is via a sense, and only via a sense, that a proper name
is related to an object." [1979a, p. 124] It follows that if the context principle is a principle about
sense, it is automatically also a principle about reference. (We may also say that there are two basic
principles at work here: (*i*) *the context principle for sense* and (*ii*) *the principle that sense determines
reference.* Taken together they imply (*iii*) *the context principle for reference.*)

number words)! As we have seen, if one does not follow this advice, one is in danger of concluding that number words stand for something mental, and thus that arithmetic is subjective. However, the basic error here does not consist in these conclusions—they are just the symptoms of a deeper error. What is really problematic, according to Frege, is the *general approach* exemplified by this kind of psychologism: to look at single, individual words; to come up with some entities, conceived of in themselves; and to connect the two directly. And the context principle is invoked to guide us away from this general approach, not just from its psychologistic application. (The principle is thus also directed against, say, certain formalists who, after looking at individual numerals, jump to the conclusion that numbers must be the numerals themselves.) —That is to say, by appealing to the context principle Frege wants to cure the disease, not just the symptoms.

If this is Frege's real goal, a question suggests itself in connection with his *platonism.* Namely, is he not inconsistent, i.e., is his own platonist position not another instance of what he is opposed to in general with his context principle? This question is particularly pressing if Frege is interpreted as a metaphysical platonist—since a metaphysical platonist explanation of the meaning of number words follows exactly the same general path as that criticized in psychologism: to look at individual words, to conceive of corresponding objects in themselves, and to associate the two directly. (The only difference is that the mental entities invoked in psychologism as the meaning of number words are replaced by corresponding "abstract objects" in metaphysical platonism. Yet clearly the same violation of the context principle occurs.)

Now, should we really interpret Frege as being so obviously inconsistent? I do not think so, at least if there is an alternative. (The alternative will be to interpret him not as a metaphysical, but as another kind of platonist.) But let me dwell a bit more on Frege's uses of the context principle at this point, since they allow for interesting comparisons to Wittgenstein's views.

More Anti-Psychologism (in Frege and Wittgenstein). If we compare Frege's appeal to the context principle in the context of his attack on psychologism to our earlier discussion of Wittgenstein (in Section II), two interesting connections suggest themselves. First, the psychologistic explanation of the meaning of number terms just discussed results precisely from an application of the Augustinian picture. Thus Wittgenstein's general criticism of this picture applies to this case. Second, and more strikingly, this criticism turns out to be very much in line with Frege's attack on psychologism—in fact, in retrospect Wittgenstein's criticism looks like a generalization of Frege's. I suggest that what we have here is not just a parallel, or a mere similarity; Wittgenstein is clearly influenced by Frege.

The main reason this influence has not found much attention so far is, I suppose, the prevalence of the usual interpretations: of Frege as a metaphysical platonist, of Wittgenstein as an anti-realist, and of their relation as that between polar opposites.[17] On the other hand, it is not hard to find evidence that Wittgenstein himself did *not* see his relation to Frege as purely antagonistic. In particular, he mentions Frege's context principle explicitly, and approvingly, in *Philosophical Investigations*. Thus he observes:

> We may say: *nothing* has so far been done, when a thing has been named [by ostention]. It has not even *got* a name except in a language game. [§49]

And then he adds:

> This is what Frege meant, too, when he said that a word has meaning only in the context of a sentence. (*ibid*)

In other words, Wittgenstein takes his own criticism of the Augustinian picture to be in agreement with Frege's use of the context principle. (In a number of other passages, e.g., §10, Frege's context principle is almost as much on the surface, as we will see later.)

Somewhat more implicit, but no less striking, is a second piece of evidence. Namely, Wittgenstein's own *argumentation* in the case of psychological language (leading up to his rejection of a "private language") seems to be directly influenced by Frege's criticisms of psychologism—even with respect to some of its *details*. As an illustration take again Wittgenstein's well-known discussion of the role of private entities (or states, processes, etc.), analogous to "beetles in boxes", for explaining the meaning of words such as 'pain'. About them he says:

> The thing in the box has no place in the language game at all; not even as a *something,* for the box might even be empty. — No, one can 'divide through' by the thing in the box; it cancels out, whatever it is. That is to say: if we construe the grammar of the expression of sensation on the model of 'object' and 'designator' the object drops out of consideration as irrelevant. [1958, §293]

As I read this passage, Wittgenstein does not deny that human sensations or feelings, such as pain, exist (in some sense). In fact, to do so would be absurd in his eyes. Rather, his suggestion is that in the case imagined, the language game with the private beetles (used as an "object of comparison"), whatever is in the box is *irrelevant*—the beetle, be it there or not, is "not a something" *as far as an explanation of meaning goes.* Analogously, in the case of ordinary words such as 'pain': if we appeal to sensations as completely private entities, then they do not, even cannot, play the explanatory role assigned to them.

---

[17]See in particular [Dummett, 1973]; compare also [Baker and Hacker, 1980] (especially Chapters 4 and 8) and [Baker and Hacker, 1984]. I should note that both Dummett and Baker and Hacker bring up a number of the individual points I make in this paper—but they do not put the pieces of the puzzle together in the right way. (The fact that they don't has always been a puzzle for me. The main reason in Dummett's case seems to be his insistence on the difference between "truth-conditional" and "assertability-conditional" views, coupled with his conviction that the latter is superior. In the case of Baker & Hacker the main reason seems to be their overly strong antagonism toward Frege.)

Compare this with Frege's arguments against psychologism. Both Frege and his opponent are interested in explaining the meaning of arithmetic expressions, say of 'the number two'. Now suppose, along the lines of psychologism, that I associate some mental entity with this expression, for instance, a certain mental picture. Can this association be used as the basis for an explanation of meaning? Frege thinks it cannot, amongst others for this reason: other people may have different ideas in their minds, these ideas may change, and for some such ideas may be completely absent—the box may contain a different beetle, its content may change, and it may even be empty. Also, like Wittgenstein, Frege is here not concerned with the *existence* of the mental; rather he calls into question the *explanatory role* of mere mental ideas with respect to the objective, public meaning of arithmetic terms.[18]

In his later writings Frege adds further depth to his criticism of psychologism. Thus he notes in the Introduction to Volume 1 of *Basic Laws of Arithmetic:*

> If every man meant something different by the name 'moon', namely one of his own ideas, much as he expresses his own pain by the cry "Ouch", then of course the psychological point of view would be justified; but an argument about the properties of the moon would be pointless: one person could perfectly well assert of his moon the opposite of what the other person, with equal right, said of his. If we could not grasp anything but what was within our own selves, then a conflict of opinion, a mutual understanding would be impossible, because a common ground would be lacking, and no idea in the psychological sense can afford us such a ground. There would be no logic to be appointed arbiter in the conflict of opinions. [1967a, p. 17]

In this passage Frege focuses again on a view according to which the meaning of our words are just private mental ideas. Here he emphasizes what such a view entails: It makes all our judgments subjective, i.e., agreements and disagreements turn out to be impossible; there does not remain any "common ground" (any common understanding) from which to arbitrate disputes. (Remember that ideas are subjective, and thus completely private, according to the view under discussion.) For Frege this conclusion is clearly unacceptable. In particular, it amounts to a *reductio ad absurdum* of such psychologism with respect to mathematics—agreements and disagreements are clearly possible in mathematics. His basic diagnosis of what has gone wrong is that our use of words has been misunderstood.

Again, Wittgenstein clearly agrees with this diagnosis. In fact, in his own attack on the Augustinian picture, especially as applied to psychological words such as 'pain', he pushes Frege's line of thought even further. Thus he asks (amongst others): if the Augustinian picture gave us the right explanation con-

---

[18]Frege argues both against the claim that such mental ideas constitute the *sense* and that they constitute the *reference* of arithmetic terms (compare fn. 16); sense *and* reference are objective according to him.

cerning the meaning of words such as 'pain', could we even agree or disagree with *ourselves?* Even that seems problematic. What is at issue here is this: have we (along the lines of the Augustinian picture) been provided with enough of a criterion for judging applications of such words to be correct or incorrect even when applied to our *own* mental processes and states?[19]

Frege's Constructive Use of the Context Principle. So far I have discussed what Frege means by "asking for the meaning of a word in isolation"; and I have clarified his (and Wittgenstein's) arguments against doing so. That is to say, I have discussed his *critical* use of the context principle. But what about the other side of the coin, "to explain the meaning of words as they are used in the context of sentences"? In other words, what does it mean for Frege to follow the context principle in a *constructive* way? In order to answer this question, it is useful again to first look at *Foundations of Arithmetic,* the work in which the principle is mentioned explicitly. After that we will also consider his later writings (where the context principle still plays a role, if somewhat less obviously).

In *Foundations* Frege's central concern is to clarify our understanding of the notion of "number". An important part of this is to give an account of what number terms "mean". If we go beyond Frege's criticisms of inadequate views (as discussed above), his own positive account consists of two main parts: (*i*) He analyses our ordinary use of arithmetic terms, including their use in informal arithmetic; thus he says:

> It should throw some light on the matter to consider number in the context of a judgment which brings out its basic use. [1884, p. 59]

(*ii*) He gives an outline for a formal and rigorous reconstruction of arithmetic, within his logicist framework. Now, two of Frege's direct invocations of the context principle occur in this second connection, i.e., his logicist reconstruction. To quote the first more fully:

> Only in [a complete sentence] do words really have a meaning. . . . It is enough if the sentence as a whole has a sense; it is this that confers on its parts also their content. [p. 71]

And the second, also quoted more fully, reads:

> Only in the context of a sentence do words have meaning. Thus our concern becomes this: to explain the sense of a sentence in which a number word occurs. [p. 73][20]

---

[19]This is not *all* that is at issue for Wittgenstein here (in his private language argument and in related considerations). My claim is only that the line of thought I have sketched is a *basic part* of his discussion.

[20]In the original German the added parts are: "Es genügt, wenn der Satz als Ganzes einen Sinn hat; dadurch erhalten auch seine Theile ihren Inhalt" [1884, p. 71]. And: "Es wird also darauf ankommen, den Sinn eines Satzes zu erklären, in dem ein Zahlwort vorkommt" [p. 73].

Later, in *Basic Laws of Arithmetic,* Frege continues with the second part of his account; that is, he makes his "explanation of the sense of arithmetic sentences", and thus of "the content of their parts", more complete and systematic. The corresponding reconstruction of arithmetic will turn out to be most important for us in the end. However, we should consider the first part of the account, too, since Frege's reconstruction will be guided by it.

Frege makes several related observations about our "basic use" of number terms. For example, in our everyday sentences we often use number terms with the definite article, as in "the number two". We also say things like "the number two is even"; that is, we often use 'the number two' in subject position, complemented by a predicate term—here 'is even'. Furthermore, even if we sometimes seem to use number terms in purely adjectival form, as in "there are nine planets in the solar system", such sentences can be transformed into a form so that the number terms appear again only in subject position, as in "the number of planets in the solar system=the number nine". Facts such as these show that number terms function in many ways like terms such as 'the Moon', 'the black chair in my apartment', etc.—in post-Fregean terminology: they are both used as "singular terms"; in his own terminology: both 'the Moon' and 'the number nine' are used as *object names.*

The following is interesting to note in this connection: With respect to some of these observations (e.g., the first two above) Frege just stays on the "surface" of language, i.e., he follows ordinary grammar. But with respect to others he goes "deeper". Thus his claim that the adjectival use of numerical terms is reducible to a substantival use involves moving from mere observation about ordinary grammar to some further, deeper analysis, namely an analysis of the "logic" of our terms as used in ordinary sentences. A central result of this analysis is: "The content of a statement of number is an assertion about a concept." [1884, p. 59] A simple illustration, one that should also make this result plausible in itself, is the following: the statement "there are nine planets in the solar system" contains an assertion about the concept "planets in the solar system", namely the assertion that nine objects "fall under" it, i.e., are subsumed by it. It is such results about "content" in which Frege is really interested; that is, he is interested in *logical content,* as revealed by *logical analysis.*

Frege's sensitivity to ordinary language in *Foundations* shows again a striking similarity to what Wittgenstein does in his *Investigations.* In fact, Frege's logical analysis, in the sense just described, concerns exactly the "grammar" of words in Wittgenstein's sense; and Frege analyzes both their "surface grammar" and their "depth grammar" (cf. [Wittgenstein, 1958, §664]). Once more this does not look like a fortuitous parallel to me; it is another case of Frege's direct influence on Wittgenstein. On the other hand, there certainly remain important differences between the two in this connection. In particular, analyzing the ordinary use of arithmetic terms is for Frege only the first step towards a systematic, logicist *reconstruction* of arithmetic. In other words, his real goal is a *scientific* one; in his own words:

> Now our concern here is to determine a concept of number usable for the purposes of science. [1884, p. 69]

In contrast, the later Wittgenstein does not have any comparable scientific goal; he aims only at clearing up certain kinds of *philosophical confusion.*

In his criticism of J.S. Mill's views in *Foundations* Frege clarifies further what exactly his aim is: he wants a scientific reconstruction of "pure", as opposed to "applied", mathematics. He accuses Mill of mixing up the two:

> Mill always confuses the applications that can be made of an arithmetic proposition, which often are physical and do presuppose observed facts, with the pure mathematical proposition itself. [1884, p. 13]

As it turns out, Mill always focuses on the relation of arithmetic operations (such as addition) to physical operations (such as the combination and arrangement of pebbles). Relatedly, Mill thinks that there is a role for empirical observations in connection with justifying arithmetic results. In sharp contrast, Frege's main concern is with statements like "2 + 3 = 5" or "There are infinitely many prime numbers" seen as parts of pure mathematics. And he denies that empirical observations can play any role in justifying such statements.

Frege's general aim is, thus, a scientific reconstruction of pure arithmetic. I suggested above that this reconstruction is guided by his analysis of ordinary linguistic usage, especially the usage of number terms in informal arithmetic judgments. But what exactly does this guidance amount to? Frege's analysis of ordinary language and informal arithmetic has led him to the conclusion that number terms are usually used as "object names". That is to say, they are, in a sense important to logic, used *like* 'the moon'. Suppose, then, we want to build that conclusion into a rigorous, systematic reconstruction of arithmetic. This leads to the question: how do we "define the sense of a sentence in which a number words occurs" given that it is supposed to function as an object name? More particularly, Frege asks himself the following question:

> [F]or every object there is one type of sentences which must have a sense, namely recognition-statements, which in the case of numbers are called identities. . . . The concern, therefore, [is] this: to fix the sense of a numerical identity. . . . [1884, p. 116][21]

In other words, the question is in particular: how should we analyze and treat equations, i.e., sentences in which number terms occur on both sides of '=' (the equality sign)?

---

[21]"Es gibt nun eine Art von Sätzen, die für jeden Gegenstand einen Sinn haben müssen, das sind die Wiedererkennungssätze, bei den Zahlen Gleichungen genannt. . . . Es [kommt] nun darauf an, den Sinn einer Zahlengleichung festzustellen. . . . " [1884, p. 116]

As a first attempt to answer this last question Frege considers the use of "contextual definitions" of a certain form (see [1884, p. 73 ff.]). Such definitions were used in the geometry of Frege's time, e.g., the definition of "direction of a line" in terms of the notion of "parallelism".[22] In this example the sense of a sentence such as 'the direction of line a = the direction of line b' is defined in terms of the sense of 'line a is parallel to line b'. Could we proceed analogously in arithmetic, now using the notion of "equinumerosity" (1-1-mappability)? That is to say, what about defining the sense of sentences such as 'the number of Fs = the number of Gs' in terms of 'F is equinumerous to G' (where 'F' and 'G' are "concept names")? In the middle parts of *Foundations* Frege first defends such contextual definitions with respect to several apparent general problems. However, in the end he rejects them, i.e., he thinks they are inadequate for his purposes. One reason for this rejection is that this whole method is not encompassing enough; it only allows us to treat sentences of one particular *kind*. What Frege needs is a method for defining the sense of *all* relevant kinds of sentences.[23]

Frege's next step is to develop such a more encompassing method. Basically it consists of an extended attempt to *reduce arithmetic to logic*. This amounts to the following: (*i*) all arithmetic notions (and all less basic logical notions) are defined in terms of more basic logical notions; (*ii*) the most basic (undefinable) logical notions are determined by means of logical laws. In the second half of *Foundations* Frege first indicates informally how to do (*i*) (at least for some central arithmetic notions). In *Basic Laws of Arithmetic* he is then more rigorous and systematic with respect to both (*i*) and (*ii*): he formulates precise, formal definitions for all the terms used; and he specifies explicitly the basic logical laws needed in his system. An example (and a crucial part of such a reduction of arithmetic to logic) is to define the meaning of number words in terms of the notion of "extension of a concept"; Frege stipulates: 0 (the number zero) is identical with the extension of the concept "equinumerous with 'x is not identical with itself'"; similarly, 1 (the number one) is identical with the extension of the concept "equinumerous with 'x is identical with 0'"; etc.

At this point it may appear that the context principle does not play a big role any more with respect to Frege's reconstruction of arithmetic. If so, it would not be crucial to his constructive project in the end, contrary to what I have suggested. (One may even be tempted to wonder: did he implicitly reject it at this point, together with the "contextual definitions" mentioned?) On the other hand,

---

[22]For some interesting historical remarks, compare here [Wilson, 1992, pp. 149–180].

[23]For instance, the method cannot be used with respect to defining the sense of 'the number 9 = Julius Caesar' (the so-called "Julius Caesar problem"). It also cannot be used for sentences such as '17 is prime' (a sentence of pure arithmetic). Notice that these are two *different* kinds of examples. (Thus, it is not only Julius Caesar who poses a problem here, as one may be led to think by parts of Frege's discussion.)

we have already seen that Frege repeats the context principle explicitly—and approvingly—in his summary, i.e., at the end of *Foundations*. More importantly, a remaining question is: how is the meaning of, say, "extension of the concept 'x not is identical with itself'" determined according to Frege? At one point in *Foundations* he says merely: "I assume that it is known what the extension of a concept is" [1884, p. 80, fn.] (cf. also p. 117). But then he adds, briefly but significantly:

> How we think of [extensions of concepts] emerges clearly from the basic assertions we make about them. [1884, p. 80]

It seems to me that this passage is once again a direct appeal to the context principle, now explicitly at the basic level of extensions. Thus, in Frege's mature system the principle still plays a crucial role. It now applies to extension terms; it guides us in understanding their meaning. Furthermore, the principle then applies still to number terms, too—indirectly, via explicit definitions of numbers in terms of extensions. Notice also that in *Basic Laws* the "basic assertions" by means of which the meaning of extension terms is determined are his basic logical axioms (including his infamous Axiom V).

To sum up, my suggestion is that Frege's context principle underlies his *entire* reconstruction of arithmetic, both in *Foundations* and in *Basic Laws*. In particular, it is not, as some interpreters have suggested, an idea he gives up after *Foundations*. And in fact, there is direct textual evidence that Frege did not give up the context principle. He reaffirms it explicitly (in a new, more general form) in the following passage in *Basic Laws:*

> The name of a first-level function of one argument has a *meaning* (*means* something, is *meaningful*) if the name which results from filling its argument place by a meaningful object name always has a meaning. An object name has a meaning if the name which results from filling with it the argument place of the meaningful name of a first-level function of one argument always has a meaning. [Similarly for functions of several arguments]. [1967a, p. 84][24]

As it appears here, the context principle has turned into a more formal principle (as befits the formal setting of *Basic Laws*). But it is not hard to see that this reformulated principle contains the original context principle from *Foundations*. (Just consider the case of names for "propositional functions", i.e., functions referred to by sentence names with an object name replaced by a variable.)

---

[24]In German: "Ein Name einer Function erster Stufe mit einem Argumente hat dann eine *Bedeutung* (*bedeutet* etwas, ist *bedeutungsvoll*), wenn der Eigenname, der aus diesem Functionsnamen dadurch entsteht, dass die Argumentstelle mit einem Eigennamen ausgefüllt wird, immer dann eine Bedeutung hat, wenn dieser eingesetzte Name etwas bedeutet. Ein Eigenname hat eine Bedeutung, wenn der Eigenname immer eine Bedeutung hat, der dadurch entsteht, dass jener die Argumentstelle eines bedeutungsvollen Namens einer Function erster Stufe mit einem Argumente ausfüllt. . . . " [1967a, p. 45–46]

Notice also the following: the first half of the reformulated principle reflects exactly the standard way of defining functions in mathematics; that is, mathematical functions are defined by determining their values for all arguments. Frege's additional suggestion, in the second half of the principle, is simply to say: conversely for objects! In other words, his context principle treats object names and concept names, and thus objects and concepts, in a converse, complementary way.[25]

Conclusions about the Context Principle and Frege's Platonism. I want to end my discussion in this section with some general conclusions about the context principle and its use in Frege's writings. These conclusions will allow me to identify and criticize, at least briefly, some of the ways in which the context principle has been misunderstood in the literature. They will also form the basis for my subsequent reinterpretation of Frege's platonism.

My most basic observation is the following: Frege's various appeals to the context principle, both in his criticisms of other views and in his own constructive project, occur in the context of explaining the meaning of *various* arithmetic expressions, including that of number words. Consequently, the principle is clearly not just meant, as one may suspect at first, to explain the meaning of "syncategorematic" expressions (in Russell's sense, e.g., the '*dx*' in Calculus).[26] It is also not *just* meant to explain the meaning of concept words (and thus the nature of concepts), as has been suggested in the literature.[27] Instead, Frege applies the context principle *both* to concept names and to object names as they occur in arithmetic. He even adds:

> This observation [that psychologism can be avoided following the context principle] is suitable, it seems to me, to throw on quite a number of difficult concepts, among

---

[25]This procedure is not circular in any vicious way, as may be suspected. That is to say, we do not have to start with one side in order to determine the other. Instead, the sense of both kinds of names is (ultimately) determined together, namely by means of basic laws (in Frege's logical system, seen as a whole).

[26]Compare Russell's "On Denoting" in [Russell, 1956b]. Notice, by the way, that Russell has no appreciation at all for Frege's context principle; his notions of "logical atomism", "acquaintance", etc., all point in the opposite direction. (Compare here Peter Hylton's interpretation of Russell as a "platonic atomist" in [Hylton, 1990].) Russell is, thus, a good illustration for what happens when vague intuitions along the lines of the Augustinian picture are brought into the form of a philosophical theory. As such he was probably the original target of Wittgenstein's criticisms.

[27]For references, see Michael Dummett, "The Context Principle" in [Dummett, 1981]. Dummett himself agrees that these narrow interpretations of the context principle are inadequate. Compare also [Milne, 1986] Milne mentions another simple, indeed simplistic, proposal for how to interpret Frege's context principle: that it just has to do with "disambiguation", i.e., with distinguishing the meanings of ambiguous words in different sentences (e.g., of a word such as 'bank', which can mean either "a place to keep money" or "the slope of a river"). Any real attention to Frege's use of the context principle in *Foundations of Arithmetic* makes quickly clear, I think, that this is not what it is about.

them that of the infinitesimal, *and its scope is not restricted to mathematics either.*
[1884, pp. 71–72; my emphasis][28]

Thus Frege's context principle is meant to apply quite *generally,* even beyond mathematics.

Next, Frege's context principle is not, as it may be tempting to think, meant as a defense of "contextual definitions" (in the sense mentioned earlier, e.g., the cited definition of "direction of a line"). In particular, it does not tell us to look at only *one kind* of sentences (e.g., only identity-statements) if we want to explain the meaning of a word. Rather, we have to look at *all kinds* of sentences in which the word in question occurs (or can occur). A related and even more basic observation is the following: the context principle does not tell us to look at *only one sentence* in which a word occurs. It is easy to be misled into this view if one focuses merely on Frege's explicit formulations of the principle in *Foundations*. Admittedly, most of them are in the form: "Don't study the meaning of a word in isolation, but in *a* sentence!" Nevertheless, if we look at Frege's actual *use* of the context principle, in particular in his systematic reconstruction of arithmetic, it is hard to deny the following: he appeals to it within the analysis of a whole *system* of judgments, and thus of sentences. The relevant "context" must, thus, be more than one sentence.

This last suggestion—that we have to understand "context" more broadly than as a single sentence—is both controversial and crucial for my interpretation of Frege. Let me therefore dwell on it a bit more. A good illustration, one that should help to prove my general point, is provided by Frege's analysis of the distinction between "concept terms" and "object terms", together with his argument that number terms are object terms. For Frege both the distinction and the argument are based on a systematic analysis of the logical relations that hold between all our judgments. But if so, then they are based on an analysis of a whole system of sentences, namely all the sentences we can use to make these judgments.

How exactly does Frege make his distinction? And how does his argument proceed? Roughly, there are four steps. (Notice that in each step we have to look at all the sentences in which the relevant terms occur.) (*i*) In *Begriffsschrift* Frege develops his new logic, including a new analysis of quantification. Within it we encounter a basic difference between two kinds of terms: first-order versus second-order (and higher-order) terms. This difference is constituted by facts about which inferences are counted as correct and which not.[29] (*ii*) Next, it turns out that in the applications of logic to ordinary language, object terms, say 'the

---

[28]"Diese Bemerkung scheint mir geeignet, auf manche schwierige Begriffe wie den des Unendlich-kleinen ein Licht zu werfen, und ihre Tragweite beschränkt sich wohl nicht auf die Mathematik" [1884, p. 71–72].

[29]Some examples are: from "for all x: $F(x)$" it is correct to infer "$F(a)$"; likewise, from "for all X: $X(a)$" it is correct to infer "$G(a)$"; but, from "for all x: $F(x)$" it is *not* correct to infer "$F(G)$".

Moon' and 'Gottlob Frege', occur as first-order expressions, while concept terms, say 'is blue' and 'is a logician', occur as second-order expressions. (*iii*) In *Foundations* and in *Basic Laws of Arithmetic* Frege shows (or tries to show) that his new logic can be used for a systematic reconstruction of all arithmetic judgments and inferences; and in this reconstruction number terms, say '7', occur as first-order expressions, while concept terms, say 'is prime', occur as second-order expressions. In other words, number terms turn out to function, logically speaking, like ordinary object terms. Finally, there is one more step, often overlooked: (*iv*) According to Frege, what he has given us is not just a possible reconstruction, rather it is the *right* one (or so he thinks). But if all of this is the case, number terms really *are* object terms, i.e., Frege has revealed their "true natures".[30]

Frege's thesis that number terms are object terms is not just an isolated syntactical or logical point. Rather, it is intimately connected with his thesis that *numbers are objects.* This brings me to my final observation about Frege's context principle (and it leads us back to the question of how to understand his platonism). Based on paying attention to the actual use of the context principle in *Foundations* and *Basic Laws,* one can see, I suggest, that it is ultimately a *metaphysical principle* for him—not *just* a semantic principle, also not *just* an epistemological principle, as has been claimed in the literature.[31] The context principle guides Frege's answer to the question what numbers are, or what their nature is (namely logical objects); and that I take to be a paradigmatic metaphysical issue.

Going beyond the context principle now, Frege's argument for the thesis that numbers are logical objects exemplifies the *explanatory reversal* which is at the core of this paper. Let me summarize the argument again in order to highlight its crucial features. It consists of four main steps: (1) Frege studies the use of number words in ordinary sentences, i.e., in ordinary language and informal mathematics; that is, he studies how they function in our usual judgments and inferences. He concludes, amongst others, that ordinary number words play the role

---

[30]Compare Frege's article "Function and Concept" in [1984, pp. 137–156]; there he says about the distinction between *first-order* and *second-order functions:* "It is founded deep in the nature of things" (p. 156).

[31]For a merely epistemological interpretation of the context principle, see [Haaparanta, 1985]. For a merely semantic interpretation (within the framework of Donald Davidson's views), see [Wallace, 1977, pp. 144–164]. For a (more implicit) semantic and epistemological, but not metaphysical, interpretation, see [Burge, 1986, pp. 97–154] and [Burge, 1992, pp. 633–650], also included in this collection. Closest to my own interpretation of Frege's context principle comes Michael Dummett, especially in his early article "Nominalism" in [Dummett, 1978], at a few points also in [Dummett, 1991]. However, when it comes to drawing conclusions with respect to Frege's *platonism* (its interpretation and its appraisal), I disagree with Dummett in crucial respects. Similarly, Crispin Wright, in [Wright, 1983], comes close to Dummett's, and thus to my interpretation in certain respects (and he develops a more sympathetic interpretation of Frege's platonism than Dummett). But in his case, too, there remain certain differences. I developed my interpretation independently of Wright's. I do not have space to go into more detail concerning my differences with Dummett and Wright here.

of object terms, not of concept terms. (2) This conclusion, together with his new logic, guide Frege in his rigorous, systematic reconstruction of arithmetic. His initial conclusion about number words finds, then, a reflection within this reconstruction: in it number terms play again the role of object terms, not that of concept terms (or function terms); more precisely, they function as first-order object names. (3) Frege grounds his reconstruction in explicit definitions and basic laws; these definitions and laws allow (supposedly) to derive all the usual arithmetic propositions. In this context the meaning of number terms is defined in terms of the meaning of certain extension terms; and the meaning of extension terms is, in the last respect, determined by means of the basic logical laws. (4) Finally, based on some additional considerations, Frege argues that his is, in some sense, the right reconstruction. If so, it captures the "true nature" of numbers.

It is not my intention to defend Frege's whole account as contained in these four steps. In fact, I think there are serious problems with it, especially with respect to (3) and (4) (and thus with Frege's logicism). As to (3): The most basic problem is, of course, that Frege's system turns out to be inconsistent, as Russell's antinomy shows.[32] And Gödel's Incompleteness Theorem for arithmetic introduces deep additional complications. As to (4): We know now, after the work of Russell, Zermelo, and others, that alternative reductions of arithmetic are possible (reductions to type theory, to set theory, etc.). Comparing Frege's reduction to these, it is hard to see why it should be superior, i.e., the "right" reduction (even supposing it were consistent). Also, and more fundamentally, it is hard to see why *any* of these reductions should capture the "true nature" of numbers. In fact, all reductionist accounts assign additional, non-arithmetic properties to numbers; and these properties seem inappropriate in an answer to the question what the nature of numbers is.[33]

Yet, I think that in one respect Frege's approach is still very interesting, even attractive: its *order of explanation*. To repeat, Frege's aim is to explain the mean-

---

[32]It is interesting to note in this connection that Frege gives up his identification of numbers as *extensions* after he has been informed of Russell's antinomy, since at that point extensions seem fundamentally suspect to him—but he does *not* conclude that this forces him to give up the more general thesis that numbers are *objects*. As one piece of textual evidence consider what he says in "Number and Arithmetic" (1924–25), i.e., shortly before his death: "I, for my part, never had any doubt that numerals must designate something in arithmetic, if such a discipline exists at all. And that it does is surely hard to deny; we do, after all, make statements of number" [1979a, p. 275]. Compare also the following (charming) report by the young Wittgenstein: "The last time I saw Frege, as we were waiting at the station for my train, I said to him 'Don't you ever find any difficulty in your theory that numbers are objects?' He replied: 'Sometimes I seem to see a difficulty—but then again I don't see it' " (recorded in Peter Geach's "Frege", in [Anscombe and Geach, 1963, p. 130]).

[33]Michael Dummett discusses some of Frege's reasons for preferring his construction of the natural numbers over those of others (e.g., Dedekind's) in [Dummett, 1991a] (see in particular Chapter 23). For a critique of both Frege and Dummett on these issues compare W.W. Tait's "Frege versus Cantor and Dedekind: on the Concept of Number" (this volume).

ing of number words in a rigorous way. He notices that in order to give such an explanation we need to look carefully at all the sentences, or all the judgments, in which number terms are used. Consequently, he first analyzes and then reconstructs all arithmetic judgments in a systematic way. As a result of this reconstruction, the sense of all arithmetic sentences is determined, in the following sense: (*i*) It is specified, in an explicit and perspicuous way, which roles the various kinds of expressions are allowed to play in arithmetic sentences—i.e., the *logico-syntactic use* of all relevant expressions is fixed. (*ii*) It is determined, in a systematic and objective way, how arithmetic sentences follow from the basic axioms of the system (if they do), thus when they are true and when false—i.e., the *truth-grounds* of all relevant sentences are fixed. But if the sense of all arithmetic sentences is determined in this way, then (remember the context principle) the meaning (the "sense" and the "reference") of number words occurring in them is explained, too—(*i*) and (*ii*) together *constitute* this explanation.[34]

If this is right, what follows for Frege's platonism? It is simply the following: We have determined that number terms play the role of object terms in arithmetic sentences; in addition, these sentences are objectively true or false depending on whether they or their negations follow from our basic axioms; and all the axioms needed are logical axioms. Thus numbers are logical objects, *since that is what it means to be a logical object.* Notice, furthermore, that along these lines the *objectivity of arithmetic* is not explained via the appeal to a simply postulated realm of abstract objects. Rather, it is the basic logical axioms (together with definitions and rules of inference) which give arithmetic judgments their objectivity. And this is exactly what Frege says in passages such as the following:

> My explanation [of number] lifts the matter onto a new plane; it is no longer a question of what is subjectively possible, but of what is *objectively definite*. For in fact, that one proposition *follows* from certain others is something *objective*. . . . . [1884, p. 93; my emphasis][35]

The position we have arrived at is far from metaphysical platonism. I propose to call this new position "contextual platonism", since it is guided by the context principle. My suggestion is, thus, that *Frege is a contextual, not a metaphysical platonist.*

I am well aware that this reinterpretation of Frege flies in the face of conventional wisdom, i.e., the received views about him.[36] For that reason it is probably

---

[34]Exactly the same holds for function words in arithmetic. Note in this connection what Frege says in "Function and Concept": "The first time where a scientific expression appears with a *clear-cut meaning* is where it is required for the statement of *law*. This case arose as regards functions upon the discovery of higher Analysis. Here for the first time it was a matter of setting forth *laws* holding for functions in general." [1984, pp. 137–138; my emphasis]

[35]I will come back to this passage, and to the general issue of "objectivity", in Section IV.

[36]This remark needs some qualification: With respect to my general approach towards Frege, I see myself in agreement with certain ideas expressed in recent writings by Cora Diamond, Thomas Ricketts, W.W. Tait, and Joan Weiner, to some degree also with those by Crispin Wright and Michael

necessary for me to expound it further (in particular, the remark about objectivity just made). Let me then devote one more section of this paper to it, i.e., to a further clarification and defense of my interpretation—and also of contextual platonism itself. (After that I will come back to Wittgenstein, specifically to his adaptation of the context principle.)

IV. FREGE'S CONTEXTUAL PLATONISM AND HIS RATIONALISM

Let me sum up again the main results of Section III: If we examine Frege's critical and constructive use of the context principle carefully, a new interpretation of his platonsim suggests itself. He turns out to be a *contextual platonist,* not a metaphysical platonist. The core of contextual platonism is a new explanation of the meaning of number terms and the nature of numbers, one that is characterized by its *reversed order* (relative to metaphysical platonism)—platonism is turned "upside-down" (or rather "downside-up"). Since my account of this reversal may have gone by rather quickly, I now want to explain it more. I also want to give additional evidence for my interpretation of Frege. And I want to explore its consequences further, especially concerning what one may call Frege's *rationalism.*

I will proceed as follows: First, I will highlight the exact sense in which contextual platonism reverses the order of explanation inherent in metaphysical platonism. Second, I will show how all of Frege's platonist remarks, in *Foundations* and in his later writings, can be understood along contextual lines. Third, I will add some reflections on Frege's invocation of basic logical laws and on their objectivity. It is with respect to the latter issue that, in my view, a mystery remains about how exactly to understand Frege. Frege appeals to "reason" in this connection, a notion he never really clarifies. At the end of this section, I will distinguish two rather different ways in which this appeal can be understood: as embodying *internal* or *external rationalism.*

Frege's Reversed, Contextual Platonism. As I interpret Frege, his platonism starts with a look at our arithmetic sentences, seen as used in a whole system of arithmetic judgments. For him this does not mean just to accept this system uncritically. Rather, he analyzes it, by reflecting on our ordinary usage of terms and by applying his new logical tools. This leads him to a systematic reconstruction of arithmetic consisting of the following three steps (compare Section III):

Dummett (compare fns. 1, 17, 31, and 45). However, I do not think that these ideas have attained the status of "conventional wisdom". On the contrary, interpreting Frege as a metaphysical platonist seems to me to be still the most widespread and dominant approach.

(*i*) All arithmetic notions are reduced to logical notions, in particular the notion of "number" to that of "extension"; (*ii*) the logical notions, in turn, are determined in a system of logical judgments, a system grounded in fundamental logical laws (i.e., fundamental axioms and rules of inference); and (*iii*) these logical laws find a justification in "reason". Seen as a whole, this reconstruction is what determines the *sense* and the *truth-value* of all arithmetic *sentences,* in a rigorous, systematic way. And remember:

> It is enough if a sentence taken as a whole has a sense; it is this that confers on its parts also their content. [1884, p. 71]

Thus, the *sense* and the *reference* of arithmetic terms, including *number words,* is also fully determined in Frege's reconstruction.

What, then, is the *nature of numbers?* Well, the meaning of numbers terms has been defined in terms of the meaning of extension terms. And extension terms are used as object names, in objectively true or false statements. But that means that extensions, as the referents of extension terms, are objects. Thus numbers, as the referents of number terms, are *objects,* too. More precisely: number terms refer to *logical* objects, i.e., objects whose identity is completely determined by logical laws. Finally, all of this also clarifies what the nature of arithmetic *knowledge* is. Such knowledge amounts to knowledge of our explicit definitions, our basic logical laws, and what follows from both. (In *Foundations* and *Basic Laws* one of Frege's main goals is to establish, in a rigorous and systematic way, exactly this kind of knowledge.)

What I have just recounted is how a contextual platonist, i.e., someone guided by the context principle, explains the meaning of number words, the nature of numbers, and the status of arithmetic knowledge. Let me make the *conceptual order* underlying this kind of explanation even more explicit—and thus its difference to the explanation we saw earlier. In contextual platonism we proceed as follows:

1. We start from our *logical laws,* i.e., our basic logical axioms and rules of inference. (They are fundamental for thought in general). The ultimate justification of these laws is understood in terms of the notion of "reason". Relatedly, our *knowledge* of these laws is based on "reason" (ultimately at least).

2. We then explain the *truth/falsity,* and thus also the *objectivity,* of arithmetic sentences in terms of whether they follow from our logical laws or not. In particular, we determine the truth/falsity and the objectivity of *existence* claims along these lines. And all of this is done within the framework of a rigorously reconstructed system of arithmetic.

3. Next, a reflection on our systematic reconstruction shows that number words are *used* as object names in arithmetic sentences, not as concept

names. But this means that they *refer to objects,* and thus that numbers *are objects.* More precisely, numbers reveal themselves to be *logical* objects, since the truth/falsity of the arithmetic sentences containing them turn out to be completely determined by logical laws.

4. At the same time, our reconstruction, being a logicist reduction, shows in what *arithmetic knowledge* consists. It turns out to be just logical knowledge, namely: knowledge of the basic logical axioms, of logical definitions, and of what follows from both.

Recall at this point how one proceeds in metaphysical platonism: One starts from primitive notions of "object", "existence", and "reference"; one then uses these to explain "truth" and "objectivity"; and at the end one adds a primitive notion of "mathematical perception". In contextual platonism, in contrast, the notions of "object", "existence", and "reference" are not primitive; they are explained notions, as is that of "arithmetic knowledge". What is primitive, instead, are the notions of "logical law" and "reason". This is the sense in which contextual platonism proceeds in *reversed order* relative to metaphysical platonism.

Two aspects of the *context principle,* as used by a contextual platonist, also stand out now. First, this principle is built right into this explanation, namely on level three. As such it is a central part of explaining what the notions of "object", "existence", etc., amount to in the case of arithmetic. But that means the context principle is part of a *metaphysical* explanation. Second, this piece of metaphysics is intimately tied up with *semantic* and *epistemological* considerations. Along the lines of contextual platonism questions about what it means for a term to have reference (semantics), questions about the nature of its referent (metaphysics), and questions about how we know about both (epistemology) are all connected—they all find answers when we look at two things: (*a*) the *logico-syntactic function* of the term, i.e., the way it fits into all relevant sentences; (*b*) the *truth-ground* of judgments made by means of these sentences, i.e., their ultimate justification. In the case of our main example: number terms are used as object terms in objectively true/false arithmetic judgments, thus numbers are objects; and our arithmetic judgments find their ultimate justification in logical laws (supposedly), thus numbers are logical objects.

We are now also in a good position to clarify certain semantic issues further. Earlier I talked about the fact that a metaphysical-platonist explanation involves a semantic account that is *compositional* and *truth-conditional.* As I said, in the literature it is often assumed that these two features single out a particular, unique position in the philosophy of mathematics: "platonism". But now it is not hard to see that contextual platonism involves a compositional and truth-conditional semantics, too. Consequently, we have to be more careful here—these two features do not pick out a unique position (at least not if invoked without further qualifications). Some simple examples can serve to illustrate that point.

First, take the sentences 'the biggest prime number is odd' and '$1-1+1-1\pm \ldots = 1/2$'. In both cases we run into a problem if we try to determine the truth value of the corresponding sentence. The reason is that the expressions 'the biggest prime number' and '$1-1+1-1\pm\ldots$' have no reference; thus we cannot put the parts of the sentences together to determine their truth-values. Notice that this is an explanation a contextual platonist can give, too, not just a metaphysical platonist. The contextual platonist will point out the following: The fact that these expressions do not have reference can be proven from our basic logical and arithmetical laws. That is to say, there are well-known mathematical proofs which establish that there is no biggest prime number and that the infinite sum in question does not converge (at least as construed in standard analysis). But then for a contextual platonist, not just for a metaphysical platonist, the meaning of a sentence depends on the meanings of its constituent words. In this sense both contextual and metaphysical platonism involve a compositional semantics. Second, consider a sentence like '17 is prime'. Clearly a contextual platonist, not just a metaphysical platonist, can say: This sentence expresses the fact that an object, referred to by '17', has a property, referred to by 'is prime'. And the sentence is true if and only if the object 17 actually is prime, i.e., falls under the concept "is prime". Thus truth and meaning are closely related, and the contextual platonist account of meaning is also truth-conditional. (Of course, the contextual platonist will add: the fact that 17 is prime simply amounts to the fact that the corresponding proposition follows from arithmetic axioms and definitions.)

There is, of course, an important difference with respect to the notions of "compositionality" and "truth-condition" as involved in metaphysical and contextual platonism. In metaphysical platonism one starts with the meaning of words; and one then uses them to explain the meaning and the truth of the sentence. In contextual platonism, on the other hand, one does not assume that words and their meanings are explanatorily *prior* to sentences and their meanings, or to their truth-conditions. What is *prior,* instead, are our basic laws and definitions. Put metaphorically, in the metaphysical version the way the meaning of expressions is composed and the way truth-conditions are understood is "bottom-up", i.e., from words up to sentences. In the contextual version it is "top-down", i.e., from sentences down to words (in fact, from a whole system of judgments down to words).

Making Sense of Frege's Platonist Remarks. At this point I anticipate the following doubt: Is contextual platonism, with its reversed order of explanation, really Frege's position? More particularly, can one understand all of his "platonist" remarks within this framework? Those interpreters who insist on reading Frege as a metaphysical platonist will most likely assume that one cannot do that.[37] Let me now show in detail that one can do so, indeed that it is not hard. I also want to discuss some further passages from Frege's writings—passages

---

[37]See [Burge, 1992] for a recent, sophisticated reading of Frege as a metaphysical platonist. Characteristically, his interpretation is based on a collection of "platonist" remarks from Frege's writings (all of which can be interpreted along my lines, as I am about to argue.)

which make perfect sense if he is read as a contextual platonist, but not if he is read as a metaphysical platonist.

Recall Frege's most strikingly "platonist" claims (as quoted in Section I): that numbers are "definite, self-subsistent objects", even if they are "not spatial [or temporal] objects"; that "number is no whit more an object of psychology or a product of mental processes than, let us say, the North Sea"; that "arithmetic is no more psychological than, say, astronomy"; that "the mathematician cannot create things at will"; and that we must recognize a "third realm", distinct from the realms of physical objects and of mental ideas. Now, the first thing to note about these Fregean claims is that most of them occur in the context of his criticism of psychologism. Thus their primary function is negative: to signal that his own position is different from psychologism. But can we also make sense of them in a more positive way, in particular along contextual platonist lines? Let me begin with the claim that numbers are "definite, self-subsistent objects".

According to contextual platonism, there is an important difference between objects and concepts. It is explained via the different logico-syntactic uses of object terms and concept terms. And Frege has shown that number terms are used as object terms, not as concept terms. In addition, he has pointed out that we use these terms in objectively true or false sentences. But then it is perfectly legitimate to conclude that numbers are "objects"—as I said, that is what it means to be an object according to contextual platonism. Next, numbers are "definite" in the following sense: we have precise, objective laws that determine the truth value of the sentences in which number words occur. Furthermore, one way to understand the "self-subsistence" of numbers is also related. Namely, traditionally "properties" have been said to be *not* self-subsistent—presumably they only "subsist" in the objects which have them. But numbers are objects, not properties, as we have just seen; in that sense they are then self-subsistent.

For textual evidence that this is exactly how Frege often thinks about "self-subsistence," consider the following passage:

> The self-subsistence which I am claiming for numbers is not to be taken to mean that a number word signifies something when removed from the context of a proposition, *but only to preclude the use of such words as predicates or attributes, which appreciably alters their meaning.* [1884, p. 72; my emphasis]

But there is also another way in which "self-subsistence" is understood by Frege, namely in the sense of "mind-independence". Consider in this connection a mental entity, say one of the ideas (in the psychological sense) entertained by me right now. This idea depends in its existence on my mind; that is, if my mental activity ceased, or if I thought of something else for a while, the idea itself would cease to exist. As Frege sometimes puts it, the idea needs a "bearer", it can only exist "in someone's mind"—and as such it is *not* self-subsistent. But, so Frege, numbers are not like that; in particular, they are not mental entities.

Remember here also that Frege's context principle is supposed to apply rather widely ("its scope is not restricted to mathematics", [1884, p. 72]). As I propose to interpret the principle, it applies thus even to expressions for physical entities. Consequently, if pressed, Frege would explain the sense in which, say, chairs are "definite objects" in exact parallel to the mathematical case: by appealing to the logico-syntactic function of the corresponding words and the objective truth grounds of the corresponding sentences. And chairs, like numbers, are also "self-subsistent": that is, they, too, are not properties, but objects; and they do not exist "in people's minds", but in the physical world. To put the latter point more positively: the ultimate justification of existence claims concerning chairs does not depend on what is true of the mental; likewise for existence claims about numbers.

I hasten to add: this is not to say that there are no important differences between these two cases for Frege. Both the logico-syntactic function of physical and arithmetic object words and the truth grounds for the corresponding sentences are not *exactly* the same. With respect to truth grounds, or ultimate justification, the situation is roughly as follows: The truth-values of statements about physical objects are objectively determined by empirical facts and physical laws, to be ascertained by observation, scientific induction, and related considerations. On the other hand, the truth-values of statements about numbers are determined by arithmetic definitions and arithmetic laws (which, according to Frege's reconstruction, can be reduced to logical definitions and laws). Thus both are independent of what is true of the mental—but in different ways. For textual evidence note, once more, the following passage from *Foundations,* now quoted in its entirety:

> But, it will perhaps be objected, even if the earth is really not imaginable, it is at any rate an external thing, occupying a definite place; but where is the number 4? It is neither outside us nor within us. And, taking those words in their spatial sense, that is quite correct. To give spatial co-ordinates for the number 4 *makes no sense;* but the only conclusion to be drawn from that is that 4 is not a spatial object, not that it is not an object at all. Not every object has a place. [1884, p. 72; my emphasis]

Frege acknowledges here that number words and words for physical objects differ in this respect: while it is perfectly normal to use predicates involving spatio-temporal location in connection with 'the earth', it "makes no sense" to do so in connection with number words. It is exactly in this sense that numbers are "not spatial (or temporal) objects" for Frege. At the same time they are still objects—Frege's notion of "object" is broad enough to cover not just physical objects, but also logical, even (mind-dependent) mental objects.[38]

Such a distinction between physical, mental, and logical objects corresponds exactly to Frege's *three realms.* The "first realm" contains physical objects, the

---

[38]Frege uses the term 'wirklich' to distinguish physical from logical objects. Thus the earth, unlike the number 4, is "wirklich" in the following senses: (*i*) it can be located in space-time; (*ii*) it interacts causally with other physical objects; and, more particularly, (*iii*) it produces effects on our senses, i.e., it can be seen, touched, etc. (Note that "existent", as "wirklich" is sometimes translated, is very misleading, since numbers certainly do exist for Frege, but they are not "wirklich".)

"second realm" contains mental entities; and then there is a "third realm", a realm containing numbers (amongst others). Frege introduces the term 'third realm' in his "Thoughts". In this essay he is, as the title suggests, mainly concerned about certain other "inhabitants" of the third realm, namely *thoughts*. For him thoughts are those things that are expressed by our sentences and contained in our judgments. And as in the case of numbers, the expressions with which we refer to such thoughts function as object names in objectively true or false judgments. Thus thoughts, too, are "objects" and "self-subsistent". (But are they equally "determinate"? From a contextual platonist perspective this leads to the question: what exactly determines their properties and relations—maybe also some logical laws? Unfortunately, Frege never gives us a rigorous answer to that question.)[39]

What about Frege's claims that numbers are "not the object of psychology", that they are "not the product of mental processes", and that "the mathematician cannot create things at will"? I suggest that in order to make sense of these remarks we have, once more, to look at the truth grounds of arithmetic judgments. In particular, we have to consider the truth grounds for arithmetic existence-claims. From a contextual platonist perspective the question to ask is: How are claims about the existence of numbers ultimately justified? Frege answers that they are justified insofar as they follow from basic logical laws (and definitions)—and these logical laws are neither psychological nor physical laws. But then it follows that numbers are neither "the product of mental processes" nor "created" (or, for that matter, "destroyed") by mathematicians. In fact, it does again not even make sense to say that numbers "come into existence" or "go out of existence"; they just exist (supposing that the corresponding existence claims in fact follow from our basic logical laws).

Of course it is true that we, as human beings, have come up with particular *formulations* of our logical laws at some point in space and time. Similarly, one may perhaps be able to locate our (implicit or explicit) *adherence* to these laws in space-time. And it makes sense to ask at what point someone has *shown* for the first time that a certain existence claim follows from our basic laws. But these are all just observations about us as human beings (or maybe about mathematics as a human practice); as such they have a mere psychological character (perhaps also sociological or historical). Crucially, they are *not* observations about numbers *per se*—since they are not about the *validity* of our basic laws and about what *follows* from them. To confuse these two sides is, as we may say,

---

[39]Notice that Fregean thoughts are *intentional entities* (unlike objects such as the moon or the number three and concepts such as "is prime", all of which are *extensional entities,* i.e., have extensional criteria of identity). With respect to the "definiteness" of such thoughts, one may, thus, want to consider the kind of laws proposed by Alonzo Church in his "logic of sense", an intensional logic based on Fregean ideas; see Church's "A Formulation of the Logic of Sense and Denotation" in [Church, 1951] and its sequels. However, there remain serious difficulties with such an approach (well-known formal problems, but also questions about applicability).

a *category mistake;* in Frege's terms, it is to confuse "being true" with "taking to be true". This also clarifies why numbers, just like the Moon and Julius Caesar, are not "objects of psychology" (while mental ideas and thought processes concerning each of them are).

I conclude, altogether, that there remains not much of a mystery with respect to interpreting Frege's platonist remarks, i.e., his claims that numbers "exist", in a "separate realm", as "self-subsistent, determinate objects", etc. Likewise, there remains not much of a mystery in connection with his corresponding claims about arithmetic "thoughts" or "truths", say the Pythagorean theorem: they, too, "exist" in the "third realm", etc. That is to say, both kinds of claims can be understood from the perspective of contextual platonism, not just from that of metaphysical platonism.

Let me now quickly turn the tables. I want to present four pieces of textual evidence which seem to me to speak directly *against* the *usual interpretations* of Frege as a metaphysical platonist. Two of them we have already encountered, the other two are new. First, consider again the following passage about "self-subsistence" from *Foundations:*

> The self-subsistence which I am claiming for numbers is not to be taken to mean that a number word signifies something outside of the context of a proposition, but only to preclude the use of such words as predicates or attributes, which appreciably alters their meaning. [1884, p. 72]

As we have seen, this passage is clear on a contextual platonist reading. But, I submit now, it seems very hard to make sense of it from the point of view of metaphysical platonism. In particular, how are we to understand its last part along those lines?

Second, we have also already encountered the following comment about the non-spatial nature of numbers:

> But where is the number 4? It is neither outside us nor within us. And, taking those words in their spatial sense, that is quite correct. To give spatial-coordinates for the number 4 makes no sense. [1884, p. 72]

According to my interpretation, Frege presents a logico-syntactic observation in this passage, i.e., an observation about which predicates it makes sense to apply to numbers. And how else could we understand it, in particular along metaphysical platonist lines?

Third, and in addition to what we have seen so far, there is the following general remark about "independence" in *Foundations:*

> [F]or what are things independently of reason? To answer that would be as much as to judge without judging, or to wash the fur without wetting it. [1884, p. 36]

But in connection with arithmetic objects we can now observe the following: it is metaphysical platonists (as well as proponents of psychologism) who try to "wash the fur without wetting it"; since they try to explain what numbers are without considering the basic judgments we make about them. And Frege is explicitly opposed to any such attempt.[40]

Finally, consider the following passage about "arithmetic knowledge":

> In arithmetic we are not concerned with objects which we come to know as something alien from without through the medium of the senses, but with objects given directly to reason and, as its nearest kin, utterly transparent to it. [1884, p. 115]

Frege denies here the existence of any special problem about "access" to arithmetic objects. Furthermore, his appeal to reason in this passage sounds fundamentally different from postulating an extra "intellectual sense", i.e., a special kind of mathematical "perception" (analogous to our usual senses). Both observations speak again directly against a metaphysical platonist reading of his position. On the other hand, if one interprets him as a contextual platonist, these things all make sense.[41]

At the same time, Frege's use of the notion of "reason" in my last two quotations does bring up a question, one I have avoided so far, namely: Suppose he is a contextual platonist. Then it is, as I have argued, not all that mysterious how to understand his notions of "object", "existence", and "reference", given the notions of "(basic) logical law" and "reason". But what about these latter notions? More particularly: In which sense are we to understand the status, or the ultimate justification, of our *basic logical laws?* And how is this justification related to *reason?* Indeed, what does "reason" here amount to in the first place? In my view, all of these are questions one has to face if one wants to understand the real sense in which logic and arithmetic are objective for Frege.

Objectivity, Basic Laws, and Rationalism. We have already touched on Frege's views about objectivity twice. First, Frege's criticisms of psychologism is prompted by the observation that this approach makes logic and arithmetic subjective, both in terms of their content (one sense of psychologism) and the nature of their basic laws (another sense of psychologism). Second, Frege himself connects the objectivity of logic and arithmetic with the fact that our corresponding judgments can be grounded in basic logical laws (and precise, explicit defini-

---

[40]One has to be careful here to distinguish between "being independent of reason" and "being mind-independent". That is, one has to separate "reason", understood in an objective sense, from "mind", understood in a psychological sense. In Frege this distinction parallels exactly that between "thoughts", seen as objective entities, and "thinking", seen as a mental process.

[41]So as not to be misunderstood: The access problem, as described by me in Section I, concerns the possibility of gaining access to a postulated *realm of mathematical objects* (a Model-in-the-Sky). I would claim that Frege never takes *this* problem seriously; in the passage cited he even denies it directly. It is, of course, true that Frege wonders about our ability to "grasp" *thoughts* (compare especially "Thoughts"). Still, "grasping" a thought (i.e., understanding it) seems rather different from "perceiving" a number (in some quasi-sensual way). In addition, even with respect to our ability to grasp thoughts, Frege never entertains any fundamental *skeptical* doubts.

tions). I now want to pay closer attention to his second idea, both as expressed in
Foundations and in his later writings.

In *Foundations* Frege makes only very few remarks about objectivity. His
basic view is hidden in the following long passage about geometry:

> Space, according to Kant, belongs to appearance. For other rational beings it might
> take some form quite different from that in which we know it. Indeed, we cannot
> even know whether it appears the same to one man as to another; for we cannot, in
> order to compare them, lay one man's intuition of space beside another's. Yet there is
> something *objective* in it all the same; everyone recognizes the same geometrical
> *axioms*, even if only by his behavior, and must do so if he is to find his way about
> the world. *What is objective in it is what is subject to laws, what can be conceived
> and judged, what is expressible in words.* What is merely intuitable is not communi-
> cable. To make this clear, let us suppose two rational beings such that projective
> properties and relations are all they can intuit—the lying of three points on a line, of
> four points on a plane, and so on; and let what the one intuits as a plane appear to the
> other as a point, and vice versa, so that what for the one is the line joining two points
> for the other is the line of intersection of two planes, and so on with the one intuition
> always dual to the other. In these circumstances they could communicate quite well
> and would never realize the difference between their intuitions, since in projective
> geometry every proposition has its dual counterpart; any disagreements over points
> of aesthetic appreciation would not be conclusive evidence. Over all geometrical
> *theorems* they would be in complete agreement, only translating the words differ-
> ently into their respective intuitions. With the word 'point', for example, one would
> connect one intuition and the other another. We can therefore still say that this word
> has for them an *objective meaning,* provided only that by this meaning we do not
> understand any of the peculiarities of their respective intuitions. [1884, pp. 35–36;
> my emphasis]

In order to understand this passage as a whole, in particular Frege's remarks
about "intuition", one would have to examine in detail his views on geometry
(something not attempted in this paper). However, one aspect is clear just from
looking at the quote itself: Frege does not appeal to some primitive notion of
"geometric object", or to some postulated "geometric realm", in order to explain
the objectivity of geometry. Instead, he draws our attention to our geometric
laws. Thus the crucial line is:

> What is objective . . . is what is subject to laws, what can be conceived and judged,
> what is expressible in words. (*ibid*)

In other words, what different people "intuit" is subjective (it may vary, etc.).
Nevertheless, geometry is objective; and this is due to its laws—it is these laws
which determine the "objective meaning" of geometric terms.

To be sure, for Frege there are important differences between geometry, on
the one hand, and logic and arithmetic, on the other. Still, the same basic insight
about objectivity carries over from geometry to logic and arithmetic: in both
cases it is *laws* (together with explicit definitions) which determine the objective
meaning of our terms; and they do so by making objective *judgments* and

inferences possible. As further evidence, remember the way Frege describes
what he has done for arithmetic:

> Whether, as our attention shifts, we reach *y* may depend on all sorts of subjective
> contributing factors, for example on the amount of time at our disposal or the extent
> of our familiarity with the things concerned. Whether *y* follows in the φ-series after
> *x* has in general absolutely nothing to do with our attention and the circumstances in
> which we move it. . . . My explanation lifts the matter onto a new plane; it is no
> longer a question of what is subjectively possible but of what is *objectively definite.*
> For in fact, that one proposition *follows* from certain others is something *objective,*
> something independent of the laws that govern the movements of our attention.
> [1884, p. 93, my emphasis]

The context here is a consideration about whether a certain number *y* follows
another number *x* in a series of numbers. Frege's claim is that arithmetic facts
such as these do not depend on how our attention shifts or on other psychological conditions; rather, they depend on what follows from arithmetic definitions
and laws.

This leads, of course, immediately to another question: How should we think
about the status of our arithmetic and logical laws? More particularly, in which
sense, if any, are they objective; or what is their ultimate justification?[42] The first
step in Frege's response is this: All arithmetic laws reduce to logical laws; that
is, our usual arithmetic laws can (supposedly) be proved using only logical laws
(and some explicit definitions). Similarly for less fundamental logical laws: they
can be reduced to more basic ones. But then the question becomes: what about
the *basic* logical laws?

All Frege says in *Foundations* about the justification of basic logical laws is
this:

> [T]hey neither need nor admit of proof. [1884, p. 4]

Later, in *Basic Laws of Arithmetic,* he is somewhat more explicit. Thus, in its
Introduction he makes clear what logic can and cannot give us in this connection:

> The question why and with what right we acknowledge a law of logic to be true,
> logic can answer only by *reducing* it to other laws of logic. Where that is not possi-
> ble, *logic can give no answer.* [1967a, p. 15; my emphasis]

He continues more speculatively, but also very carefully:

> If we step *outside of logic* we may say: we are, by our own nature and by external
> circumstances, compelled to make judgments; and if we make judgments, we cannot
> reject this law—of Identity, for example—; we must acknowledge it unless we wish

---

[42]Notice that these are not just questions about the subjective justification of beliefs. The question is
what makes arithmetic judgments *objectively correct;* in other words, what is at issue is arithmetic
truth.

to reduce our thought to confusion and finally to renounce all judgment whatever. *I shall neither dispute nor support this view;* I shall merely remark that what we have here is *not a logical conclusion.* What is given is not a reason for something's *being true,* but for our *taking it to be true.* Furthermore: this impossibility of our rejecting the law in question does not hinder us in supposing beings who reject it; but it does hinder us in supposing that these beings are *right* in so doing; and it also hinders us in having *doubts* whether we or they are right. (*ibid;* my emphasis)

And this is immediately qualified again:

> At least this is *true of myself.* If other persons presume to acknowledge and doubt a law in the same breath, that seems to me *an attempt to jump out of one's own skin,* something against which I can only urgently warn. (*ibid,* my emphasis)

To paraphrase: Biology and psychology (in conjunction with sociology and history) may be able to give us an account of why we take a logical law to be true (perhaps in terms of evolutionary considerations); but such an account will not tell us why the law is true. Logic, on the other hand, can reduce less basic to more basic laws; but it cannot justify the most *basic* logical laws—in other words, it cannot justify itself.

As Frege notes in the passages just quoted, our logical laws have a certain kind of normativity: these laws express how we *ought* to argue, not just how we *in fact* argue. In his essay "Thoughts" he comes back to this very aspect. There he calls our logical laws "laws of thought", or "laws of truth"; and such laws are carefully distinguished from psychological "laws of thinking":

> People may very well interpret the expression 'law of thought' by analogy with 'law of nature' and then have in mind general features of thinking as a mental occurrence. A law of thought in this sense would be a psychological law. And so they might come to believe that logic deals with the mental process of thinking and with the psychological laws in accordance with which this takes place. But that would be misunderstanding the task of logic, for *truth* has hereby not been given its proper place. Error and superstition have causes just as much as correct cognition. Both taking something false to be true and taking something true to be true come about in accordance with psychological laws. A derivation from these laws, and an explanation of a mental process that ends in *taking something to be true,* can never take the place of *proving* what is taken to be true. [1984, pp. 351–352; my emphasis]

And a little later he adds:

> In order to avoid any misunderstanding and to prevent the blurring of the boundary between psychology and logic, I assign to logic the task of discovering the *laws of truth,* not the *laws of taking things to be true* or *of thinking.* (*ibid;* my emphasis)

Thus for him logic is not concerned about thinking, seen as a psychological process. If it were, it would be part of psychology, i.e., of empirical science. But logic is exactly not empirical, or *a posteriori;* it is *apriori,* as he insists.

Our considerations so far have clarified the status of logical laws mostly in terms of saying what they are not, for Frege. The remaining, really difficult question is whether he also has something positive in mind when he talks about their *apriori* nature, or about their ultimate *justification*. Throughout his writings there are only a very small number of remarks about this issue; and they all contain no more than vague, ambiguous hints. We have already encountered two from *Foundations*. Let me now quote them more fully:

> It is in this way that I understand *objective* to mean what is independent of our sensations, intuition and imagination, and of all constructions of mental pictures out of memories of earlier sensations, but not what is independent of *reason*. For what are things independently of reason? To answer that would be much as to judge without judging, or to wash the fur without wetting it. [1884, p. 36; my emphasis]

And:

> On [my] view of numbers the charm of work on arithmetic and analysis is, it seems to me, easily accounted for. Paraphrasing a well-known sentence one might say: *reason's* proper object of study is itself. In *arithmetic* we are not concerned with objects which we come to know as something alien from without through the medium of the senses, but with objects given directly to *reason* and, as its *nearest kind,* utterly *transparent* to it. [1884, p. 115; my emphasis]

Again, Frege appeals to "reason" in this connection, unfortunately without explaining his understanding of this notion more.

These two cryptic passages from *Foundations* find an indirect echo in some of Frege's very early and very late writings. There he does not talk about reason itself; but he gives lists of certain "faculties" or "sources of knowledge", in particular one for empirical science, one for logic, and one for geometry. For example, already in his dissertation "On the Geometric Representation of Imaginary Forms in the Plane" (1873) Frege talks about "our intuitive faculty" in connection with geometry. In his late, unpublished "Sources of Knowledge of Mathematics and the Mathematical Natural Sciences" (1924–25) he mentions three "sources of knowledge": "1. sense perception, 2. the logical source of knowledge, and 3. the geometric and temporal sources of knowledge"; and he adds that the "logical source" is "wholly inside us", calling it also "the logical disposition alive in man". Finally, Frege mentions "an *apriori* mode of cognition" in connection with arithmetic in "Numbers and Arithmetic" (1924–25), another late, unpublished manuscript.[43]

All these remarks, like Frege's claims about the *apriori* nature of arithmetic and logic, have a rather *rationalist* sound to them. They suggest a connection from Frege to Kant, to Leibniz, or even further back (maybe all the way to Plato). Thus, in various of his writings Leibniz already discussed various

---

[43]See Gottlob Frege, CP, p. 1, and PW, pp. 267, 269, and 275–277, respectively.

"sources of truth"; and both for Leibniz and Kant our knowledge of logic and arithmetic is *apriori*. More particularly, Frege could have agreed with the following passage from Kant's *Logic*:[44]

> In logic we do not want to know how the understanding is and thinks and how it hitherto has proceeded in thinking, but how it *ought* to proceed in thinking. Logic must teach us the *correct* use of the understanding, i.e., that in which it is in *agreement with itself*. [Kant, 1988, p. 16; my emphasis]

Here Kant, like Frege, notices the normativity of logical laws. And what he says about "the understanding" might be closely related to some Fregean remarks about "reason" and "arithmetic knowledge". However, I should be cautious with respect to such comparisons. For one thing, it is not easy to be clear about what Kant means by the understanding being "in agreement with itself". Furthermore, Frege's, Kant's, and Leibniz's notions of "reason", "logic", etc., are not exactly the same. Still, it is interesting to note that Frege uses their rationalist terminology in this whole connection.[45]

Internal versus External Rationalism (and Platonism about Laws). Is there anything else one can say about Frege's (if not Kant's and Leibniz's) understanding of "reason", in spite of the scarcity of remarks about it in his writings? One possibility is, of course, to conclude that Frege simply did not have any further, i.e., clearer and more definite, understanding of this notion. In other words, maybe "reason" was a concept at the limits of what he thought about. Yet, just to say that is not very satisfying—it amounts to no more than giving up at this point. Let me then take one brief stab at what Frege *could* have meant. A distinction between two opposite possibilities should be helpful here: according to the first possibility reason is *internal,* according to the second it is *external.*

First, some remarks about reason as internal. According to this alternative, what "reason" deals with is constituted by nothing more than our system of logical laws itself (say higher-order quantificational logic, as clarified and made explicit by Frege in his main writings). Consequently, all justifications of logical and arithmetic judgments can only appeal to what one can do "within" this system, not to anything "outside" it. The justification for all non-basic logical or arithmetic judgments is then simply the fact that they follow from our basic

---

[44]See [Kant, 1988]; in connection with Leibniz compare, say, his short papers "Primary Truths" and "The Source of Contingent Truths" in [Leibniz, 1989].

[45]I owe the quote from Kant's *Logic* to Cora Diamond (see [Diamond, 1991] Introduction II, p. 29). Let me add that I think it would be well worth clarifying Frege's relation to Kant (and Leibniz) further. For some first steps in this direction compare [Sluga, 1980], [Gabriel, 1986], [De Pierris, 1988], and [Weiner, 1990]. Note in this connection that there are some similarities between my interpretation of Frege's platonism and Joan Weiner's. However, unlike me she does not focus on his use of the context principle.

logical laws. Furthermore, concerning a basic law of logic we can talk about justification only in a weak, degenerate sense: the sense that it fits consistently into our system of judgments (a system constituted in part by this very law). Let me call this view about reason, justification, and objectivity *internal rationalism*.

I think there is an attractive line of thought leading to the conclusion that Frege was, at least implicitly, an internal rationalist. Notice, first, that it seems plausible in itself to assume that justification always presupposes some background of logical laws; since what could be meant by "justification" if there were no such laws to appeal to at all? Next, it also seems plausible (at least to me) that there is no real alternative to the particular system of logical laws we have now; and Frege would be the first to agree.[46] Furthermore, if this is so, it seems unnecessary to mention our logical system all the time when talking about justification; indeed, it would be quite tedious. But then the fact that Frege fails to make this system explicit becomes understandable: he just assumes it as the fixed background. Finally, and most importantly, it also becomes possible to make sense of some otherwise quite obscure Fregean claims. In particular, consider his thesis that our basic logical laws "neither need nor admit of proof". If we simply assume our usual system of logic as the "background logic", then these laws really do not need a proof; they are just a constitutive part of the underlying system. And they admit only a degenerate proof, namely the one-line proof of stating them as axioms (assuming here that the basic laws under consideration are logically independent from each other, which is partly what makes them "basic").

What is the alternative to such an "internal" interpretation? Well, one may want to suggest that Frege's appeal to reason is an appeal to something "beyond", or "outside of", our usual system of logic, i.e., an appeal to something *external*. This would mean that justification in logic and arithmetic proceeds by relying on some kind of "external measure", something that allows us to decide which logical and arithmetic laws are correct—even in the case of basic laws. Let me call the corresponding view *external rationalism*.

The problem with external rationalism is immediately that it is hard to specify what this "something", the "external measure", could possibly be. Note that for Frege it cannot reduce to empirical facts, e.g., facts about the way we, as human beings, think (given the ways in which he criticizes psychologism). Likewise, it cannot consist in the success of our usual ways of thinking, or similar pragmatic considerations (although Frege does not deny such success). Furthermore, Frege never appeals to God, a *deus ex machina,* in connection with justifying logic and arithmetic, as rationalists like Descartes might do. But what else remains? One may have the vague intuition of some ghostly "structure of

---

[46]Frege did not know about intuitionist, quantum-mechanical, and other recent proposals for "alternative logics"; thus it would be anachronistic to demand from him their consideration. Furthermore, it is questionable whether these proposals really provide an alternative framework; compare here [Tait, 1983, pp. 173–95].

thought" against which the way we reason can be measured. In other words, one may be led to some kind of *metaphysical platonism about laws,* i.e., the assumption that basic logical laws "exist" somewhere "outside"—an assumption that is supposed to explain the objectivity of logic in some deep way. However, is this not again just a misleading picture, in fact as misleading as the platonist picture about objects discussed in Section I?

This last remark suggests a more general similarity between external rationalism and metaphysical platonism, as discussed earlier. Not only do both of these views appear to rely on vague intuitions, i.e., mere pictures, they also share the following feature: they both involve the appeal to something *transcendent,* i.e., something that goes beyond what we say and how we argue—indeed, something by means of which what we say and how we argue can be *adjudicated.* In other words, both appeal to some "transcendent measure of correctness". Internal rationalism and contextual platonism, on the other hand, do not appeal to any such measure; they both stick to what is *immanent.*[47]

Is Frege an internal or an external rationalist? I have argued (and am convinced) that he is a contextual, not a metaphysical, platonist about objects. But I can only wish that he is an internal, not an external, rationalist, and in particular not a metaphysical platonist about laws; since then his position would be clearer (and more acceptable) to me. Unfortunately, I cannot point to much textual evidence to support this interpretation. Then again, there is not much evidence for *any* interpretation in this connection. In addition, even if someone insisted that sometimes, say in his article "Thoughts", Frege "sounded" like more than an internal rationalist, the following question would remain: In which clear, positive sense could "laws of thought" be a "transcendent measure" of correctness for logic and arithmetic? If there is no such sense, my reaction is: why burden Frege with a view that it seems impossible to substantiate?[48]

V. WITTGENSTEIN'S EXTENSION OF THE CONTEXT PRINCIPLE

Wittgenstein is directly opposed to metaphysical platonism, as we saw earlier. And he is not exactly a contextual platonist either, as we will see now. At the same time, he is fundamentally sympathetic to Frege's *context principle.* In Sec-

---

[47]It does not follow that from an immanent perspective any criticism of what we have done in logic and arithmetic so far is impossible. But such criticism can only rely on *internal criteria,* e.g., consistency, clarity, scope, coherence, and usefulness. For an internal rationalist and contextual platonist there is nothing to appeal to beyond these well-known criteria.

[48]My own view is that external rationalism, especially in the form of metaphysical platonism about laws, is *not coherent* in the end, i.e., that it cannot be spelled out in any substantive, non-question-begging way. However, I will not try to defend this view here. Note that at certain points in [Burge, 1992], Burge seems to attribute something like metaphysical platonism about *laws* to Frege; thus he says (p. 645, end of fn. 16): "Frege sees the whole logical structure, not just objects, in a Platonic fashion". Unfortunately, he does not clarify much what this is supposed to mean.

tion II we already discussed Wittgenstein's critical use of that principle. More particularly, we studied the way in which his criticism of the Augustinian picture is an extension of Frege's criticism of certain psychologistic views. But Wittgenstein, like Frege, also uses the context principle in a more constructive way; and in doing so he clarifies it further and extends its range of application. I now want to consider this constructive use—in its general form and with respect to the particular cases of psychology and mathematics. This will lead us to Wittgenstein's notions of *grammar* and *criterion;* and it will lead us to my thesis that he can be seen as a *grammatical realist* (at least with respect to psychology).

The Context Principle and the Notion of Grammar. With respect to Wittgenstein my focus in this paper is on his later writings, in particular on *Philosophical Investigations.* However, the context principle comes up already in earlier texts, at a number of places. In fact, positive considerations of Frege's principle occur in almost all of Wittgenstein's writings, from the *Tractatus* all the way to *Last Writings.* It is interesting to compare his most striking reiterations and reformulations of the principle.

Recall, first, Frege's two main formulations of the context principle:

> One must ask for the meaning of words in the context of sentences, not in isolation. [1884, p. X; similarly on p. 116]

> Only in the context of a sentence do words have meaning. [1884, p. 73; also on p. 71]

Now consider the following sequence of remarks in Wittgenstein's writings:

> Only in the context of the sentence does a name have meaning. [1922, 3.3] (1918)

> A name has meaning, a sentence has sense, in the calculus to which it belongs. [1974a, p. 63] (1932–34)

> Only in the practice of a language can a word have meaning. [1978, VI, 41] (1943–44)

> Only in the stream of life do words have their meaning. [1982, § 913] (1948–49)[49]

Clearly these formulations are not only direct echoes of Frege, they are also variations on a theme. The theme—the context principle—gets developed further and further by Wittgenstein. In particular, his views about the relevant context expand: from "sentence" over "calculus" and the "practice of a language" (or "language games") to the "stream of life".

---

[49]In the original German: "Nur im Zusammenhang des Satzes hat ein Name Bedeutung." [1922, 3.3] "Ein Name hat Bedeutung, ein Satz hat Sinn, im Kalkül welchem er angehört." [1974a, p. 63] "Nur in der Praxis einer Sprache kann ein Wort Bedeutung haben." [1978, VI, 41] Finally: "Nur Im Fluss des Lebens haben die Worte ihre Bedeutung." [1982, §913]

Briefly, what does change and what remain constant in this development? Most fundamentally, throughout his writings Wittgenstein keeps insisting that we have to look at the *use* of words when explaining their meaning. Thus he says already in the *Tractatus*:

> In order to recognize a symbol by its sign we must observe its meaningful use. [1922, 3.326]

> If a sign has *no use,* then it is meaningless. . . . (If everything behaves as if a sign had meaning, then it does have meaning.) [1922, 3.328]

And what we have to pay attention to with respect to this use, according to the *Tractatus*, is what it reveals about the *logical form* of an expression. As Wittgenstein puts it:

> A sign determines a logical form only together with its logico-syntactic use. [1922, 3.327]

But why is it so important to consider the logical form of a word? It is because this form reflects the logical form of the object to which the word, as a name, refers. That is to say, the logical form shows what *kind* of an object it is for which the name stands. If we look back to Frege, this thesis should sound familiar. In particular, remember that for Frege the fundamental difference between objects and concepts shows itself in the different logico-syntactic uses of object names and concept names.[50]

Moving ahead to Wittgenstein's later writings, in particular to *Philosophical Investigations,* the same basic focus on the use of words occurs, now in the following form:

> Let the use of words teach you their meaning. [1958, p. 220]

Or (as we have already seen):

> Now what do the words of this language *signify?* — What is supposed to show what they signify, if not the kind of use they have? [1958, §10]

Once again, the use of a word reflects the identity of its referent (if it has one). Now, at this point Wittgenstein also insists on another point, namely: we cannot *derive* this use of words from some direct, primitive connection to the world. Thus he says:

> Don't always think that you read off your words from the facts; that you map these into words according to rules. [1958, §292]

---

[50]Of course it is true that the *Tractatus* Wittgenstein rejects Frege's distinction between objects and concepts; in a Tractarian world there are only objects (with different logical forms). Nevertheless, the two thinkers agree, I think, with respect to their *fundamental perspective:* both focus on what the use of words in sentences shows us, since both follow the context principle.

For Wittgenstein—as for Frege—it is rather the other way around: the use of a word is *prior,* relative to its referent which is *posterior,* with respect to an explanation of what the word means. What that amounts to is this: Wittgenstein's writings, from early to late, exhibit the same basic *reversal in the order of explanation* as Frege's (now seen relative to the Augustinian picture in general); and this reversal is again guided by the *context principle.*[51]

However, not everything stays the same when we go from the early to the later Wittgenstein; in fact, there are some significant changes. Most importantly, in Wittgenstein's writings after the *Tractatus* the notion of "logical form" is replaced by that of "grammar". Thus he remarks in the *Investigations:*

Grammar tells what kind of object something is. [1958, §373]

This transition—from logical form to grammar—is at the core of one of Wittgenstein's central moves in his later writings, namely: away from looking at language as a system structured in terms of a crystalline logical "scaffolding" and used to "picture" the world; towards looking at it as a "language game", i.e., as intimately tied up with various practices and deeply embedded in the "stream of life".

Wittgenstein's transition goes through at least two stages. In the first stage, from his early writings (including the *Tractatus*) to those of the early 1930s (in particular *Philosophical Grammar*), the Tractarian conception of language is replaced by that of language as a *calculus.* Correspondingly, the notion of "logical form" is replaced by that of "role in the calculus" [1974a, p. 63]—a first meaning of "grammar". In the second stage, through the late 30s and up to Wittgenstein's mature writings in the 1940s (in particular *Philosophical Investigations*), he shifts from looking at language as a calculus to looking at it as a *language game.* Thus, the notion of "role in the calculus" is replaced with that of "role in the language game"—a second, more mature meaning of "grammar". The reason for this second shift is Wittgenstein's recognition that language does not function mechanically; that is, words do not "apply themselves", according to some hidden rules.[52] Thus Wittgenstein writes later (reflecting back on *Philosophical Grammar*):

---

[51]As I mentioned, in this paper I am focusing on Wittgenstein's *later* writings. For more on treating the *Tractatus* along the lines indicated compare [Ishiguro, 1969, pp. 20–50], [McGuinness, 1981, pp. 60–73], Peter Winch's "Language, Thought, and World in the Tractatus" in [Winch, 1987, pp. 3–17]; and [Diamond, 1991], in particular Chapter 6: "Throwing away the Ladder: How to Read the *Tractatus*".

[52]As W.W. Tait has reminded me, for the later Wittgenstein this is true in two senses: (*i*) Many of our usual words are simply not governed by strict, general rules (see Wittgenstein's discussion of "family resemblance"; for instance, in connection with "game"); (*ii*) even insofar as there are such rules, these do not apply themselves (see his discussion of "rule-following", in particular with respect to "+2").

One would like to speak of the function of a word in *this* sentence. As if the sentence were a mechanism in which the word had a particular function. But what does this function consist in? How does it come to light? For there isn't anything hidden—don't we see the whole sentence? The function must come out in operating with the word in the calculus. [1958, §559]

In much of the *Investigations* Wittgenstein's main aim is, then, to develop a conception of the "function of words" which is less mechanical than that in his middle writings.[53]

Any substantive discussion of how, according to the later Wittgenstein, we "operate with words" has to take into account his various considerations about *rule-following*. (For him how we operate with, say, 'red', 'pain', and '+2' are prime examples of "following a rule".) However, I do not want to digress too much. Thus I will restrict myself to only one general observation in this connection (relating "rule-following" and "grammar"). Namely, for the later Wittgenstein the following three things do *not* determine the grammar of a word (at least not independently from our practices): (*i*) the world, in itself; (*ii*) what has gone on in our minds, or our brains, in past applications; and (*iii*) some mysterious, transcendent structure of rules. Correspondingly, he rejects three kinds of explanations for how we use language (including logical and mathematical language): (*i*) empiricist explanations according to which the world in itself "tells us" how to use words; (*ii*) psychologist explanations according to which some act of the mind or brain, i.e., purely internal "intentionality", is enough; and (*iii*) rationalist explanations according to which everything is determined by some "hidden" logic, a logic transcending the world, what we think, and what we do. (The third rejection shows that Wittgenstein is *not* an *external rationalist*.)

Like Frege, Wittgenstein always sees the context principle as a *general* principle. But unlike Frege, he works out its general application in considerable detail; that is, he applies the maxim "grammar tells what kind of object something is" explicitly to a number of different cases (including that of words for ordinary physical objects and people). In *Philosophical Investigations* one case finds Wittgenstein's special attention: *psychological* language. In Section II we considered some of his critical remarks in connection with it. Now I want to add a brief review of his constructive remarks, i.e., those in which he starts to investigate the grammar of words such as 'pain', 'understanding', etc. This review will also illustrate further his general notion of "grammar"; and it will lead us to his notion of "criterion", as well as to my thesis that he is a "grammatical realist".[54]

---

[53]For more on Wittgenstein's general shift from a "calculus conception" to a "language-game conception" of language, see again [Gerrard, 1991b].

[54]Wittgenstein never defines (at least not in any strict sense) what the "grammar" of a word is supposed to be; similarly for "criterion". Instead, he shows how to *use* these notions by considering various examples. Thus I take it to be important to consider some of these examples.

The Notion of Criterion and Grammatical Realism. As is well known, Wittgenstein rejects "inner pointing" as the sole basic for the meaning of a word such as 'pain'. More precisely, he denies that the meaning of this word is based on some simple act of inner ostention. Likewise, he denies that the word 'understanding' obtains its meaning simply by being attached to a process in the mind or brain. We may say, then, that Wittgenstein is not an "empiricist" with respect to psychological language—someone who thinks that one can just *read off* the meaning of psychological words from the brain or from the mind. But he is also not an "anti-realist", in several senses—not in the sense of denying the *existence* (or occurrence) of pain and understanding; not in the sense of *reducing* such pain and understanding to mere *physical* states or processes; and also not in the sense of reducing them to mere categories of *behavior.* Instead, he says in *Remarks* (somewhat cryptically):

> Not empiricism and yet realism in philosophy, that is the hardest. [1978, VI, 23][55]

On the basis of remarks such as this, I suggest that Wittgenstein is a *grammatical realist,* in particular with respect to psychology. In other words, for him cases of pain and understanding are "real", i.e., they do exist or occur—but their reality (and nature) cannot be understood independently from the grammar of 'pain' and 'understanding'.

How exactly does Wittgenstein think about the *grammar* of such words? Two basic and complementary observations need to be made here (at least). First, our usual *logico-syntactic use* of 'understands' and 'is in pain' is *similar* in important ways to the use of, say, 'is five feet tall'. In particular, in both cases these expressions can be preceded by names, definite descriptions of people, or pronouns. Also, in both cases the resulting expressions can be used in sentences by means of which we make *objective judgments.* It is such similarities which allow us to say that understanding and pain are "states" or "processes". (Wittgenstein also notes that it does not make sense to attribute understanding or pain to mind-less objects. Put the other way around, the attribution of such states or processes, or at least the possibility of such attributions, are prerequisites for attributing a mental life to someone or something'. In that sense understanding and pain are "mental".)

Wittgenstein's second basic observation in this connection is the following: States or processes such as "understanding" and "pain" are also *different* in important respects from, say, "being five feet tall". In particular, there are differences with respect to the kinds of *criteria* used for evaluating the correctness of

---

[55]Wittgenstein makes this remark in connection with mathematics. However, if I am right that his treatments of mathematics and psychology are parallel, it applies equally to psychology. For an interesting discussion of this passage, compare Cora Diamond's "The Realistic Spirit" in [Diamond, 1991, pp. 39–72]. She interprets it in a broader way—but I think our two interpretations are compatible.

the corresponding judgments. Crucially, in the case of "understanding" and "pain", unlike the case of "being five feet tall", these criteria include observations about behavior. As Wittgenstein puts it:

> Let us remember that there are certain *criteria in a man's behavior* for the fact that he does not understand a word: that it means nothing to him, that he can do nothing with it. And *criteria* for his 'thinking he understands', attaching some meaning to the word, but not the right one. And, lastly, *criteria* for his understanding the word right. [1958, §269; my emphasis]

Passages such as this show that for Wittgenstein the correct use, and thus the meaning, of 'understanding' is somehow intimately connected with certain kinds of behavior. However, having noticed this connection, we must immediately resist the temptation to think that it amounts to a *reduction*—it does *not* for Wittgenstein (thus he is not a behaviorist). The main reason is, very briefly, that for him the role of criteria, in particular in the case of behavioral criteria, is not exactly that of necessary or sufficient conditions.[56]

For my purposes in this paper one thing is crucial about Wittgenstein's discussion of psychological language. Namely, he always focuses on two aspects of the grammar of words: (*i*) logico-syntactic facts, i.e., facts about how these words fit into sentences; (*ii*) criterial facts, i.e., facts about how the truth and falsity of sentences containing them is determined. But if this is so, a close parallel to Frege's approach to arithmetic reveals itself; compare: (*i*) Frege's logico-syntactic distinction between object names and concept names, and his related observation that number terms function as object terms; (*ii*) his focus on the truth grounds of arithmetic statements, as reconstructed on the basis of logical definitions and laws. Consequently, Wittgenstein's *grammatical realism* in the case of psychology parallels Frege's *contextual platonism* in the case of arithmetic.

Given my suggestion that Wittgenstein is a "grammatical realist", another possible misunderstanding should be prevented at this point. Namely, according to me Wittgenstein is *not,* as may be falsely inferred, siding with "realism" as that notion is widely used today in the literature; *nor* is he on the side of "anti-realism". In fact, from the point of view developed here the usual opposition of "realism versus anti-realism" reveals itself as rather *misleading* (and to call Wittgenstein a "grammatical realist" is intended to point in a different direction,

---

[56]For more on "criteria", including their difference to necessary and sufficient conditions, compare [Baker and Hacker, 1980]. Notice that with his use of the notion of "criterion" Wittgenstein clearly goes *beyond* Frege. In fact, I think that here we have reached an important point where the two thinkers begin to *differ* in their views—Wittgenstein's notion of "criterion" leads to a kind of *anti-reductionism* (in particular in the case of psychology) that is quite foreign to Frege's general reductionist tendencies (as exhibited mostly in the case of arithmetic). It would be worth exploring this difference further, but I cannot do so in this paper. (In retrospect, I think that this divergence may well be more important than the two "remaining differences" discussed later in this section.)

one orthogonal to the realism-vs.-antirealism dichotomy). Notice in this connection what Wittgenstein says about the case of mathematics in his *Lectures:*

> [We get into] queer trouble: one asks such a thing as what mathematics is about—and someone replies that it is about numbers. Then someone comes along and says that it is not about numbers but about numerals; for numbers seem very mysterious things. And then it seems that mathematical propositions are about scratches on the blackboard. That must seem ridiculous even to those who hold it. [1975, p. 112]

As I read this passage, Wittgenstein distances himself in it *both* from metaphysical platonism *and* from its opposites, e.g., from simple kinds of formalism. At other points he discusses such formalist views also under the name of 'finitism' (thereby misusing the latter term somewhat); and he compares finitism to "behaviorism" in psychology. Thus he writes in his *Remarks:*

> Finitism and behaviorism are quite similar trends. Both say, but surely, all we have here is. . . . Both deny the existence of something, both with a view to escaping from a confusion. [1978, II, 61.]

Similarly in his *Lectures,* now in a more critical and categorical tone:

> Hence we want to see the absurdities both of what the finitists say and of what their opponents say—just as we want in philosophy to see the absurdities both of what the behaviorists say and of what their opponents say. Finitism and behaviorism are as alike as two eggs. The same absurdities, and the same kind of answer. Both sides of such disputes are based on a particular kind of misunderstanding—which arises from gazing at a form of words and forgetting to ask yourself what's done with it, or from gazing into your own soul to see if two expressions have the same meaning, and such things. [1975, p. 111]

Wittgenstein's position is, thus: Both "finitism" and "behaviorism" are attempts to "escape from a confusion". Namely, finitism attempts to avoid metaphysical platonism (and thus the "access problem" and questions about the "mysterious nature" of numbers); behaviorism attempts to avoid certain forms of psychologism and dualism (with their corresponding problems about "privacy" and questions about the "mysterious nature" of mental states). But both finitism and behaviorism are themselves still based on a fundamental "misunderstanding"—in fact, as much so as the views to which they are opposed.

The source of this misunderstanding is, in Wittgenstein's view, that most philosophers involved in these debates (formalism *versus* platonism, behaviorism *versus* dualism, etc.) have been careless with respect to the way they think about the meaning of words. In particular, they have neglected to look carefully at "what's done with words". Consequently, they have gotten stuck in simplistic dogmas. As Wittgenstein puts it in the *Investigations* (now very generally):

> For this is what disputes between Idealists, Solipsists and Realists look like. The ones attack the normal form of expression as if they were attacking a statement; the

others defend it, as if they were stating facts recognized by every reasonable human being. [1958, §402]

And he proposes the following way out:

What we have to do is to accept the everyday language game and to note false accounts of the matter as false. [1958, p. 200]

One thing I have done in this paper is to look in some detail at Wittgenstein's (and Frege's) criticisms of "false accounts" of the matter, especially in the cases of our psychological and mathematical language games. But I have also pointed out some positive results. In other words, Wittgenstein's (and Frege's) investigations into the grammar of words go beyond just "accepting the everyday language games"—they help us to understand these language games better (at least with respect to some of their philosophical aspects).

Remaining Differences between Frege and Wittgenstein. So far I have argued that Wittgenstein's philosophical perspective agrees with Frege's in a fundamental way, namely with respect to the context principle and the corresponding reversal of metaphysics. In this sense the simple opposition between Frege the "arch-platonist" and Wittgenstein the radical "anti-realist" turns out to be inadequate and misleading. Nevertheless, clearly Wittgenstein does not agree with Frege on *everything*. In order to avoid the misunderstanding that this is what I am suggesting, let me add a few remarks about remaining *differences* between them. I will mention two in particular: (*i*) In his later writings Wittgenstein calls into question the usefulness and coherence of any strong notion of *meaning*—including Frege's notion of "sense" or "thought"; (*ii*) he proposes a view of logic and arithmetic as mere collections of *techniques*—not, like Frege, as systems of truths.

First to "meaning"; already in the *Blue Book* (1934–35) Wittgenstein remarks critically:

Frege ridiculed the formalist conception of mathematics by saying that the formalists confused the unimportant thing, the sign, with the important, the meaning. Surely, one wishes to say, mathematics does not treat of dashes on a bit of paper. Frege's idea could be expressed thus: the propositions of mathematics, if they were just complexes of dashes, would be dead and utterly uninteresting, whereas they obviously have a kind of life. And the same, of course, could be said of any proposition: Without a sense, or without the thought, a proposition would be an utterly dead and trivial thing. And further it seems clear that no adding of inorganic signs can make the proposition live. And the conclusion which one draws from this is that what must be added to the dead sign in order to make a live proposition is something immaterial, with properties different from all mere signs. But if we had to name anything which is the life of the sign, we should have to say that it was its *use*. [1960, p. 4]

He clarifies what he is opposed to as follows:

> The mistake we are liable to make could be expressed thus: We are looking for the use of the sign, but we look for it as though it were an object *co-existing* with the sign. [1960, p. 5]

And he adds:

> As a part of the system of language, one may say, the sentence has life. But one is tempted to imagine that which gives the sentence life as something in an occult sphere, accompanying the sentence. (*ibid*)

On the surface what Wittgenstein rejects here is any postulation of an "occult sphere" of "meanings" (parallel to the realm of "abstract objects" in metaphysical platonism). On closer inspection it becomes clear that what he is primarily concerned about is the postulation of a notion of "meaning" (or "sense", "thought") according to which the meaning of words is *independent* from, or *prior* to, their use.

If there was such an independent notion of "meaning", we could explain and adjudicate our usual use of words by means of it. In other words, we would have an *external motivation and measure* for this use (and thus, presumably, for logic and arithmetic). But, so Wittgenstein, isn't this idea just an illusion? Or as he puts it in *Philosophical Investigations,* is appealing to such "meaning" not "turning a knob not connected to the mechanism"? (see [1958, §270]). Notice here that if Frege was an *external rationalist,* he would be guilty of exactly this mistake with respect to "senses" or "thoughts". In the passages above Wittgenstein seems to interpret him as such.

But even if he took Frege's notion of "thought" or "sense" as not being so strong, i.e., even if he took it as not so independent from use, Wittgenstein would still be opposed to it. There are several reasons for this further opposition; let me briefly mention three: First, in most cases we do not have clear and strict enough *criteria of identity* for such "senses". Second, too much of a reification of "senses" obscures the strong *context-sensitivity* of linguistic meaning. And third, even if we assume the first two problems to be not so decisive, the appeal to "senses" just does not *explain* much. Put differently, the more we recognize the lack of clear identity conditions for "thoughts", their context dependency, and similar phenomena, the less is left to be explained by them. Consequently, Wittgenstein urges: why not give up the notion of "thought" or "sense"; why not talk directly about "use"? It seems that for most purposes talk about "use" is all one needs; and such talk is much less prone to lead into empty philosophical puzzles.

A second remaining disagreement between Wittgenstein and Frege concerns the question whether logic and arithmetic should be seen as collections of *propositions* or not. Frege defends the view that they should, most explicitly in his article "Thoughts". In his terminology, the question is whether logic and arithmetic are "sciences", i.e., bodies of substantive "truths"; and his answer is affirmative. Wittgenstein proposes instead: logic and arithmetic are mere collections of *techniques*. Crucially, such techniques cannot be said to be either true or false; they are just more or less useful (in a variety of ways).

The general background to this counter-proposal is worked out in Wittgenstein's *Philosophical Investigations*. There he points out the countless ways in which we use language: "Giving orders, and obeying them; describing the appearance of an object; . . . reporting an event; . . . forming and testing a hypothesis; . . . making up a story; . . . asking, thanking, cursing, greeting, praying" [1958, §23]. He calls this a "multiplicity of language games". And immediately before giving this list he explains:

> But how many kinds of sentences are there? Say assertion, question, and command? — There are *countless* kinds: countless different kinds of use of what we call "symbols", "words", "sentences". And this multiplicity is not something fixed, given once and for all; but new types of language, new language games, as we may say, come into existence, and others become obsolete and get forgotten. (We can get a *rough picture* of this from the changes in mathematics.) Here the term "language game" is meant to bring into prominence the fact that the speaking of language is part of an activity, or of a form of life. [1958, §23]

Immediately after it he adds:

> It is interesting to compare the multiplicity of the tools in language and of the ways they are used, the multiplicity of kinds of word and sentence, with what logicians have said about the structure of language. (Including the author of the *Tractatus Logico-Philosophicus*.) (*ibid*)

The "logicians" here include Frege, Russell, and the Wittgenstein of the *Tractatus*. These thinkers have only paid attention to language as a means for making assertions, in particular in the cases of logic and arithmetic. And combined with Frege's notion of "sense" or "thought," such attention leads directly to viewing mathematics as a body of truths.

As indicated, Wittgenstein suggest instead to think of mathematical sentences as expressing techniques. Relatedly, he sometimes likens mathematical statements to *rules* or *imperatives*; as such they say: do this, do that! In *Remarks on the Foundations of Mathematics* he gives a number of simple examples, amongst them "$25 \cdot 25 = 625$". He analyzes this sentence as saying the following: If you want to determine that you have 625 objects, arrange them in groups of 25 objects and count these groups, up to 25! Thus, Wittgenstein analyzes the arithmetic sentence as expressing a technique, rule, or imperative for what to do in *practical applications*.

Such an analysis corresponds to Wittgenstein's general idea that our understanding of mathematical terms, or of words in general, is ultimately tied to how we use them in simple, everyday applications. It is along these lines that he says early on in the *Investigations:*

Now think of the following use of language: I send someone shopping. I give him a slip marked "five red apples". He takes the slip to the shopkeeper, who opens the drawer marked "apples"; then he looks up the word "red" in a table and finds a color sample opposite it; then he says the series of cardinal numbers—I assume that he knows them by heart—up to the word "five" and for each number he takes an apple of the same color as the sample out of the drawer. — It is in this and similar ways that one operates with words. — But how does he know where and how he is to look up the word 'red' and what he is to do with the word 'five'?" — Well, I assume that he *acts* as I have described. Explanations come to an end somewhere. — But what is the meaning of the word "five"? — No such thing was in question here, only how the word "five" is used. [1958, §1]

Here the "meaning", or better the use, of the word 'five' is put in the context of a practical procedure: that of counting from one to five while correlating numbers with objects. Notice that there are certain immediate advantages to such an analysis. Most importantly, it suggests a new understanding of the *apriori* character of arithmetic (or at least of simple, applied arithmetic). Namely, if we ask why arithmetic statements are not subject to empirical verification or falsification, Wittgenstein can answer: it is because they express rules, and rules are not true or false—just more or less useful.[57]

However, this interesting suggestion—to be found mostly in *Remarks on the Foundations of Mathematics* and in other writings from the 1930s—is never fully worked out in Wittgenstein's later writings. Thus it is not clear just how seriously he takes it in the end. Also, he never explicitly addresses the question whether an analysis along these lines can be carried through for *all* of mathematics, i.e., beyond simple, applied arithmetic—and it seems rather problematic that it can. How, for instance, is the analysis supposed to be extended to algebraic number theory, complex analysis, and advanced set theory, especially if we regard these fields as parts of pure mathematics? Furthermore, does it help with respect to more complex application of mathematics, say that of differential geometry in Relativity Theory? etc. In the end it seems to me that an approach which treats pure mathematics (including arithmetic) as consisting of a body of propositions has a better chance of being applicable and illuminating. Thus, Frege's "propositional" point of view seems more appropriate in these cases than Wittgenstein's "imperative" one after all.[58]

---

[57]Wittgenstein's fascination with this answer seems to motivate his interest in the whole approach. His general stance towards non-empirical statements, including simple applications of logic and arithmetic, is worked out more in *On Certainty* [Wittgenstein, 1979b]. There he speaks of them metaphorically as part of "the riverbed of our thoughts" (§97); he likens them to "the axis" which is fixed, but around which other thoughts "rotate" (§152); and he says that such statements are not themselves "measured" empirically, but that they are part of the "measure" (i.e., they function as rules, methods, etc.). (§151, 318, 476, etc.) In my view Wittgenstein is here up to something interesting. However, his ideas never get fully worked out; and it is not clear how extensively they can be applied.

[58]Wittgenstein seems not to have known much about advanced mathematics; and what he knew he partly misunderstood (e.g., the roles logic and set theory can play as regular parts of mathematics).

Final Observations about the Relation between Frege and Wittgenstein. As just explained, Wittgenstein is opposed to certain aspects of Frege's general views about *meaning.* In particular, he objects to Fregean "senses" or "thoughts". In addition, he entertains the idea that logical and arithmetic sentences express techniques, rules, or imperatives, an idea which is undeniably opposed to Frege's *platonism*—even if Frege is interpreted as a contextual platonist. Nevertheless, with respect to this second issue Wittgenstein's opposition to Frege is not as complete as it might appear now. This brings me back to two final observations about *similarities* with respect to their basic outlooks.

Let us assume, first, that Wittgenstein completely endorses an analysis of mathematics as consisting merely of techniques, not of truths. Then he is clearly not a contextual platonist (much less a metaphysical platonist). Nevertheless, he does not disagree with Frege on a *fundamental* level—at bottom both of them study how logical and arithmetic words are *used* in sentences. Their disagreement concerns merely the question *how* to think about our use of logical and arithmetic *sentences.* In their respective answers Wittgenstein concentrates on simple applications of logic and arithmetic, and he analyzes them in terms of his notion of "technique"; Frege, on the other hand, aims at a systematic reconstruction of pure logic and arithmetic, by means of his new logical tools.

But, second, it not so clear that Wittgenstein completely and finally endorses the view of mathematics just attributed to him; or it is not so clear how far he means it to apply. Undoubtedly he plays with it as a general idea for a while, in particular in his *Remarks on the Foundations of Mathematics.* And in *Philosophical Investigations* he maintains at least that there is something right about it in the context of simple, applied mathematics (such as shopping in a grocery store). At the same time, he now explores other, differing ideas, too. Consider for example the following very general remark from the *Investigations:*

> Think how many different kinds of things are called "description": description of a body's position by means of its co-ordinates; description of a facial expression; description of a sensation of touch; or of a mood. [1958, §24]

Now, what about the following suggestion: why can we not say that sentences in pure arithmetic, say, form a *special class* of "descriptions"? The difference between it and other classes would not be hard to explain along Wittgensteinian lines: we just have to look at how the truth of various kinds of descriptions is to be *determined*—by means of mathematical proofs, by means of empirical observations, by means of introspection, etc. Keeping in mind such *criterial* differences, we could, then, maintain that arithmetic contains "descriptive" truths after all, couldn't we?

As it turns out, Wittgenstein's later writings on mathematics, in particular *Lectures* and *Remarks,* do contain a number of specific passàges which go exactly in this direction. Thus, in some of them Wittgenstein recognizes, even emphasizes, the importance of *proof* in mathematics. For instance, he remarks:

> The proof is part of the surroundings of the [mathematical] sentence. [1978, VII, 70]

And:

> The proof belongs to the background of the sentence, to the system in which the sentence has an effect. [1978, VII, 74]

In passages such as these Wittgenstein, very much like Frege, points to our whole system of mathematical judgments in connection with understanding mathematical expressions. And he points out that what holds this system together is proof (and calculation).

Sometimes Wittgenstein makes the same point about proof also in a more concrete way, in connection with particular examples (from pure mathematics). Thus, he remarks about theorems concerning roots of equations in analysis:

> If the proposition 'A quadratic equation has two roots' stood alone, it would be as meaningless as '$25 \cdot 25 = 625$' would if it stood alone outside any system of multiplication—although it is English and it looks all right. [1975, p. 155]

And even in the case of Russell's system of logic, usually an object of attack, he admits:

> The symbols '$(x).\phi x$' and '$(\exists x).\phi x$' are certainly useful in mathematics, so long as one is acquainted with the technique of proofs for the existence or non-existence to which Russell's signs refer *here*. [1978, V, 13]

Note that Wittgenstein connects the *existence* of numbers (and of other mathematical objects) with "techniques of proof". For him the meaning of "existence" in mathematics has, thus, to do with how we *prove* existence claims. This idea is, I think, exactly in line with Frege's contextual approach; indeed, it makes it more explicit and clarifies it further.

To be sure, according to Wittgenstein one has to be careful when talking about "existence" in the case of mathematics—carelessness may lead to the misunderstanding that one is promoting metaphysical platonism. Because of this danger, he writes:

> It looks like obscurantism to say that . . . mathematics does not treat of signs, or that pain is not a form of behavior. But only because people believe that one is asserting the existence of an intangible, i.e., shadowy, object side by side with what we all can grasp. Whereas we are only pointing to different modes of employment of words. [1978, III, 76]

It is exactly in order not to lead people back into such "obscurantism" that Wittgenstein often stresses the differences between various kinds of descriptions, in particular between those used in mathematics, psychology, and physics. But he also admits:

> I will have to stress the differences between things, where ordinarily the similarities are stressed, though this, too, can lead to misunderstandings. [1975, p. 15]

In the end we should realize the following: There are *important similarities and important differences* between describing the fact that a table is four feet long, describing the fact that my headache has gone away, and describing the fact that 17 is prime. Furthermore, Frege usually stresses the similarities, while Wittgenstein usually stresses the differences; and from the point of view developed in this paper these are *two sides of the same coin.*

Finally a brief observation about the personal relation between Frege and Wittgenstein: It is well known that Wittgenstein, throughout his life, showed great respect for Frege. Thus, in the *Tractatus* (1918) he talks about his debt to "Frege's great works"; in *Culture and Value* (1931) he lists Frege as one of his main influences; and in *Zettel* (1945–49) he says: "The style of my sentences is extraordinarily strongly influenced by Frege. And if I wanted to, I could establish this influence where at first sight no one would see it."[59] If I am right, Frege's influence on Wittgenstein is not just one of style; it is quite *substantive.* Maybe Wittgenstein's awareness of that fact also explains his continued respect?

---

[59]See [1922, p. 3], [1980b, p. 19], and [1970, §712]. Another indication of Wittgenstein's continued respect, even admiration, for Frege is the fact that late in the 1940s he persuaded Peter Geach and Max Black to work on a translation of Frege's main works (resulting in their *Translations from the Philosophical Writings of Gottlob Frege,* Basil Blackwell: Oxford, 1952); compare here [Monk, 1990], especially Chapters 7, 8, and 26.

8

Thomas Ricketts

TRUTH-VALUES AND COURSES-OF-VALUE IN FREGE'S *GRUNDGESETZE*

In the opening sections of *Die Grundgesetze der Arithmetik,* Frege informally explains the meanings of the primitive signs of his logical notation, his begriffsschrift, and illustrates the use of his notation by examples that paraphrase back and forth between begriffsschrift and colloquial language. In the midst of all this, in §10, Frege interrupts his exposition in order to identify the two truth-values with selected courses-of-values: the True is equated with the course-of-values of Frege's horizontal function, the function that maps the True to the True and everything else to the False; the False is similarly equated with the course-of-values of a concept under which it alone falls. The point of and basis for these identifications is, however, obscure. Given Frege's untypical unclarity here, it might be thought that Frege offers these identifications in order to clarify or further specify the ontological standing of truth-values. After all, Frege assimilates sentences to proper names and maintains that the truth-values, the True and the False, are the objects meant by these names. Some might then think that Frege identifies the truth-values with specific courses-of-values in order to tell us *what* truth-values are.[1]

It is not, however, truth-values that are at issue in §10. Frege takes anyone who judges to have an implicit grasp of what truth-values are. In his essay "On Sense and Meaning," he says, "We are therefore driven to acknowledge the truth-value of a sentence as its meaning. . . . These two objects [the True and the False] are acknowledged, if only implicitly, by anyone who judges something to be true, and so even by the skeptic" [1892a, p. 34/1984, p. 163]. Frege is, of course, well aware that his treatment of sentences as proper names is unfamiliar and that his thesis that sentences mean truth-values " . . . may appear arbitrary and contrived," and so requires motivation [1891, p. 14, fn. 6/1984, p. 145].

---

[1]Joan Weiner adopts this approach to Frege's identification of truth-values with courses-of-values in [Weiner, 1990, appendix A]. See especially p. 286. Tyler Burge follows it as well in [Burge, 1986]. See especially pp. 136–137 and p. 139.

However, once these points are in place—Frege's correlative conception of proper names and objects, the assimilation of sentences to proper names, and the identification of truth-values as the putative meanings of sentences—Frege acts as if there are no further issues, no need for further elucidation, concerning truth-values. Frege's introduction of truth-values in the *Grundgesetze* gives further confirmation here. In §2, Frege briskly introduces truth-values as the meanings of sentences, referring the reader to "On Sense and Meaning" for further support for this view. Thereafter, Frege freely speaks of the two truth-values in introducing the primitive signs of the begriffsschrift. Here he finds a transparent, unassailable, and accessible starting point for the exposition of his notation. The clarity attaching the notion of a truth-value is almost immediately reflected in the begriffsschrift itself. In §5 Frege introduces the horizontal function and points out that a begriffsschrift sentence of the form

$$\Delta = -\Delta$$

is true just in case the proper name replacing "Δ" means a truth-value. We thus see in such sentences a compound begriffsschrift predicate that picks out a concept under which just the truth-values fall. For Frege to grasp the sense his explanations confer on this predicate is to understand fully what truth-values are.

The title Frege gives to §10—"More exact determination of what the course-of-values of a function is supposed to be"—indicates a very different motivation for the identification of truth-values with courses-of-values.[2] But how is this stipulative identification to answer any pressing questions about courses-of-value? An answer to this question will help us appreciate better how Frege, before the shock of Russell's 1902 letter, understood his positing of courses-of-value. More importantly, scrutiny of Frege's answer shows his posit of courses-of-value, quite apart from the paradox, to be incompatible with the view of clarity and rigor that accompanies his universalist conception of logic. In §10 Frege points out an indeterminacy in his earlier introduction of courses-of-value and tries to remedy it. Frege concedes that his remedy does not completely eliminate this indeterminacy. By his own admission, Frege does not grasp with the clarity that logic requires of any scientific notion what courses-of-value are.

I

Frege holds to a universalist view of logic. There is a single body of logical principles that mediates demonstrative inference in any subject matter whatsoever. The universal applicability of these principles is understood substantively,

---

[2]Other commentators have noted that it is courses-of-value, not truth-values, that are at issue in §10. See [Dummett, 1981, chap. 19, pp. 400–427]. See also [Thiel, 1976, pp. 287–299].

thanks to Frege's understanding of quantifiers. Frege's quantifiers and variables are intrinsically unrestricted: each quantifier generalizes over all the items of a given logical type—objects, first-level functions of one argument place, etc. Logical principles themselves set forth maximally general truths whose statement, in addition to quantifiers, requires only the fundamental topic-neutral vocabulary that every discipline employs, vocabulary like the negation sign and the identity sign. The generality of logical principles secures their universal applicability and enables Frege to conceive of the begriffsschrift as a framework that, with the addition of the basic vocabulary and laws of the special sciences, can be expanded into a single system that embraces all of science. In the foreword to his first codification of logic in the 1879 monograph, *Begriffsschrift*, Frege compares his logical system to Leibniz's idea of a *characteristica universalis* and *calculus ratiocinator*:

> We can view the symbols of arithmetic, geometry, and chemistry as realizations of the Leibnizian idea in these particular areas. The begriffsschrift offered here adds a new domain to these; indeed the one situated in the middle adjoining all the others. Thus, from this starting point, we can begin to fill in the gaps in existing formula languages, connect their hitherto separate domains to the province of a single formula language and extend it to fields which up to now have lacked such a language. [1879, p. vi]

The formalization of the sciences in this single system, properly accomplished, is to display epistemic dependencies among the sciences; for within such a system, we will be able to determine the ultimate grounds for the truth of scientific laws by proving them from more general laws.[3] In the 1879 monograph, Frege presents a codification of logic in order to investigate the extent to which the truths of arithmetic are provable from logical laws. To this end, in the final part of the book, he produces the second-order definition of the ancestral of a relation and proves some central theorems in theory of such relations. Frege does not, on the basis of this achievement, even tentatively, conjecture the truth of logicism. Rather, at the end of the foreword, he says:

> As I said at the beginning, arithmetic was the starting point of the line of thought that led me to my begriffsschrift. Therefore, I intend to apply it first to this science by trying to dissect [*zergliedern*] its concepts further and to provide a deeper grounding for its propositions. [1879, p. viii]

Frege's analysis of the concept of number unfolds in his next book, *The Foundations of Arithmetic*, especially §§45–69.

---

[3]This ideal of systematizing all of science within a single language shapes Frege's redefinitions in [Frege, 1884, §3] of Kant's four epistemological pigeon holes. See also Frege's discussion of the importance of systems in mathematics and science generally toward the end of his career in [Frege, 1914] in [1983, p. 261/1979a, p. 241ff.].

Frege seeks " . . . to assign Number its place among our concepts" [1884, §21], by considering statements of Number—statements like "Here are four companies," "Here are five hundred men," and "Mars has two moons"—that exhibit the original and basic use of number to answer the question "How many?" [1884, §45]. Comparing them to universal affirmative statements and existential statements, Frege claims that a statement of number contains an assertion about a concept. The statement "All whales are mammals" asserts the subordination of the concept *whale* to the concept *mammal.* The statement "There are whales" asserts that the concept *whale* is non-empty. Similarly, a statement of number sets forth how many objects fall under a given concept. Moreover, as Frege observes, it seems that the numerical property assigned to a concept *F* by a statement of the form "There are exactly *n* things that *F*" can be specified in logical terms in the now familiar way by use of object quantifiers and the identity sign. Frege argues that these specifications are not the desired definitions of individual numbers, for " . . . in truth we have only fixed the sense of the phrases 'the number 0 belongs to' 'the number 1 belongs to'; but we have no authority to pick out 0 and 1 here as self-subsistent objects again" [1884, §56].

While Frege's specification perhaps defines the predicate "the number 1 belongs to," it does not define the numerical element of the predicate, the phrase "the number 1". Frege's ontological categories track his logical ones—I believe that this is the import of his context principle. Objects are what proper names putatively mean; similarly for concepts and predicates. Proper names are segmented as meaningful expressions in language by Leibniz's law, an inference Frege considers logically fundamental. Proper names are then the expressions that flank the identity sign in singular equations. Predicates are the expressions obtained by removing proper names from statements.[4] By these logical standards, the numerals that figure in arithmetic are paradigmatic proper names. As Frege puts the point:

> I have already drawn attention above to the fact that we speak of "the number 1", where the definite article serves to class it as an object. In arithmetic this self-subsistence comes out at every turn, as for example in the identity $1 + 1 = 2$. . . . And equations are, of all the forms of statements, the most typical of arithmetic. [1884, §57, pp. 68 ff.]

---

[4]See especially [1884, §§51, 60, and 65 ft.nt. 2]. The notion of a predicate, and its generalization, incomplete expression, is set forth more starkly in later writings like "Function and Concept". I believe that there is a great deal of continuity between *Foundations* and Frege's post-1891 writings on this point, as evidenced particularly by the discussion of relational predicates in [1884, §70] and by Frege's citations in the 1892 paper "On Concept and Object" [1892b] of the linguistic hints he presents in *Foundations* to explain the concept-object distinction. For further discussion of Frege's context principle, see my "Objectivity and Objecthood" [1986a, §3].

Moreover, statements of number can themselves be paraphrased as equations—"The number of Mars's moons is identical with 2" rather than "Mars has 2 moons."

This logical-grammatical treatment of arithmetical statements shapes Frege's task. His problem is to define in logical terms a first-level concept, the concept of (cardinal) number, and to identify objects falling under this concept with the positive integers 0, 1, 2, ... Frege does not present matters so starkly in *Foundations*, and understandably so. In the introduction to the book in a context in which the positive integers are at issue, Frege concedes that the concept of number appears unanalyzably simple. It is then entirely opaque what could count as a definition of this concept. Frege's strategy here will be to characterize in logical terms the distinguishing mark (*Kennzeichen*) that individuates numbers. He will then attempt to define a second-level function, the *Number of* function, that associates every concept with objects that are thus individuated. These objects are Frege's numbers.

Frege states the following principle, one previously set forth by Cantor, to give the distinguishing mark of numbers:

The number of F = the number of G if and only if as many objects are F as are G;

and he provides the now familiar second-order rendition of the right hand side of this generalized biconditional. Once we appreciate the logical character of the right-hand side, it is tempting to take this statement alone to be the desired logical definition of number. Frege resists this proposal, on the grounds that the biconditional does not determine whether the man Julius Caesar is identical with the number of Martian moons, or in indeed with the number belonging to any concept. The trouble is that Cantor's principle presupposes rather than supplies a concept of number in that it says that the concept of number satisfies a certain higher order constraint.[5]

Two very basic features of Frege's approach lie behind this curious sounding argument. First, for Frege any proper name position is accessible to first-level quantification, and Frege's first-level quantifiers are unrestricted. Frege's understanding of quantifiers thus commits him to the view that every concept has sharp boundaries—it must be determinate for each object, whether it falls under

---

[5]Frege raises the Julius Caesar point first in §56 in arguing against taking the quantificational specification of "the number 1 belongs to" as the definition of the number 1. Frege considers whether Cantor's principle might serve as a definition of Number via the discussion in §§64–67 of the formally parallel proposal to take the biconditional:

The direction of line a = the direction of line b if and only if line a is parallel to line b,

to define directions. In §66 he raises the Julius Caesar point against this proposed definition, maintaining that this biconditional does not decide whether England is identical with the direction of the Earth's axis. This application of the Julius Caesar point is the one directly relevant to my discussion.

the concept or not. Accordingly, if expressions of the form "the number of F" are to be admitted as meaningful proper names in equations like "The number of G = the number of F", then

$$(\text{There exists } x)(\text{the number of } G = x)$$

must also be admitted as a meaningful sentence and

$$\text{the number of } G = [\xi]$$

as a meaningful predicate that designates a concept under which each object falls or fails to fall. Hence, if N is any meaningful proper name

$$\text{the number of } G = N$$

must be a meaningful equation.[6] Second, Frege distinguishes definitions from the axioms and theorems of a science. Formally, definitions set forth explicit notational abbreviations. As the definiendum is eliminable from any sentence in which it occurs on the basis of its definition, definitions add no content to a science.[7] Cantor's principle is not an explicit definition of the phrase "the number of F." If we try to construe it as a definition, it is a definition of the phrase, "the number of F = the number of G". Viewed as a definiendum, this phrase is an unsegmented expression of a relation over concepts, not an equation.[8] In particular, Frege does not take Cantor's principle to set forth a contextual definition of the concept of number. In *Foundations,* just as in later writings, Frege is antipathetic to contextual definitions. Furthermore, as I read it, Frege's context principle plays no substantive role in justifying the introduction of numbers. The context principle encapsulates Frege's identification of logical and ontological categories and so fixes the form that a definition of number must take.[9] A definition of "the number of F" must take the form of the stipulation of an equation

---

[6]Charles Parsons pointed out the connection between Frege's treatment of equations like "the number of F = Julius Caesar" and his view of quantification in [Parsons, 1983, pp. 158–159].

[7]While this view of definitions is more sharply expressed in later writings, I believe that it informs *Foundations* as well. The principal difference between *Foundations* and later treatment of definitions is Frege's understanding and accommodation of the referential presuppositions of definitions. For further discussion, see my "Generality, Meaning, and Sense in Frege" [1986], especially §§4–5. Here I am indebted to Weiner's discussion of Frege's view of definition in [1990, chap.3, pp. 82–102]. I believe that Weiner establishes the basic continuity in Frege's conception of definitions throughout his career.

[8]Indeed, taken as a definition, Cantor's principle is a definition of the two-place *second-level* relation of equinumerosity (same cardinality).

[9]See *Foundations* §60, the last sentence. *Foundations* §63 does not propose the introduction of numbers via contextual definition. Rather, the unusual sort of definition Frege here commends is his version of our abstractive definitions that introduce "new" objects as equivalence classes of familiar objects. I think the terms Frege uses here to describe abstractive definitions are explained by his view of concepts and extensions that I discuss below.

that joins this definiendum with an expression of the same logical category built up using only logical vocabulary.

Frege goes on in *Foundations* to define the Number belonging to the concept *F* as the extension of the concept *equinumerous with the concept F,* thus coyly and offhandedly introducing extensions. Frege does not in *Foundations* state the fundamental logical law for extensions that will become Basic Law V in *Grundgesetze:*

The extension of *F* = the extension of *G* if and only if exactly the same objects are *F* as are *G,* i.e, if and only if the concepts *F* and *G* are coextensive.

He does silently presuppose it in arguing in §72 that the proposed definition of number satisfies Cantor's principle. The motivation for this abrupt introduction of extensions is somewhat veiled in *Foundations.* Earlier in *Foundations* Frege has rejected any notion of collection or set as too vague to be serviceable for mathematics.[10] What best corresponds in Frege's thought to the mathematical idea of a set is Frege's notion of a concept:

The concept has a power of collecting together [*die sammelnde Kraft*] far superior to the unifying power of synthetic apperception. By means of the latter it would not be possible to join the inhabitants of Germany together into a whole; but we can certainly bring them all under the concept "inhabitant of Germany" and number them. [1884, §48, p. 61][11]

Why then does Frege introduce extensions in addition to concepts? I have already briefly indicated how I take Frege's understanding of the concept-object distinction to be rooted in his understanding of the logical segmentation of language into proper names and predicates. Frege alludes to this type-theoretic understanding of the concept-object distinction in the third and final guiding principle he adumbrates in the introduction to *Foundations,* "never to lose sight of the distinction between concept and object." We have seen how Frege takes numerals to be proper names. Given the concept-object distinction and his analysis of arithmetic discourse, Frege cannot identify numbers with concepts under which equinumerous concepts fall. Frege attempts to circumvent this difficulty by introducing extensions that are to be *objects* that, via Basic Law V, can serve as surrogates for concepts.[12] Frege can thus define a concept of number that

---

[10]See [1884, §§23, 28, and 41].

[11]See also "Formal Theories of Arithmetic" [Frege, 1886, p. 96/1984, p. 114]. Charles Parsons has distinguished those elucidations of the notion of set that draw on intuitions concerning collections and intuitions concerning the items a predicate is true of, noting that Frege is the best example of a thinker who draws only on the latter motivation. My brief remarks on concepts indicate how Frege viewed this distinction. See Parsons's illuminating discussion in, "Some Remarks on Frege's Conception of Extension" [Parsons, 1976], p. 265ff.

[12]The seriousness with which Frege takes this logical grammatical point is evident in post-paradox writings where Frege recurs to the logical role of numerals as proper names. See "Aufzeichnungen für Ludwig Darmstaedter" (1919) in [1983, pp. 276ff./1979a, p. 276]; "Tagebucheintragungen über

identifies numbers with certain extensions. By means of this definition, Cantor's Principle can be derived from Basic Law V; and in the second order setting of the 1879 version of begriffsschrift, Cantor's principle suffices for the derivation of arithmetic. Thus, Frege's analysis of arithmetical discourse meshes with the formal requirements for the development of arithmetic within the begriffsschrift extended by a theory of extensions.[13]

Frege says very little about extensions in *Foundations*. There are some indications that Frege's reticence reflects unspecified uncertainty concerning extensions.[14] I see, however, a great deal of continuity between *Foundations* and Frege's later writings—in this case between Frege's introduction of extensions into the construction of number informally presented in *Foundations* and his later introduction of courses-of-values of functions.[15] I think that Frege's coyness in introducing extensions has, in considerable measure, a pedagogical source. Frege's concept-object distinction can consistently be adhered to only in a language, like Frege's begriffsschrift, that has separate vocabularies of quantifiers and variables for generalizing into proper name and predicate positions respectively. In light of the failure of the 1879 monograph to find an audience, Frege intended *Foundations* to be a non-technical, broadly accessible presentation of the application of his logical work to arithmetic. I believe that Frege, in writing *Foundations,* is aware of the awkwardness of language—above all his use of the contrasting first-level predicates "object" and "concept"—that Kerry will exploit in his criticism of Frege's view of concepts in *Foundations*. Discussion of extensions and their relation to concepts, especially an informal statement of Basic Law V like the one just given, would only have drawn undesired attention to this awkwardness and the expository difficulties it creates for Frege's position.

How though is Frege's definition of number supposed to solve the problem that led us to it, the Julius Caesar problem? After all, Basic Law V stands to extensions as Cantor's principle stands to numbers: as the latter does not define the concept of number, so the former presupposes, and does not define, the con-

---

den Begriff der Zahl," (1924) in [1983, p. 282/1979a, p. 263]. Also, although Frege talks in *Foundations* as if second-level concepts have extensions, following Warren Goldfarb, I take Frege's *Foundations* definition of number to be properly formalized by: the Number of $F = \,'e$[there exists $G(e = \,'aG(a)$ & F is equinumerous with G].

[13]Here I am indebted to George Boolos's discussions of Frege's construction of number in "The Consistency of Frege's *Foundations of Arithmetic*" [Boolos, 1987] and "The Standard of Equality in Number" [Boolos, 1990a]. Charles Parsons observed that Cantor's Principle suffices in a second order setting for arithmetic in his article "Mathematics, Foundations of" in *The Encyclopedia of Philosophy* [Parsons, 1967].

[14]See especially the concluding paragraph of *Foundations* §107. Mark Wilson has suggested that in *Foundations* Frege may be uncertain about the extensional identity standards of the concept-representing objects, thinking that something more "intensional" might be preferable. See his paper "Frege: the Royal Road from Geometry" [Wilson, 1992, p. 172].

[15]For a different view, see [Burge, 1984, pp. 3–34].

cept of extension. Frege does not return to discuss the Julius Caesar problem. However, in a footnote to his introduction of extensions in his definition of number, he remarks, "I presuppose that it is known what the extension of a concept is."[16] The concept of extension is an undefined primitive; the clear suggestion is that we know what extensions are and know that Julius Caesar is not one.[17]

In his 1891 paper "Function and Concept," Frege assimilates concepts to functions whose range is the truth-values; he correspondingly generalizes the notion of the extension of a concept to that of the course-of-values of a function. Basic Law V is the claim that the courses-of-value of functions f and g are identical just in case f and g return the same values for the same arguments. Some of the motivations Frege presents for accepting Basic Law V are, I think, thin. For instance, in *Grundgesetze* vol. II §146 he says that in accepting Basic Law V we acknowledge something that two coextensive functions have in common. Given Frege's function-object distinction, this acknowledgment, it might be urged, is properly expressed by the use of the second-level predicate that has the second-level coextensiveness relation as its meaning. In a retrospective, post-paradox discussion of Basic Law V Frege notes the analogies between the second order relation of coextensiveness and identity. He says that the analogy here "almost compels us to transform a sentence asserting the mutual subordination of concepts into a sentence expressing an identity."[18] However, Frege's admission in the foreword to *Grundgesetze* that Basic Law V may be controversial testifies to the weakness of this motivation.[19]

Frege presents his most compelling motivation for Basic Law V in his most extensive pre-paradox discussion of it in *Grundgesetze* vol. II, §§146–147. The immediately preceding sections criticize mathematicians who, Frege says, purport to create mathematical objects—Dedekind's stipulation of the existence of real numbers corresponding to Dedekind cuts is a prime example. In §146 Frege remarks that his introduction of courses-of-values in volume one of *Grundgesetze* might be taken to be a similar creation of mathematical objects. He responds that the equivalence set forth in Basic Law V should be viewed as a fundamental logical law; he notes that it is not, by his standards, a definition.[20] Frege criticizes Dedekind's introduction of new mathematical objects as ad hoc: there are no general rules specifying the circumstances under which such introductions are legitimate. In contrast, Basic Law V sets forth once and for all the

---

[16][1884, §68, ft.nt. 1, p. 80] The remark is repeated at the end of the book in §107.

[17]See Frege's discussion of the question whether England is the direction of the earth's axis in [1884, §66].

[18]"Über Schoenflies: die Logischen Paradoxien der Mengenlehre," [1906a] in [Frege, 1983, pp. 197ff./1979a, p. 182]. After the quoted passage, Frege notes, that the acceptance of this transformation amounts to the introduction of new objects.

[19][1893, p. vii]. Note how Frege claims here that mathematicians have been making tacit use of Basic Law V.

[20]See also "Function and Concept" [1891, p. 10/1984, p. 142].

means for grasping and recognizing logical objects with which mathematical objects are identified. Frege says:

> Without such a means, a scientific grounding for arithmetic would be impossible. For us, [Basic Law V] serves the purpose that, for other mathematicians, the creation of new numbers is supposed to reach. So, from the eight functions whose names are enumerated in vol. I §31, we hope, as from seeds, to develop the full wealth of objects and functions that mathematics treats.[21]

Frege's most compelling motivation for Basic Law V is thus the explicit general basis he believed Basic Law V to give for mathematical practice: Basic Law V promised to be a codification of the means for the introduction of "new" objects into mathematics via abstractive definitions, a means applicable both in arithmetic and analysis on the one hand and geometry on the other. Mark Wilson, in a recent illuminating and instructive paper, "Frege: The Royal Road from Geometry," persuasively maintains that Frege was led to Basic Law V as the means for identifying the non-euclidean elements required by projective geometry.[22] *Foundations* alludes to this role, for the directions of lines—whose definition in §68 is Frege's model for the definition of number—are the projective geometer's points at infinity. Moreover, the general method Basic Law V seems to offer for the introduction of mathematical objects distinguishes it in Frege's eyes from Cantor's principle, even though these share the same logical form. Simply positing Cantor's principle would have the same ad hoc character Frege finds in Dedekind's construction of the real numbers. In §147 Frege notes that the mathematicians' talk of functions, sets, and classes—their use of first-level predicates and associated definite descriptions here to specify objects—can be construed as making use of Basic Law V. He goes on to remark: "With this transformation we do not do anything really new; rather we do it with full consciousness and with appeal to a basic logical law" [1903, §147].

II

In part one of the *Grundgesetze,* Frege explains his logical notation, his begriffsschrift, in order to instruct his readers in its use. By the end of these sections, readers are supposed to be able to figure out what thought is expressed by each begriffsschrift sentence. They are then in a position to use the sentences to make assertions in the course of constructing gap-free proofs in the formal system Frege sets forth. Central to the explanations and examples Frege provides are the

---

[21]*Grundgesetze* vol. II [1903, §147].
[22][Wilson, 1992], see especially pp. 163–174. Weiner also notes this use of Basic Law V and urges that Frege propounded Basic Law V as a codification of a basic mathematical inference. See [Weiner, 1990, p. 189].

stipulations of meaning that introduce the primitive function names of the begriffsschrift. In the very early sections, Frege introduces the horizontal, the negation sign, the universal quantifier over objects, and course-of-values names. The stipulation for the universal quantifier illustrates the pattern for the introduction of all of these names except the last.

> Let "$(x)\phi x$" mean the True, if the value of the function $\phi(\xi)$ for each argument is the True, and otherwise the False. [1893, p. 12][23]

Frege's later discussion in §32 makes it clear how he expects his readers to use these stipulations. The stipulations of meaning for the primitive names are supposed to determine the conditions under which any begriffsschrift sentence means the True. The sense of the sentence is then, Frege says, " . . . the thought that these conditions are fulfilled."

Frege's stipulations are, of course, couched in colloquial language and do not constitute definitions of the primitive begriffsschrift signs. For Frege, definitions are properly set forth inside a formalization of a science, once the primitive vocabulary is in place, by the definitional stipulation of an equation or generalized equation whose left hand side is a proper name or function name constructed from primitive signs and whose right hand side is the new name. The definition introduces the new name as a definitional abbreviation of the old one, with the same sense and meaning.[24] Definitions thus presuppose that the primitive signs from which the definiens is constructed have a fixed sense and meaning. Frege, accordingly, sharply distinguishes the introduction of new vocabulary into a system by definition and the explanation of the sense and meaning of the primitive vocabulary.[25] This is the task of elucidations. Elucidations are informal, extrasystematic remarks that attempt to convey, hint at, and point towards the sense and meaning that is to be attached to a primitive sign. At the beginning of the *Grundgesetze,* in the introduction that precedes the exposition of the system, Frege says:

> It will not always be possible properly to define everything, precisely because we must endeavor to get down to the logically simple that, as such, is not really definable. I must then content myself with hints that point toward what I intend. I must above all strive to be understood. Therefore, I will try to develop matters gradually and not immediately at the outset attempt to reach full generality and definitive expression. [1893, p. 4, my translation][26]

---

[23]Frege goes on to state the conventions for quantifier scope required to clarify his talk of the function associated with any universal quantification.

[24]See [1893, §§27 and 33]. In the case of definitions of function names, free variables fill the argument places of the function names.

[25]See [Weiner, 1990], especially in chapter 6.

[26]Frege discusses the difference between definitions and elucidations in his letter of Hilbert of 27.12.99(letter XV/3) [1980, pp. 36–37]. He returns to this point in "Über die Grundlagen der Geometrie" [1906b, pp. 302–303] in [Frege, 1984, pp. 301–302]) and, in his posthumously published papers, in "Logik in der Mathematik" [1914] in [1983, p. 224/1979a, pp. 207–208].

The introduction of the universal quantifier just quoted illustrates one way in which elucidations may be imprecise. Here Frege uses a definite description of the form "the function . . . " to speak not of objects, but of functions. The stipulation, by his lights, does not have the sense and meaning he intends it to point toward.[27]

Frege is cognizant of the novelty of his courses-of-values. In the definitive setting of *Grundgesetze,* Frege cannot simply assume a knowledge of what courses-of-values are: a straightforward elucidation that stipulates that the meaning of " $\,'e\phi(e)$ " is the course-of-values of the function $\phi(\xi)$ would be useless.[28] In "Function and Concept" Frege analogizes courses-of-values to the curves that provide an intuitive [*anschaulich*] geometrical representation of the values some functions return for various arguments.[29] In particular, analytical geometry associates the same curve with real-valued functions that return the same values for the same arguments. Frege's comparison thus helps his readers understand what Basic Law V requires of courses-of-values. However, once the form of Basic Law V is grasped, given the generality of Frege's notion of function, the analogy is of no further use in elucidating courses-of-values. Furthermore, as we have seen, Frege rejects the notion of an assemblage or collection of items as excessively vague. He remains throughout his career highly critical of so-called extensional presentations of the notion of class that he believes draw on this crude notion. Frege comments in a manuscript, "An aggregation consists of its parts. . . . An extension of a concept has its existence [*Bestand*] in a concept, not in the objects that belong to it; these are not its parts."[30] He cannot then draw on talk of collections of things to elucidate his conception of courses-of-values. Given Frege's cross-cutting distinctions of sense versus meaning and function versus object, a more "intensionalist" approach will also be of little service. Talk of a rule for classifying objects or for associating objects with each other will at best direct attention to the sense or the meaning of a function name, not the course-of-values. At worst, such talk may direct attention to the function name itself or to psychological processes.

Frege cannot then communicate the sense and meaning of the name of the course-of-values function with the direct stipulations of meaning he uses to introduce the other primitive begriffsschrift names. Instead, he introduces

---

[27]Frege alerts his readers to this pervasive awkwardness of his elucidations, citing "On Concept and Object" [1892b] in *Grundgesetze* §4, ft.nt. 1, p. 8. Frege's stipulation for the universal quantifier also runs afoul of strict adherence to the use-mention distinction by quantifying into quotation marks.

[28]Having introduced course-of-values names in *Grundgesetze* §3, Frege does employ this stipulation in §9 to specify, on the model of his treatment of the universal quantifier in §8, the function associated with the course-of-values designated by any course-of-values name.

[29]"Function and Concept" [1891, pp. 8–9/1984, pp. 141–142]. Burton Dreben pointed out to me the importance of this passage for the elucidation of the notion of a course-of-values.

[30]"Über Schoenflies" [1906a] in [1983, p. 199/1979a, p. 183]. See also "A Critical Elucidation of some Points in E. Schröder's *Vorlesungen über die Algebra der Logik*" [1895, p. 455/1984, p.228].

course-of-values in *Grundgesetze* §3 by stipulating the equivalence of the two sides of the instances of Basic Law V:

I use the words

"the function $\phi(\xi)$ has the same course-of-values as the function $\psi(\xi)$"

generally as meaning the same [*gleichbedeutend*] as the words

"the functions $\phi(\xi)$ and $\psi(\xi)$ always have the same value for the same argument."

In effect then, Frege introduces courses-of-values as objects whose criterion of recognition is set forth in Basic Law V. There is, it seems, nothing else positive to say by way of elucidating what courses-of-value are.

Frege opens §10, maintaining that the stipulations that introduce courses-of-value names in §3 do not fully determine the meanings of these names. He then identifies two selected courses-of-value with the True and the False, arguing that these identifications are consistent with the §3 stipulations. At the end of the section, Frege observes that these identifications, while alleviating the indeterminacy left by the introduction of course-of-value names, still do not completely fix their meanings. In the remainder of this section, I take up the first two points of §10; section III discusses the indeterminacy left after the stipulations of §10.

At the beginning of §10 Frege avers that the stipulation of §3 does not completely fix the meanings of course-of-value names. He says:

> We have only a means of always recognizing [*Wiedererkennen*] a course-of-values, if it is designated by a name like " $\varepsilon\phi(e)$ ", by means of which it is already recognizable as a course-of-values. But so far, we can neither decide whether an object is a course-of-values that is not given to us as such, and to what function it may perhaps correspond, nor decide in general whether a given course-of-values has a given property, if we do not know that this property is connected with a property of the corresponding function. [1893, §10, p. 16, my translation]

As Cantor's principle is to the concept of number, so Basic Law V is to the concept of a course-of-values. Not surprisingly, these considerations exactly parallel those that Frege advanced in *Foundations* in considering whether Cantor's principle supplies a concept of number.[31] Recall the form and content of Basic Law V. Frege's first-level functions map objects to objects; second-level functions map functions to objects. Basic Law V posits a second-level function that maps first-level functions to the same object just in case they return the same value for the same argument. Let us call this third-level condition that Basic Law V imposes on the course-of-values function *the extensionality condition*. While the extensionality condition does provide a criterion of recognition

---

[31]Michael Dummett emphasizes the parallels between the *Foundations* discussion of Cantor's principle and *Grundgesetze* §10 especially as regards the Julius Caesar problem in [Dummett, 1981, chap. 19].

for courses-of-value, it does not tell us what objects are courses-of-value; nor does it fix whether any particular object is the course-of-values of a particular function. Apart from course-of-value names, sentences that designate truth-values are the only other proper names that Frege has up to §10 introduced into his formalism. Frege's explanation of the meaning of course-of-value names does not settle whether any courses-of-value are truth-values. Accordingly, Frege's stipulations of meaning through §9 do not fix the meaning, the truth-value, of equations that join a sentence to a course-of-values name. With the failure, then, of Frege's stipulations to fix a meaning for these "mixed" equations, the Julius Caesar problem threatens to appear within the begriffsschrift itself.

Here in §10 Frege does not, as in *Foundations,* just assert the indeterminacy his stipulations leave in the meaning of course-of-values names by calling attention to mixed equations. The passage just quoted is followed by what Michael Dummett has dubbed Frege's permutation argument. The permutation argument is an obscure and compressed argument to establish this indeterminacy. On the next page, Frege adapts and expands the permutation argument to attempt to show the consistency of his identification of truth-values with certain courses-of-value. This second use of the permutation argument holds the interpretive key to the first use. Let us examine it first.

Frege declares that the indeterminacy in the meanings of course-of-values names is remedied, if on introduction of the name of a function into the system, " . . . it is determined what values the function returns for courses-of-values as for all other arguments." As regards the functions meant by the horizontal and the negation sign, this is done, once we settle whether the truth-values are courses-of-values, and if so, which ones. Since the only names of objects that have been introduced thus far are names of truth-values and courses-of-value, Frege thinks that settling this issue handles identity as well. Frege now argues that the identification of the two truth-values with distinct courses-of-value is consistent with the stipulation of §3 that courses-of-value satisfy the extensionality condition. Frege supposes that this stipulation holds for names of the form "$\tilde{n}\phi(n)$". Let $L(\xi)$ and $M(\xi)$ be first-level functions that differ in the value they return for some argument. So, $\tilde{n}(M(n) \neq \tilde{n}(L(n))$. Let $X(\xi)$ be the following permutation over objects: $X(\tilde{n}L(n)) =$ the True, and conversely $X(\text{the True}) = \tilde{n}(L(n))$; similarly $X(\tilde{n}M(n)) =$ the False and conversely; any other object is mapped by $X(\xi)$ to itself. Frege now observes that names of the form "$X(\tilde{n}\phi(n))$" satisfy the stipulation of §3. He concludes that it is consistent with the stipulation of §3 to identify the True and the False with two arbitrarily selected courses-of-value. Note that Frege's formulation of this argument presupposes that the truth-values have already been identified.

I see Frege's argument here as an informal higher order argument for the generalization:

(A) If there is a second-level function satisfying the extensionality condition, then, given any two distinct first-level functions, there is a second-level function satisfying the extensionality condition that maps one of the first-level functions to the True and the other to the False.[32]

The generality of the conclusion is signaled by Frege's use of "$\bar{n}\phi(n)$" rather than course-of-values names. But how might this conclusion be thought to demonstrate the consistency with Basic Law V of the stipulation that the True and the False are particular courses-of-value of distinct functions?

Frege has no semantic conception of logical consequence or consistency. For him, consistency is logical irrefutability. The stipulations identifying certain courses-of-values with truth-values are consistent with Basic Law V, if there is no refutation of them from Basic Law V using just logical means. Suppose that the identification of the truth-values as the courses-of-value of two particular functions were, using Basic Law V, logically refutable. The only information about courses-of-value used in the refutation would be that contained in Basic Law V. So, generalizing the argument, it could be shown that there is no function satisfying the extensionality condition that maps the particular functions to the truth-values. Hence, via generalization (A), Basic Law V itself could be refuted. Frege thus takes the truth of the generalization (A) to show the consistency of the identification of truth-values with courses-of-value with Basic Law V.

This argument displays the attitude toward consistency and consistency proofs Frege voices elsewhere. Apart from establishing the truth of a sentence, to show a sentence consistent, first find a suitably related sentence; then establish the truth of the related sentence; finally observe that were the sentence in question to be logically refutable, there would be a parallel logical refutation of the related sentence.[33] So, for Frege, assurance of the consistency of a sentence comes from the proof of a related sentence, a proof that might be formalized in the begriffsschrift. The observation that were the sentence in question to be logically refutable, so would the proven sentence, is treated as an unformalized upshot that Frege leaves unspoken. This rudimentary view of consistency proofs reflects two deep-seated features of Frege's conception of logic: the absence of a

---

[32]Frege explains quantifiers over first-level functions in §§20 and 25 and introduces variables over second-level functions in §25. In §20 Frege first states Basic Law V. In the context of his explanation of second-level functions, Frege clearly takes the statement of Basic Law V to add no debatable substance to the stipulations of §§3 and 9. See *Grundgesetze* §20, p. 36. I believe that Frege phrases his argument as he does in order not to draw on ideas he has yet to explain and, perhaps, in order to minimize the awkwardness that for him accompanies any informal talk of functions. I then attach no significance to the fact that Frege's informal argument is not explicitly formulated in higher order terms, and take Frege's elucidation of course-of-values names to be in essence the statement of Basic Law V.

[33]See [1884, §95, p. 106]; "Formal Theories of Arithmetic" [1886, p. 103/1984, p. 120], and, most importantly, Frege's letter to Hilbert 6.1. 1900 [1980, pp. 47–48].

notion of logical consequence and a certain antipathy toward the concept of truth.

There is no overarching, independently characterizable relation of logical consequence that Frege is trying to mirror in terms of formal derivability. Frege takes for granted our ability to infer, to recognize one truth on the basis of another. He aims to provide a language in which generality, predication, identity, negation, etc., are explicitly, uniformly, and perspicuously expressed so as to then state axioms and inference rules that suffice for the rigorous, non-enthymematic reconstruction inside the system of intuitively valid arguments. That the principles of logic Frege sets forth "suffice for all cases" is, as Van Heijenoort has observed, an experimental matter.[34] The only assurance Frege has of the comprehensiveness of his codification of logic is success in expressing a broad range of argumentation from mathematics and the mature sciences as gap-free proofs within the framework of the begriffsschrift. This experimental attitude toward the codification of logic is manifest in Frege's attempt to win affirmation of Basic Law V by maintaining that it is implicit in colloquial mathematical proofs. A further indication of this attitude is the fact that Frege never claims that the inferences capturable in the system of *Grundgesetze* exhaust all logical inferences.

The syntactic codification of quantificational inference makes metamathematics possible, in particular the mathematically rigorous investigation of formal derivability in formalizations of various mathematical theories. But Frege introduces his formalism in order to use it to state the gap-free proofs that will establish the logicist conjecture. He shows no inclination to treat his formalism as an object of mathematical investigation. As I noted at the outset, Frege's begriffsschrift is a framework for universal science: with the addition of the requisite vocabulary, the laws and facts uncovered by the special sciences are expressible in it. For Frege, truth is scientific truth: there are no truths not expressible in this framework. Nothing in Frege's philosophy precludes, as we would put it, formalizing the logical syntax of the begriffsschrift within the framework of the begriffsschrift, treating the construction of begriffsschrift derivations as a notational game. Frege, however, would see little point to this exercise. Sentences, considered only as series of marks or sounds, are of no interest to Frege. They are of interest only in that they express thoughts and so, when produced with asserting force, may be used to publicly manifest the acknowledgment of the truth of a thought. For Frege, logical provability or inferability is no more a notational notion than assertability. To infer something is to acknowledge the

[34]Jean van Heijenoort, "Logic as Calculus and Logic as Language" [1967a, pp. 326–327]. For Frege's expression of this attitude, see [1884, §91] and "On Mr. Peano's Conceptual Notation and My Own" [1897, pp. 362–363/1984, p. 235]. A full treatment of this point requires discussion of the relationship between Frege's experimental attitude toward the adequacy of a codification of logic and his universalist conception of the subject matter of logical laws.

truth of one thought on the basis of the acknowledgment of truth of other thoughts in accordance with logical laws.[35] Accordingly, a discussion of syntactic manipulations standing alone would not then for Frege be a discussion of provability. One would have to present as well the basis for taking series of sentences constructed according to certain formal rules to be proofs.

Just here the view of truth that accompanies and supports Frege's universalist conception of logic bars scientific theorizing about provability. Frege states his inference rules as permissions. The following formulation of *MP* can stand in an example of the sort of rule Frege states:

> From a conditional and the antecedent of the conditional, the consequent may be inferred.

The rule licenses the assertion in begriffsschrift proofs of the consequent of a conditional on the basis of the earlier assertion of the conditional and its antecedent. From a contemporary perspective, we would say that the basis for the permission that the rule grants is the soundness of the rule under the intended interpretation of Frege's formalism. Formulation of this basis requires, however, the use of a truth predicate. I have argued elsewhere that Frege's view of truth bars the serious, scientific use a truth predicate, for truth is not a property of the thoughts that sentences express.[36] In this sense then, there is no statable basis for the permissions that Frege's inference rules grant, and thus no scientific theorizing about provability. There is, in the end, just the rigorous, explicit construction of proofs in the begriffsschrift. Consistency claims are then extrasystematic invitations to observe that were some claim refutable, we would then be able to refute something else whose truth has been established.

In sum, as Frege views them, consistency arguments are not explicitly metalogical arguments. On this reading then, Frege's argument in *Grundgesetze* §10 is not a proto-model theoretic argument: it employs no notion of varying interpretations of a formalism and draws on no semantic notion of logical consequence.[37] Far from showing an interest in metalogical questions, §10 marks the

---

[35]See "On the Foundations of Geometry" [1906c, p. 387/1984, p. 318].

[36]For further discussion of Frege's views on truth and inference, see my "Objectivity and Objecthood" [1986a, §2], and "Frege, the *Tractatus,* and the Logocentric Predicament," [1985, pp. 6–9]. The most serious textual challenge to this interpretation is, I believe, Frege's exploratory attempt to make sense of independence proofs in the third part of "On the Foundations of Geometry" [1906c, pp. 423–430/1984, pp. 333–340].

[37]Frege believes that the use in logic of a notion of varying interpretations is, at best, a confused way of getting at what should properly be expressed by variables. See [1906c, pp. 307–309, 384–393/1984, pp. 306–308, 315–324]. Other detailed interpretations of the argumentation in *Grundgesetze* §10 I am familiar with see Frege as using some notion of varying interpretation. I include among these [Dummett, 1981, pp. 403–404] and [Dummett, 1991a, pp. 211, 219], [Moore and Rein, 1986, pp. 375–384], and [Schröder-Heister, 1987, pp. 69–77]. Thiel's discussion in "Wahrheitswert und Wertverlauf" [1976] of §10 is less clear, as Thiel gives no interpretation of the notion of determination that is operative in Frege's argumentation.

distance between Frege's attitude toward consistency and modern, post-Hilbert-ian attitudes.

Frege now proceeds to identify the True with the course-of-values of a concept under which the True and only the True falls, and likewise for the False. These concepts are designated by begriffsschrift expressions and are, independent of Frege's identifications and Basic Law V, provably not coextensive. It needs to be emphasized that in making these identifications, Frege is not arbitrarily identifying the True with some already identified object. On the contrary, I have stressed that Frege takes it to be clear and unquestionable what truth-values are. Nor is Frege settling by fiat a factual matter that properly belongs to judgment, to science.[38] Until the course-of-values function has been introduced, no sense has been given to the question, "Is the True identical with the course-of-values of some function?" Frege offers his stipulative identifications in the course of explaining to us what second-level function he intends by the function name " $\varepsilon\phi(e)$ ", i.e., one that maps $-(\xi)$ to the True. Frege might have identified the truth-values with the courses-of-value of other functions. Or he might have stipulated that neither is the course-of-values of any function. Or, perversely, he might have identified one, but not the other, truth-value with a course-of-values.

Let us now return to Frege's first use of the permutation argument. All Frege's §3 stipulation tells us about the course-of-values function is that it maps extensionally identical first-level functions to the same object. This condition says nothing about which object the course-of-values function associates with what function.[39] The first and truncated version of the permutation argument is to gloss and substantiate this conclusion:

> Let us assume that
>
> $$X(\xi)$$
>
> is a function that never returns the same value for different arguments. Then the very same criterion for recognition [Kennzeichen zur Wiedererkennung] is valid for objects whose names have the form " $X(\varepsilon\phi(e))$ " as for the objects signs for which have the form " $\varepsilon\phi(e)$ ". Namely then, " $X(\varepsilon\phi(e)) = X(\alpha\psi(a))$ " means the same as " $(a)(\phi(a) = \psi(a))$ ". From this it follows that by means of the identification of the meaning of " $\varepsilon(\phi(e)) = \alpha(\psi(a))$ " with that of " $(a)(\phi(a) = \psi(a))$ ", the meaning of a name like " $\varepsilon(\phi(e))$ " is in no way fully determined, not at least if there is a function like $X(\xi)$, whose value for a course-of-values as argument is not always this very thing. [1893, §10, p. 16, my translation]

It may look as if Frege, assuming Basic Law V, here argues that there is another second-level function satisfying the extensionality condition. This conclusion,

---

[38]Here I think that [Moore and Rein, 1986] misses the point of the clarification of courses-of-values that §10 offers in *"Grundgesetze, Section 10"* in *Frege Synthesized.*
[39]Thiel frames the conclusion of the permutation argument in similar terms in [1976, p. 293].

though, is too weak for Frege's purposes.[40] Given Basic Law V, one can define a permutation that interchanges the courses-of-values of two provably non-coextensive concepts and, as above, define a second function allegedly satisfying the extensionality condition. Frege would not take such a permutation of courses-of-value to reveal an indeterminacy in the meaning assigned to course-of-values names; for the truth-value of all mixed equations formed from course-of-value names and the new names are fixed by Basic Law V and the definition of the permutation. We have in effect, by means of the defined permutation, relabeled courses-of-value. Frege's point here, rather, is that as far as Basic Law V goes, *any* object might be the course-of-values of a particular function.[41] What though does this casually stated, nebulous point come to for Frege?

Frege's positive explication of courses-of-value is exhausted by the observation that the second-level courses-of-values function satisfies the extensionality condition. All we know from this introduction about courses-of-value is what can be inferred from this observation; and this is not enough, Frege argues, to determine whether an arbitrary object, one not identified as a course-of-values, is the course-of-values of a particular function. Frege begins with an informal proof of the higher-order generalization:

> (B) if $X(\xi)$ is a permutation over objects, then its composition with the course-of-values function satisfies the extensionality condition.

(B) is the related claim that here in the first permutation argument plays the role that (A) plays in the second. The conclusion that Frege's explication does not fix the meaning of course-of-values names is the upshot of a schematic consistency argument that exploits this generalization. Let y be an object and N a proper name for y that, on the elimination of any defined names, contains no mention of the course-of-values function. Consider the equation

$$(1)\ N = \text{'}e\phi(e).$$

The first permutation argument is supposed to show that (1) is not logically decidable from Basic Law V.

First, suppose (1) were refutable from Basic Law V. Let $X(\xi)$ be a permutation defined using N that interchanges y with $\text{'}e\phi(e)$. By (B), everything that is known about the course-of-values function from Frege's introduction holds for

---

[40]This is more or less the way that Dummett understands the first permutation argument in [1981, chap. 19], see especially pp. 402–403. Dummett observes that it is not clear why Frege should take this result to show an indeterminacy in the meanings of course-of-values names and that Frege's identification of truth-values with courses-of-values does not address this sort of referential inscrutability. In my attempt to arrive at an interpretation of Frege's permutation argument that better fits it into both §10 and Frege's philosophy generally, I have been aided by Dummett's probing discussion of *Grundgesetze* §10 in [1981]. Moore and Rein also raise these points [1986].

[41]Thiel similarly understands the point of the permutation argument [1976, p. 293].

this composition. But then, any refutation of (1) from Basic Law V could be transformed into a refutation of

$$N = X('e\phi(e)),$$

contradicting the existence of the permutation $X(\xi)$.

Second, suppose (1) were provable from Basic Law V. Let $X(\xi)$ be a permutation defined using N that interchanges y with $'e(\text{not }\phi(e))$. As $'e\phi(e)$ is not identical to $'e(\text{not }\phi(e))$, from (1) it follows that

$$N \neq X('e\phi(e)).$$

Once again however, given (B), the assumed proof of (1) can be transformed into a proof of

$$N = X('e\phi(e)),$$

again contradicting the existence of $X(\xi)$.[42]

This argument shows that Frege's introduction of course-of-value names gives rise to the Julius Caesar problem within the begriffsschrift, if there are proper names that are not course-of-value names. Sentential names of truth-values do not present the truth-values as courses-of-values. By their use, a permutation $X(\xi)$ can be defined in logical terms, giving a particular example within the begriffsschrift of the indeterminacy Frege presents in the first permutation argument in general terms. Thus understood, Frege's use of the first permutation argument is not then, as Michael Dummett has claimed, an "aberration" [1991a, p. 211, fn 1].

III

Frege's identification of truth-values with courses-of-value makes only a small contribution to determining the meanings of course-of-values names. After all, these stipulations do not settle whether Julius Caesar himself is the course-of-values of some function. In general, it appears that the complete determination of meanings for course-of-values names requires stipulations that settle for each object, whether that object is the course-of-values of some function. In a footnote toward the end of §10 Frege explores the possibility of generalizing his treatment of truth-values by declaring each object to be identical with the course-of-values of a concept under which it alone falls, i.e., $x = 'e(x = e)$. Frege rejects this suggestion: in conjunction with Basic Law V, applied to courses-of-

[42]Although Moore and Rein reconstruct the permutation argument in semantic terms in their [1986], their reconstruction is similar in structure and purpose to mine. I have benefited from their paper, especially pp. 380–381.

values themselves, it implies the course-of-values of any concept is the sole object falling under the concept.[43]

In the final paragraph of section 10, Frege says that course-of-values have been determined "so far as it is here possible." He warns, however, if names of functions not already definable are introduced into the system, then it must be stipulated what values they yield for courses-of-values as arguments. Recall that Frege intends the begriffsschrift to be a framework for the language of all of science. He envisions adding to the logical core presented in *Grundgesetze* the primitive vocabulary required for the expression of the laws and facts uncovered by the special sciences. Perhaps Frege's strategy is this. Since the only objects named in the logical core are truth-values and courses-of-values, Frege takes his identifications of truth-values with courses-of-values to clarify what courses-of-values are, and so to fix a meaning and sense for every begriffsschrift sentence so far as possible at this initial stage in the development of the language. As the begriffsschrift is expanded to incorporate the special sciences, there will be a family of specifiable concepts that partition objects. Moreover, the stipulations that are to be made in introducing new primitive vocabulary will determine whether the objects falling under each of the concepts in this family are courses-of-value. The stipulations would then fix whether any given object is a course-of-values. Nothing more, Frege might claim, can be required by way of an elucidation of what courses-of-value are.

Frege says at the very end of §10 that the stipulations that settle the values that a newly introduced primitive first-level function returns for courses-of-value as arguments can be seen equally as a determination of that function as of courses-of-values. This claim is curious. Frege does not treat the §10 stipulations as further determinations of the horizontal function or the identity relation. Why shouldn't he hold, for example, that the sense and meaning of the euclidean geometrical predicate "point" is fully explicable apart from any special stipulation of whether points are courses-of-value? After all, throughout his career, Frege adheres to an attenuated Kantianism that posits a distinct cognitive capacity for geometrical knowledge. So, why shouldn't any stipulation here be an elucidation solely of courses-of-value? Why treat "point" differently from the horizontal function sign? Perhaps the reason is this. Logical vocabulary is used in every science; and logical laws and inferences are applied in the acquisition of knowledge in any science. Once Basic Law V is admitted as a fundamental logical principle, a determination of whether points are courses-of-value is required to fit geometry into the framework for universal science that the begriffsschrift provides. Hence, the stipulation counts equally as an elucidation of what points are and what courses-of-values are.

---

[43] Assume $x = \text{'}e(x{=}e)$. Then $\text{'}ef(e) = \text{'}a(\text{'}ef(e){=}a)$. Then, by the §3 stipulation, $(x)(fx = (\text{'}af(a){=}x))$. So $f(\xi)$ is a concept under which only $\text{'}ef(e)$ falls.

Frege himself never extended the begriffsschrift to incorporate the basic vocabulary of any special science. How might Frege have incorporated the predicate "point" into an extension of the begriffsschrift to include geometry? Following the precedent set by Frege's treatment of truth-values, this could be done by stipulating that each point is identical with the extension of a concept under which it alone falls, i.e., If Point(x), then $x = \,'e(x=e)$. Might Frege have been prepared to follow this policy quite generally so that every object would end up the course-of-values of some function? This policy might be thought inconsistent with Frege's rejection in a footnote to §10 of the stipulation that every object not given to us as a course-of-values is to be identified with the course-of-values of a concept under which only it falls. However, Frege confirms in this footnote that it is possible to stipulate any object y that is, like the truth-values, given independently of courses-of-value to be identical with $'e(e=y)$. What Frege rejects are *general* stipulations to this effect that use predicates like "object not given to us as a course-of-values."

Might Frege's view that logical objects are courses-of-value give him motivation to refrain from identifying geometrical and physical objects with courses-of-value? After all, Frege rejects a conception of objecthood that makes spatiality, temporality, or causal powers constitutive of objecthood. In this connection Frege contrasts actual [*wirklich*] with unactual objects, and he asserts that numbers are examples of unactual objects. Frege also believes that logic is a science with its domain of investigation and accompanying ontology, an ontology that includes at least some courses-of-value. Perhaps then Frege took this status of unactuality to be intrinsic to courses-of-value so that he was prepared to stipulate, in expanding the begriffsschrift to incorporate the vocabulary of the special sciences, that e.g., points are *not* courses-of-value. In contrast, as truth-values certainly are for Frege logical objects, there is no objection on ontological grounds to their identification as courses-of-value. Attribution of this view to Frege does not, however, fit well with his consideration in §10 of the prospects for identifying objects generally, or broad ranges of objects, with the extensions of concepts under which they alone fall.[44]

Nevertheless, it must be admitted that the position to which Frege is forced at the end of §10 does not comport with his understanding of the presuppositions of judgment—his understanding of clarity, rigor, and content—that accompany the universalist conception of logic. In numerous places, Frege insists that in order for a sentence to express a thought that belongs to science, that may properly be judged true or false, the names in that sentence must express a sense that

---

[44]The view also does not fit with the passage in Frege's August 2, 1902, letter to Russell discussed in the penultimate paragraph of this paper. If courses-of-value were intrinsically unactual, it would be a straightforward matter whether the objects falling under most concepts that figure in science were courses-of-value.

determines a meaning.[45] In the case of function names, this meaning must be a function of the appropriate type that yields a determinate value, a definite object, for every argument. The following passage from Frege's 1914 manuscript "Logic in Mathematics" expresses an attitude he holds throughout his career:

> We must distinguish between the history and the system of science. In history we have development; in a system, fixity (Starrheit). A system can be extended; but what once stands must remain, or else the entire system must be thrown over in order that a new one be built. Only in a system does science come to completion.[46]

However, at the end of §10, Frege admits in effect that he has not given his course-of-values function name a determinate meaning. As a result, Frege is not in a position to attribute to himself a grasp of what second-level function " $'e\phi(e)$ " is to mean. Towards the end of *Foundations,* Frege rhapsodizes:

> On this view of numbers the charm of work on arithmetic and analysis is, it seems to me, easily accounted for. We might say, indeed, almost in the well-known words: the reason's proper study is itself. In arithmetic we are not concerned with objects which we come to know as something alien from without through the medium of the senses, but with objects given directly to our reason, and, as its nearest kin, utterly transparent to it. [1884, §105, p. 115]

But in *Foundations* Frege assumes knowledge of what extensions of concepts are. In §147 of the second volume of *Grundgesetze,* Frege is more cautious:

> If there indeed are logical objects—and the objects of arithmetic are such—then there must be a means of grasping them, of knowing [*erkennen*] them. The basic logical law that permits the transformation of the generalization of an equation into an equation for us serves this purpose. Without such a means, a scientific grounding of arithmetic would be impossible. [1903, §147, p. 149, my translation]

Frege should hesitate here; for, by his own admission at the end of §10, with only a partial grasp of courses-of-values, Basic Law V cannot serve this purpose.

The strain in Frege's views is visible in his August 2, 1902, letter to Russell. In his July 24 letter, Russell had said, "Every day I understand less what generally 'extension of a concept' means." Frege responds:

> You ask how it can be known that something is a course-of-values. This is indeed a difficult point. Now, all objects of arithmetic are introduced as courses-of-values. Whenever a new object to be considered is not introduced as a course-of-values, we must at once answer the question whether it is a course-of-values, and the answer is probably always no, since it would have been introduced as a course-of-values if it was one. [1980, p. 142][47]

---

[45]See "On Sense and Meaning," [1892, pp. 31ff., p. 41/1984, pp. 161ff., p. 169]; [1893, p. xxi and §28, p. 45]; "Logik" [1983, pp. 141ff./1979a, pp. 129–130].

[46]"Logic in Mathematics," [1914] in [1983, p. 261/1979a, pp. 241ff.].

[47]I am grateful to Richard Heck for calling this passage to my attention.

The objects of arithmetic are introduced as courses-of-value in that Frege envisions that from the definitions of the arithmetical vocabulary, it will be provable that the objects falling under the concepts defined are courses-of-value. Frege now confronts again the indeterminacy in his conception of courses-of-value by considering how we might discover whether some object not introduced as a course-of-value is one. Frege assumes that a meaningful vocabulary used to designate the object is in place. The object is not given as a course-of-values in that it is not provable from the definitions and stipulations that introduce the vocabulary that figures in the designation that the object designated is a course-of-values. Frege lamely suggests that in this case, the object probably is not a course-of-values. But is it, or is it not? If we have a grasp of courses-of-value and a grasp of what the object is, a grasp of the sense of its designation, then, perhaps drawing on scientific knowledge, we should understand what considerations are relevant to settling the question. On the one hand, Frege appears here to have forgotten how in §10 he identified truth-values, objects not introduced as courses-of-value, with courses-of-value; and he has lost sight of the problematic conclusion of §10—a full and sharp grasp of what courses-of-values are is attained only globally with the introduction of further non-logical vocabulary in the expansion of the begriffsschrift to encompass universal science. On the other hand, Frege realizes that he cannot represent the difficulty here as a purely epistemic one that arises in the setting of a sharp conception of courses-of-value.

Russell's paradox makes urgent what is already apparent in §10: by his own standards of clarity, Frege lacks a sharp conception of courses-of-value. To introduce names for logical objects with the desired features into the begriffsschrift, Frege needed a designation of a specific second-level function that satisfied the extensionality condition. By his own standards of clarity and rigor, he had a right, at best, only to the existential generalization of this condition. Frege's surviving correspondence contains a partial draft of a letter to the American mathematician E. V. Huntington. The draft was apparently written in 1903, after Russell's communication of the paradox. Frege criticizes Huntington's talk of the object denoted by "2 *o* 3". Frege says:

> Now what does "2 *o* 3" mean. We could assume very different rules of combination. If we take the sum, then 5 is determined, if the product, then 6 . . . but we cannot recognize from the sign what rule to take. . . . There seems to me to be here a mixture of two different kinds of signs, namely those that designate or mean and those that merely indicate. This sign "*o*" seems to me to be a hermaphrodite [*Zwitter*]. . . . Unclarity over the sense of the sentence in which this sign occurs arises from this hermaphrodite character. [1980, pp. 58–59][48]

---

[48]Frege to Huntington XVIII/1 (undated). See also Frege's comment in a 1910 letter (letter XXI/9) to Jourdain on Russell's characterization of universal algebra [1980, p. 182].

I have argued that the criticism Frege makes of Huntington applies, after a fash-ion, to his own introduction of courses-of-value.

9

W.W. Tait

FREGE VERSUS CANTOR AND DEDEKIND: ON THE CONCEPT OF NUMBER*

There can be no doubt about the value of Frege's contributions to the philoso-phy of mathematics. First, he invented quantification theory and this was the first step toward making precise the notion of a purely logical deduction. Sec-ondly, he was the first to publish a logical analysis of the ancestral $R*$ of a rela-tion R, which yields a definition of $R*$ in second-order logic.[1] Only a narrow and arid conception of philosophy would exclude these two achievements. Thirdly and very importantly, the discussion in §§58–60 of the *Grundlagen* defends a conception of mathematical existence, to be found in [Cantor 1883] and later in the writings of Dedekind and Hilbert, by basing it upon considerations about meaning which have *general* application, outside mathematics.[2]

Michael Dummett, in his book [Dummett 1991][3] on Frege's philosophy of mathematics, is rather stronger in his evaluation. He writes "For all his mistakes and omissions, he was the greatest philosopher of mathematics yet to have writ-ten" (P. 321). I think that one has to have a rather circumscribed view of what constitutes philosophy to subscribe to such a statement—or indeed to any

---

*This paper is in honor of my colleague and friend, Leonard Linsky, on the occasion of his retire-ment. I presented the earliest version in the Spring of 1992 to a reading group, the other members of which were Leonard Linsky, Steve Awodey, André Carus, and Mike Price. I presented later versions in the autumn of 1992 to the philosophy colloquium at McGill University and in the autumn of 1993 to the philosophy colloquium at Carnegie-Mellon University. The discussions following these pre-sentations were valuable to me, and I would especially like to acknowledge Emily Carson (for com-ments on the earliest draft), Michael Hallett, Kenneth Manders, Stephen Menn, G.E. Reyes, Teddy Seidenfeld, and Wilfrid Sieg and the members of the reading group for helpful comments. But, most of all, I would like to thank Howard Stein and Richard Heck, who read the penultimate draft of the paper and made extensive comments and corrections. Naturally, none of these scholars, except pos-sibly Howard Stein, is responsible for any remaining defects.

[1]Frege (1879). Dedekind (1887) similarly analyzed the ancestral $F*$ in the case of a one-to-one func-tion F from a set into a proper subset. In the preface to the first edition, Dedekind stated that, in the years 1872–78, he had written a first draft, containing all the essential ideas of his monograph.
[2]However, it was only in the hands of Wittgenstein, in *Philosophical Investigations,* that this critique of meaning was fully and convincingly elaborated.
[3]All references to Dummett will be to this work, unless otherwise specified.

ranking in philosophy of mathematics. If I had to choose, I would perhaps rank
Plato first, on grounds of priority, since he was first, as far as we know, to conceive of the idea of a priori science, that is science based on primitive truths
from which we reason purely deductively. But, if Plato seems too remote, then
Frege still has some strong competitors even in the nineteenth century, for example Bolzano, Riemann, Weierstrass, and, especially, Cantor and Dedekind. Contributing to Dummett's assessment is, I think, a tendency to make a sharp distinction between what is philosophical and what is technical and outside the
domain of philosophy, a sharper distinction between philosophy and science
than is historically justified or reasonable. Thus, we read that Frege had answers
(although not always the right ones) "to all the philosophical problems concerning the branches of mathematics with which he dealt. He had an account to offer
of the applications of arithmetic; of the status of its objects; of the kind of necessity attaching to arithmetic truths; and of how to reconcile their a priori character
with our attainment of new knowledge about arithmetic." (p. 292) The question
of existence of mathematical objects, their 'status', certainly needed clarification; but, otherwise, are these the most important philosophical problems associated with the branches of mathematics with which he dealt? Surely the most
important philosophical problem of Frege's time and ours, and one certainly
connected with the investigation of the concept of number, is the clarification of
the infinite, initiated by Bolzano and Cantor and seriously misunderstood by
Frege. Likewise, the important distinction between cardinal and ordinal numbers, introduced by Cantor, and (especially in connection with the question of
mathematical existence) the characterization of the system of finite numbers to
within isomorphism as a simply infinite system, introduced by Dedekind, are of
central importance in the philosophy of mathematics. Also, the issue of constructive versus non-constructive reasoning in mathematics, which Frege
nowhere discussed, was very much alive by 1884, when he published his *Grundlagen*. Finally, although Frege took up the problem of the analysis of the continuum, his treatment of it appeared about thirty years after the work of Weierstrass, Cantor, Dedekind, Heine, and Meray (the latter four in 1872) and,
besides, was incomplete. What it lacked was, essentially, just what the earlier
works supplied, a construction (at least up to isomorphism) of the complete
ordered additive group of real numbers. Whether Frege had, as he thought,
something to add to that construction in the definition of the real numbers is a
question on which I shall briefly comment in §VII, where I discuss the analogous question of Frege's versus Dedekind's treatment of finite cardinal numbers.
The issue here concerns the matter of applications. It is true that Frege offered
an account of application of the natural numbers and the real numbers and that
this account structured his treatment of the real numbers and possibly, as Dummett suggests, his treatment of the natural numbers. But there is some question

as to whether his account of application should enhance his stature as a philosopher.

However, more important to me in this paper than the question of Frege's own importance in philosophy is the tendency in the literature on philosophy to contrast the superior clarity of thought and powers of conceptual analysis that Frege brought to bear on the foundations of arithmetic, especially in the *Grundlagen,* with the conceptual confusion of his predecessors and contemporaries on this topic. Thus, in [Dummett 1991], p.292: "In Frege's writings, by contrast [to those of Brouwer and Hilbert], everything is lucid and explicit: when there are mistakes, they are set out clearly for all to recognize." Aside from the contrast with Brouwer, I don't believe that this evaluation survives close examination. Frege's discussions of other writers are often characterized less by clarity than by misinterpretation and lack of charity, and, on many matters, both of criticism of other scholars and of substance, his analysis is defective. Dummett agrees with part of this assessment in so far as Volume II of the *Grundgesetze* (1903) is concerned. He writes

> The critical sections of *Grundlagen* follow one another in a logical sequence; each is devoted to a question concerning arithmetic and the natural numbers, and other writers are cited only when either some view they express or the refutation of their errors contributes positively to answering the question. In Part III.1 of *Grundgesetze,* the sections follow no logical sequence. Each after the first . . . is devoted to a particular rival mathematician or group of mathematicians. . . . From their content, the reader cannot but think that Frege is anxious to direct at his competitors any criticism to which they lay themselves open, regardless of whether it advances his argument or not. He acknowledges no merit in the work of those he criticizes; nor, with the exception only of Newton and Gauss, is anyone quoted with approbation. The Frege who wrote Volume II of *Grundgesetze* was a very different man from the Frege who had written *Grundlagen:* an embittered man whose concern to give a convincing exposition of his theory of the foundations of analysis was repeatedly overpowered by his desire for revenge on those who had ignored or failed to understand his work. (pp. 242–243)

Concerning the relative coherence of the two works, Dummett is surely right. But I think that, in Frege's treatment of other scholars, we can very well recognize the later Frege in the earlier one. Establishing this purely negative fact about Frege would be, by itself, very small potatoes. But unfortunately, his assessment of his contemporaries in *Grundlagen* and elsewhere lives on in much of the philosophical literature, where respected mathematicians, such as Heine, Lipschitz, Schröder, and Thomae, are regarded as utterly muddled about the concept of number, and great philosophers, such as Cantor and Dedekind, are treated as philosophical naifs, however creative, whose work provides, at best, fodder for philosophical chewing. Not only have we inherited from Frege a poor regard for his contemporaries, but, taking the critical parts of his *Grundlagen* as a model, we in the Anglo-American tradition of analytic philosophy have inherited a poor vision of what philosophy is.

I

The conception of sets and of ordinal and cardinal numbers for which Cantor is perhaps best known first appeared in print in 1888 and represents a significant and, to my mind, unfortunate change in his position. He first introduced the concept of two arbitrary sets, finite or infinite, having the same power in [Cantor 1878]. In [Cantor 1874] he had already in effect shown that there are at least two infinite powers (although he had not yet defined the general notion of equipollence). Prior to 1883, all of the sets that he had been considering were subsets of finite-dimensional Euclidean spaces, all of which he had shown to have the power of the continuum. New sets, the number classes, with successively higher powers, were introduced in [Cantor 1883]. So here, for the first time, he obtained sets which might have powers greater than that of the continuum. In this connection, it should be noted that, although he defined the concept of a well-ordered set and noted that the ordinal numbers corresponded to the order types of well-ordered sets,[4] the ordinal numbers themselves were defined *autonomously* and not as the order types of well-ordered sets.[5] Indeed, in general, the only well-ordered set of order type α available to him was the set of predecessors of α. In discussing what had been gained by his construction of the ordinals, the application to well-ordered sets is mentioned only *second,* after the founding of the theory of powers. For Cantor, at this time, the construction of the number classes was essential to the theory of powers. In speaking of their significance, he writes

> Our aforementioned number classes of determinately infinite real whole numbers [i.e. the ordinals] now show themselves to be the natural uniform representatives of the lawful sequence of ascending powers of well-defined sets. [Cantor 1932, p. 167]

Just prior to this he wrote that "Every well-defined set has a determinate power", so his view at that time was that every infinite well-defined set is equipollent to a number class.[6] In particular, he notes in the 1883 paper that neither the totality of

---

[4]Cantor 1932, p.168.

[5]Frege obviously appreciated this point. In [1884, §86] he wrote, "I find special reason to welcome in Cantor's investigations an extension of the frontiers of science, because they have led to the construction of a purely arithmetical route to higher transfinite numbers (powers)."

[6]At the beginning of §3 of [1883], Cantor explicitly states as a 'law of thought' that every set can be well-ordered. His assertion that the powers form an absolute infinity seems to imply that the construction of the number classes is to be continued beyond the finite number classes. He isn't explicit about how one proceeds to construct the αth-number class for limit ordinal α, but presumably, if its power is to be the next highest after those of all the β number classes for $\beta < \alpha$, we should take it to be the union of the number classes of smaller index. But *when* should we introduce the αth number class for limit α? If we require that α be already obtained in some earlier number class, then the only

all ordinals nor the totality of all cardinals has a power. It follows then that neither is a well-defined set.

It was in "Mitteilungen zur Lehre vom Transfiniten" (1887–88) and, later, in "Beiträge zur Begründung der transfiniten Mengenlehre" (1895–97) that Cantor introduced the much-criticized abstractionist conception of the cardinals and ordinals. To quote from the "Beiträge":

> By the "power" or "cardinal number" of M we mean the general concept, which arises with the help of our active faculty of thought from the set M, in that we abstract from the nature of the particular elements of M and from the order in which they are presented. . . . Since every single element m [of M], if we abstract from its nature, becomes a 'unit', the cardinal number . . . [of M] is a definite aggregate composed of units, and this number has existence in our mind as an intellectual image or projection of the given aggregate M. [Cantor 1932, p. 282–283]

In the analogous way, he introduced the *order type* of a linearly ordered set *M:*

> By this we understand *the general concept which arises from* M *when we abstract only from the nature of the elements of* M, *retaining the order of precedence among them.* . . . Thus, the order type . . . is *itself an ordered set* whose elements are pure units. . . . (p. 297).

In particular, ordinal numbers are identified in the "Mitteilungen" and the "Beiträge" with the order types of well-ordered sets. It would be interesting to conjecture about the reasons for the change from the point of view of [1883] to that of [1887–88]; but I shall not go into that here, other than to register my regret.[7] Husserl, who notes in [Husserl 1890] the change with approval, defends the later definition and, as does Cantor, argues that the essential principle that, if two sets are equipollent, then they have the same cardinal, is derivable from it. (Two sets are *equipollent* or, as Cantor expressed it, *equivalent* if they are in one-to-one correspondence.) But the argument is not entirely clear: Why should abstraction from two equipollent sets lead to the *same* set of 'pure units'? And the conception of the cardinal number as a set plays no other role in Cantor's theory. We shall discuss this further in §VIII.

---

ordinals Cantor's scheme yields are those less than the least fixed point $\alpha = \aleph_\alpha$. But if, as seems perfectly consistent with Cantor's ideology, we require only that the cofinality of α be obtained in some earlier number class, then the ordinals that would be obtained are precisely those less than the least weakly inaccessible cardinal (i.e. the least *regular* fixed point of $\aleph$). After his proof in Cantor (1891–92) that the power of a set is strictly less than that of its power set, possibly higher powers are obtained. The analogous hierarchy of powers leads to the least strongly inaccessible cardinal. Not until [Zermelo, 1930] does it seem that anyone pursued this 'constructive' approach to set theory, to obtain ordinals beyond the least strongly inaccessible cardinal.

[7]The assimilation of the theory of ordinals to the more general theory of order types may be part of the explanation. The discovery that a set is strictly less in power than its power set does not seem to be part of the explanation, since the "Mitteilungen" precedes that discovery.

II

In §71 of "Was sind und was sollen die Zahlen?" (1888), Dedekind defines the notion of a 'simply infinite system' M with respect to a one-to-one function $\phi:M{\to}M$. Namely, there is an element of e of M which is not in the range of ϕ, and M is the least set containing e and closed under ϕ. ϕ is said to *order M*, and e is called the *base element* of M (with respect to ϕ). He then goes on to introduce the simply infinite system of natural numbers:

> 73. Definition. If, in considering a simply infinite system [*M*] ordered by the mapping ϕ, we completely disregard the particular nature of the elements, retaining only their distinguishability and considering only those relationships in which they are placed to one another by the ordering map ϕ, then these elements are called *natural numbers* or *ordinal numbers* or simply *numbers,* and the base element [*e*] is called the *base element* of the *number series* [*M*]. In consideration of this freeing of the elements from every other content (abstraction) one can with justice call the numbers a free creation of the human intellect [*menschlichen Geistes*].

When M is a simply infinite system with respect to the map ϕ and base element e, let us call the triple $M={\langle}M,\phi,e{\rangle}$ *a simply infinite set.* We may denote the system of numbers by $N={\langle}N,',1{\rangle}$. Dedekind goes on to cite his proof in §134 that all simply infinite sets are isomorphic, in order to show that arithmetic depends only on the axioms of the (second order) theory of simply infinite sets and not on the choice of any particular such system[8]. The step from M to N is an instance of Cantor's abstraction in the case of ordered sets.

III

The response in the literature on philosophy of mathematics to Cantor's and Dedekind's abstractionist treatment of numbers has generally been negative.

An early direct attack on Cantor is contained in [Frege 1891], a review of [Cantor 1890] (which includes the "Mitteilungen".)[9] In what must count as one of the more impertinent passages in the history of philosophy, he writes:

> If Mr. Cantor had not only reviewed my *Grundlagen der Arithmetik* but also read it thoughtfully, he would have avoided many mistakes. I believe that I have done there already a long time ago what he is here trying in vain to do. Mr. Cantor repeats (p. 13) a definition he had given in his review of my book as his own intellectual prop-

---

[8]The axioms in question are

$$\forall x(e{\neq}\phi(x))$$
$$\forall xy(\phi(x)=\phi(y){\to}x=y)$$
$$\forall Z[e{\epsilon}Z{\wedge}\forall x(x{\epsilon}Z{\to}\phi(x){\epsilon}Z){\to}\forall x(x{\epsilon}Z)].$$

[9]A more virulent attack, which Frege chose not to publish, is contained in a partial draft of that review [Frege 1979, p. 68–71].

erty. It seemed to me at the time that it differed from mine, not in its essentials, but only in its wording . . . I now see that the truths I enunciated in my book were not, after all, like coins dropped in the street which anybody could make his own simply by bending down. For Mr. Cantor goes on to give some other definitions (pp. 23 and 56) which show that he is still firmly ensconced in an antiquated position. He is asking for impossible abstractions and it is unclear to him what is to be understood by a 'set', even though he has an inkling of the correct answer, which comes out faintly when he says (p. 67 n.): 'A set is already completely delimited by the fact that everything that belongs to it is determined in itself and well distinguished from everything that does not belong to it.' This delimitation is, of course, achieved by characteristic marks and is nothing other than the definition of a concept. On this point compare my proposition (*Grundlagen,* §46): ' . . . the content of a statement of number is an assertion about a concept'. [1984, p. 179]

And shortly after:

. . . we once again encounter those unfortunate ones which are different even though there is nothing to distinguish them from one another. The author evidently did not have the slightest inkling of the presence of this difficulty, which I dealt with at length in §§34 to 54 of my *Grundlagen.*

The page references are to [Cantor 1890]. But the 'other definitions (pp. 23 and 56)' are the "Mitteilungen" versions of the above quoted definitions of power and order type, in [Cantor 1932], p. 387 and p. 422, respectively. The definition given 'as his own intellectual property' in Cantor's review [1885] of [Frege 1884] and which he 'repeats' is clearly the definition of the cardinal number or power of an aggregate [*inbegriff*] or set as 'that general concept under which all and only those sets fall which are equivalent to the given set.' [Cantor 1932, p. 380]. Frege's own definition is that the number $N_x F(x)$ of F's, where F is a concept, is the extension of the second level concept 'is equipollent to F'. Frege had thought that it differs only in wording from his own, because he thought that it is inessential whether one speaks of a general concept here or of its extension and because he thought, incorrectly (see §XII below), that Cantor's notion of a set could be understood to mean 'extension of a concept' in his sense.[10]

In [1883], §1, Cantor writes "Every well-defined set M has a power, such that two sets have the same power when they [are equipollent]" The passage from this, in response to the question "What *is* the cardinal of M?", to the definition of the cardinal of M as the general concept under which fall precisely those sets equipollent to M, surely owes nothing to Frege. In defining the cardinal number of M as a 'general concept', it seems clear that Cantor did not have in mind Frege's technical notion of a concept; rather, he was following the traditional view according to which, for example, the numeral '10' is a common name, under which falls all ten-element sets. (For example, see Aristotle's

---

[10]See the footnote at the end of §68 of [Frege, 1984] and his reply in [Frege, 1984], p. 120, to Cantor's review [Cantor 1932, pp. 440–441]

Physics, 224a3–16.) Moreover, as we shall see, Cantor had already pointed out, implicitly in his 1883 paper and explicitly in his review of [Frege 1884], that it is a mistake to take the notion of a set (i.e. of that which has a cardinal number) to simply mean the extension of a concept. Finally, the very definition of equinumerosity in terms of equipollence, applied to sets *in general,* is due to no one but Cantor—not to Hume, Kossak, or Schröder, whom Frege cites but who were concerned entirely with finite sets. See §X below. As for Frege, who did intend the definition to apply also to the infinite, he was not only anticipated by Cantor by seven years, but even after that time and, presumably, after having read [Cantor 1883] (to which he refers in his 1884 paper), he was unaware of the difficulties involved in treating the infinite. See §XII below.

But Frege is right that Cantor crucially modifies his definition of the power of a set *M* when he goes on to define it, not merely as a concept under which fall all sets equipollent to *M,* but also as an equipollent set of pure units: the concept becomes a paradigm instance of itself. Frege's own conception of abstraction (although he disapproves of the term) is, as we shall see, in agreement with the view that abstracting from the particular nature of the elements of *M* would yield the concept under which fall all sets equipollent to *M.* His target was the idea that abstraction leads to the paradigm set of pure units. We have already noted a difficulty with this idea, at least with respect to the work to which Cantor wanted to put it. But Frege's own arguments against Cantor's conception, that he cites from §§34–54 of his 1884 paper, are invalid. See §VIII below.

A very influential attack on Dedekind's theory occurs in Russell's *Principles of Mathematics* [1903]:

> Moreover, it is impossible that the ordinals should be, as Dedekind suggests, nothing but the terms of such relations as constitute a progression. If they are anything at all, they must be intrinsically something; they must differ from other entities as points from instants, or colours from sounds. (p. 249)

Russell's point is often expressed by saying that it is impossible that objects should 'have only structural properties'. The confusion that lies behind this objection is discussed in §VII. His criticism is echoed in [Dummett 1991]. In Chapter 5, comparing Frege's and Dedekind's treatment of the foundations of arithmetic, Dummett writes

> One of the mental operations most frequently credited with creative powers was that of abstracting from particular features of some object or system of objects, that is, ceasing to take any account of them. It was virtually an orthodoxy, subscribed to by many philosophers and mathematicians, including Husserl and Cantor, that the mind could, by this means, create an object or system of objects lacking the features abstracted from, but not possessing any others in their place. It was to this operation that Dedekind appealed in order to explain what the natural numbers are. His proce-

dure differed from the usual one. Husserl . . . supposed that each individual cardinal number was created by a special act of abstraction: starting with any arbitrary set having that number of elements, we abstract from all properties possessed by the individual members of the set, thus transforming them into featureless units; the set comprising these units was then the relevant cardinal number. Cantor's variation on this account was a trifle more complex: we start with an ordered set, and abstract from all the features of the individual members, but not from their ordering, and thus obtain their [sic] order type; next, we abstract from the ordering relation, and obtain the cardinal number as an unordered set of featureless units, as before. Frege devoted a lengthy section of *Grundlagen*, §§29–44, to a detailed and conclusive critique of this misbegotten theory; it was a bitter disappointment to him that it had not the slightest effect. (p.50)

In questioning that "the mind could, by this means, create an object or system of objects lacking the features abstracted from, but not possessing any others in their place", Dummett seems to be merging Russell's criticism with another: Is it abstract objects to which we should object or is it their creation by the mind? The same double-barreled objection arises immediately after when, discussing Russell's reaction to (and misunderstanding of) Dedekind, Dummett writes that Dedekind "believed that the magical operation of abstraction can provide us with specific objects having only structural properties: Russell did not understand that belief because, very rightly, he had no faith in abstraction thus understood." (p. 52) Dummett is taking 'abstraction' here to be a psychological term.

Dedekind's philosophy of mathematics was that mathematical objects are 'free creations of the human mind', as he says in the Preface. The idea, widely shared by his contemporaries, was that abstract objects are actually created by operations of our minds. This would seem to lead to a solipsistic conception of mathematics; but it is implicit in this conception that each subject is entitled to feel assured that what he creates by means of his own mental operations will coincide, at least in its properties, with what others have created by means of analogous operations. For Frege, such an assurance would be without foundation: for him, the contents of our minds are wholly subjective; since there is no means of comparing them, I cannot know whether my idea is the same as yours. (p. 49)

So Dummett believes that Cantor's and Dedekind's operation of abstraction is psychologistic.

Frege himself does not criticize Dedekind's treatment of the number concept on grounds of psychologism when he discusses it in the introduction to the *Grundgesetze I* (1893). And, in his review of [Cantor 1890], he makes the criticism rather mildly when he writes: "Besides, the verb 'abstract' is a psychological expression and, as such, ought to be avoided in mathematics." (p. 181) But this is by no means his principal attack on Cantor's conception of cardinal and ordinal numbers. *His* reference to his refutation of what Dummett calls the 'misbegotten theory' of Cantor is not to §§29–44 in his 1884 paper, but to §§34–54, in which psychologism is not the issue.

IV

Actually, Dedekind did not say in the Preface that mathematical objects are free creations of the human mind. He did say this of the natural numbers, and there is little doubt that he would have said it also of the real numbers; but it is too hasty to reduce his 'philosophy of mathematics' to a psychologistic reading of this metaphor. Indeed, this tendency to attack forms of expression rather than attempting to appreciate what is actually being said is one of the more unfortunate habits that analytic philosophy inherited from Frege. If one reads §73, quoted above, the metaphor of 'free creation' is justified by the fact that we arrive at the system of numbers by abstraction, by freeing the elements from every other content. Therefore, it is reasonable to conclude that Dedekind's conception is psychologistic only if that is the only way to understand the abstraction that is involved. And we shall see that it is not.

The difficulty with abstraction as a psychological operation would be that what is abstracted is mental, that what I abstract is mine and what you abstract is yours. (See [Frege 1884, §§26–27].) We are no more communicating when I say, "$0<1$", meaning that my 0 is (my) less than my 1, and you say, "No, $1<0$", meaning that your 1 is (your) less than your 0, than when I say, "I am shorter than Jones," and you say, "No, I am taller than Jones". Of course, this does not mean that you and I cannot argue objectively about your, my, or some third party's mental states as an empirical question. But when we discuss the nature of arithmetic truth, that is not what is going on: on whatever grounds I might be seduced into thinking that I am expressing something about *my* mental states when I assert that $0<1$, you would, on the same grounds, be seduced into thinking that you are expressing something about *your* mental states when you assert that $1<0$. Frege's point is that the objectivity of mathematics demands that we both resist this seduction.

So Frege's argument against psychologism in the context of abstraction is not that the source of judgment about the abstracted objects is not in some sense to be found in the common human psyche, but rather that the objects abstracted should not be found in the individual psyche.[11] For example, he himself ultimately traces the source of logical principles to our logical disposition. [Frege 1979, p. 269.] So the objectivity of logic rests, for him, upon the fact that we are disposed to agree in logical judgment.[12] The same point is illustrated by his defense of Kant's conception of geometry as objective in [Frege 1884, §26].

---

[11]There is of course another side to psychologism, which Frege discusses and opposes in [1884], p. x and §60. There the issue is the confusion of the logical with the psychological, e.g. of the senses of words or sentences with our (psychological ideas). But it would seem that Dummett's charge against Dedekind is not this, but that he is taking the *reference* of number words to be ideas.

[12]It should be noted that Frege does not observe, as Wittgenstein later did in the *Investigations,* that objectivity requires not only agreement in the judgment concerning the laws of logic, but also agree-

Space, according to Kant, belongs to appearance. For other rational beings it might take some form quite different from that in which we know it. Indeed, we cannot even know whether it appears the same to one man as to another; for we cannot, in order to compare them, lay one man's intuition of space beside another's. Nevertheless, there is something objective in space all the same; everyone recognizes the same geometrical axioms, even if only by his behavior, and must do so if he is to find his way about in the world. What is objective in it is what is subject to laws, what can be conceived and judged, what is expressible in words. What is purely intuitable is not communicable.

The abstractionism of neither Cantor nor Dedekind is subject to the criticism that it is psychologistic: For neither of them are numbers psychological objects nor are the laws of number to be understood in any way as subjective.

V

Concerning the notion of abstraction, Frege writes:

> For suppose that we do, as Thomae demands, "abstract from the peculiarities of the individual members of a set of things", or "disregard, in considering separate things, those characteristics which serve to distinguish them". In that event we are not left, as Lipschitz maintains, with "the concept of the number of the things considered"; what we get is rather a general concept under which the things considered fall. The things themselves do not in the process lose any of their special characteristics. For example, if I, in considering a white cat and a black cat, disregard the properties which serve to distinguish them, then I get presumably the concept "cat". [1884, §34]

There is a serious misunderstanding of both Thomae and Lipschitz in this passage, which we shall take up later. But the point I want to make here is that Frege is not really correct about abstraction resulting always in concepts, at least not if he is referring to the traditional meaning of the term 'abstraction'. For example, although it is true that Aristotle regards attributes such as 'white' (the concept 'x is white', for Frege) to be obtained by abstraction, he also regards geometric objects such as lines and surfaces to be obtained by abstraction from sensible things (*Metaphysics* 1061^{a}29).

But, of course, there is a sense in which no object is really created by this latter kind of abstraction. The geometric magnitude, e.g. the line segment or the plane figure, was for Aristotle just the sensible substance; but in geometry we regard it, not *qua* sensible object, but only with respect to those properties it has in virtue of its extension. On this view, truths about a geometric object are simply truths about the sensible object, but restricted to the language of geometry.

---

ment drawing consequences, i.e. in moving from premises to conclusion (computing according to a rule).

Analogous to this is the so-called 'forgetful functor' by means of which we pass, say, from a ring $\langle M,+,.\rangle$ to the corresponding group $\langle M,+\rangle$. But these cases are somewhat different from the case of the abstraction of the power $|A|$ from the set A. For if A is equipollent to the set B, then $|A|=|B|$. But this does not imply that $A=B$. Hence, we cannot regard $|A|$ as really being just A, taken in abstraction, unless 'taking in abstraction' has the power to identify distinct sets. Or rather, since Frege is certainly right that the process cannot literally identify distinct things, the process of abstraction in this case must be understood to create new objects. Nevertheless, there is something common to Aristotle's conception of geometry, right or wrong, and the abstraction of cardinal numbers. Namely, sentences about the abstract objects have a canonical, truth-preserving, translation into sentences about the objects from which they are abstracted. In the case of cardinals, the objects from which the powers are abstracted are sets. The relation $\sim$ of equipollence is clearly an equivalence relation among sets and it respects the relation

$$X \leq Y$$

of X being equipollent to a subset of Y as well as the operations of *sum* or *disjoint union*

$$\Sigma_{i \in I} X_i$$

(i.e. the set $\{(i,a)|i \in I \ \& \ a \in X_i\}$) and *cartesian product*

$$\Pi_{i \in I} X_i$$

of a family $\langle X_i | i \in I \rangle$ of sets. In view of this fact, the order relation $\leq$ among the cardinals and the arithmetical operations of addition and multiplication on cardinals may be defined by

$$|X| \leq |Y| \leftrightarrow X \leq Y$$

$$\Sigma_i |X_i| = |\Sigma_i X_i|$$

$$\Pi_i |X_i| = |\Pi_i X_i|.$$

It follows that any proposition about the arithmetic and ordering of cardinal numbers translates into a proposition about sets, providing only that '$=$' is translated as '$\sim$', '$\leq$' is interpreted as the corresponding relation between sets, and 'Σ' and 'Π' are interpreted as the corresponding operations on families of sets. The one difficulty with this translation is that we are passing from the cardinal $|X|$ to the set X, and it could happen that X is itself a set containing cardinals or whose transitive closure contains cardinals;[13] and so the translation does not

---

[13]The transitive closure of a set X is the least transitive set which includes X. A set X is transitive if $Y \in X$ and $b \in Y$ imply that $b \in X$.

entirely eliminate reference to cardinals. But, assuming the well-ordering principle, we can always take the representative X of the cardinal $|X|$ to be a pure set, i.e. one, such as the corresponding initial von Neumann ordinal, whose transitive closure contains only sets.

Of course I am not accurately presenting Cantor's abstractionist conception of the cardinals here, since for him they are sets of pure units. But I will leave this aside for the moment, noting only that it is entirely inessential to the reduction.

In any case, what seems to me to be essential to this kind of abstraction is this: the propositions about the abstract objects translate into propositions about the things from which they are abstracted and, in particular, the truth of the former is founded upon the truth of the latter. So the abstraction in question has a strong claim to the title *logical abstraction*: the sense of a proposition about the abstract domain is given in terms of the sense of the corresponding proposition about the (relatively) concrete domain.[14]

Dedekind's treatment of the finite ordinals is also a case of logical abstraction, providing that we assume given some simply infinite set $M=\langle M, \phi, e \rangle$, such as the system of finite von Neumann ordinals. We introduce the simply infinite set $N=\langle N,',1 \rangle$ of finite ordinals by stipulating that $M \cong N$. As we noted, the isomorphism is unique. In terms of this isomorphism, any arithmetical proposition, i.e. proposition about N, translates into a proposition about M. Moreover, because all simply infinite sets are isomorphic, the truth value of the arithmetical proposition does not depend upon the particular simply infinite set M.[15]

Of course, this treatment depends upon having a simply infinite set M to begin with, from which to abstract N. Dedekind in fact showed that it suffices to have a so-called Dedekind infinite set $\langle S, \phi \rangle$, i.e. a set S with a one-to-one function Φ from S into a proper subset of S. As Frege had essentially done previously, Dedekind notes that, if e is an element of S which is not a value of Φ and M is the intersection of all subsets of S which contain e and are closed under ϕ, then $\langle M, \phi, e \rangle$ is a simply infinite set.[16]

One may ask: What is the point of logical abstraction? That is, instead of abstracting the simply infinite set of numbers from an already given simply infinite set M, why did Dedekind not simply take the system of numbers to *be* this latter system? Similarly, noting that every ordinal or cardinal is the order type or

---

[14]Dummett (1991), pp. 167–168, uses the term 'logical abstraction' for the construction of the abstract objects as equivalence classes. But it is not clear why we should call this construction 'logical'.

[15]For further discussion of Dedekind's conception, see [Parsons, 1990] and [Tait, 1986; 1993].

[16]Dedekind in fact 'constructs' such a Dedekind infinite set, where S is the domain of all objects of thought and $\phi(x)$ is the thought of x. He argues that his ego is in S but is not a thought; and so $\langle S, \phi \rangle$ is a Dedekind infinite set. Frege begins, in effect, with the Dedekind infinite set $\langle S, \phi \rangle$ in which S is the totality of all cardinals and $\phi(m)=n$ means that n is the cardinal of some concept F and, for some b in the extension of F, m is the cardinal of '$Fx \ \& \ x \neq b$'. See [Frege, 1884, §76].

cardinal of a unique von Neumann ordinal, why not take this pure set to *be* the ordinal or cardinal? Dedekind discussed this question, not in connection with his monograph on the natural numbers, but in a letter to Weber about his earlier monograph, [Dedekind, 1872], on the irrational numbers.[17] He explains why he takes an irrational number to be *represented* by the corresponding Dedekind cut rather than defining it to *be* that cut. His argument is that to identify the real numbers with cuts—or with the objects in any other representation of them—is to endow them with properties which have nothing to do with them *qua* numbers but only to do with a particular and arbitrary representation of them.[18] Dummett seems to entirely misunderstand Dedekind's point here when he writes of the latter's refusal to identify the real numbers with the cuts: "Dedekind's resort to construction was not a means of avoiding labor. It was due solely to his philosophical orientation, according to which mathematical entities are to be displayed as creations of the human mind." (p. 250).

An objection often leveled at the abstractions of Cantor and Dedekind is that the abstractions do no work—they play no role in proofs. Of course Cantor intended his conception of cardinals as sets of pure units to do work, namely to yield the equivalence of the equinumerosity of two sets with their equipollence; but this is not convincing. But it would seem that logical abstraction, as it is described here, does play a role, not in proofs, but in that it fixes grammar, the domain of meaningful propositions, concerning the objects in question, and so determines the appropriate subject matter of proofs. For example, proving the categoricity of the axioms of simply ordered sets fixes the sense of all propositions in the pure theory of numbers; but it would not do so if numbers were sets, since the sense of $0 \epsilon 1$ is not fixed.

In Dedekind's final judgment of the matter, it is not clear that his foundation of arithmetic (as opposed to the foundation of the theory of real numbers) should be regarded as abstractionist. In the well-known letter to Keferstein in 1890,[19] in which he explained the argument of "Was sind und was sollen die Zahlen?", Dedekind casts a somewhat different light upon his foundation of arithmetic and, in particular, his construction of the simply infinite set from the Dedekind infinite set of all objects of thought. He writes:

> . . . the question arose: does such a system *exist* at all in the realm of our ideas? Without a logical proof of existence it would always remain doubtful whether the

---

[17]*Werke*, vol. 3, pp. 489–490. This letter was brought to my attention by Howard Stein. Cf. [Stein, 1988].

[18]Dedekind's argument is close to Benacerraf's in his paper "What numbers could not be": The latter argues that there is no one representation of the numbers by sets and so nothing intrinsic to the notion of number itself which decides the answer to the question "Is $0 \epsilon 2$?", for example. Hence, *no* representation of the numbers as sets should be regarded as *defining* the numbers.

[19][Dedekind, 1932, p. 490].

notion of such a system might not perhaps contain internal contradictions. Hence the need for such proofs. [von Heijenhoort, p. 101]

What is stressed here is not the abstractionist reduction of arithmetic to some-thing else, but rather the question of the *internal* consistency of arithmetic itself. In this respect, Dedekind was the precursor of Hilbert's view that mathematical existence is established when one has proved completeness and consistency.[20] In view of this, there is all the more reason to question Dummett's psychologistic reading of Dedekind—in particular when he writes:

> For Dedekind, however, the process of creation involved the operation of psycholog-ical abstraction, which needed a non-abstract system from which to begin; so it was for him a necessity, for the foundation of the mathematical theory, that there be such systems. That is why he included in his foundation for arithmetic a proof of the exis-tence of a simply infinite system, which had, of necessity, to be a non-mathematical one. (p. 296)

VI

There is another objection to Dedekind's foundation of arithmetic raised by Dummett: the characterization of N as a simple infinity does not tell us whether it is the system of numbers beginning with zero or beginning with one (or begin-ning with some other number)—in other words, it does not tell us whether 1 is really zero or one. But why hasn't Dedekind eliminated that ambiguity by *telling* us that 1 is the number one? Another way to state Dummett's objection is this: Dedekind proves (§126) the general principle of definition by primitive recur-sion according to which we may define unique functions F and G on N such that

$$F(m,1) = m \qquad\qquad G(m,1) = m'$$

$$F(m,n') = F(m,n)' \qquad\qquad G(m,n') = G(m,n)'.$$

The ambiguity in question then concerns whether it is F or G that is to be called 'addition', and Dedekind himself opts for the latter. Dummett suggests that we could eliminate the ambiguity by identifying the system of numbers with, say, the structure $N^+ = \langle N,',1,G \rangle$ rather than with N. But that is surely inadequate *unless we then specify that G is to denote addition!* After all, no matter what number we take "1" to denote, the function G is well-defined on N. But, if we must specify that G is addition in N^+, then we might as well stick with the struc-ture N and specify that 1 is the number one. Dummett introduces this topic in the

---

[20]Of course, when second order logic is involved, completeness and consistency are not purely for-mal notions, because of the incompleteness of formal higher-order logic. But categoricity and exis-tence of a model suffice to establish these properties, both in Dedekind's case and in Hilbert's case of Euclidean geometry.

context, not of Dedekind's theory, but of Benacerraf's 'neo-Dedekindian' thesis "that structure is all that matters, since we can specify a mathematical object only in terms of in the structure to which it belongs". He objects to eliminating the ambiguity by passing from N to N^+, not because it doesn't work, but because he believes that it betrays Benacerraf's thesis. N is already characterizable to within isomorphism as a simple infinity and G is definable in the structure N. Therefore it is contrary to Benacerraf's thesis to consider the structure N^+ instead of N as giving the structure of the numbers. So Benacerraf's thesis is false. (P. 53) But, having noted that N^+ is simply a definitional expansion of N, how can Dummett believe that substituting the former for the latter would determine which number '1' denotes?

But putting this aside, it is clear that, for Dummett, it is the fact that Dedekind's definition of the numbers does not 'intrinsically' determine for the number $1''$, say, whether it is the cardinal of two-element sets or the cardinal of three-element sets that is the defect in Dedekind's treatment of number. He writes

> Frege and Dedekind were at odds over two interconnected questions: whether or not the use of natural numbers to give the cardinality of finite totalities is one of their distinguishing characteristics, which ought therefore to figure in their definition; and whether it is possible, not merely to characterize the abstract structure of the system of natural numbers, but to identify the natural numbers solely in terms of that structure. Unlike Frege's, Dedekind's natural numbers have no properties other than their positions in the ordering determined by their generating operation, and those derivable from them; the question is whether such a conception is coherent. (p. 51)[21]

In consequence of the above alleged ambiguity in the meaning of "1", he writes of Benacerraf's thesis

> The thesis is false, and the example Benacerraf chose to illustrate it is the very one that most clearly illustrates its falsity. The identity of a mathematical object may sometimes be fixed by its relation to what lies outside the structure to which it belongs; what is constitutive of the number 3 is not its position in any progression whatever, or even in some particular progression, nor yet the result of adding 3 to another number, or of multiplying it by 3, but something more fundamental than any of these: the fact that, if certain objects are counted 'One two, three', or, equally, 'Naught, one, two', then there are three of them. The point is so simple that it needs a sophisticated intellect to overlook it; and it shows Frege to have been right, as

---

[21]Of course, Dummett does not mean that Frege and Dedekind were at odds over whether the structure of the system of numbers could be characterized: this was not a question that Frege even considered in [1884]. In his [1893] he formalizes (without citation) Dedekind's proof of categoricity (after having given a new proof of Dedekind's principle of definition by primitive recursion, again without citation) in his system. Cf. [Heck, 1993].

against Dedekind, to have made the use of the natural numbers as finite cardinals intrinsic to their characterization. (p. 53)

There are several difficulties with Dummett's assessment in this connection. One concerns the dominance in his argument *here* of the role of numbers as cardinals: Why should we single out one kind of application of the natural numbers as being of their essence?[22] We have already noted that Dedekind focused on a different one; namely, their role as ordinals or counting numbers. Thus, Dummett notes (p. 51) as a point of criticism of Dedekind's account that whereas he defines the addition of natural numbers by the recursion equations for G, i.e. as ordinal addition, Frege defines it as cardinal addition. But of course it is precisely what one would expect from someone who is analyzing the notion of finite *ordinal* or counting number that he would define addition as ordinal addition. What is surprising is that Dummett should find, in the case of finite numbers, that 'giving cardinality' is a more 'distinguishing characteristic' than serving as counting number. He even writes about Frege that "[H]e assumed, as virtually everyone else at the time would have done, that the most general application of the natural numbers is to give the cardinality of finite sets." (p. 293), although he then goes on to point out that Cantor took the ordinal numbers to be primary: in his generalization of the cardinals and ordinals into the transfinite, it is the ordinals that he called 'numbers'. With an apparent reversal of judgment, he also suggests *here* that the notion of ordinal is the more fundamental one.[23] One must also put Dedekind on the side of the ordinal numbers. Kronecker also, in his "Über den Zahlbegriff" (1887), writes, "I find the natural starting point for the development of the number concept in the *ordinal numbers*." But anyway, when we are speaking of applications, what about the role of the natural numbers in the foundation of analysis, e.g. in the foundation of the theory of rational and real numbers? Even if we attempt to go the route of [Frege 1903] and construct the real numbers as ratios, the natural numbers must function as exterior multipliers on any system of magnitudes? That is, there must be the operation $n.x$ defined for numbers n and quantities x by $1.x=x$ and $n'.x=n.x+x$ (when $n>0$)[24]. As Frege himself noted in [Frege 1884, §19], in his criticism of Newton's definition of numbers in terms of ratios, the definition of the relation of

---

[22]Stein [1988] raises this question as a mild criticism even of the "und was sollen" part of the title of Dedekind's monograph.

[23]One must question this judgment. For example, the proof in affine geometry that all lines contain the same number of points is not a counting argument.

[24]Actually, it suffices to define the notion that a pair (x,y) of magnitudes are equimultiples of the pair (a,b). We could do this, using Frege's (and Dedekind's) analysis of the ancestral F^* of a function F, without introducing the natural numbers. Namely (x,y) is an equimultiple of (a,b) iff $(a,b)F^*(x,y)$, where $F(c,d)=(c+a,d+b)$. But then we have essentially introduced the (positive) natural numbers; namely, they are the ratios $x:a$, where (x,x) is an equimultiple of (a,a).

'having the same ratio' between pairs of like magnitudes presupposes the operation $n.x.$[25]

What makes one of these applications of the natural numbers privileged, so that it, rather than others, should be one of their 'distinguishing characteristics'?

VII

So far as the application of the numbers as cardinals is concerned, what is wrong with Dedekind's definition (§161) (also given in Kronecker's paper) of 'The set X has cardinal n' as meaning that X is equipollent with the set $\{1,...,n\}$? It should be noted that, if this analysis is acceptable, then a certain argument that Frege repeats over and over again fails. The argument appears in "On formal theories of arithmetic" [Frege 1984, pp. 112–121] as an a priori argument for logicism:

> ... the basic propositions on which arithmetic is based cannot apply merely to a limited area whose peculiarities they express in the way in which the axioms of geometry express the peculiarities of what is spatial; rather, these basic propositions must extend to everything that can be thought. And surely we are justified in ascribing such extremely general propositions to logic. (p. 112.)

Frege's point appears to be endorsed in the foreword to the first edition of [Dedekind 1887]

> In speaking of arithmetic (algebra, analysis) as part of logic I mean to imply that I consider the number concept entirely independent of the notions or intuitions of space and time, that I consider it an immediate result from the laws of thought.

But there is a difference in their arguments. Dedekind's point, echoing Bolzano (who, in turn, quotes Aristotle)[26], is in effect an expression of unwillingness to admit, in reasoning about numbers, any principles drawn from alien sciences. Frege's argument, on the other hand, is bound up with the idea that the definite description 'the number of x such that $\phi(x)$' should apply to any concept $\phi(x)$ at all and not just to those concerning which we have some special source of knowledge. (We can count anything.) We find this argument repeated many times in [Frege 1884]. In §14, discussing Kant's conception that arithmetic is founded on intuition, Frege contrasts arithmetic and geometry:

---

[25]Dummett [1991, p. 73] writes that Frege "flounders somewhat, and fails to make the simple point as cleanly as he ought", the simple point being that Newton's definition is of the positive real numbers whereas Frege is concerned with the natural numbers. But, of course, the positive real numbers, with the operation $+1$, form a Dedekind infinity in terms of which a simple infinity may be constructed. So in fact it is essential to Frege's point that Eudoxos's definition already involves the numbers as multipliers.

[26]Bolzano [1817, Preface] (p. 160 in the translation [Russ, 1980]); *Posterior Analytics* 75ᵃ39.

The fact that this is possible shows that the axioms of geometry are independent of one another and of the primitive laws of logic, and are consequently synthetic. Can the same be said of the fundamental propositions of the science of number? Here, we have only to try denying any one of them, and complete confusion ensues. Even to think at all seems no longer possible. The basis of arithmetic lies deeper, it seems, than that of any of the empirical sciences, and even than that of geometry. The truths of arithmetic govern all that is numerable. This is the widest domain of all; for to it belongs not only the existent [*Wirkliche*] not only the intuitable, but everything thinkable. Should not the laws of number, then, be connected very intimately with the laws of thought?

In §19, in the discussion of Newton's definition of number as a ratio between like magnitudes, Frege again presents the argument for logicism from the universal applicability of number. We have already mentioned one objection that he raised to Newton's definition. But his second objection is this:

[W]e should still remain in doubt as to how the number defined geometrically in this way is related to the number of ordinary life, which would then be entirely cut off from science. Yet surely we are entitled to demand of arithmetic that its numbers should be adopted for use in every application made of number, even although that application is not itself the business of arithmetic. Even in our everyday sums, we must be able to rely on the science of arithmetic to provide the basis for the methods we use. And moreover, the question arises whether arithmetic itself can make do with a geometric concept of number, when we think of some of the concepts in it, such as the number of roots of an equation or of the numbers prime to and smaller than a given number. On the other hand, the number which gives the answer to the question *how many?* can answer among other things how many units are in a length.

In §40, where he is discussing the problem of how one could understand cardinal numbers as sets of 'pure units', he considers the possibility of the units being points in space/time. He again writes:

The first doubt that strikes us about any such view is that then nothing would be numerable except what is spacial and temporal.

But, of course, on Dedekind's analysis, this line of argument is fallacious: *Whatever* simple infinity we take the system of numbers to be, the question of whether the extension of a concept is equipollent to $\{1, \ldots, n\}$ makes sense. In §42 Frege continues:

Another way out is to invoke instead of spatial or temporal order a more generalized concept of series, but this too fails in its object; for their position in the series cannot be the basis on which we distinguish the objects, since they must have already been distinguished somehow or other, for us to have been able to arrange them in a series.

But this is a strange idea. Why can't we have a series all of whose members are identical? Frege is confusing the notion of a series with that of a linearly ordered set $\langle A, < \rangle$ (where, for x and y in A, $x<y$ implies that x and y are distinct). Why does Frege preclude the series $(a,a, \ldots ,a)$? His response is:

When Hankel speaks of our thinking or putting a thing one or twice or three times, this too seems to be an attempt to combine in the things to be numbered distinguishability with identity. But it is obvious at once that it is not successful; for his ideas or intuitions of the same object must, if they are not to coalesce into one, be different in some way or other. Moreover we are, I imagine, fully entitled to speak of 45 million Germans without having first to have thought or put an average German 45 million times, which might be somewhat tedious.

But to regard the number n as an n-element sequence whose members are identical is not to say that the things numbered must be identical. Frege's second point surely betrays his confusion. To say that there are 45 million Germans is to say that there is a set of Germans which is equipollent to $\{1, \ldots, 45,000,000\}$—and, again, *this is quite independent of how the numbers are defined.*

Schröder's proposal to define the numbers as expressions, i.e. sequences of atomic symbols, is essentially the same as Hankel's proposal, except that Schröder decides against the expressions 11 . . . 1 because, for example, three, identified with 111, might be confused with one hundred and eleven. So he wishes to use the expressions $1+1+ \ldots +1$ instead. This may be silly, but it is not open to Frege's objection in §43 that "This passage shows that for Schröder number is a *symbol*. What the symbol expresses, which is what I have been calling number, is taken, with the words 'how many of these units are present', as already known." Why shouldn't numbers be symbols? 111 is, in any case, a different symbol than 3. Why not take the latter to denote the former? In truth, there is an objection, namely, the objection that numbers are numbers and symbols are symbols and that the grammar of the one is different from the grammar of the other. In essence, this is the objection of Dedekind to any reductionist account of the natural numbers or the real numbers. But it cannot be Frege's objection, since he will make numbers be extensions of concepts!

Presumably, Dedekind's analysis of "The set X has n elements" won't do for Frege, as Dummett understands it, because it does not make "the use of natural numbers to give cardinality of finite sets . . . one of their distinguishing characteristics". But we are owed a definition of 'distinguishing characteristic', as well as of 'intrinsic property'. Since Dedekind's treatment is being contrasted with Frege's in this connection, we should presumably look to Frege to find cases of distinguishing characteristics and intrinsic properties. The two cases with which this presents us are the cardinal numbers and the real numbers. In both instances, the numbers are defined as equivalence classes: A set has the cardinal number n iff it is an element of n and a pair of like magnitudes has the real number r iff it is an element of r. Of course, one problem in the case of cardinal numbers is that this definition is inconsistent for $n>0$, since there is no set consisting of all sets of power n. But let us restrict the equipollence relation to subsets of some infinite set A, so that n is an equipollence class of the subsets of A. To be sure, for sets X which are not subsets of A, the statement that X has cardinal n will no longer be equivalent to the assertion that it is an element of n; and so it will not be a 'defining characteristic' of n that X has cardinal n. But, even for subsets X of A, why does its being an element of n make the fact that it has cardinal n a defining characteristic or intrinsic property of n? The relation ϵ of set membership (or 'being in the extension') is being given a distinguished role without any indication of why this should be so. For example, suppose that we instead define the cardinal numbers to be the equipollence classes of non-empty subsets of A and define 'X has cardinal n' to mean that $X \cup \{X\} \epsilon n$ (assuming for this that A contains all of its finite subsets). Then $\{\emptyset\}$ will no longer be a cardinal of any subset of A, the set of all unit subsets of A will be the cardinal of the null set and, in general, the cardinal of an n-element subset of A will be the equipollence class of all $n+1$-element subsets of A. Why is the relation $X \epsilon n$ between X and n to be preferred to the relation $X \cup \{X\} \epsilon n$?

The same considerations apply to Frege's rejection of earlier treatments of the real numbers on the grounds that they do not adequately account for applications. Given a (linearly ordered) system of magnitudes, any ratio $a{:}b$ of magnitudes from that domain is equal to a ratio $r{:}1$ in any connected ordered field, and so can be assigned the 'real number' r. It has yet to be made clear why it would be preferable to treat the real number of the pair (a,b) *as* the ratio, i.e. as the equivalence class of all pairs (c,d) (from any system of magnitudes) such that $a{:}b \equiv c{:}d$—leaving aside the question of the consistency of doing so.

Finally, as used by Dummett, the term 'structural property' is at the least misleading.

> There is no absolute notion of 'structural property'. It is only relative to a specific structure, e.g. $\langle M, e, \phi \rangle$, on M that we may speak of the structural properties of the objects of M, namely the properties definable in terms of the structure (in the example, in terms of e and ϕ, with individual quantifiers ranging over M, second-order quantifiers over subsets of M, etc.)

Thus, when Dummett speaks of "objects or systems of objects lacking the features abstracted from, but not possessing any others in their place" or of Dedekind's natural numbers as having "no properties other than their positions in the ordering determined by their generating operation, and those derivable from them" or of "specific objects having only structural properties", he is guilty of confusion. What is true of the numbers on Dedekind's account is that it is possible to specify a structure on them, e.g. N or $\langle N, ' \rangle$ or $\langle N, < \rangle$, in terms of which they are characterizable to within isomorphism by finitely many axioms. But *this* can hardly be the basis of a metaphysical objection to them.

From this it is clear that the objection of Russell and Dummett cannot reasonably be about the paucity or kind of properties that Dedekind's numbers have nor about the fact that they can be categorically determined in terms of a structure which distinguishes some of those properties. Perhaps the objection is, rather, that they are *given* to us only in terms of that structure. In Dummett's words, the question is "whether it is possible, not merely to characterize the abstract structure of the system of natural numbers, but to identify the natural numbers solely in terms of that structure". But what more is required to 'identify' the numbers, even on Frege's own grounds? The sense of every arithmetical proposition A is fixed: A is true just in case it can be derived from the axioms for a simple infinity. Moreover, we lack no account of the application of the numbers on this foundation. The idea that the numbers can be identified or, perhaps, further identified in terms of some particular application of them is, as we have seen, neither a very clear idea nor a desirable one.

At the end of the day, I think that, for Russell and for Dummett, the objection to Dedekind's treatment of the natural numbers is that, for Dedekind, they are just numbers and not something else as well. For Dedekind, the question "What are the numbers?" could only be answered by exhibiting their structure. For many writers since Frege, the question has rather meant: "What *besides* numbers are the numbers?" This becomes clear in the case of Dummett in his discussion of 'structuralism', when he writes:

> On the stronger interpretation, structuralism is the doctrine that mathematics in general is solely concerned with structures in the abstract sense, that is, with systems left no further specified than as exemplifying the structure in question. This doctrine has, again, two versions. According to the more mystical of these, mathematics relates to *abstract structures,* distinguished by the fact that their elements have no non-structural properties. The abstract four-element Boolean algebra is, on this view, a specific system, with specific elements; but, for example, the zero of the algebra has no other properties than those which follow from its being the zero of that Boolean algebra—it is not a set, or a number, or anything else whose nature is extrinsic to that algebra. This may be regarded as Dedekind's version of structuralism: for him the natural numbers are specific objects; but they are objects that have no properties save those that derive from their position in 'the' abstract simply infinite system (sequence of order type ω).

VIII

There is an aspect of Cantor's abstractionist conception of ordinal and cardinal numbers that I have so far ignored and which was the main target of Frege's attack. Namely, the cardinal number of a set is to be itself a set, equipollent to the given set, and its elements are to be 'pure units'; and the order type of an ordered set is to be itself an ordered set of 'pure units', isomorphic to the given ordered set.

Consider just the case of cardinals. Clearly the idea of a cardinal as a set of pure units—call it a *cardinal set*—is inessential to the foundation of the theory of cardinals on logical abstraction, at least as that kind of abstraction is described in §V. But what did Cantor actually mean by speaking of pure units? There are two ways in which we might try to understand his idea of the cardinal set corresponding to the set M as a set of 'pure units'. One is that the units, the elements of a given cardinal set, should be obtained by abstracting from the particular properties that distinguish the elements of M from one another and thus should be indistinguishable in some sense from one another. That is the way in which Frege understands Cantor. The other interpretation is that the abstraction concerns, not the individuating properties of the elements relative to one another, but rather the individuating property of the set itself, for example the concept of which it is the extension. On this interpretation, the cardinal set C corresponding to a set M is to be constituted of unique elements, specified in no way other than that they are the elements of C and that C is equipollent to M. Thus, the cardinal sets are not sets of points in Euclidean space or of numbers or of sets, or of apples or etc. Once we decide in the first place that the cardinal number of M should be a set equipollent to M, then the argument for Cantor's conception of the cardinal set, on this interpretation, is exactly Dedekind's argument that the system of numbers is a 'creation of the human spirit': The cardinal set corresponding to M should not be a set of points or of numbers or of apples or of sets (as in the case of the initial von Neumann ordinals). The things that we may say about these other kinds of sets would be ungrammatical when speaking of cardinal numbers. Now, the role that Cantor would have his doctrine that cardinal numbers are sets of pure units play in the theory of cardinals is to infer the equivalence of Card(M)=Card(N) and the equipollence of M and N, and only this. It is clear from this that it is the *second* interpretation of his doctrine that is correct, and that Frege has entirely misunderstood him when he refered to his *Grundlagen* for a refutation of Cantor's doctrine.

As a matter of fact, Cantor's motivation for the conception of cardinals as cardinal sets is weak: one is introducing one cardinal set by 'abstraction' corresponding to each equipollence class, but one is not analyzing the notion that M is equipollent to N *in terms of* the notion of cardinal number. Abstraction, as Frege says, is strong lye. To abstract the cardinal set corresponding to M from M, we must specify what it is from which we are abstracting. The only possible answer is that we are abstracting from all properties and relationships of M except those which respect the equipollence relationships of M. So we do not derive the equipollence of M and N from Card(M)=Card(N); rather, the former notion is built into the latter. (Frege makes essentially the same point in criticizing Husserl's formulation of Cantor's doctrine.) Moreover, Dedekind's argument from grammar applies to Cantor's doctrine of cardinals as sets, itself: it is ungrammatical to ask whether a particular object is an element of a particular cardinal number. So I think that Cantor's view that cardinal numbers are sets of pure units is ill-conceived.

But Frege's claim was that it is *incoherent*. But certainly, on the second interpretation, which I think that we must accept as the correct one, the theory of cardinal sets is perfectly coherent. We may take the pure units in a cardinal set to be atoms (i.e. non-sets or *urelements*). If κ and λ are distinct von Neumann cardinals (i.e. initial von Neumann ordinals), we may even assume that the corresponding cardinal sets C_κ and C_λ are disjoint sets of atoms. So the question is whether or not we can coherently assume that, corresponding to every von Neumann cardinal κ, there is a set C_κ of atoms which is equipollent to κ such that, for distinct von Neumann cardinals κ and λ, $C_\kappa \cap C_\lambda = \emptyset$. But we can construct a standard model M of this assumption together with the axioms of second order set theory with urelements from a standard model of second-order set theory with a strongly inaccessible cardinal.[27] Moreover, any permutation of the elements of the cardinal set C_κ induces an automorphism of M in an obvious way. For example, all of the cardinal sets C_λ and all pure sets (i.e. whose transitive closures contain no atoms) are fixed points of this automorphism. So, in any reasonable sense, even on Frege's mistaken interpretation of Cantor's doctrine, it is perfectly coherent. Of course, there is a property that distinguishes the element b of C_κ from all of the other elements, namely the property $x=b$. But, however Frege was reading Cantor, surely it would have been unreasonable of him to suppose that Cantor either overlooked this or would have denied it.

The suggestion of incoherence of the notion of the cardinals being sets of pure units seems to arise for Frege from two sources. One source is Leibniz's Principle of the Identity of Indiscernibles: If nothing distinguishes between two 'pure units' in the cardinal-set C, then they must be the same; and so every cardinal number must be 0 or 1. For example, recall that, in his review of Cantor, Frege writes of "those unfortunate Ones which are different even though there is nothing to distinguish them one from another" (p. 270). He goes on to say: "The author evidently did not have the slightest inkling of the presence of this difficulty, which I deal with at length in §§34–54 of my *Grundlagen*." Unfortunately, the discussion in these sections is interwoven with a discussion, beginning at §29, of quite another notion, that of a 'unit', as well as with Frege's view of abstraction. But, concerning the issue at hand, he writes in §35:

> We cannot succeed in making different things identical simply by dint of operations with concepts. But even if we did, we should then no longer have things in the plural, but only one thing; for, as Descartes says, the number (or better, the plurality) in things arises from their distinction.

The first sentence of this passage refers to his argument in §34 that abstraction cannot produce new objects ('make distinct things identical'). His correction of Descartes, choosing the term 'plurality' over 'number', illustrates another source of confusion in his discussion of other authors. By a number, Descartes meant

---

[27] Take the domain to be $V_{\kappa+\kappa}$, where κ is the least inaccessible cardinal. The sets of rank $\leq \kappa$ are taken to be atoms, except for the null set, which is taken to be the null set. The sets in $V_{\kappa+\kappa}$ of rank $>\kappa$ thus become the non-null sets of rank $<\kappa$ over the set of atoms. The elements of C_μ, for μ a cardinal $<\kappa$, are the atoms $\mu \times \{\mu\}$.

essentially a set and, as we shall see below, that was a common usage of the term in earlier times. Moreover, the passage cited in Descartes' *Principia* (Part I, §60) in no way supports Frege's point. 'Distinct' there means only 'not identical', not 'distinguished by some property', and Descartes is distinguishing three different kinds of 'distinction': real, modal, and rational. Nowhere in this discussion (§§60–62) does he imply that non-identity of P and Q requires there to be some property possessed by one of them and not the other. But there can be no doubt that Frege himself subscribed to this principle: In *Grundlagen* §65 he takes as his own definition of identity (being the same object) Leibniz's.[28]

> Things are the same as each other, of which one can be substituted for the other without loss of truth.

But, of course, this principle doesn't tell us anything until we know in which propositional contexts $F(x)$ the substitution may occur. For example, any two distinct objects will be distinguished by the context '$x \epsilon M$', where M is a set which contains one but not the other.

Frege himself might defend against this by insisting that '$x \epsilon M$' is not a primitive concept and must be replaced by the concept $F(x)$ of which M is the extension. And, presumably, $F(x)$ cannot itself be defined in terms of the identity relation, since otherwise $x=b$ distinguishes the object b from all other objects and Leibniz's principle is trivialized. I have already expressed the view that it would have been entirely unreasonable for Frege to have supposed Cantor to have rejected this trivial form of Leibniz's principle or to have overlooked it in formulating his doctrine of cardinal numbers as sets of pure units. So Frege's objection would then be that there is no such concept $F(x)$, not already involving the identity relation, which distinguishes between two 'pure units' of the cardinal-set.

But of course this whole line of argument presupposes the validity of the non-trivial form of Leibniz's principle, and, in Frege's case, it seems hard to defend. Certainly no point in Euclidean space is distinguished from any other by a concept, unless that concept itself is defined by reference to specific points, since the space is homogeneous. But there is a difficulty with individuating points by means of concepts which themselves refer to points. For example, the points p and q may be distinguished by the concept 'x is between r and s', which is satisfied by p and not by q. But then q satisfies a corresponding concept 'x lies between t and u, e.g. where (p,r,s) is congruent to (q,t,u). The problem is that our grounds for calling these two concepts distinct is only that (r,s) and (t,u) are distinct (i.e. non-identical) pairs of points: the individuation of such concepts presupposes the individuation of pairs of points and so, ultimately, of points. Hence, there is a circle.[29] Of course, since Frege believed that Euclidean geometry is the

---

[28]He later rejected this as a *definition* (cf. Frege [1984, p. 200]), but he continued to affirm its validity.
[29]Leibniz did not face this difficulty. For him, the principle of identity of indiscernibles applies to substances (which have no real relations), and not to ideal things such as points in space.

science of physical space, he may have believed that any two points are distinguished by empirical, non-geometric concepts, e.g. by physical scalars. But it would be hard to accept the non-trivial form of Leibniz's principle as a metaphysical principle based upon such a belief.

The other source of the appearance of incoherence in the notion of a cardinal number as a set of pure units is the argument that, if cardinal numbers are sets at all, then, for example, $1+1$ must equal 1. In §35 Frege writes:

> Jevons goes on: "Whenever I use the symbol 5 I really mean
>
> $$1+1+1+1+1$$
>
> and it is perfectly understood that each of these units is distinct from each other. If requisite I might mark them thus
>
> $$1'+1''+1'''+1''''+1'''''."$$
>
> Certainly it is requisite to mark them differently, if they are different: otherwise the utmost confusion must result. . . . The symbols
>
> $$1', 1'', 1'''$$
>
> tell the tale of our embarrassment. We must have identity—hence the 1; but we must have difference—hence the indices; only unfortunately, the latter undo the work of the former.

Frege and Jevons collaborate in a confusion here. Jevons problem is that he is thinking of 5 as a set of five elements on the one hand and as $1+ \ldots +1$ on the other. If the different occurrences of '1' do not denote different unit sets, then Jevons worries that $1+ \ldots +1$ will not yield a set of five elements. *But that is because he thinks that, if cardinals are sets, then their addition is just their union.* But even if we take cardinal numbers to be sets, $m+n$ does not denote union of m and n; it denotes the cardinal of their disjoint union. Frege (§38) somewhat misses the point here: He thinks that Jevon's problem arises from confusing 'unit' with 'one' and of treating numbers as 'agglomerations'. He is right that one cannot take the units in 5 to be the unit in 1 since there are five of the former and only one of the latter. But Jevons' equation $5=1+1+1+1+1$ leads to this identification, not because he thought that numbers are sets (after all, the von Neuman cardinals are sets), but because he confused the addition of cardinals with the union of sets. Frege's argument, were it valid, would not simply be an argument against cardinals being sets of pure units, *it would be an argument against the cardinal of a set* M *being a set equipollent to* M *at all.* I am persuaded by Dedekind's grammatical argument that numbers are not sets; but Frege's line of argument would exclude even the *representation* of cardinals by initial von Neumann ordinals.

Of course, Frege might have made the argument that, since the identification of cardinals with sets does not admit the identification of cardinal addition with set-theoretic union, then there is no point in regarding cardinals as sets at all. But this is not the argument that he gave.

IX

One problem with reading the literature on the number concept prior to Cantor, Dedekind, and Frege is that, aside from Bolzano, the authors generally have not fully distinguished the notion of a set and tended to subsume it under a more general notion of a 'multitude' or 'plurality'. Anything with proper parts was regarded as a plurality—a line segment, Socrates, a heap of stones, a flock of sheep. It was understood from the time of Plato that number does not unambiguously apply to pluralities. Socrates is one but has many parts, the flock of ten sheep also includes a plurality of twenty sheeps' eyes and a plurality of forty sheeps' legs, etc. Aristotle explicitly understood that assigning number to pluralities in this sense requires a prior choice of the parts to be numbered.[30] He referred to this as a choice of 'unit': To assign numbers to line segments, for example, we must first choose a particular line segment as the unit of measurement. This conception, that what can be numbered, the ἀριθμὸς, is some object (in a generalized sense that admits flocks of sheep, the aggregate of planets, etc.) relative to a partition—a choice of unit—, survived even into the late nineteenth century in the form of the rejection of the null set: no object can be partitioned into zero parts. There was also a surviving conceptual difficulty with unit sets, which is reflected in the sometime rejection of the number 1 by the classical Greeks: if what can be numbered is an object X relative to a choice of unit, the unit set of X would be X qua part of X, which was indistinguishable from X.[31]

Indeed, Frege reveals some of this confusion about the concept of a set in *Grundlagen*, §28, where he is discussing the notion that a number is simply a set. He writes:

> Some writers define the number as a set or multitude or plurality. All of these views suffer from the drawback that the concept will not then cover the numbers 0 and 1. Moreover, these terms are utterly vague: sometimes they approximate in meaning to "heap" or "group" or "aggregate" [*"Aggregat"*], referring to a juxtaposition in space, sometimes they are so used as to be practically equivalent to "number", only vaguer.

In *Paradoxien des Unendlichen* (1851), Bolzano had already made a distinction between what he called an '*Inbegriff*' and a set:

> There exist aggregates [*Inbegriffe*] which agree in containing the selfsame members, and nevertheless present themselves as *different* when seen under different aspects or under different conceptions, and this kind of difference we call 'essential'. For

---

[30]Aristotle, *Metaphysics,* Book X, Chapters 1 and 2.
[31]*Metaphysics* 1052^{b}31. Also see the second quote below from Bolzano's *Paradoxien des Unendlichen.*

example: an unbroken tumbler and a tumbler broken into pieces, considered as a drinking vessel. We call the ground of distinction between two such aggregates their *mode of combination* or their *arrangement*. An aggregate whose basic conception renders the arrangement of its members a matter of indifference, and whose permutation therefore produces no essential difference, I call a *set* . . . (§4)

Bolzano's 'Inbegriff' seems to be Frege's 'Aggregat'—a plurality with the unit chosen. But it is fair to say that even Bolzano had not entirely liberated the notion of a set from that of an aggregate and, in particular, could not accommodate unit sets, since in §3 he writes, "For if *A* were identical with *B,* it would of course be absurd to speak of an aggregate composed of the objects *A* and *B*". Moreover, Bolzano uses the term 'Teil' to refer to elements of a set, suggesting, too, that the element/set relation is not entirely distinguished from the part/whole relation. Notice also that Cantor did not clearly distinguish between Bolzano's notions of Inbegriff and Menge in the quote above from [Cantor 1895–97, p. 282], in as much as he speaks of obtaining the power of the *set [Menge] M* by abstracting both from the nature of its elements and *from the order in which they are given.*[32] Yet, when he speaks of a set as "already completely delimited by the fact that everything that belongs to it is determined in itself and well distinguished from everything that does not belong to it", it would seem that he intends the notion of a set to be independent of the order of its elements.

A further difficulty with reading the pre-twentieth century literature on the number concept is manifested in Frege's "[these terms] are so used as to be practically equivalent to 'number', only vaguer". The fact is that the term "number", in the sense of the whole numbers, often really did just mean a (finite) set—in the somewhat confused sense of 'set' that we have just discussed. So a 'number' is given only relative to the choice of unit. This meaning goes back to the Greek meaning of ἀριθμὸς which came to be translated as "number". Thus at the beginning of Book VII of the Elements, Euclid has these definitions

1. A unit is that with respect to which each of the things that exist is called one.

2. A number is a multitude composed of units.

In (1884), §29, Frege writes that Euclid "seems to mean by the word 'μονάς' sometimes an object to be numbered, sometimes a property of such an object and sometimes the number one." But the meaning is clear. In Definition 1 Euclid says that numbering begins with the choice of unit, of what is to be counted— what is to be called one. Definition 2 then defines a 'number' (an ἀριθμὸς) to be a set of such units. It is true that 'unit' in Definition 1 refers to a property and in Definition 2 to objects having that property. But that is a frivolous objection. We use the word 'man' sometimes to refer to a property and sometimes to men.

---

[32]Of course, Cantor had been concerned with point sets in Euclidean space, and this is what he had in mind in this passage.

So things may be called 'one' after the choice of unit in the same way that men may be called 'man'. It is because Frege does not understand that 'one' is a *common* name, applying to all units (once the unit has been chosen), that he misunderstands Euclid. Similarly, also in §29, he misunderstands [Schröder 1873, p. 5], when he quotes "Each of the things to be numbered is called a unit" and then goes on to object:

> We may well wonder why we must first conceive of the things as units, instead of simply defining number right away as a "set of things", which would bring us back once again to the view just discussed.

Here he is referring to his discussion in §28, partly quoted above. But he can't have it both ways: if he believes that the term 'set' can only refer to heaps and the like, then he should also agree that number can be assigned only after the choice of unit.

Hume also uses the term 'number' to mean a set. In §63, discussing how the notion of equinumerosity should be defined, Frege writes:

> Hume long ago mentioned such a means: "When two numbers are so combined as that the one has always an unit answering to every unit of the other, we pronounce them as equal." This opinion, that equality of numbers must be defined in terms of one-to-one correspondence, seems in recent years to have gained widespread acceptance among mathematicians.

Frege goes on to say that the definition of numerical equality in terms of one-to-one correspondence raises certain "logical doubts and difficulties". In particular, he writes, "It is not only among numbers that the relation of equality [*Gleichheit*] is to be found. From which it seems to follow that we ought not to define it specially for the case of numbers". The ambiguity of the German "Gleichheit" as between "equality" and "identity" helps (along with Austin's translation) to hide a confusion here: It is quite clear, even just from the passage in Hume's *Treatise* that is quoted (Bk. I, Part III, Sect. I), that by 'number' Hume is referring to finite sets and that, when he speaks of equality of numbers, he is not referring to the identity relation but to the relation of equinumerosity, *which indeed is to be defined specially for the case of 'numbers', i.e. sets*. The 'logical doubts and difficulties' were created by Frege's incorrect reading, not by Hume's conception.

[Bolzano 1851] also used the term 'number' for sets. In §8 he attempts to characterize "*finite* or *countable multitudes*, or quite boldly: *numbers*".

Certainly the term 'number' did not *always* refer to a set. Thus people spoke of 'the number ten' and of the set (and number) of prime numbers less than n, etc. But, on the one hand, there seems to be no obstacle to understanding number in these contexts as referring to species of finite sets—just as one might speak of the animal, man, or of the number of species in a certain genus. Into the nineteenth century, every theorem of number theory could be understood as a statement about an arbitrary finite set, free from any assumption of the existence of an infinite set. Moreover, there was always the resource (exploited in analytic number theory) of regarding the natural numbers as embedded in the system of real numbers. The move towards treating the natural numbers as forming an autonomous system of objects dates from later in the century. It required the explicit admission of the actual infinite into mathematics, and the motivation would seem to be the arithmetical foundation of the system of real numbers. Rational numbers are constructed from natural numbers and real numbers are, for example, sets of rationals. If the natural numbers are not to form an autonomous system of objects, then it is hard to make sense of this construction.[33]

X

In [Frege 1884, §62], Frege raises the question of the meaning of "the number which belongs to the concept F is the same as that which belongs to the concept G". We have already quoted his attribution to Hume of the definition of this concept as meaning equipollence. He goes on to cite Schröder, Kossak, and [Cantor 1883] as well. Dummett writes, "By the time that Frege wrote Grundlagen, the definition had already become a piece of mathematical orthodoxy, though Frege undoubtedly gave it its most exact formulation and its most acute philosophical defense." (pp. 142–143) But Frege's citation of earlier authors is misleading. We have already noted his misunderstanding of Hume. But there is another and more compelling respect in which his citation is misleading and, in particular, slights Cantor's contribution. I do not mean the fact that Frege refers to [Cantor 1883] rather than to his earliest published definition of equality of power, [Cantor 1878].[34] Rather, I refer to the fact that *the other authors cited were concerned only with finite 'numbers'*, i.e. sets, and not with the general notion of cardinal number which applies to infinite sets. Frege and Cantor, on the other hand were concerned with the general notion of cardinal. The extension to this general notion was not a trivial matter. As late as 1851, in his monograph just cited, Bolzano, who did understand the notion of set to include infinite sets, had argued that the characterization of numerical equality in terms of one-to-one cor-

---

[33]Dummett's explanation (pp. 133–134) of why *Frege* required that the numbers be objects is unconvincing. His explanation is that 0, . . . ,n have to be objects in order to prove that n has a successor, namely the number of $\{0, . . . ,n\}$. In other words, we need a set (i.e. extension of a concept) with $n+1$ elements. But, whether or not we count the object, call it n^*, which Frege takes to be the number n *as* the number n, it is an object in his system and so the set $\{0^*, . . . ,n^*\}$ still exists. Indeed, eliminating the middle man and making no commitment at all about the nature of the numbers, we may replace k by the von Neuman ordinal $N_k = \{N_0, . . . ,N_{k-1}\}$ in Frege's argument.

[34]Not, as Dummett cites, [1874]. In this paper, Cantor does not define the general concept of equipollence, although he does produce the first significant result concerning infinite powers.

respondence, though correct for finite sets, could not be applied to infinite sets. His reason was the traditional obstacle to a coherent theory of infinite numbers: It would then happen that infinite sets could be numerically equal to proper subsets of themselves. (§23) *It was Cantor, in (1878), who took this bull by the horns and forever separated the notion of proper subset from that of proper numerical inequality.* (See [Cantor 1932, p.119].) Quite clearly the *general* analysis of the concept of having the same cardinal number, finite or infinite, can be attributed only to Cantor.

XI

One must wonder why Dummett wrote that Frege gave the definition of equinumerosity in terms of one-to-one correspondence of sets "its most exact formulation and its most acute philosophical defense". (pp. 142–143) The definition is quite clear in the above quote from Hume once one understands that by 'number' he means the thing to be numbered, the set. But anyway it is stated with admirable clarity by both Bolzano and Cantor, even though the former did not accept it as the definition of equinumerosity in the case of infinite sets. As for a defense, who was attacking it and why was defense needed, philosophical or otherwise? Certainly one attack that needed to be answered was Bolzano's, which we have already mentioned. Cantor responded to this and Frege made no mention of it at all.[35] Another attack came from Cantor himself, who in (1883), §2, distinguished the two conceptions of number, cardinal and ordinal, which essentially coincide in the finite case but not in the infinite. On the ordinal conception, it is not abstract sets but well-ordered sets to which number applies. Again, this analysis was undertaken by Cantor, not by Frege.[36]

What *did* Frege contribute to this question? The problem as he saw it is formulated in [Frege 1884, §39], as a dilemma:

> If we try to produce a number by putting together different distinct objects, the result is an agglomeration [*Anhäufung*] in which the objects contained remain still in possession of precisely those properties which serve to distinguish them from one another; and that is not a number. But if we try to do it in the other way, by putting together identicals [*Gleichem*], the result runs perpetually together into one and we never reach a plurality.

But distinguish two questions which, in his discussion of earlier authors, Frege tended to confuse: What are the things to which number applies? And, what are

---

[35] Although both Cantor and Dedekind cite Bolzano's fundamental work on the nature of the infinite, I have found no reference at all to him in the published works of Frege.

[36] Indeed, from the discussion in [Frege, 1884, §86], it seems likely that he did not even understand Cantor's concept of a well-ordered set at that time.

numbers? The first horn of his dilemma concerns the first question. And the things to be numbered are not 'agglomerations' but sets, which indeed arise by 'putting together' different distinct objects. These sets *were* called 'numbers' by some of these authors, and this is one source of Frege's confusion. The second horn of Frege's dilemma can concern only the view that the numbers themselves are sets of pure units. The argument is that, if the units are not distinguished by their properties, then they will be identical. We have already discussed this view and concluded that the notion of cardinal number as a set of pure units, though unattractive, is by no means incoherent. Distinct units are indeed distinguished by their properties; but when from a set of two cats, one white and one black, we 'abstract' the number two as a set of pure units, the units are not white and black, respectively, and they are not cats.

But also, unlike Frege, I find no sign of the conception of number as set of pure units in the quotes from other authors that he offers in [Frege 1884] (in contrast to Cantor in his later writings and to Husserl's book). His reading seems to me to have been misdirected by two related things: his interpretation of "*gleich*" to mean identity and his failure to understand the historical use of the term "number" to mean what is numbered. For example, in §34, where he begins the discussion of whether the units are *gleich*, he refers to the *very same page* (p. 5) of [Schröder 1873] from which the quote "Each of the things to be numbered is called a unit" (cited in §28) came. He now paraphrases Schröder as giving as the reason we call things "units" that it ascribes "to the items that are to be numbered the necessary identity (Gleichheit)". Clearly Schröder could not mean here that the things are being identified with each other. He means rather that they are being identified *as* the things to be counted. Indeed, in §54, Frege quotes p. 7 of the same work on the notion of a unit: "This generic name or concept will be called the denomination of the number formed by the method given, and constitutes, in effect, what is meant by its unit." As further evidence of Frege's confused reading of other authors, let me repeat part of the quote cited above from [Frege 1884, §34]:

> For suppose that we do, as Thomae demands, "abstract from the peculiarities of the individual members of a set of things", or "disregard, in considering separate things, those characteristics which serve to distinguish them". In that event we are not left, as Lipschitz maintains, with "the concept of the number of the things considered"; what we get is rather a general concept under which the things considered fall. The things themselves do not in the process lose any of their special characteristics.

If we put together Thomae's "abstract . . . set of things" with Lipschitz's "the concept of the number . . . ", then it seems that we are abstracting from the particular nature of the elements of a *set* to obtain the number of the set. But if we read only what Lipschitz wrote, then we are, in considering separate things, disregarding those characteristics which serve to distinguish them and are left with the concept of the number [*anzahl*] of the things in question. But by "anzahl" here Lipschitz means the set. So Frege is in complete agreement with Lipschitz: The set (or concept whose extension is the set) is obtained by abstracting from the differences among the elements of the set.

The citation of Thomae is equally misleading. *His* ultimate concern is with the theory of analytic functions and so with the complex numbers. He is sketching the construction of these numbers from the natural numbers. His account is 'formalistic', in the sense that he treats the natural numbers as signs and the real numbers as infinite sequences of signs. This account is by no means as defective as Frege makes it out to be (e.g. in [Frege 1903, pp. 96–139]);[37] but that is not my point here. The numbers, being for Thomae signs, are certainly not sets of pure units. The context of the above quote from Thomae is this:

> We assume that one can count, i.e. that one is in the position to abstract from the peculiarities of the individuals in a set of objects and assign successive distinct names to distinct such sets of objects. Each individual of the set is called a unit, and, as a consequence of the required abstraction from all distinctive peculiarities, one may replace any unit by any other. *The units are equal to one another.* [Thomae 1880, p.1]

The units are *equal*, not identical. The sense in which they are equal is explained: one can be substituted for any other without altering the name assigned, i.e. the number.

Frege's proposed solution to his dilemma is to be found in §§46–48 and in §54: The things to which number applies are concepts or extensions of concepts. This is consistent with his view that Cantor's notion of a set can only be understood as the extension of a concept. Concerning the notion of a unit, Frege points out (§54) that the term was used with two senses: For the concept and for the objects that fall under the concept. Indeed, we saw that this was true of Euclid. But Frege seems to have thought that this was a source of confusion, whereas one would think that it would have been a commonplace observation: "Man" is sometimes used to denote a particular man and sometimes to denote the property of being a man. The difference between 'man' and 'unit' in this respect is that the meaning of the former is fixed and the meaning of the latter is relative and must be specified in any context—as meaning 'man in the room' in one context, 'sheep in the flock' in another, etc. It is to this relativity that Schröder refers when he speaks of it as a *generic* name or concept.

XII

Ultimately, Frege's contribution with respect to the definition of equinumerosity was to replace Cantor's sets as the objects of number attributions by concepts. Indeed, his proposal in his review of Cantor is that we should understand the

---

[37]And Frege's treatment of the 'formalism' of [Heine, 1872] in [1903] is totally unjustified.

term 'set' to refer to extensions of concepts. Perhaps it is this idea that Dummett thinks renders the definition more precise. *In the case of finite numbers,* Frege's proposal would indeed have clarified the discussion of number among his contemporaries: the meaning of choosing a unit and of all units being equal is well analyzed in terms of choosing a concept, in something like Frege's sense of concept. The number of people in the room is an attribute of the concept '*x* is in the room', where *x* ranges over people. It is only a pity that he needed to so discredit other authors, from Euclid to Thomae, in order to make his contribution.

But notice that, in the above example, we do not really have Frege's notion of concept, since *x* ranges over people and, for Frege, the variable ranges over all objects. In the example given, the appropriate concept for Frege would be '*x* is a person in the room'. But, when we admit Fregean concepts in general, that is, concepts of the form *F(x)*, where *x* ranges over 'all objects', then Frege's idea that number is attributable to concepts goes wrong. In the case of *infinite* numbers, the fact is that Cantor had already noted in the [Cantor 1883] that there are concepts, for example, the concept that *x* is an ordinal (or cardinal), which do not have a power. In his note to §4 he writes:

> [E]ach of the number classes, and hence each of the powers, is associated with an entirely determinate number of the absolutely infinite totality of numbers, . . . Thus the different powers also form an absolutely infinite sequence.

The 'absolute infinite' is contrasted with a determinate infinite, which has a power. His much maligned review of Frege's *Grundlagen* in 1885 may also be read as spotting immediately what is wrong with Frege's conception. He writes:

> The author comes upon the unfortunate idea—and it appears that he is following in this respect a suggestion of Überweg in his *System der Logic,* §53—of taking what is called in Scholastic logic [*Schullogik*] the 'extension of a concept' as the foundation of the number concept. He entirely overlooks the fact that the 'extension of a concept' in general may be quantitatively completely indeterminate. Only in certain cases is the 'extension of a concept' quantitatively determinate: Then it has of course, if it is finite, a definite number or, in the case it is infinite, a definite power. For such a quantitative determination of an 'extension of a concept' the concepts of 'number' and 'power' must already be given from another source, and it is a *reversal of direction* if one undertakes to found the latter concepts on that of 'extension of a concept'. [Cantor, 1932, p. 440]

Although neither Frege nor Cantor's editor, Zermelo,[38] understood him in this way, it is reasonable to believe that the concepts he had in mind, whose extensions are quantitatively indeterminate, are '*x* is an ordinal' and '*x* is a cardinal'. One might question this on the grounds that he does not explicitly name these concepts; but, since he doesn't give *any* examples, that would be an objection to *any* attempt to interpret his remark that there are quantitatively indeterminate

---

[38][Cantor, 1932, p.441]

extensions of concepts. Moreover, he had recently published his 1883 paper and [Frege 1884] referred to it; so it would have been not unreasonable to assume that the reader of the review and, in particular, Frege would know that the totalities of ordinals and powers have no power. But most importantly, other interpretations—such as that he is referring to non-sortal concepts, such as 'water', or to concepts whose extensions are indefinite, such as 'living creature'—make no sense of Cantor's subsequent remark about reversal of direction. The point of that remark, it seems to me, must be that the number classes are in place to serve as a measure for an infinite totality being a determinate infinity, i.e. having a power. The number classes would play no conceivable role in distinguishing sortals from non-sortals or well-defined concepts from ill-defined ones. Again, Cantor's reference to Überweg's *System der Logik*, §53, although it does not seem to be particularly apt, lends some support for my interpretation of his review. Überweg is speaking, not of concepts there, but of representations [*Vorstellungen*]. Stripped of Überweg's psychologistic conception of them, they come closest to what Frege means by a 'concept'. Concepts for Überweg, on the other hand, are of a restricted kind of representation (§56). The extension of a representation (§53) consists of other representations. Thus the relation between representation and elements of the representation conforms not at all to Frege's sharp distinction between concept and object. An individual is in an extension by way of having its individual representation in the extension. Concerning number, Überweg writes:

> The formal relation of the subordination of many representations under the same higher one leads to the concept [*Begriff*] of number which, in its original sense [*as Anzahl*], is the determination, by means of a unit, of the plurality [*Vielheit*] of individuals of the extension. (§53)

I do not understand the role of the unit in this conception. Shouldn't the plurality of individuals in the extension be determined already by the representation itself? But anyway, in an earlier passage, and perhaps closer to Frege's conception, Überweg writes:

> Only on the basis of concept formation can *numerals* be understood; for they presuppose the subsumption of similar objects under the same concept. (§47)

I can't find any grounds in this for thinking that Cantor understood Frege's concepts to include non-sortals or concepts whose extensions are not well-defined.

It is easy to misunderstand Cantor's review because, for many, the primary question is to be formulated by asking whether a given totality is a set. If it is, then it has a cardinal number. Indeed, in his later papers, in which he seems to have abandoned his autonomous theory of ordinals and powers, this question is primary. But in the 1883 paper and in his review of Frege, Cantor's understanding was that the theory of the number classes is primary and with it, the theory of infinite cardinals *as the powers of the number classes*. Our question of whether a totality is a well-defined set *is* precisely his question of whether it is 'numerically determinate'—in other words, whether it is finite or equipollent to one of the number classes. It is for this reason that Cantor speaks of a reversal of direction. One cannot define the cardinals simply to be the extensions of second-order concepts of the form 'equipollent to F', since not every concept F has a cardinal.

Frege's reply [1984, p. 122] to Cantor's review shows that he thinks that Cantor's remark is aimed at his definition of $N_x Fx$, the number of F's, as the extension of the concept 'equipollent with F', and is pointing out that *this* concept might or might not be numerically determinate. Frege responds that is of no consequence, since this concept does not have to have a number in order to *be* the number $N_x Fx$. But Cantor means that F might itself be quantitatively indeterminate, so that $N_x Fx$ does not exist. On explanation for Frege's interpretation of Cantor's criticism, and one which lends some support to it, is Cantor's assertion that Frege took the notion of the extension of a concept as the foundation of the number concept. My suggested reading of this requires that we understand him to be saying that, for Frege, it is the extension of concepts which have number; but Frege's actual definition in the *Grundlagen* attributes number to the concept, and it is the number itself which is an extension of a concept. On the other hand, although Frege does not explicitly speak of higher level concepts in the *Grundlagen*, his official definition of $N_x F(x)$ makes it the extension of a second level concept, so that its elements are themselves first level concepts. It is not at all unreasonable to suppose that Cantor would understand this by taking the elements of $N_x F(x)$ to be the corresponding extensions of the concepts.

Of course, even with the misunderstanding, Frege should have taken heed. If there is *any* concept whose extension does not have a cardinal, then Frege's analysis fails. *Even if it were concepts to which number should be attributable, one would need to distinguish, on some other grounds, as Cantor insisted, those concepts which do have number from those which don't.* Frege might have responded that the concept 'equipollent with F' is a second-level concept, and that it is only first-level concepts to which number is attributable. But in [Frege 1893], which implicitly postulates as an object an extension of each first-level concept, this response fails; for every second-level concept induces the first-level concept of the corresponding extensions. In particular, the second-level concept 'equipollent with F' yields the first-level concept 'equipollent with the extension of F'.

There tends to be a picture of Frege as a tragic victim of fate: by his very virtue, namely his insistence on precision, he committed himself explicitly to a contradiction that was already implicit in mathematical thought. But in fact his assumption in the *Grundgesetze* that every concept has an extension was an act of recklessness, forewarned against by Cantor already in 1883 and again, explicitly, in his review in 1885.

10

Joan Weiner

HAS FREGE A PHILOSOPHY OF LANGUAGE?*

Has Frege a philosophy of language? Most contemporary writers would say he has. And, while some might agree that Frege's early philosophical writings are restricted to issues concerning logic and arithmetic, few express any doubt that Frege's 1892 paper, "On Sense and Meaning" is meant as the beginning of some sort of philosophy of language. Part of the explanation of this might be that it seems clear to most contemporary writers first that, as Michael Dummett says, "However Frege is to be interpreted, there will *be* such a thing as the philosophy of language" [Dummett, 1981, p. 40] and, second, that if there *is* such a thing as the philosophy of language, Frege made important contributions to it. Those contributions, of course, are to be found in "On Sense and Meaning", among other writings. In the chapter of *The Interpretation of Frege's Philosophy* titled "Was Frege a Philosopher of Language?" Dummett writes,

> Frege says that, while all sciences have truth as their goal, the predicate 'true' defines the subject-matter of what he calls 'logic'. [1979a, p. 128]. . . . Now the notion of truth, as the object of philosophical enquiry, has always been recognized by philosophers as closely allied to that of meaning. [p. 37]

Even if this is so, philosophers may differ on what the nature of the alliance might be. Dummett has made it clear that, on his view, the notion of meaning has to do with features of language that are in no way exhausted by what is expressed in logical laws. But is Frege concerned with meaning in this sense? I will argue that, by insisting that he is, we place obstacles in the way of providing a coherent interpretation of Frege's writings. I will argue, in particular, that, supposing we understand meaning as Dummett does, then on Frege's view the philosophical treatment of the notion of truth is closely allied, not with meaning, but with science. Frege's logical investigations answer to what he views as the most fundamental standards of science. And one consequence of taking these standards seriously is that, if a semantic theory or a theory of meaning must consist of truths, there can be no such theories.

---

*I would like to thank Mark Kaplan for extensive comments on earlier drafts of this paper. My final revisions were influenced by many helpful and interesting discussions with participants at the conference.

I

Why think the traditional reading of Frege causes difficulties for interpreting his writings? One reason is that this reading is not easily reconciled with some of Frege's explicit claims about his aims and achievements. One of these appears in a jotted note, from Frege's *Nachlass* apparently dated August 1906 and labeled "What may I regard as the result of my Work?" It begins,

> It is almost all tied up with the concept-script. a concept construed as a function. a relation as a function of two arguments. the extension of a concept or class is not the primary thing for me. unsaturatedness both in the case of concepts and functions. the true nature of concept and function recognized [1979a, p. 184]

There is no immediate conflict. To say that Frege meant to contribute to a theory of meaning is not to deny the importance of his contribution to logic. But this comment does place a burden on the reader who takes a contribution to the theory of meaning as one of Frege's aims. Frege's explicit assessment of his achievement suggests that, insofar as he intended to contribute to a theory of meaning, this contribution, too, is tied up with his concept-script. What is the relation of Frege's contribution to the theory of meaning and his logical achievements?

Although Dummett recognizes that this relation is important, his characterizations of the relation are not always very convincing. He writes that the syntactic analysis embodied in Frege's symbolic notation,

> expresses Frege's conception of the way in which sentences are to be viewed as having been constructed out of their components; and its point lies in the fact that it serves as a base for the semantic theory embodied in his theory of reference. [1981, pp. 151–152]

But this is very different from Frege's description of its point. When Frege first attempted to set out this syntactic analysis in 1879, he characterized it as a means for expressing all content that is of significance for inference and as a means of preventing presuppositions from sneaking into inferences unnoticed. No theory of reference is mentioned. This is not very surprising, since Frege did not have a theory of reference in 1879. Nor is there textual evidence that, in 1879, Frege was planning to introduce a theory of reference. That is, there is no compelling evidence that, on Frege's view, the point of his 1879 introduction of his symbolic notation was that it could serve as a base for a semantic theory. Frege may, of course, have changed his mind about the sort of contribution his symbolic notation constituted. But Dummett's characterization does not appear in Frege's later writings either.

A few pages later, Dummett again characterizes the relation between theories of reference and logic—this time reversing the relation. He asks what the notion of reference is for and answers,

> In logic, we need the notion of reference, or of semantic value in order to characterize validity; but, more generally, we need it as the basis for a theory of sense: it has a point if, and *only* if, it plays a role in our account of sense. What, then, do we need a theory of sense for? We need it as forming a large part of a theory of meaning, that is, of a theory that will explain in virtue of what features of our use of them our sentences bear the meanings they do. [1981, p. 157]

Unlike the previous quote, this suggests that a need for a theory of reference arose from the demands of Frege's logic—a more plausible story. It also suggests that a need for a theory of reference will arise from any attempt to develop a theory of meaning (or, as Dummett says elsewhere, an account of the workings of language FPL 83). Dummett seems to have identified two distinct projects to which Frege wished to make a contribution: the development of a logic and the development of a theory of meaning. Both projects, according to Dummett, require a theory of reference.

There can be no doubt that Frege meant to be developing a logic. He said so repeatedly. But Frege did not say he was developing a theory of meaning. Thus any evidence that he meant to be doing this must be indirect. And the evidence is, at best, equivocal. For instance, Dummett claims that Frege's project requires a definition of what it is to be a proper name. If Frege did mean the syntactic analysis embodied in his symbolic notation to be a contribution to an analysis of the workings of language, then Dummett's claim is not unreasonable. On the other hand, Frege does not think that he needs to give a definition of what it is to be a proper name. What are we to infer? Dummett infers that Frege has made a mistake for, Dummett says, "Such an attitude is not acceptable." (1973, p. 54) But this conclusion is not inevitable. No definition of 'proper name' is required for purposes of setting up a logical notation and logical laws. Nor is one required for purposes of explaining what his Begriffsschrift does. Frege's failure to offer a definition of "proper name" can be interpreted either as an error or as an indication that Frege was not concerned with the workings of language. If we insist, as Dummett does, that Frege was concerned with the workings of language, this is not the only error.

Another error, according to Dummett, is Frege's claim that a sentence is the proper name of one of two objects, the True and the False. Dummett characterizes this as "disastrous" [1991b, p. 242]. One of the interesting features of this disaster is its location. We have all found ourselves in the position of having committed ourselves to views that we would rather deny. But typically these commitments are made without full awareness. Taken in isolation, some of Dummett's remarks might lead the naive reader to imagine that Frege's claim that sentences are proper names appears somewhat late in his writings about language. The naive reader might suspect that at some point Frege realized that he had already made this commitment and decided, given his options and other commitments, that the appropriate response was to stand behind this unfortunate consequence.

The actual situation is different. Frege did not originally claim that sentences were names of truth-values. It is probably true that he came to realize that details of his logic committed him to this. But there is no indication in his writings that he was reluctant to embrace this consequence or that he thought it conflicted with other views he held—particularly views about language. Indeed, in the writings that precede his assimilation of sentences to proper names, there *is* no philosophy of language for which this consequence could cause trouble. The first article that seems to address linguistic meaning as an object of philosophical investigation is "On Sense and Meaning". And the bulk of that paper is devoted to Frege's argument that it is appropriate to take sentences as names of the True and the False. The 'disaster' is right up front. There is an obvious alternative to Dummett's characterizations of Frege's claim not only as 'disastrous' but also as 'tragic', an 'absurdity', a 'ludicrous deviation' and a 'gratuitous blunder' [1973, p. 184]. The alternative is to consider the possibility that Frege is not interested in contributing to the sort of theory of meaning Dummett advocates. To see why it should be considered, let us look more closely at the nature of the disaster.

It is obvious, of course, that the view of sentences as proper names does not come from the demands of a theory of meaning. The demands that motivate this view come, Dummett says, from Frege's theory of reference. Moreover, according to Dummett, a theory of reference plays a necessary role both for Frege's logic and for his theory of meaning. Evidently, then, the view that sentences are proper names should arise from the demands of logic. The explanation is simple. It is an essential part of Frege's logical notation to show how the truth-value of a complex sentence is dependent on its composition. Sentences can, themselves, be parts of sentences. And, as it turns out, a sentence's contribution to the truth-value of a sentence in which it appears can only be explained if sentences are names of truth-values. This is the argument Frege gives in "On Sense and Meaning". Also, in the preface to volume 1 of *Basic Laws,* the work in which Frege presents the revised version of his logic, he indicates that the introduction of truth-values as objects for which sentences stand is useful for purpose of the logic. As he says in the preface, this makes everything "sharper and simpler". In addition, it is an important part of the characterization of functions needed to make his logical regimentation clear. Thus the arguments in "On Sense and Meaning" play a role in Frege's exposition of his altered logical notation in *Basic Laws.*

If we insist that Frege was developing a theory of meaning we are, it seems, required to ascribe many serious and inexplicable blunders to him. Why, then, does it seem so evident that he was? There are two obvious answers. The first is that not *all* the views expressed in "On Sense and Meaning" are needed for Frege's logic. I will put this answer aside for the moment and return to it later. The second is that a theory of meaning must underlie logic. This seems to be Dummett's answer. At many points his discussions suggest that the demands of a theory of meaning should have priority over those of logic. (See, e.g., [1973, pp.

669–671], [1981, pp. 19, 37–38, 63, 157].) In his discussion of the assimilation of sentences to proper names he writes that this assimilation

> does not accord with our strong intuition that sentences are not of the same syntactic or semantic category as proper names, and this implies, at least within a Fregean framework, that the things they stand for will be of different logical types too. [1991b, pp. 242–243]

This may seem to contradict Frege's dictum that criteria for decisions about logic should not be derived from language which is "unreliable on logical questions" [1984, p. 381]. But Dummett does not mean these intuitions to come directly from an examination of natural language. A correct theory of meaning is not to be understood as an accurate account of the actual functioning of natural language. Dummett says,

> no systematic theory of meaning will fit our linguistic practice as it actually is: but so much the worse for our linguistic practice, which ought to be revised so as to accord with such a theory. [1981, p. 30]

He goes on to say that Frege's theory is meant to apply to natural language, "in so far as it does function properly" [1981, p. 31]. In Dummett's view logic must be responsible, not to our *actual* use of language, but to a systematic theory of meaning that fits with what is right about our actual use of language. And, again, the content of this theory cannot be constituted by logical laws. What is right in our actual language goes beyond those bounds.

It is difficult, however, to reconcile this view of the relation between logic and theories of meaning with Frege's writings. The assimilation of sentences to proper names is a direct result of one of the central features Frege mentions in his 1906 note: the construal of concepts as functions. This assimilation is itself manifested in Frege's logical laws. And there is no indication that the logical laws must answer to a theory of meaning. For Frege says,

> The questions why and with what right we acknowledge a law of logic to be true, logic can answer only by reducing it to another law of logic. Where that is not possible, logic can give no answer. [1967a, p. 15][1]

Nor is this merely the only answer logic can give: it is the only sort of answer available. Frege considers only one sort of answer we might get if we

---

[1] Of course, according to Dummett, Frege uses the term 'logic' both for what we understand as logic and for the theory of meaning [1981, p. 63]. Indeed, more often Dummett simply claims that Frege's term 'logic' should be understood as 'theory of meaning' (See, e.g., [1973, pp. 669–670], [1981, pp. 36–37]). However, even if we were to agree with Dummett that, at some points, Frege's use of the term 'logic' can be replaced with 'theory of meaning', the laws of logic to which Frege refers here are clearly what we would describe as laws of logic. If we read the other occurrence of 'logic' as 'theory of meaning', then it is clear that the theory of meaning must answer to the laws of logic rather than the other way around.

"step away from logic". It is that "we are compelled to make judgments by our own nature and by external circumstances." And this, Frege tells us, is not an answer to the question. Thus, insofar as Frege takes himself to have presented a correct logic in *Begriffsschrift* or *Basic Laws,* if his logic conflicts with a theory of meaning—so much the worse for the theory of meaning.

But even if there is reason to believe that Frege did not hold the view of the relation between logic and theory of meaning that Dummett attributes to him, Frege might still have intended to contribute to a theory of meaning. Even if the demands of logic have priority, the notions of reference and sense introduced in "On Sense and Meaning" still seem to belong, at least, to a semantic theory and, perhaps also, to a theory of meaning. But do they? Can we really find views about language in Frege's writings that are not part of his attempt to exposit or defend his logic or his views about what his logic does?

As we have seen, Dummett thinks that the point of a theory of sense is its contribution to a theory of meaning. But is this the point of Frege's comments about sense? On the standard view, the evidence that these comments express Frege's concern with language is that these comments go beyond what is needed for his logic. For the sense, or cognitive value, of an expression is what is communicated by use of the expression. It is what one understands when one understand the expression. And, if this is what the sense of an expression is, then it seems apparent that different expressions whose content is logically equivalent can express different senses. Our intellectual limitations guarantee that, for most of us, there will be pairs of logically equivalent sentences both of which we use for purposes of communication yet which we also believe do not express logically equivalent thoughts. This is supported by at least one passage in which Frege says that, when sameness of reference (or meaning) is not self-evident, there must be a difference in sense [1980, p. 152].

But, for all the apparent importance of communication and understanding in this characterization of sense, there remains a puzzle to be solved about the relation of sense and logic. After all, Frege himself claims in a letter to Husserl that "the only possible means of deciding whether two sentences express the same thought is that their contents are logically equivalent" [1980, p. 70]. And, in a different letter to Husserl, Frege says, "equipollent propositions have something in common in their content, and this is what I call the thought they express" [1980, p. 67]. Dummett dismisses these passages with the remark that we should not hold Frege to something he only says in a letter [1981, p. 325]. Dummett's response might be convincing if the claims in these letters were truly isolated aberrations. But they are not.

A more careful look at Frege's remarks about sense shows that it would be precipitous to dismiss the evidence of what Frege says in the letters to Husserl. For, if sense contains content beyond what is expressible in Begriffsschrift, Frege would need another term for the content that is expressed by his notation. In fact, Frege often uses the term "sense" as a term for the content expressed by

Begriffsschrift. One of the aims of Frege's Begriffsschrift was to set out a nota-tion adequate to express possible contents of judgment. He says, in the preface to Begriffsschrift, that his notation is meant to express all and only the content with significance for the inferential sequence [1879, p. 5]. It would thus seem that a possible content of judgment is exhausted by what has significance for the inferential sequence. And, as he says in "On Concept and Object", a companion paper to "On Sense and Meaning", what he called 'possible content of judg-ment' in Begriffsschrift, combined what he now designates as 'thought' (the sense of a sentence) and truth-value (its reference or meaning). If sense is meant to be what is expressed by Begriffsschrift, then it is not clear how there can be a difference in sense when there is logical equivalence. The assimilation of same-ness of sense to logical equivalence is also suggested by several other remarks. One of these is that the truth of a logical law is immediately evident of itself, from the sense of its expression [1984, p. 405].

I do not take any of this to show that sameness of sense is logical equiva-lence. Rather, it is clear that there is a role to be played by sense in Frege's attempt to explain what his logic does. Indeed, one might argue that Frege is wrong about the significance of his notion of sense—that the notion, as described in "On Sense and Meaning", is not simply a part of the earlier notion of possible content of judgement. But, if so, it is clear that there is a tension exhibited in Frege's remarks—a tension between the role sense seems to play in Frege's explanation of his logic and the role it seems to play in a theory of meaning. If Frege did regard his introduction of sense as a contribution to a the-ory of meaning then, at the very least, he should not have said that sense is a part of what he earlier called "possible content of judgement". Perhaps Frege simply never faced this tension. But, as before, there is an alternative interpretation. It may be that Frege did not mean to be developing a theory of meaning. It seems only reasonable, at this point, to address these issues by examining Frege's view of what his logic does.

II

The laws of logic cannot, of course, be independent of meaning. The content of a sentence that has significance for the inferential sequence is probably part of its meaning. But it does not follow that Frege has any need for a *theory* of mean-ing. Nor does this follow from Frege's claim that the laws of logic are the laws of truth. The significance of his claim is abundantly clear from his writings. It is that the laws of logic are meant to be applicable whenever our interest is in establishing truths. They are the ultimate basis of every science. Such assertions appear throughout Frege's writings. Thomas Ricketts describes these sorts of passages as expressing the view that logic is the maximally general science. But the roots of this maximally general science, according to Ricketts, lie not so much in science and scientific inference as they do in a conception of everyday agreements and disagreements. Ricketts writes,

> When I disagree with you, there arises an issue between us: either your assertion or my denial must be wrong. This issue is addressed when we reason together, when we attempt to locate further truths from which the original assertion or its opposite may be inferred. So, Frege adopts as his starting point our common understanding of language. This understanding includes a shared appreciation of elementary implications, of the basis that the assertion of one statement provides for the assertion and denial of others. [1986b, p. 173]

After all, it is not only in scientific contexts that we view ourselves as concerned with truth. When Frege says, "Thought is in essentials the same everywhere" [1884, p. III] and when Frege writes about logic as something "to be appointed as arbiter in the conflict of opinions" [1967a, p. 17], these claims must be understood, according to Ricketts, as applying to everyday reasoning.

On Ricketts' interpretation, Frege's notion of Bedeutung does not originate in an attempt to provide a theory of reference but, rather, in an attempt to explain generality and its quantifier representation in Begriffsschrift. On this interpretation, Frege's aim is to contrast "variables which indefinitely indicate [*andeuten*] anything, with names, which mean [*bedeuten*] some single thing." [Ricketts, 1986b, p. 177]. This has nothing to do with identifying a means by which names hook onto the world or separating names into those that do and those that do not. But it involves a presupposition, according to Ricketts. And this presupposition is that any name that is not a variable means some single thing. What is the significance of this presupposition?

Although Frege writes, in the preface to *Begriffsschrift,* that his logical notation is a means for preventing any presupposition from sneaking into an inference unnoticed, he also acknowledges, fairly early in his career,[2] that there are presuppositions involved in the use of his Begriffsschrift. He says,

> The rules of logic always presuppose that the words we use are not empty, that our sentences express judgments, that one is not playing a mere game with words. [1979a, p. 60]

But this presupposition seems innocuous. If all we are presupposing is that our apparent assertions do not amount to gibberish, the presupposition is no part of the content of the argument. The status of this presupposition appears to change, however, after the formulation of the sense/meaning distinction. Ricketts argues that Frege draws this distinction as a response to his recognition of the existence of meaningless names and that this recognition is forced on Frege by his conception of logic. And, according to Ricketts, once Frege claims that names have

---

[2]This is from a dialogue with Bernard Pünjer who, according to the editors of Frege's *Posthumous Writings,* died in 1885.

both sense and meaning but that the laws of logic apply only to sentences all of whose terms have meaning, the presuppositions involved in the application of the laws of logic acquire substance.

Consider the use of definite descriptions. In our ordinary understanding of inference, definite descriptions function as proper names. On our everyday understanding of the inferential relations, a claim that, for example, the F is a G is an instance of the generalization, 'Everything is a G'. It ought, then, to be immediately inferable from the generalization.[3] The claim that the expression 'the F' has meaning is not part of the content expressed by a rendering of the argument in Begriffsschrift. It is a presupposition. But, unlike the innocuous presupposition that we are not mouthing gibberish, this presupposition appears to have substance. We can think that we are inferring in accord with the logical laws, but be mistaken. A definite description, on Frege's view, has meaning for purposes of logic only if it picks out precisely one object. And this is something that must be demonstrated. Nor is the problem limited to definite descriptions. 'Odysseus' is one of Frege's examples of a name with sense but not meaning. Someone who thought that Odysseus was a historical figure might believe she is making inferences about Odysseus but would have, inadvertently, wandered into the realm of fiction.[4] It seems, then, that before we are permitted to apply logical laws we must assure ourselves that all the expressions we use have meaning. Ricketts writes,

> Presumably, the investigation of presuppositions belongs to the science of semantics, the science that examines what, if anything, a given name or sense of a name means. [1986b, p. 190]

Thus, Ricketts argues, Frege does find himself in need of a semantic theory—although the recognition of this need does not merit the celebration Dummett accords it. For this need is in direct conflict with Frege's conception of logic.

I have far more sympathy for the Ricketts interpretation than I have for Dummett's. I, too, have argued that the sense/meaning distinction is Frege's response to the recognition of the existence of meaningless names and I have argued that his logical laws are the most general laws of science. (See [Weiner, 1990, pp. 66–67, 104–105].) But my interpretation of the notion of a most general science is rather different from Ricketts' and one upshot is that, on my interpretation, the situation is nowhere near as grim as Ricketts suggests. On my interpretation, Frege does not need a semantic theory and the predominant

---

[3]Or, almost immediately. In Frege's actual system the proof requires, first, the use of an instance of Basic Law IIa (in contemporary notation: $(x)Fx \rightarrow Fa$) and, then, the use of Modus Ponens. The point is that it should be inferable from the generalization without the use of any additional facts.

[4]Frege says that if he uses the expression 'that lime-tree' without realizing that the expression doesn't designate anything, then he has "wandered into the realm of fiction without knowing it or meaning to" [1984, p. 362]. Frege also says that the name 'Odysseus' doesn't designate anything [1979a, p. 191]. Thus, it does not seem unreasonable to describe someone who thinks that 'Odysseus' does designate a historical person as having wandered into the realm of fiction.

reading of "On Sense and Meaning" is a misreading. My difference, both with Dummett and with Ricketts, has to do with the relation of logic, as Frege conceives it, to ordinary language and ordinary reasoning. It also has to do with our different assessments of the importance of Frege's treatment of proper names.

Let us look at some passages in which Frege describes the aims of his logic and the relation between logical laws, truth, and science. Let us look, in particular, at the extent to which Frege thinks the laws of truth should apply to our everyday language and our everyday reasoning.

First, everyday language. One of the hallmarks of Dummett's interpretation is his insistence that Frege's comments about what is required of a logically perfect language should apply to everyday language as well. Dummett claims that the primary difference between Begriffsschrift and ordinary language is that the expression of a thought in ordinary language includes content that is not relevant to inference—content that obscures the thought expressed. His image of what goes on when a sentence of ordinary language is translated into Begriffsschrift is that of purification [1981, p. 32]. He says, "there is no suggestion that it is meant to express more rarefied thoughts than can be put into the words of natural language" [1981, p. 18].

In fact, however, there is more than a suggestion.[5] One of Frege's earliest comments about the relationship between his logical notation and language is the following passage from the preface to *Begriffsschrift*.

> I believe that I can best make the relation of my ideography [*mein Begriffsschrift*] to ordinary language [*Sprache des Lebens*] clear if I compare it to that which the microscope has to the eye. Because of the range of its possible uses and the versatility with which it can adapt to the most diverse circumstances, the eye is far superior to the microscope. Considered as an optical instrument, to be sure, it exhibits many imperfections, which ordinarily remain unnoticed only on account of its intimate connection with our mental life. But, as soon as scientific goals [*wissenschaftliche Zwecke*] demand great sharpness of resolution [*die Schärfe der Unterscheidung stellen*], the eye proves to be insufficient. The microscope, on the other hand, is perfectly suited to precisely such goals, but that is just why it is useless for all others.
>
> This ideography [*Begriffsschrift*], likewise, is a device invented for certain scientific purposes [*wissenschaftliche Zwecke*], and one must not condemn it because it is not suited to others. [1879, p. 6]

A microscope does not show us what we are able to see with the naked eye but is likely to be obscured. The microscope shows us something that cannot be seen with the naked eye. Frege's image suggests that his notation *does* express something that cannot be expressed in natural language. Indeed, Frege gives an example of what such a thing would be like in section 24 of *Begriffsschrift,* where he

---

[5]That is, there is more than a suggestion that Frege's logical notation enables one to express thoughts that may not be expressible in natural language. I'm not sure that such thoughts are more rarefied than those expressible in natural language.

says, about a property F's being hereditary in an f-sequence.

> We see, incidentally, that it can become difficult and even impossible to give a rendering in words if very involved functions take the places of F and f [1979, p. 57]

So, just as a microscope and an eye have different uses, natural language and Begriffsschrift have different uses. The defects of natural language that Frege identifies later are almost always identified as 'logical defects'. Why correct the logical defects of natural language? The most likely reason is that one wants to apply logical laws in everyday contexts as, on Ricketts' interpretation, Frege seems to want. But this does not exactly fit with what Frege says in his comparison of his notation with the microscope. The use of the microscope becomes important when scientific goals demand a sharpness of resolution for which the eye is insufficient. Similarly, Frege says that his notation is a device invented for scientific goals. It is, like the microscope, a tool for science. Natural language, like the eye, is unsuited for these peculiar purposes. But Frege also emphasizes the advantages of the eye over the microscope. The eye is, for most purposes, superior to the microscope, which is "useless" for all goals other than those for which it was designed. Begriffsschrift, too, is designed for particular scientific purposes and should not, he says, be condemned because it is not suited to others. Thus there seems to be no justification for eliminating the defects of natural language.

These two points, first, that natural language has a different purpose from logically perfect languages and, second, that a logical notation is to be viewed as a tool for science appear in both Frege's early and late writings.[6] So why does it seem that the laws of logic ought to apply to everyday statements? The answer is that Frege says, not only that his notation is to be used for scientific goals but, also, that it is to be used whenever our concern is with truth. Perhaps it is not

---

[6]Although Dummett concentrates on Frege's many comments about the features of natural language that aren't related to truth-value, e.g., coloring and shading, as I have indicated above, this is not the only sort of difference Frege recognized. Frege also says that the requirements that guided the formation of natural language do not include the requirements of logic. See, e.g., [1984, p. 400], and the passage from his letter to Peano quoted below [1980, pp. 114–115]. Further, he suggests at least once that the defects of natural language have a salutary effect. In an early paper, "On the Scientific Justification of the Concept-Script" [1972, p. 86], he says,

> The shortcomings stressed are rooted in a certain softness and instability of ordinary language [*der Sprache*], which nevertheless is necessary for its versatility and potential for development. In this respect, ordinary language [*Die Sprache in dieser Hinsicht*] can be compared to the hand, which despite its adaptability to the most diverse tasks is still inadequate. We build for ourselves artificial hands, tools for particular purposes, which work with more accuracy than the hand can provide.

A significant part of this paper is devoted to the description of a Concept-Script as a tool for science [1972, pp. 83–86]. In addition to this passage and the microscope passage from *Begriffsschrift*, the view of the Concept-Script as a technical tool appears in his latest papers. (See [1984, pp. 380, 397–400].) If we do need a logically perfect technical tool, why require that ordinary language be logically perfect as well?

that natural language needs to be replaced in all its uses with a non-defective language but, rather, that natural language should be replaced in those contexts in which our concern is with truth. This is, in fact, what Dummett says at one point [1981, p. 30]. So there appears to be a tension here. Surely, scientific research does not exhaust the circumstances in which our concern is with truth.

Or does it? It is interesting to examine the passages in which Frege says that proper names must have a meaning. He says this is required if the sentences in which they appear are to have truth-values [1979a, p. 191], [1984, p. 226]. He writes, for example,

> Now a proper name that designates nothing has no logical justification, since in logic we are concerned with truth in the strictest sense of the word; it may on the other hand be used in fiction and fable. [1984, p. 226]

The only unusual features of this passage is that Frege mentions the requirement that proper names have meaning without *also* mentioning that this requirement comes from the demands of science.[7] Furthermore, Frege says, two pages after above passage, "Proper names without any meaning are illegitimate in science" [1984, p. 228]. And there are a number of passages in which Frege *only* mentions science [1984, pp. 148, 223, 241, 298], [1979a, p. 232]. But, typically, when Frege mentions this requirement, both truth and science are mentioned. He says, for example, in a discussion of the name 'Odysseus',

> The question of truth would cause us to abandon aesthetic delight for an attitude of scientific investigation. [1984, p. 163]

and

> The thought, though it is devoid of meaning, of truth-value, is enough, but not for science [*der Wissenschaft*]. [1979a, p. 122]

In two other explanations of when we need proper names to have meaning, he says that it happens when we are after "truth in the scientific sense" (*Wahrheit im wissenschaftlichen Sinne*) [1979a, p. 186], [1979a, p. 188]. Is Frege also interested in truth in a non-scientific sense? There is no indication that he is.[8]

---

[7] It is one of only two passages I have found in which Frege mentions this requirement but does not also say that it comes from the demands of science.

[8] But note that this is not to say that Frege means to be restricting his notation to serving the aim of establishing truths of natural science. Recall that, in a passage quoted above, not only psychology, but also metaphysics is called a science. The distinction here is between the use of language to find our way about everyday circumstances and its use in systematic attempts to establish truths. (See, e.g., [1972, pp. 85–86].) As I will elaborate shortly, the point is that finding our way about in everyday life does not require us to establish truths. There is also evidence that Frege views the aim of establishing general laws to be an intrinsic feature of science. See, e.g. [1984, pp. 133, 137–138], [1979a, p. 136].

Indeed, he writes in "Thoughts", "What I have in mind is that sort of truth which it is the aim of science to discern" [1984, p. 352].

There is another odd feature of these passages. In most of them Frege recognizes just two realms of discourse—science and fiction. In a few such passages he talks instead of the realms of truth and fiction. Why doesn't the subject of everyday communication come up? There is no obvious answer. Should we, nonetheless, attempt to draw morals about everyday communication from these passages? Suppose we want to do so. Everyday communication must be appropriately categorized. It is surely not fiction. Hence it seems reasonable to infer that Frege means us simply to understand everyday communication as assimilable under the truth category. But this will not fit with an interpretation that accounts both for Frege's remarks about natural language and for his remarks about what is required for truth.

To see this, let us recall the difficulties that Frege gets into, according to Ricketts. In our reasoning we presuppose that everyday proper names have meaning, but, because this presupposition is substantive, our application of logical laws needs to be justified. Consequently, Ricketts argues, the application of logical laws depends on a semantic science that decides these substantive questions. The problem with interpreting Frege as Ricketts does, however, is that there *is* no substantive issue here. Supposing our interest is in truth in the scientific sense, we need no science of semantics to determine whether or not our everyday proper names have meaning. We already know the answer. They do not. Why not?

Recall, first, that on the Ricketts interpretation, the name/bearer relation is not a prototype for the relation of an expression to its meaning. Indeed, the notion of meaning is not originally regarded as involving a relation between words and non-linguistic entities. On the position with which Frege starts, expressions that are not variables are, if they are not gibberish, meaningful. It is only after the introduction of the sense/meaning distinction that we have any reason to talk about a relation between an expression and what it means. At that point the question of whether or not an expression means something becomes substantive. But this, Ricketts argues, creates a problem for Frege. We can now apply logical laws to everyday inferences only if we make the substantive presupposition that our expressions are meaningful. Ricketts' argument comes from a consideration, not of everyday proper names, but of definite descriptions. In order to use such expressions as 'the F' in our inferences, we must presuppose that they pick out unique objects. But the presupposition is not exactly as Ricketts describes it. We cannot simply ask whether or not a definite description picks out a unique object. Definite descriptions are complex expressions. And a complex expression can be meaningful only if its constituents are. Moreover, the constituents of definite descriptions are concept-expressions. And a concept-expression is meaningful only if it has a sharp boundary, that is, only if for each object it either determinately holds or fails to hold. Frege says,

> If something fails to display a sharp boundary, it cannot be recognized in logic as a concept, just as something that is not extensionless cannot be recognized in geometry as a point, because otherwise it would be impossible to set up geometrical axioms. [1984, p. 133]

However, the failure to display sharp boundaries is almost universal among the concept-expressions of natural language.

There are several morals. One moral is that, for Frege, there is no substantive issue about the truth of our presuppositions in everyday reasoning. Our presuppositions are simply false. Our terms will be meaningful only if, first, we replace our defective everyday concept-expressions with non-defective terms and, second, we have rules that prevent the introduction of a definite description that does not pick out a unique object—that is, our terms will be meaningful only if we replace our language with a logically perfect language. The use of a logically perfect language requires no presuppositions. Thus Frege has no need for a semantic theory for natural language. And, finally, the logical laws cannot be applied in our everyday reasoning.

But this may seem to be less a solution than a relocation of the problem. After all, Frege's strategy for introducing his logical laws is to rely on our common understanding of everyday sentences. And this common understanding is constituted by an agreement about its use in the expression of correct inferences. If logical laws do not, in fact, apply—if we cannot, in fact, distinguish good everyday inferences from bad, what happens to our claim to be communicating? Worse, it seems that we have lost our ability to disagree and our right to view ourselves as expressing truths in everyday language. Is it reasonable to attribute such a view to Frege? And, if so, how can his work have any interest for us?

III

I will start with the first question. Elsewhere I have argued at length that there can be no doubt that Frege believed, for almost all his career, that concepts must have sharp boundaries [Weiner, 1990, pp. 92–97]. The above quotation about the need for sharp boundaries is from a paper published in 1891, but the same view appears in *Foundations,* which was published in 1884. And in the second volume of *Basic Laws,* which was printed in 1903, Frege says that something that appears to be a concept but does not have sharp boundaries is "wrongly termed a concept" [1952, p. 139] and is "an inadmissible sham concept" [1952, p. 145].[9] Nor is there any evidence that Frege considered a special standard of admissibil-

---

[9]This has important, and largely unrecognized, consequences for what metaphysical views can be attributed to Frege. I have discussed this issue in [Weiner, 1995].

ity for concepts used in everyday language. In the second volume of *Basic Laws*, for instance, his strict standard of admissibility is explicitly applied to the question "Are we still Christians?" There seems to be little alternative but to deny that Frege thinks the laws of truth apply to everyday conversation. But before we throw up our hands and abandon Frege's writings as the ravings of a lunatic, let us consider some of his remarks about natural language.

Perhaps the most interesting remark appears in a letter to Peano. Frege writes, about the sharp boundary requirement,

> a sign for a concept whose content does not satisfy this requirement is to be regarded as meaningless from the logical point of view. It can be objected that such words are used thousands of times in the language of life. Yes; but our vernacular languages are also not made for conducting proofs. And it is precisely the defects that spring from this that have been my main reason for setting up a conceptual notation. The task of our vernacular languages is essentially fulfilled if people engaged in communication with one another connect the same thought, or approximately the same thought, with the same proposition. For this it is not at all necessary that the individual words should have a sense and meaning of their own, provided only that the whole proposition has a sense. [1980, pp. 114–115]

It is interesting to notice that everyday language involves communicating *approximately* the same thought and that subsentential parts might lack not only meaning, but also sense. There is a suggestion in the rest of the paragraph that, among these subsentential parts, may be concept-expressions that we think of as being determinately true or false of certain objects but as undetermined elsewhere. Let us consider an example. In a letter dated 1882, Frege writes,

> Bald people for example cannot be enumerated as long as the concept of baldness is not defined so precisely that for any individual there can be no doubt whether he falls under it. [1980, p. 100]

And, of course, bald people cannot be enumerated. The term "bald" is, according to Frege, meaningless. Nonetheless most of us are pretty confident that we know what it means to be bald. Indeed, most of us who have young friends over the age of four are pretty confident that *they* know what it means to be bald. But none of us, whether four or forty, is likely to claim that there is a sharp demarcation between those who are bald and those who are not—let alone that it can be definitively stated whether or not the sun is bald. How do we use this term in everyday language and what would Frege regard as permissible?

There is no reason to think that Frege would object to my asking to be introduced to someone I identify as 'the bald man in the corner'. In such a situation, it is not particularly important that it be *true* that there is a bald man in the corner. I can still achieve my aim if the person I have indicated is a woman or a man who has all his hair covered by a skullcap that matches his skin. It is important only that I have made it clear who I meant to identify.

But this still may not be very satisfying. After all, instead of wanting to be introduced, I might want to inform. Suppose I tell my companion that the bald man in the corner is one of my logic students. Once again, it is only important that I have identified someone, not that my description uniquely fits that person. Well, then, suppose I tell my companion that some of my logic students are bald. This is exactly the sort of situation that Frege describes in the letter to Peano. It suffices for communication that we both associate approximately the same thought with the sentence.

It is a consequence of Frege's views that most everyday sentences do not express real thoughts—senses that have truth-values. But he does not claim that we ought not to make assertions in everyday life. Similarly, it is a consequence of Frege's views that the laws of logic do not apply to these defective assertions. But just as we may have perfectly good practical reasons for making defective assertions, we may have perfectly good practical reasons for making defective inferences. It is not that we are especially prohibited from making everyday inferences. Rather, if our interest is in truth, we should not be content with sham concepts. So when *do* we care about truth?

Suppose that, instead of wishing to meet the bald person in the corner, I wish to avoid becoming bald myself. According to some recent advertisements, I should ask my doctor about minoxidil.[10] And, since I am not inclined to trust doctors, I might want information that allows me to decide for myself whether or not minoxidil will prevent baldness. I have now wandered into the realm of science. And, suddenly, Frege's objections to inadmissible sham concepts no longer sound inappropriate. First, I will need to stop talking about baldness, for it would be more accurate to describe my aim as that of having more hair rather than less. Actually, I want to prevent hair loss and/or increase hair growth. Thus I will want to start thinking about degree of hair loss or growth. Degree of hair loss or growth is still a pretty vague concept, and if I am to evaluate the minoxidil research I will have to settle on a precise concept that is of interest to me.

It seems that most researchers have now agreed that the unit for measuring hair growth or loss should be the amount of hair found growing on a square centimeter of scalp. Beyond that, there is some disagreement. For instance, in a January 1989 article in *Clinical & Experimental Dermatology* two standards are suggested. One of these is total hair density (THD), which was measured by taking the mean of hair counts on several square centimeters of scalp. The other, meaningful hair density (MHD) relies on counts only of hairs greater than 40 microns in diameter and greater than 30mm in length. Degree of hair loss or

---

[10]Minoxidil is a drug which, until recently, was primarily used to treat high blood pressure. One of its side effects, for some people, appears to be increased hair growth. The observation of this side effect motivated research on the use of minoxidil as a treatment for baldness. In recent years minoxidil has been widely marketed for this use.

growth, then, is to be measured by mean change in THD or MHD. On the other hand, a paper in the December 1990 issue of the *Journal of Investigative Dermatology* offers a different recommendation: that the measure be taken from only one square centimeter from the front of the scalp and that degree of hair loss or growth be determined by change in total weight of hair from the defined area.

Does this show that the minoxidil investigators are taking Frege's sharp boundary requirements seriously? At first it may not seem so. After all, shouldn't they have defined what it is to be a hair? Frege says, of course, that not everything can be defined, and the minoxidil investigators might respond that there is no need to define what it is to be a hair. But, one might argue, isn't it just that *for their purposes* such a definition is unnecessary? Isn't there, nonetheless, a question about how many connected cells (and of what sort) it takes to make up a hair? In order to answer to this we must remember that the decisive issue is not whether or not there is a definition. It *matters* what their purposes are. Frege writes,

> I would demand the following from a true conceptual notation: It must have simple modes of expression for the logical relations; . . . These forms must be suitable for combining most intimately with a content. . . . The symbols for denoting content are less essential. They can be easily created as required, once the general logical forms are available. If the analysis of a concept into its ultimate components does not succeed or appears unnecessary we can be content with temporary symbols. [1972, p. 88]

If the minoxidil investigators do not study or examine cells, there may be no need for them to identify a relation between cells and hairs. The decisive issue is whether or not, given the investigators' understanding, it is determinately true or false of each object that it is a hair. What is of importance is that the world be divided up into yeses and noes.[11]

But surely there are, at least theoretically, boundary cases. Suppose, for instance, I were to take a hair, remove one cell at a time, and, after each removal, ask an investigator, "Is this a hair?" It does not seem unreasonable to assume that at some point the investigator would become unsure. If so, this would show that the common understanding of the primitive term 'hair' was vague, hence defective. This argument deserves closer inspection.

Notice, first, the disanalogy between the reason given here for thinking that the term 'hair' is vague and the reason given earlier for thinking that the term 'bald' is vague. We all know that baldness is a vague concept—we've all classified some people as borderline-bald. Hair is different. Has anyone really found

---

[11]Or, at least, what is important for *concept words* is that the world be divided into yeses and noes. This isn't to say that a categorical ranking or a degree-of-baldness ranking should be prohibited. In that case, there would still be a sharp boundary requirement—there would have to be sharp boundaries between each category (or a sharp measure).

themselves in a situation where the appropriate classification of an object is as a borderline hair? It is by no means obvious that there is any vagueness ingrained in our understanding of what it is to be a hair. Thus the objection that the minoxidil investigators are relying on a vague primitive term requires argument. Now consider the argument.

The argument that the term 'hair' is vague is based on a view of hairs as complex entities whose status *as* hairs depends on their constituents. Without the assumption that hairs can be altered by successive removal of individual cells, there would be no reason to believe in the existence of borderline cases. The minoxidil investigators could forestall the objection that the term 'hair' is vague by viewing the complex structure (and dimensions) of hairs as a part of their investigation and giving a definition of the term 'hair'. However, this would not be very helpful. Supposing such a definition were given, the next target would probably be the term 'cell'.

From Frege's point of view, something is wrong with this. It is not only that, as Frege says, not everything need be defined. Suppose that the minoxidil investigators *do* define 'hair'. What would the status of that definition be? Frege says,

> When we look around us at the writings of mathematicians, we come across many things which look like definitions, and are even called such, without really being definitions. Such definitions are to be compared with those stucco-embellishments on buildings which look as though they supported something whereas in reality they could be removed without the slightest detriment to the building. We can recognize such definitions by the fact that no use is made of them, that no proof ever draws upon them. [1979a, p. 212]

The minoxidil investigators will have no use for definitions of 'hair', let alone definitions of 'cell'. Such definitions could be removed without detriment. That is, they could be removed *provided* the term 'hair' is not vague. Thus, the important question is not whether we can use information about the structure of hairs to argue that the term 'hair' is vague. Rather, the important question is whether the term 'hair' is vague. But what kind of question is this?

A concept-expression is vague if it is indeterminate, for some object, whether or not the concept applies. Are there borderline cases of hairs? Consider what it would be for a minoxidil investigator to answer 'yes'. If there are borderline cases, then investigators will expect occasionally to find objects growing out of their subjects' heads which are neither determinately hairs nor determinately not hairs. What is an investigator to do in such a situation? There is no indeterminate category for measurements. Either the investigator will include this object in the weight and count or not. But to include this object in the weight and count is to assume that it is a hair. To exclude the object is to assume that it is not. Thus, there is no way for the individual investigator to acknowledge the existence of a borderline case. The nature of the enterprise requires precise boundaries.

There may, however, be a different way to make out the claim that there are borderline cases. Suppose one investigator calls over two others and asks, "What do you think—is this a hair?" And suppose these others disagree. Does this show that there *is* a borderline case? To answer this, let us consider Frege's comments about the use of primitive expressions in science. Since such expressions cannot be defined, he says, "something else must enter in" [1984, p. 300]. He calls this 'something else' elucidation (*Erläuterung*). What is the purpose of elucidation? Frege says that it

> serves the purpose of mutual understanding among investigators, as well as of the communication of the science to others. . . . Someone who pursued research only by himself would not need it. The purpose of elucidations is a pragmatic one; . . . And here we must be able to count on a little goodwill and cooperative understanding, even guessing. [1984, p. 301]

The issue is pragmatic. The investigators must come to an agreement—either the object in question will be included among the hairs and weighed or it will be excluded. If certain sorts of objects are routinely classified differently by different investigators the results may be biased. Agreement is required, not just in this case, but in general. If there are liable to be apparent borderline cases, then the investigators should get together and go over a number of cases in succession until it becomes clear that their classifications will be uniform. Moreover, ideally this agreement will be reached in advance of the experiment. If there are borderline cases and if ad hoc decisions involving classification are permitted, then, once again, the results may be biased. Finally, it does not matter much where the border is drawn, as long as the investigators understand it the same way.[12]

One might respond that Frege's position is unrealistic. Perhaps the *minoxidil* investigators will want to set their standards in advance. But in other scientific contexts, this may be a mistake. Sometimes an experiment may show us that we were not using the most interesting concepts. It is important to see, however, that the demands of science need not, indeed, could not, be satisfied from the very beginning. In the first stages of a science, Frege notes, we *must* use ordinary words [1979a, p. 207]. But the aim of science is not merely to establish individual truths. Frege says, "A science is a system of truths" [1979a, p. 168]. His demands are not the demands of a scientific treatment that precedes the truly systematic one [1984, p. 302]. But, he says, "science only comes to fruition in a system" [1979a, p. 241].

---

[12]Although the situation that I have described above is fanciful, my characterization of what the investigators should do in advance of the experiment is not. In the course of my own epidemiological research, I have had occasion to discuss this issue with physicians conducting clinical trials, and my characterization above stems largely from these discussions. While most articles in medical journals do not contain extensive discussions of the nature of the efforts to insure that the classifications of the investigators will be uniform, they often include partial descriptions of these efforts.

But what if we make a mistake? Suppose we develop a systematic science that proves inadequate, are we then forever committed? No. In such a case, Frege says, it must be demolished and replaced by a new structure [1979a, p. 279]. Finally, what if an agreement about the meaning of the primitive terms cannot be reached? Frege says,

> we must have confidence that such an understanding can be reached through elucidation, although theoretically the contrary is not excluded. [1984, p. 301]

What does this show about Frege?

Frege's sharp boundary requirement is widely regarded as implausible. In spite of the prominence this requirement has in Frege's writings, most commentators devote little space to it. It is, as Ricketts has emphasized, a consequence of Frege's taking logic as the maximally general science, that quantifiers range over everything and, hence, that concepts be everywhere defined. In order for us to enumerate bald people, for instance, the sun must be either determinately bald or determinately not bald. But the maximally general nature of logic is not enough to explain why vagueness should be prohibited. Indeed if, as Ricketts argues, it is our everyday disputes and judgments that provide the model for gapless logical inferences, then it is difficult to see why vagueness should be prohibited. I have tried to show that the solution to this problem is that systematic scientific investigation—not everyday disputes—provides Frege with his model. It is not enough to see that, for Frege, logic is maximally general. We must also see that, for Frege, logic is the maximally general *science*.[13]

The point about the minoxidil investigators is that, whether or not their actual work is beyond reproach, their inferences require precise classifications. The investigation of the efficacy of minoxidil for preventing baldness itself requires the introduction of precisification not found in everyday reasoning. The act of measuring total hair density on a particular region of a subject's scalp, for example, requires that every object found growing in that region of the scalp be a hair or not. The logical laws (the laws of truth) require sharp boundaries. Why should the laws of truth require sharp boundaries? Because the realm of truth *is* the realm of science. If, as Dummett argues, it is not enough to regard Frege as a philosopher of logic, then Frege should be regarded not as a philosopher of language, but as a philosopher of science.

---

[13] I do not mean to be claiming that the standards and requirements of the minoxidil researchers (or of medical researchers) are characteristic of all scientific research. My point is that Frege's sharp boundary requirement, which, viewed in isolation, may seem absurd, can also, in some contexts, seem sensible. And, as I have tried to show, it is no accident that these contexts are scientific contexts. It may also be worth mentioning that my use of this particular example was not motivated by my own experience with medical research. It was motivated, rather, by Frege's puzzling remark about enumerating bald people. My reaction was to try to think of circumstances in which one would want to enumerate bald people.

IV

In the remainder of this paper I will consider, briefly, two apparent problems for Frege's views and, then, address the issue of what Frege's views tell us about the philosophy of language. First, what of the problem Ricketts identifies? Is Frege committed to the view that substantive semantic presuppositions are required for the application of logical laws? No. Frege's starting point is, as Ricketts says, our common understanding of language, but this common understanding is not an end point. The logical laws are applicable only to assertions expressed in a logically perfect language. We do, of course, have to presuppose that the expressions of the logically perfect language have meaning. But this is rather different from the presupposition that expressions of everyday language stand for things in the world. Frege's standards of definition are meant to insure that, provided primitive terms have meaning, all defined terms have meaning. Thus, the only presuppositions are that the primitive terms have meaning. And these presuppositions need not be substantive.

To see this, it is important to begin by noticing that, for the most part, the primitive expressions will be concept- or function-expressions. It is not just that the language for Frege's logic, the most general science, has only primitive concept- and function-expressions. It also has to do with the nature of science. Frege, usually writes as if science is an attempt to establish general laws. He says, for instance, "The first place where a scientific expression appears with a clear-cut meaning is where it is required for the statement of a law" [1984, pp. 137–138]. Proper names will typically not appear in laws. It would be unlikely, then, for primitive proper names to be required for some science.

On the other hand, there are certainly points in scientific investigation when we will want to establish particular truths. Will we need a primitive proper name? It is not evident that we will. Suppose, for example, a, b, and c are lines connecting the vertices of a triangle with the midpoints of the opposite sides, and we introduce a name for the point of intersection of a and b. This name will not be a primitive expression. It seems apparent that the need for a primitive object-expression will arise when the object cannot be picked out by a description. How, then, can the primitive object-expression be given a meaning? One might suspect, as Dummett does, that ostension can be used to identify an object as the referent of a name [Dummett, 1981, pp. 143–144]. But Dummett also admits that there is no evidence for taking Frege to have believed that [Dummett, 1991b, 84]. And there is some evidence that Frege believed no such thing. Frege writes, for instance, "No beginner will get a correct idea of an angle if the figure is merely placed before his eyes" [1984, p. 56]. The beginner needs to be told what to look at. And pointing will not suffice. Concept-expressions or function-expressions will be needed. Frege continues, "If a beginner is shown how to add angles, then he knows what they are" [1984, p. 56].

Thus, the sort of presupposition involved in using a logically perfect language is a presupposition that primitive concept-expressions have meaning. But, for this, all that is required is clarity and understanding. It is not that we cannot go wrong but, rather, that there cannot be a substantive question about whether or not a primitive concept-expression has fixed meaning. To see this, consider what it would be to say that such an expression fails to have fixed meaning. There are two possibilities. The first is that there exists an object that would confound a person who believes herself to understand the expression—that is, an object that she would be unable determinately to classify as falling under or not falling under the concept, no matter how good her information. The second is that there exists an object on which two people, both of whom believe they have a common understanding of the expression, would differ. Are these substantive issues? There are, as I indicated in the discussion of the minoxidil researchers, a variety of strategies for trying to insure that these possibilities will not arise. But none is foolproof. If the notion involved truly is primitive from the point of view of the researchers, and if, in fact, it *does* have fixed meaning, there will be no way to provide a demonstration of the impossibility of the existence of borderline cases. In an important sense, the presupposition that primitive concept-expressions have meaning is just the presupposition that we understand one another—that we are not uttering gibberish.

A second apparent problem is the arbitrariness permitted. It cannot be enough, for science, to refrain from uttering gibberish. The minoxidil investigators cannot, for instance, decide to define meaningful hair density by taking counts only of hairs greater than 400 microns in diameter. Our scientific terms have to answer to something—they have to answer, it seems, to truth in the everyday non-scientific sense. The problem with restricting our hair counts to hairs with diameter greater than 400 microns is that then nobody would have any hair. We can't get our minoxidil study under way—and, indeed, would have no interest in doing so—without antecedently accepting certain everyday claims as true. Only our antecedent convictions that it is *true* that certain people are bald and *false* that certain other people are bald will motivate this work. Only these convictions will give it any content. Yet, given Frege's standards, these convictions about the truth of everyday statements are wrong. How, then, can they be used in the development of science?

Frege says,

> Research into the laws of nature employs physical instruments; but these can be produced only by means of an advanced technology, which again is based upon knowledge of the laws of nature. . . . an advance in physics results in an advance in technology, and this makes possible the construction of new instruments by means of which physics is again advanced. The application to our case is obvious. [1972, p. 89]

We must start with our understanding of everyday language as expressing truths and with our everyday standards of adjudication for disputes. But for everyday communication, we *need* a language with "a certain softness and instability" [1972, p. 86]—a language with logical defects. Our starting point will, inevitably, be with an imperfect instrument for scientific purposes. Frege is interested in everyday language only insofar as it can help in his development and explanation of a different sort of language, a language that can be a scientific tool. The true field of study for logic, Frege says, is "scientific workshops" [1979a, p. 33]. Has Frege a philosophy of language? Yes. It is that language is a tool.

Frege does seem to be committed to saying that, strictly speaking, we never utter truths or disagree with one another in everyday contexts. It is interesting to notice, however, that he need not accept such an extreme commitment. There is a respect in which Frege could view everyday statements as true. Consider his definitions of the numbers. I have argued elsewhere that their purpose is to enable Frege to replace arithmetic with a systematic science [Weiner, 1990, pp. 112–128]. The aim of replacing arithmetic with a systematic science involves introducing definitions of the everyday terms of arithmetic from primitive terms. Although the defining expressions need not have exactly the content previously associated with the term to be defined, this content does impose constraints on the acceptability of the definitions. For example, it cannot be a consequence of the definitions that $0 = 1$. One might regard this as a respect in which it is true, before Frege's definitions, that $0 \neq 1$. Supposing, then, that arithmetic can be systematized, we can view certain pre-systematic statements as truths and certain pre-systematic disputes as real, even as settleable, disputes.

I have argued that Frege did not mean to introduce a semantic theory for natural language and that semantic theories have no role to play in a logically perfect language. But it seems that Frege *has*, perhaps unwittingly, introduced a part of a semantic theory for natural language. Regardless of how Frege should be interpreted, many philosophers believe that the introduction of semantic theory in "On Sense and Meaning" constitutes an important philosophical advance. What would Frege's assessment of this semantic theory be? One might suspect that, on my interpretation, Frege would have no grounds for assessment. After all, I have suggested that he never even formulated the notion of a semantic theory. But Frege has offered criteria of evaluation that are meant to apply to all theories; and to all enterprises in which our aim is to establish truths. Must a semantic theory meet the demands of systematic science?

One may be tempted to respond that these demands, at least as Frege understands them, are only appropriately applied to natural sciences. He does say,

> What are called the humanities [*Geisteswissenschaft*] are closer to poetry, and are therefore less scientific, than the exact sciences, which are drier in proportion to being more exact; for exact science is directed toward truth and truth alone. [1984, pp. 356–357]

This may seem to suggest that the humanities are, at least partially, exempted from the demands of science. But this can provide little solace to the semantic theorists. For, as Frege goes on to say, this exemption applies to the humanities only insofar as their aim is to approach by intimation what cannot be conceptually grasped. If semantic theories are to set out truths, the demands of science apply.[14]

Can a semantic theory meet these demands? No. As I have argued elsewhere,[15] one reason has to do with the importance of functions and concepts. Every sentence has at least some of these incomplete constituents. If a semantic theory must explain how the truth value of a sentence is determined by the referents of its constituents, it must include an account of the reference of concept-expressions. But Frege repeatedly says that what can be said about objects cannot be said about concepts or functions [1984, pp. 282, 186, 189]. Suppose we have given a description of a reference relation. If, given the description, this relation can hold between a linguistic expression and an object named by the expression, then that description precludes our saying that the relation can hold between a linguistic expression and a concept named by the expression. Nor can there be a series of distinct relations that hold between linguistic expressions and, respectively, objects, concepts, second-level concepts, etc.[16] There could be only one reference relation, a relation that holds between proper names and the objects named. Thus, on Frege's view, there can be no theory of reference that plays a role in the explanation of how the truth value of a sentence is determined by the referents of its constituents.

But can there be a theory of reference for proper names? Not if the aim of that theory is to show how we succeed in talking about the world. Frege himself worries about the possibility of meaningless names. And his response is to show that these names can be appropriately defined from primitive expressions. But there can be no argument that primitive expressions stand for things in the world. When it comes to these expressions, he says, we must "be able to count on a little goodwill and cooperative understanding, even guessing" [1984, p. 300]. We may need "a meeting of minds between ourselves and others, and here we may be disappointed" [1979a, p. 259].

---

[14]Frege refers to metaphysics [1967a, p. 18], philosophy [1884, V], [1979a, p. 203], and history [1984, p. 368] as sciences.

[15]See [Weiner, 1990] Chapter 6 and [Weiner, 1995].

[16]The explanation for this is too long to give here, but it is a consequence of Frege's understanding of concepts and functions as incomplete. He says that the expressions "function" and "concept" are defective and that sentences in which they appear are either nonsensical or miss their mark (See, e.g., [1984, p. 193], [1980, pp. 136–137, 141], [1967a, p. 37], [1979a, pp. 119, 120, 122, 239, 255]. This is widely believed to be an implausible view whose consequences are unacceptable. I have argued, at length, in Chapter 6 of [Weiner, 1990] that this really was Frege's view and is an ineradicable consequence of his understanding of functions and concepts. In "Theory and Elucidation: the end of the Age of Innocence", I have argued that this consequence is not nearly as grim as it seems.

Bibliography

Ambrose, Alice, and Lazerowitz, Morris, eds. (1970) *G. E. Moore: Essays in Retrospect.* London: George Allen & Unwin.

Anderson, C. A., and Savage, C. W., eds. (1989) *Rereading Russell: Essays on Bertrand Russell's Metaphysics and Epistemology, Minnesota Studies in Philosophy of Science,* Vol. XI. Minneapolis: University of Minnesota Press.

Anscombe, G. E. M., and Geach, Peter. (1963) *Three Philosophers.* Oxford: Basil Blackwell.

Aristotle. (1980) *The Nicomachean Ethics* (tr. D. Ross). Oxford: Oxford University Press.

Armstrong, D. M. (1980) *Universals and Scientific Realism.* Cambridge: Cambridge University Press.

Asprey, W., and Kitcher, Ph., eds. (1988) *History and Philosophy of Modern Mathematics.* Minneapolis: University of Minnesota.

Austin, J. L. (1979) *Philosophical Papers.* Oxford: Oxford University Press.

Baker, G. P., and Hacker, P. M. S. (1980) *Wittgenstein: Meaning and Understanding.* Oxford: Basil Blackwell.

———. (1984) *Frege: Logical Excavations.* Oxford: Oxford University Press.

———. (1985) *Rules, Grammar, and Necessity.* Oxford: Basil Blackwell.

Baldwin, James Mark, ed. (1960) *Dictionary of Philosophy and Psychology,* Vol. II. Gloucester, MA: Peter Smith.

Baldwin, Thomas. (1990) *G. E. Moore.* London and New York: Routledge.

Barker, Stephen. (1967) "Number." In *The Encyclopedia of Philosophy.* New York: Macmillan, 526–530.

Benacerraf, Paul, and Putnam, Hilary, eds. (1983) *Philosophy of Mathematics.* Cambridge: Cambridge University Press.

Benacerraf, Paul. (1983a) "Mathematical Truth". [Benacerraf and Putnam, 1983], 403–420.

———. (1983b) "What Numbers Could Not Be". [Benacerraf and Putnam, 1983], 272–294.

Berger, Fred R. (1984) *Happiness, Justice, and Greedom: The Moral and Political Philosophy of John Stuart Mill.* Berkeley: University of California Press.

Black, Max. (1964) *A Companion to Wittgenstein's "Tractatus".* Ithaca: Cornell University Press.

Block, Irving. (1981) *Perspectives on the Philosophy of Wittgenstein.* Oxford: Basil Blackwell.

Bolzano, B. (1817) "Rein analytischer Beweis des Lehrsatzes, dass zwischen je zwey Werthen, die ein entgegengesetztes Resultat gewähren, wenigstens eine reele Wurzel der Gleichen liege". Prague. [Tr. by S. B. Russ as "A Translation of Bolzano's Paper on the Intermediate Value Theorem." *Historia Mathematica* 7, 1980.]

———. (1851) *Paradoxien des Unendlichen.* Leipzig. [Tr. by D. A. Steele as *Paradoxes of the Infinite.* London: Routledge, 1959.]

Boolos, George. (1987) "The Consistency of Frege's *Foundations of Arithmetic*". [Thomson, 1987], 3–20.

———. (1990a) "The Standard of Equality in Number". [Boolos, 1990b], 261–277.

———, ed. (1990b) *Meaning and Method: Essays in Honor of Hilary Putnam.* Cambridge: Cambridge University Press.

Bradley, F. H. (1935) *Collected Essays,* Vol. 1. Oxford: The Clarendon Press.

———. (1883) *The Principles of Logic.* London: Kegan Paul, Trench, & Co.

———. (1914) *Essays on Truth and Reality.* Oxford: Oxford University Press.

———. (1927) *Ethical Studies,* second edition. Oxford: The Clarendon Press.

Broad, C. D. (1930) *Five Types of Ethical Theory.* New York: Harcourt, Brace.

Burge, Tyler. (1984) "Frege on Extensions of Concepts from 1884 to 1903". *The Philosophical Review* 93, 3–34.

———. (1986) "Frege on Truth". [Haaparanta and Hintikka, 1986], 97–154.

———. (1992) "Frege on Knowing the Third Realm". *Mind,* Vol. 101, No. 404, 634–650. [Reprinted in this collection.]

Butler, Joseph. (1983) *Five Sermons.* Indianapolis: Hackett.

Cantor, G. (1874) "Über eine Eigenschaft des Inbegriffes aller reellen algebraischen Zahlen". *Journal für die reine und angewandte Mathematik* 77, 123–32. [Cantor (1932), pp. 115–18.]

———. (1878) "Ein Beitrag zur Mannigfaltigkeitslehre." *Journal für reine und angewandte Mathematik* 84, 242–58. [Cantor (1932), pp. 119–33.]

———. (1883) "Über unendliche lineare Punktmannigfaltigkeiten, 5". *Mathematische Annalen* 21, 545–86. [Cantor (1932), pp. 165–209] A separate edition of this, with a preface, was printed under the title *Grundlagen einer allgemeinen Mannigfaltigkeitslehre. Ein mathematisch-philosophischer Versuch in der Lehre des Unendlichen.* Teubner, Leipzig.

––––––. (1887–88) "Mitteilungen zur Lehre vom Transfiniten I, II". *Zeitschrift für Philosophie und philosophische Kritik* 91, 81–125, 252–70; 92, 250–65. [Cantor (1932), pp. 378–439.]

––––––. (1890–91) "Über eine elementare Frage der Mannigfaltigkeitslehre". *Jahresbericht der deutschen Mathematiker-Vereinigung* 1, 75–78. [Cantor (1932), pp. 278–80.]

––––––. (1895–97) "Beiträge zur Begründung der transfiniten Mengenlehre, I, II". *Mathematische Annalen* 46, 481–512; 49, 207–46. [Cantor (1932), pp. 282–56.]

––––––. (1932) *Gesammelte Abhandlungen mathematischen und philosophischen Inhalts* (ed. E. Zermelo). Berlin: Springer.

Carnap, Rudolf. (1928) *Der logische Aufbau der Welt.* Berlin: Weltkreis. [Tr. by R. George as *The Logical Structure of the World.* Berkeley: University of California Press, 1969.]

––––––. (1929) *Abriss der Logistik, mit besonderer Berücksichtigung der Relationstheorie und ihrer Anwendungen.* Vienna: Julius Springer.

––––––. (1930) "Die Mathematik als Zweig der Logik". *Blätter für deutsche Philosophie* 4, 298–310.

––––––. (1934) *Logische Syntax der Sprache.* Vienna: Springer. [Tr. by A. Smeaton as *The Logical Syntax of Language.* London: Kegan Paul, 1937.]

––––––. (1935) *Philosophy and Logical Syntax.* London: Kegan Paul.

––––––. (1942) *Introduction to Semantics.* Cambridge: Harvard University Press.

––––––. (1947) *Meaning and Necessity.* Chicago: University of Chicago Press.

––––––. (1958) *Introduction to Symbolic Logic* (tr. W. Meyer and J. Wilkenson). New York: Dover.

––––––. (1963) "Intellectual Autobiography". [Schilpp, 1963], 3–84.

Church, Alonzo. (1944) *Introduction to Mathematical Logic.* Princeton: Princeton University Press (second edition, 1956).

––––––. (1951) *Structure, Method, and Meaning* (ed. P. Henle). New York: Liberal Arts Press.

––––––. (1976) "Comparison of Russell's Resolution of the Semantical Antinomies with That of Tarski". *Journal of Symbolic Logic* 41, 747–760.

Clark, Ronald W. (1976) *The Life of Bertrand Russell.* New York: Alfred A. Knopf.

Coffa, Alberto. (1987) "Carnap, Tarski and the Search for Truth." *Nous* 21, 547–572.

––––––. (1991) *The Semantic Tradition.* Cambridge: Cambridge University Press.

Cocchiarella, Nino. (1989) "Russell's Theory of Logical Types and the Atomistic Hierarchy of Sentences". [Anderson and Savage, 1989], 41–62.

De Pierris, G. (1988) "Frege and Kantian *A Priori* Knowledge". *Synthese* 77, 285–319.

Dedekind, R. (1872) *Stetigkeit und irrationale Zahlen.* In [Dedekind, 1932]. Republished in 1969 by Vieweg, Braunschweig; English translation by W.W. Berman in 1963 in *Essays in the Theory of Numbers.* New York: Dover.

———. (1887) *Was sind und was sollen die Zahlen?* In [Dedekind, 1932]. Republished in 1969 by Vieweg, Braunschweig; English translation by W.W. Berman in 1963 in *Essays in the Theory of Numbers,* New York: Dover.

———. (1932) *Gesammelte Werke,* vol. 3 (ed. R. Fricke, E. Noether, and O. Ore). Braunschweig: F. Vieweg.

Descartes, Rene. (1971) *Descartes: Philosophical Writings* (tr. and ed. G. E. M. Anscombe and P. Geach). Indianapolis: Bobbs-Merrill Educational Publishing.

Devitt, Michael and Sterelny, Kim. (1987) *Language and Reality.* Cambridge: MIT Press.

Diamond, Cora. (1991) *The Realistic Spirit.* Cambridge: MIT Press.

Dummett, Michael. (1973) *Frege: Philosophy of Language.* New York: Harper and Row.

———. (1978) *Truth and Other Enigmas.* Cambridge: Harvard University Press.

———. (1981) *The Interpretation of Frege's Philosophy.* Cambridge: Harvard University Press.

———. (1991a) *Frege: Philosophy of Mathematics.* Cambridge: Harvard University Press.

———. (1991b) *Frege and Other Philosophers.* Oxford: Clarendon Press.

Engel, S. Morris. (1990) *With Good Reason: An Introduction to Informal Fallacies.* New York: St. Martin's Press.

Fogelin, Robert J. (1976) *Wittgenstein.* London: Routledge.

Foot, Philippa, ed. (1967) *Theories of Ethics.* Oxford: Oxford University Press.

Frankena, W. K. (1939) "The Naturalistic Fallacy". *Mind,* Vol. 48, pp. 464–77.

Frege, Gottlob. (1879) *Begriffsschrift, eine der arithmetischen nachgebildete Formalsprache des reinen Denkens.* Halle: L. Nebert. Reprinted in [Frege, 1970] and [Frege, 1977c].

———. (1884) *Die Grundlagen der Arithmetik. Eine logisch-mathematische Untersuchung über den Begriff der Zahlen.* Breslau: W. Koebner.

————. (1886) "Formal Theories of Arithmetic." *Sittzungsbericht der Jenaischer Gesellschaft für Medizin und Naturwissenschaft* 19.

————. (1891) "Function and Concept". [Frege, 1984], 137–156.

————. (1892a) "On Sense and Meaning". [Frege, 1984], 157–177.

————. (1892b) "On Concept and Object". [Frege, 1984], 182–194.

————. (1893) *Grundgesetze der Arithmetic, Begriffsschriftlich abgeleitet,* Band I. Jena: H. Pohle. Selections tr. in [Frege, 1967a].

————. (1895) "A Critical Elucidation of Some Points in E. Schröder's *Vorlesungen über die Algebra der Logik*". [Frege, 1984], 210–228.

————. (1897) "On Mr. Peano's Conceptual Notation and My Own". [Frege, 1984], 234–248.

————. (1903) *Grundgesetze der Arithmetic, Begriffsschriftlich abgeleitet,* Band II. Jena: H. Pohle.

————. (1906a) "Über Schoenflies: die Logischen Paradoxien der Mengenlehre". *Nachgelassene Schriften.* Tr. in [Frege, 1979a].

————. (1906b) "Über die Grundlagen der Geometrie I". *Jahresbericht der Deutschen Mathematiker-Vereinigung* 15.

————. (1906c) "On the Foundations of Geometry". [Frege, 1984], 293–340. Tr. of [Frege, 1906b].

————. (1919) "Aufzeichnungen für Ludwig Darmstaedter" in [Frege, 1979a], 253–257.

————. (1952) *Translations from the Philosophical Writings of Gottlob Frege* (ed. P. Geach and M. Black). Oxford: Basil Blackwell.

————. (1962) *Grundgestze der Arithmetic.* Hildesheim: Georg Olms. Reprinting of [Frege, 1893] and [Frege, 1903].

————. (1967a) *The Basic Laws of Arithmetic* (tr. and ed. M. Furth). Los Angeles: University of California Press.

————. (1967b) *Kleine Schriften.* Hildesheim: Georg Olms.

————. (1968) *The Foundations of Arithmetic: A Logico-Mathematical Enquiry into the Concept of Number* (tr. J. L. Austin). Evanston: Northwestern University Press. Tr. of [Frege, 1884].

————. (1970) *Begriffsschrift: A Formal Language Modeled upon That of Arithmetic,* (ed. J. van Heijenoort). Cambridge: Harvard University Press.

———. (1972) *Conceptual Notation* (tr. and ed. T. W. Bynum). Oxford: Clarendon Press.

———. (1976) *Wissenschaftlicher Briefwechsel.* Hamburg: Felix Meiner Verlag.

———. (1977a) *Logical Investigations* (ed. P. T. Geach). Yale: Yale University Press.

———. (1977b) "Thoughts." [Frege, 1977a], 1–30, and [Frege, 1984], 351–372.

———. (1977c) *Begriffsschrift, eine der arithmetischen nachgebildete Formalsprache des reinen Denkens.* Hildesheim: Georg Olms.

———. (1979a) *Posthumous Writings* (ed. H. Hermes et. al., tr. Peter Long and Roger White). Oxford: Basil Blackwell.

———. (1979b) "Logic in Mathematics." [Frege, 1979a], 203–250.

———. (1979c) "Über Schoenflies." [Frege, 1979a], 176–183.

———. (1980) *Philosophical and Mathematical Correspondence* (ed. B. McGuiness, tr. H. Kaal). Chicago: The University of Chicago Press.

———. (1983) *Nachgelassene Schriften.* Hamburg: Felix Meiner Verlag.

———. (1984) *Collected Papers on Mathematics, Logic and Philosophy* (ed. B. McGuinness). Oxford: Basil Blackwell.

Gabriel, G. (1986) "Frege als Neukantianer." *Kant-Studien* 77.

Gerrard, Steve. (1991a) "Two Ways of Grounding Meaning." *Philosophical Investigations,* Vol. 14, No. 2, 95–114.

———. (1991b) "Wittgenstein's Philosophies of Mathematics." *Synthese* 87, 125–142.

Gödel, Kurt. (1944) "Russell's Mathematical Logic." [Schilpp, 1944], 123–153.

Goldfarb, Warren. (1983) "I Want You to Bring Me a Slab: Remarks on the Opening Sections of the *Philosophical Investigations.*" *Synthese* 56, 265–282.

———. (1989) "Russell's Reasons for Ramification." [Anderson and Savage, 1989], 24–40.

Grandy, Richard. (1977) "A Defense of Weak Platonism." *Philosophical Studies* 32, 359–369.

Grote, John. (1870) *An Examination of the Utilitarian Philosophy* (ed. Joseph Bickersteth Mayor). Cambridge: Deighton, Bell, and Co.

Haaparanta, Leila, and Hintikka, Jaakko, eds. (1986) *Frege Synthesized.* Dordrecht: D. Reidel.

Haaparanta, Leila. (1985) "Frege's Context Principle." *Communication and Cognition,* Vol. 18, No. 1/2, 81–94.

Hall, Everett W. (1949) "The 'Proof' of Utility in Bentham and Mill." *Ethics* 60, pp 1–18.

Hayward, F. H. (1901) *The Ethical Philosophy of Sidgwick.* London: Swan Sonnenschein & Co.

Heck, R. (1993) "The Development of Arithmetic in Frege's *Grundgesetze der Arithmetik.*" *Journal of Symbolic Logic* 58, 579–601.

Heine, E. (1872) "Die Elemente der Functionenlehre." *Journal für die reine und angewandte Mathematik* 74, 172–188.

Hume, David. (1888) *A Treatise of Human Nature.* Oxford: Clarendon Press.

———. (1983) *An Enquiry Concerning the Principles of Morals.* Indianapolis: Hackett.

Hylton, Peter. (1980) "Russell's Substitutional Theory." *Synthese* 45, 1–31..

———. (1990) *Russell, Idealism, and the Emergence of Analytic Philosophy.* Oxford: Oxford University Press.

———. (1994) "Functions and Propositional Functions in *Principia Mathematica.*" *Russell and Analytic Philosophy* (ed. A. Irvine and G. Wedeking). Toronto: Toronto University Press, 342–60.

Kant, Immanuel. (1988) *Logic.* New York: Dover.

———. (1785) *Groundwork of the Metaphysics of Morals.*

Keynes, John Maynard. (1972) *The Collected Writings of John Maynard Keynes,* Vol. X. New York: MacMillan.

Kronecker, L. (1887) "Über den Zahlbegriff." Reworked and expanded version in *Werke,* 3 (ed. K. Hensel). Leipzig: Teubner, 251–274.

Ishiguro, Hide. (1969) "Use and Reference of Names." [Winch, 1969], 20–50.

Lackey, Douglas, ed. (1972) *Essays in Analysis.* New York: Braziller.

Leibniz, G. W. (1989) *Philosophical Essays* (ed. R. Ariew and D. Garber). Indianapolis: Hackett.

Lewy, C. (1964) "G. E. Moore on the Naturalistic Fallacy." *The Proceedings of the British Academy* 50.

Linsky, Bernard. (1988) "Propositional Functions and Universals in *Principia Mathematica.*" *Australasian Journal of Philosophy* 66, 447–460.

Linsky, Leonard. (1983) *Oblique Contexts.* Chicago: The University of Chicago Press.

———. (1988) "Terms and Propositions in Russell's *Principles of Mathematics.*" *Journal of the History of Philosophy,* Vol. xxvi, No. 4, 621–642.

Locke, John. (1690) *An Essay Concerning Human Understanding.*

MacIntyre, A. C. (1959) "Hume on 'Is' and 'Ought.'" *The Philosophical Review* 68.

Mackenzie, John S. (1897) *A Manual of Ethics,* 3rd edition. London: University Correspondence College Press.

Maddy, Penelope. (1984) "Mathematical Epistemology: What is the Question?" *The Monist* 67, 46–55.

Mandelbaum, Maurice. (1969) "Two Moot Issues in Mill's Utilitarianism." [Schneewind, 1969], 206–233.

Manser, Anthony, and Stock, Guy. (1984) *The Philosophy of F. H. Bradley.* Oxford: Clarendon Press.

Manser, Anthony. (1984) "Bradley and Frege." [Manser and Stock, 1984], 303–317.

McGuinness, B. F. (1981) "The So-Called Realism of the *Tractatus.*" In [Block, 1981].

Mill, J. S. (1861) *Utilitarianism.*

———. (1843) *A System of Logic.*

———. (1924) *Autobiography of John Stuart Mill.* New York: Columbia University Press.

———. (1974a) *The Collected Works of John Stuart Mill,* Vol. VIII (ed. J. M. Robson). Toronto: University of Toronto Press.

———. (1974b) *An Examination of Sir William Hamilton's Philosophy.* Reprinted in [Mill, 1974].

———. (1974c) *On Liberty.* Harmondsworth: Penguin.

Milne, Peter. (1986) "Frege's Context Principle." *Mind* 95, 491–495.

Monk, Ray. (1990) *Ludwig Wittgenstein: The Duty of Genius.* New York: MacMillan.

Moore, A. W., and Rein, Andrew. (1986). "*Grundgesetze* § 10." [Haaparanta and Hintikka, 1986], 375–384.

Moore, G. E. (1898) "Freedom." *Mind,* n. s. 7, 179–204.

———. (1899) "The Nature of Judgment." *Mind,* n. s. 8, 76–193. Reprinted in [Moore, 1986].

———. (1903) *Principia Ethica.* Cambridge: Cambridge University Press.

———. (1901) "Relative and Absolute." In J. Baldwin, *Dictionary of Philosophy and Psychology,* Vol. II., 1960.

———. (1968) "An Autobiography." [Schilpp, 1968], 3–39.

———. (1986) *G. E. Moore: The Early Essays* (ed. Tom Regan). Philadelphia: Temple University Press.

Myhill, John. (1974) "The Undefinability of the Set of Natural Numbers in the Ramified *Principia.*" In [Naknikian, 1974], 19–27.

Naknikian, George, ed. (1974) *Bertrand Russell's Philosophy.* London: Duckworth.

Parsons, Charles. (1967) "Mathematics, Foundations of." *The Encyclopedia of Philosophy.* New York: Macmillan, 188–213.

———. (1976) "Some Remarks on Frege's Conception of Extension." [Schirn, 1976], 265–277.

———. (1983) "Frege's Theory of Number." Reprinted in *Mathematics in Philosophy.* Ithaca: Cornell University Press, 150–175.

———. (1990) "The Structuralist View of Mathematical Objects." *Synthese* 84, 303–346.

Passmore, John. (1968) *A Hundred Years of Philosophy.* New York: Penguin.

Quine, W. V. O. (1969) *Set Theory and Its Logic.* Cambridge: Harvard University Press.

Ramsey, F. P. (1925) "The Foundations of Mathematics (1925)." [Ramsey, 1931], 1–61.

———. (1931) *The Foundations of Mathematics and Other Logical Essays.* London: Routledge.

Rawls, John. (1971) *A Theory of Justice.* Cambridge: Harvard University Press.

Resnik, Michael D. (1980) *Frege and the Philosophy of Mathematics.* Ithaca: Cornell University Press.

Ricketts, Thomas. (1985) "Frege, the *Tractatus,* and the Logocentric Predicament." *Nous* 19, 3–15.

———. (1986a) "Objectivity and Objecthood." [Haaparanta and Hintikka, 1986], 65–95.

———. (1986b) "Generality, Meaning, and Sense in Frege." *Pacific Philosophical Quarterly* 67, 172–195.

Rorty, Amelie. (1993) "From Passions to Sentiments: The Structure of Hume's Treatise." *The History of Philosophy Quarterly,* Vol. 10, No. 2, 165–180.

Russell, Bertrand (1895) "Review of Heymans, *Die Gesetze und Elemente des wissenschaftlichen Denkens.*" *Mind,* n.s. 5, 245–249.

———. (1903) *Principles of Mathematics.* New York: Norton.

———. (1919) *Introduction to Mathematical Philosophy.* London: Allen and Unwin.

———. (1945) *A History of Western Philosophy.* New York: Simon and Schuster.

———. (1935) *Religion and Science.* Oxford: Oxford University Press.

———. (1946) "My Mental Development." [Schilppp, 1946], 3–20.

———. (1956a) *Portraits from Memory and Other Essays.* New York: Simon and Schuster.

———. (1956b) *Logic and Knowledge.* London: Unwin Hyman.

———. (1966) "The Elements of Ethics." Reprinted in *Philosophical Essays.* New York: Simon and Schuster.

———. (1967) *Autobiography of Bertrand Russell, 1872–1914.* Boston: Little, Brown.

———. (1972) "On 'Insolubilia' and Their Solution by Symbolic Logic." Reprinted in [Lackey, 1972], 190–214.

———. (1983) *The Collected Papers of Bertrand Russell,* Vol. 1 (ed. K. Blackwell, et al.). London: George Allen & Unwin.

———. (1992) *The Selected Letters of Bertrand Russell,* Vol. 1 (ed. Nicholas Griffin). Boston: Houghton Mifflin Company.

Ryan, Alan. (1970) *John Stuart Mill.* New York: Pantheon Books.

Ryle, Gilbert. (1970) "G. E. Moore's 'The Nature of Judgment.'" [Ambrose and Lazerowitz, 1970].

Schilpp, P., ed. (1946) *The Philosophy of Bertrand Russell.* Evanston, IL: Northwestern University Press.

———, ed. (1963) *The Philosophy of Rudolf Carnap.* La Salle: Open Court.

———, ed. (1968) *The Philosophy of G. E. Moore.* La Salle: Open Court.

Schirn, Matthias, ed. (1976) *Studien zu Frege,* Vol. I. Stuttgart: Friedrich Fromman.

Schlick, Moritz. (1918) *Allgemeine Erkenntnislehre.* Berlin.

Schneewind, J. B. (1969) *Mill: A Collection of Critical Essays.* Notre Dame: University of Notre Dame Press.

———. (1977) *Sidgwick's Ethics.* Oxford: Oxford University Press

Schröder, E. (1873) *Lehrbuch der Arithmetik und Algebra für Lehrer und Studirende,* Band I. Leipzig: Teubner.

Schröder-Heister, Peter. (1987) "A Model Theoretic Reconstruction of Frege's Argumentation." *Notre Dame Journal of Formal Logic* 28, 69–77.

Seth, James. (1908) "The Alleged Fallacies in Mill's 'Utilitarianism.' " *The Philosophical Review* 17, No. 5.

Sidgwick, Henry. (1874) *The Methods of Ethics*. London: MacMillan.

––––––. (1902) *Outlines of the History of Ethics*. Indianapolis: Hackett (fifth edition, 1988).

––––––. *The Methods of Ethics* (seventh edition). Indianapolis/Cambridge: Hackett.

Sluga, Hans. (1980) *Gottlob Frege*. London: Routledge & Kegan Paul.

Specht, E. K. (1969) *The Foundations of Wittgenstein's Late Philosophy*. New York: Barnes & Noble.

Stein, H. (1988) "Logos, Logic, and *Logistike*." [Asprey and Kitcher, 1988], 238–259.

Tait, W. W. (1983) "Against Intuitionism: Constructive Mathematics is Part of Classical Mathematics." *Journal of Philosophical Logic* 12, 175–195.

––––––. (1986a) "Truth and Proof: The Platonism of Mathematics." *Synthese* 69, 341–370.

––––––. (1986b) "Wittgenstein and the 'Skeptical Paradoxes.' " *Journal of Philosophy* 83, 475–488.

––––––. (1986c) "Critical Review of Charles Parsons." *Philosophy of Science* 53, 588–606.

––––––. (1993) "Some Recent Essays in the History of the Philosophy of Mathematics: A Critical Review." *Synthese* 96, 293–331.

Thiel, Christian. (1976) "Wahrheitswert und Wertverlauf. Zu Freges Argumentation in §10 der 'Grundgesetze der Arithmetik.' " [Schirn, 1976], 287–299.

Thomae, J. (1880) *Elementare Theorie der analytischen Functionen einer complexen Veranderlichen*. Halle: Nebert.

Thomson, J. J., ed. (1987) *On Being and Saying: Essays for Richard Cartwright*. Cambridge: MIT Press.

Überweg, F. (1871) *System of Logic and the History of Logical Doctrines*. Translated by Th.M. Lindsay from the third edition of 1868. London: Longmans, Green, and Co.

van Heijenoort, Jean. (1967a) "Logic as Calculus and Logic as Language." *Synthese* 17, 324–330.

––––––, ed. (1967b) *From Frege to Gödel: A Source Book in Mathematical Logic, 1879–1931*. Cambridge: Harvard University Press.

von Humboldt, Wilhelm. (1854) *The Sphere and Duties of Government.* Tr. J. Coulthard Jr. London: J. Chapman.

——. (1969) *The Limits of State Action.* Cambridge: Cambridge University Press.

Wallace, John. (1977) "Only in the Context of a Sentence Do Words have any Meaning." *Midwest Studies in Philosophy,* Vol. II.

Weiner, Joan. (1990) *Frege in Perspective.* Ithaca: Cornell University Press.

——. (1995) "Realism *bei* Frege: Reply to Burge." *Synthese* 102.

——. (Unpublished) "Theory and Elucidation: The End of the Age of Innocence."

Whitehead, A. N., and Russell, Bertrand. (1910) *Principia Mathematica I.* Cambridge: Cambridge University Press. Second edition 1927.

——. *Principia Mathematica to *56.* Cambridge: Cambridge University Press.

Wilson, Mark. (1992) "Frege: The Royal Road from Geometry." *Nous* 26, 149–180.

Winch, Peter, ed. (1969) *Studies in the Philosophy of Wittgenstein.* London.

——. (1987) *Trying to Make Sense.* Oxford: Basil Blackwell.

Wittgenstein, Ludwig. (1922) *Tractatus Logico-Philosophicus.* [Tr. D. F. Pears and B. F. McGuiness. London: Routledge, 1961 (second edition, 1963).]

——. (1958) *Philosophical Investigations* (ed. R. Rhees, et. al., tr. G. E. M. Anscombe). Oxford: Basil Blackwell.

——. (1960) *Blue and Brown Books* (ed. R. Rhees). New York: Harper and Row.

——. (1970) *Zettel.* Berkeley: University of California Press.

——. (1974a) *Philosophical Grammar* (ed. R. Rhees, tr. A. Kenny). Oxford: Basil Blackwell.

——. (1974b) *Letters to Russell, Keynes and Moore* (ed. G. H. von Wright). Oxford: Basil Blackwell.

——. (1975) *Lectures on the Foundations of Mathematics* (ed. C. Diamond). Chicago: University of Chicago Press.

——. (1978) *Remarks on the Foundations of Mathematics* (ed. G. H. von Wright, et. al., tr. G. E. M. Anscombe). Cambridge: MIT Press.

——. (1979a) *Notebooks 1914–1916.* Chicago: University of Chicago Press.

——. (1979b) *On Certainty.* Oxford: Basil Blackwell.

————. (1980a) *Remarks on the Philosophy of Psychology* I (ed. G. E. M. Anscombe and G. H. von Wright, tr. G. E. M. Anscombe). Chicago: University of Chicago Press.

————. (1980b) *Culture and Value* (ed. R. Rhees). Chicago: University of Chicago Press.

————. (1982) *Last Writings on the Philosophy of Psychology* I (ed. G. H. von Wright et al., tr. C. J. Luckhardt and M. A. E. Aue). Oxford: Basil Blackwell.

Wollheim, Richard. (1959) *F. H. Bradley.* Penguin.

Wright, Crispin. (1983) *Frege's Conception of Numbers as Objects.* Aberdeen: Aberdeen University Press.

Zermelo, E. (1930) "Über Grenzzahlen und Mengenbereiche: neue Untersuchungen über die Grundlagen der Mengenlehre." *Fundamenta Mathematicae* 14, 339–344.

INDEX